Between Fordism
and Flexibility

Between Fordism
and Flexibility

The Automobile Industry and Its Workers

EDITED BY

STEVEN TOLLIDAY and JONATHAN ZEITLIN

BERG

Oxford / New York

Distributed exclusively in the U.S. and Canada by
St. Martin's Press, New York

Published in 1992 by
Berg Publishers, Inc.

Editorial offices:

165 Taber Avenue, Providence, RI 02906, U.S.A.

150 Cowley Road, Oxford OX4 1JJ, UK

First published in 1986 by
Polity Press in association with Basil Blackwell.

British Library Cataloguing in Publication Data applied for.

Library of Congress Cataloging-in-Publication Data applied for.

Contents

List of Contributors

Duccio Bigazzi is a Research Fellow at the Institute of Medieval and Modern History, University of Milan.

Giovanni Contini is an Industrial Archivist and Head of the Audio-Visual Section, Superintendency of Archives for Tuscany, Florence.

Knuth Dohse is a Research Fellow at the International Institute for Comparative Social Research, Science Centre, Berlin.

Rainer Dombois is a Research Fellow at the Centre for the Study of Work and the Enterprise, University of Bremen.

Ulrich Jürgens is a Research Fellow at the International Institute for Comparative Social Research, Science Centre, Berlin.

Harry Katz is Associate Professor at the New York State School of Industrial and Labor Relations, Cornell University.

Nelson Lichtenstein teaches in the Department of History, Catholic University of America.

Thomas Malsch is a Research Fellow at the International Institute for Comparative Social Research, Science Centre, Berlin.

Reiko Okayama is Professor at the Institute of Social Science, Meiji University.

Koichi Shimokawa is Professor in the Faculty of Business Administration, Hosei University.

Steven Tolliday is a Policy Advisor at the London Strategic Policy Unit.

Sylvie Van de Casteele-Schweitzer is a Research Fellow at the Institute of Contemporary History, Centre National des Recherches Scientifiques, Paris.

Giuseppe Volpato is Associate Professor in the Faculty of Economics and Commerce, University of Venice.

Paul Willman is a Lecturer at the London Business School.

Jonathan Zeitlin is a Lecturer in the Department of History, Birkbeck College, London.

Preface

This volume is based on the selected and revised proceedings of a conference on 'The International Automobile Industry and Its Workers: Past, Present and Future' held at the Lanchester Polytechnic, Coventry in June 1984. The conference was organized jointly with Paul Thompson of Essex University and was generously funded by the Economic and Social Research Council, the Japan Foundation and the King's College Research Centre, Cambridge. In addition to the conference participants, we would particularly like to thank the following people for their assistance: Tom Donnelly, Patrick Fridenson, Joe Melling, David Thoms, Paul Worm and the members of the British Working Group on the Social History of Car Workers. We would also like to thank the University of Illinois Press for allowing us to use in chapter 4 material which will appear in S. Meyer and N. Lichtenstein (eds.), *The American Automobile Industry: A Social History* (forthcoming, 1986).

Steven Tolliday and Jonathan Zeitlin

Introduction: Between Fordism and Flexibility

Steven Tolliday and Jonathan Zeitlin

The automobile industry has long occupied a central place in debates about management, technology and work in advanced industrial societies. Since the days of Henry Ford the industry has served as a model of economic expansion and technological progress based on mass production: the manufacture of standardized products in huge volumes using special-purpose machinery and unskilled labour, a system which has come to be known as 'Fordism'. But from the mid-1970s, sweeping changes in markets and technology have transformed international competitive conditions and spurred automobile manufacturers in every country to experiment with new strategies based on greater product diversity and more flexible methods of production. These shifts in competitive strategy and manufacturing methods, whose outcome is still far from certain, pose far-reaching challenges not only for the automobile companies but also for their workers and the trade unions which represent them.

This volume considers the development of the automobile industry from its origins to the present in a perspective informed by current upheavals in markets, technology and industrial relations. Like the volume itself, this introductory essay is divided into three main parts. Part I looks at the rise of mass production and the modification of the Fordist model to suit national circumstances by managers, workers and trade unions. Part II examines industrial relations in the age of Fordism, focusing on international variations in trade-union structure, bargaining strategy and job-control practices. Finally, Part III traces the recent transformations in the international automobile industry, considers how far new production and marketing strategies mark a break with Fordism, and draws out the implications for industrial relations and trade-union strategy.

I

Mass production of automobiles, as developed by Henry Ford in the half-dozen years before the First World War, depended on three basic principles: the standardization of the product, the use of special-purpose equipment,

1

and the elimination of skilled labour in direct production. More than any of his contemporaries, Henry Ford grasped the vast latent demand for cheap, reliable basic transport in the American Midwest with its prosperous but isolated farms and small towns. His Model T, ruggedly designed, easy to repair and priced well below its competitors sold in unprecedented numbers, jumping from 6,000 in 1908 to 189,000 in 1913 and 802,000 in 1917 to reach a total of 15 million by 1926.[1]

In its heyday, the T came in a single standard model and was available in 'any color as long as it was black'. The standardization of the car and its components was intended to facilitate repair by distant customers, but more importantly to permit a dramatic reduction in costs through the use of special-purpose machinery and the division of labour. Ford drew upon and elaborated the heritage of the 'American system of manufactures' as it had developed from firearms through sewing machines, agricultural equipment and bicycles towards the high-volume production of interchangeable parts. He and his engineers simplified each component as far as possible, using new materials such as pressed steel; arranged the equipment in their new Highland Park factory so that the flow of materials followed the sequence of operations; and designed first jigs, fixtures and gauges and then new special-purpose machines to ensure full inter-changeability. These 'farmer tools' could be operated by unskilled workers without a background in the industry, and Ford likewise pursued the reduction of skill requirements in vehicle assembly through the subdivision of tasks and the elimination of fitting, hallmarks of 'mass production' as he was later to define it. With the astronomical growth of sales, each of these developments reinforced the others in a constant struggle for faster throughput which gave rise to Ford's most famous innovation: the introduction of the moving assembly line in 1913.

Ford's rapid growth and dramatic innovations in production brought with them unprecedented problems of labour management. Skilled workers progressively moved into new 'indirect' services such as toolmaking, tool-setting and maintenance, joining the growing army of supervisors, inspectors, progress chasers, clerks and engineers needed to administer mass production. The workforce shot up from 1,548 in 1909 to 13,667 in 1913, an increasing proportion of which were unskilled immigrants from southern and eastern Europe, many of whom spoke no English. Turnover levels reached 370 per cent in 1913, with absenteeism rates of 10 per cent per day, creating enormous difficulties in production planning. It was in this context that Ford inaugurated his famous 'Five-Dollar Day', a profit-sharing plan designed to stabilize and integrate the workforce alongside other measures such as a Sociological Department and intensive, driving supervision.

By the First World War, Ford had synthesized his innovations in product design, production and labour management into a coherent competitive strategy whose application appeared universal. Product standardization led to economies of scale, resulting in falling unit costs which permitted price reductions, expanding the market and leading on to further economies of scale in an endless virtuous circle. The huge River Rouge complex, built at the end of the First World War, integrated from steelmaking to final assembly, with its own railways, docks and power plant was the tangible embodiment of this strategy. As sales of the Model T soared, capturing 55 per cent of the American market in 1921, Ford's prospects seemed limitless and 'Fordism' to define an international standard of modern manufacturing practice.

As Tolliday suggests in chapter 1, however, the tremendous success of Ford's competitive strategy depended in practice on specific features of the American market in this period: its enormous size, vast distances, egalitarian income distribution and homogeneous tastes. The British market was fundamentally different in each of these respects, remaining much smaller and dominated by quasi-luxury demand into the 1920s, and a strategy based on price competition and economies of scale accordingly proved far less effective than across the Atlantic. While the underdevelopment of the British motor industry allowed Ford to sell significant numbers of Model Ts before 1914, the company's hold on the British market quickly evaporated with the emergence of large-scale domestic production in the 1920s. Ford officials in Detroit refused to allow local managers to develop a model aimed specifically at the British market until 1928, and sought to impose American practices of exclusive dealerships, high day-wages and low manning levels quite unsuited to British conditions. Even once local management achieved autonomy and began to pull the company back from its nadir of the late 1920s, the influence of Detroit practice remained strong: Ford's Dagenham factory, opened in 1932 as a scaled-down version of River Rouge, proved too large for the British market until the 1950s.

British manufacturers such as Morris and Austin, Tolliday argues in chapter 1, pursued a more pragmatic strategy, competing on the basis of new models and designs as well as price and moving gradually towards higher volumes of production. Production methods accordingly remained less rigid and capital-intensive than at Ford's, with greater customization in bodywork, more adaptable equipment in machining and greater use of hand labour in assembly. In contrast to Ford, British manufacturers also relied on piecework incentive schemes rather than tight supervision to motivate the labour force; and this distinctive complex of product, production and labour strategies remained characteristic of the British motor industry until its crisis of the 1960s and 1970s.

Elsewhere in Europe, the market for automobiles also diverged sharply from the American pattern, but the attitude of local manufacturers was different.[2] As Van de Casteele-Schweitzer in chapter 2 and Bigazzi in chapter 3 show, leading French and Italian entrepreneurs such as André Citroën, Louis Renault, Marius Berliet and Giovanni Agnelli were fascinated by Fordist methods on technological grounds and sought to impose them on the market. Engineers and managers from each of these companies visited the United States on several occasions, and each time came away determined to emulate the Fordist model on a more ambitious scale. In the 1920s and 1930s, vast new factories were constructed, modelled first on Highland Park and then on River Rouge; machine tools were imported from the United

States in large numbers; product lines were drastically simplified; and valiant efforts were made to rationalize production along American lines through the use of work measurement and the introduction of the assembly line.

But as chapters 2 and 3 demonstrate, European motor manufacturers' infatuation with Fordism created major difficulties both for production management and marketing. The great leap forward to mass production ran ahead of management's ability to elaborate suitable systems of cost accounting, work scheduling, supervision and quality control, so that shop-floor realities often lagged well behind the glossy visions of the engineers. The smaller size and greater differentiation of the French and Italian markets also created obstacles for Fordist marketing strategies, and overambitious expansion projects such as those of Berliet and Citroën crashed when demand turned downwards in 1921 and again in the early 1930s. All the main manufacturers were forced to multiply models and expand their product ranges in order to maintain their sales, and as in Britain the organization of production accordingly remained less rigid and less mechanized than in the United States. None of the European manufacturers, finally, dared to emulate Ford's labour strategies in full, eschewing high day-wages in favour of piece rates, speed-up and worker flexibility as means of boosting output and adjusting to fluctuations in demand.

Despite these practical limits to the development of Fordism in Europe between the wars, the leading French and Italian automobile manufacturers continued to regard it as an ideal production strategy, to be pursued as far as the national market allowed. Certain smaller companies, such as Alfa Romeo in Italy and Mercedes–Benz in Germany followed with varying degrees of commercial success an alternative strategy of specialization on high-performance luxury cars produced with modified craft methods. But on the eve of the Second World War, Fiat, Renault, Peugeot and Citroën were all experimenting with small 'people's cars' intended to create a new mass market, as was the Volkswagen Werke in Germany under the personal sponsorship of Adolf Hitler, another of Ford's European admirers.[3]

But even as European automobile manufacturers were straining against the limits of their national markets in their efforts to emulate Fordist principles, the American market itself was changing in ways that ultimately necessitated their partial modification.[4] In the United States, the 1920s saw a growing saturation of the market for utility cars; a fall-off in the proportion of first-time buyers and the spread of used-car sales; and a slower overall growth of demand. With the emergence of what Alfred P. Sloan of General Motors called the 'mass-class' market, cars could no longer be sold effectively on the basis of price alone, and GM was able to invade the mass market from above by pricing its more comfortable and up-to-date Chevrolet only slightly above the Model T. To ensure that no one else could follow his lead, Sloan set out to produce 'a car for every purse and purpose' in four autonomous divisions, each aimed at a distinct price band; and the company also used advertising, instalment sales and annual model changes to stimulate consumer demand and outdistance its rivals. To prevent model changes disrupting production, to curb fluctuations in sales and to increase economies of scale, GM executives developed new methods of forecasting demand, raised the proportion of components purchased from outside subcontractors, and began to interchange parts across divisions. On the shop floor itself, the company moved away from Fordist practice by introducing 'semi-special' machine tools which could be adapted to new models by changes to cams and gears, increasing the proportion of toolmakers and toolsetters in the workforce; and it sought added flexibility through seasonal layoffs for production workers and the use of piece rates and group bonuses rather than a day-wage system.

GM's innovations in product and production strategy soon began to undermine Ford's grip on the American market. The Model T had become increasingly outdated despite incremental changes introduced over the years, and sales dropped off sharply after 1924 despite repeated price cuts. By 1927 Ford was forced to admit defeat and begin work on a wholly new model to restore the company's competitive position. The extreme specialization of production for the Model T made the changeover enormously difficult and expensive: all the existing machinery had to be scrapped and the factory shut down entirely for nearly a year, opening the door for the emergence of new competitors such as Chrysler. Despite an initial sales boom, the new Model A never dominated the market as the T had and periodic modifications soon proved unavoidable; by 1932 Ford had been forced to introduce a successor, the V-8. These failures in product policy in turn necessitated a retreat from some aspects of Fordism in production as well: assembly lines became shorter and machinery less specialized; vertical integration was reduced to gain flexibility; and wage rates were cut to compensate for the collapse of profits.

Thus Fordism was widely modified to permit greater flexibility in response to shifts in the market and the innovations of GM. But the triumph of what came to be called 'Sloanism' proved ambiguous in practice. During the depression of the 1930s, GM reduced the number of its divisions and increased the interchangeability of components across models to secure greater economies of scale in a contracting market, and in a postwar competitive environment of steady growth in demand and oligopolistic 'room for all' pricing policies, the Sloanist strategy of 'a model for every market' degenerated into a strategy based almost exclusively on styling and marketing competition. Once they had perfected the big V-8 engine and 3-speed automatic transmissions in the early 1950s, the big US companies turned their backs on innovation and abandoned investment in experiments that did not yield quick results. For 20 years, the only major technical innovations in the United States came in the field of air-conditioning. The styling studios were in command and led the industry through successive milestones of kitsch – the tailfins of the late forties, the port-holes of the early fifties and the panoramic windshields of the mid-fifties, all adorned with flashing chrome and lurid paintwork.

Underlying this market pattern was a commercial and competitive logic. Continuous restyling became one of GM's big selling features to defeat smaller companies who could not generate new styles and which lacked marketing power. The Big Three used their powerful advertising and dealership networks to force up the costs of competition by forcing *dis*economies of scale in body tooling on their rivals. They were ready to carry much higher fixed costs in design and tool and die equipment per vehicle in order to carry through the annual model changes that the smaller independent companies could not afford to emulate; and the latter's inability to participate in this model competition was one of the crucial factors leading to their eventual demise.

But much of this apparent product diversity remained superficial. Following GM's lead, the Big Three centralized their styling variants around a limited number of basic interior platforms and body-shells, with distinctive 'skins' placed on each, while the 'family resemblance' enabled many major stampings of body parts to be used in common over many models. Many key components, such as engines, transmissions or chassis were shared by several cars and often retained for 20 years or more. This interchangeability of components enabled American manufacturers to pursue ever greater economies of scale through vertical integration and the introduction of dedicated automation equipment such as transfer machines. In assembly, on the other hand, the proliferation of options involved enormous complexity and inhibited rationalization of the production process as a whole.[5]

In the immediate postwar period, European automobile producers followed a more classically Fordist strategy, centred on the mass production of basic transport for the newly 'democratized' markets at home and abroad. Until the late 1960s, each national market in Europe remained quite distinct and dominated by one or two domestically produced cheap small cars such as the Renault 4 and Citroën 2CV in France, the VW Beetle in Germany, the Fiat 500 and 600 in Italy and the Morris Minor and BMC Mini in the UK. With widely varying taxation structures, income distributions and road conditions, it was impossible for any single producer to dominate the European market or for any single design philosophy to prevail. This fragmentation of the European market left ample space for more specialized manufacturers of luxury cars alongside the mass producers, such as BMW, Daimler–Benz, Volvo, Jaguar and Alfa Romeo. And as incomes rose in the 1960s, European mass producers themselves began to offer a wider range of models in order to maintain their coverage of increasingly diverse national markets. But the European manufacturers, unlike their American counter-parts, did not integrate their differentiated product ranges into coherent families of models based on common components. Instead, as Volpato demonstrates in chapter 8, the Europeans maintained their practice of developing each model separately, which allowed greater scope than in the United States for continuous improvement and technical innovation, but made it difficult to match the economies of scale of their mass market best sellers across the whole of a scattered and unbalanced product line. Thus in Europe as in the United States, by the late 1960s Sloanist marketing strategies based on product differentiation coexisted uneasily with automobile manufacturers' continuing commitment to Fordist production strategies based on standardization and economies of scale.[6]

II

Thus, by the 1930s the mass production of automobiles on Fordist lines had established itself to varying degrees in most of the major industrial nations, and this process of international diffusion and adaptation gathered renewed force during the long postwar boom. In every country, the advent of large-scale car production created new problems for workers and trade unions. The size and power of the emergent companies; the rapid expansion of the labour force and the new distribution of skills within it; acute fluctuations in employment and the introduction of new payment systems all posed a major challenge to the established organizational practices of trade unions.

These distinctive features of the automobile industry came together with ideological debates within the international labour movement to suggest that the establishment of industrial unions was the key to the organization of mass-production workers, an analysis which seemed largely borne out by the experience of the 1930s. The breakthrough to mass-production unionism in the United States followed directly on the split between the American Federation of Labor (AFL) and the Committee for Industrial Organization (CIO), which paved the way for the establishment of the United Auto Workers' union (UAW) against the violent objections of the craft unions. Similarly in France, the strike wave of 1936 which organized the Renault factories was run by the Metalworkers' Federation of the Confédération Générale du Travail (CGT) which had long been committed to industrial unionism. And the situation in Britain where a variety of craft and general unions catered for the automobile industry with limited success thus appeared to be the exception that proved the rule.[7]

With greater distance from the debates of the 1930s, however, the idea of industrial unionism as the uniquely appropriate form of organization for the automobile industry – a trade-union counterpart to Fordism – seems less compelling. Two main objections stand out. Closer historical investigation of the 1930s suggests that industrial unionism was a far from sufficient condition for the breakthroughs to mass organization in France and the United States. And a broader temporal and spatial perspective suggests that under favourable conditions other forms of union organization could prove equally effective.

The first objection stresses the role of politics and the state in the breakthrough to mass organization of automobile workers. As Tolliday and Zeitlin observe in chapter 4, revisionist historians of American labour have shown that without the political context of the New Deal and the support of the Federal government first under the Wagner Act and then under the War Labor Board, it is unlikely that the newly formed industrial unions could have overcome the resistance of the giant corporations such as GM and Ford.[8] In France, as Van de Casteele-Schweitzer demonstrates in chapter 2, it was the advent to power of the Popular Front in 1936 which triggered off the factory occupations and enabled the French Communist Party and the CGT to realize their longstanding aspirations to organize these symbols of the modern proletariat. In Italy, too, as Bigazzi in chapter 3 and Contini in chapter 6 document, successful organization in the car factories depended heavily on support from the government and the law in the 1940s and again in the late 1960s and early 1970s, while industrial unions proved unable to resist determined management offensives in periods of political reaction such as the 1920s and 1950s.

In Britain, the political context of the 1930s – dominated by the National Government after the collapse of the Labour Party in 1931 – was unfavourable towards a union breakthrough in the motor industry. Some of the difficulties in organizing the industry did stem from the structure and policies of the unions concerned, notably the craft unions' attachment to the standard district rate and friendly benefits, issues of limited relevance to semi-skilled pieceworkers, and the general unions' preoccupations with sectors outside automobiles. But as Tolliday argues in chapter 1, in periods when government policies inhibited managerial resistance – the two world wars and the late 1950s and early 1960s – both craft and general unions displayed considerable capacity for creative adaptation in organizing motor workers.[9]

A further demonstration of the centrality of the political context and the variety of possible union structures compatible with mass production can be seen in the cases of West Germany and Japan in the postwar period. The German trade unions emerged from the experience of Nazism and war with a politically heightened commitment to broad, encompassing industrial organization. This went even further than in the United States, since a single union was established for the whole of the metalworking sector, and the strategy of centralized bargaining was reinforced by a legal framework which limits the right to strike to recognized unions and extends collective agreements to cover even non-unionized firms. But the political upheavals of the reconstruction period also resulted in a statutory system of works councils outside the unions' direct control. The codetermination powers and 'peace obligations' of the works councils created the conditions for informal plant bargaining which has acted as a counterweight to the centripetal pull of industry-wide negotiations.[10] In Japan, as Okayama shows in chapter 7 for the case of Toyota, industrial unionism on the American model also seemed destined to become the dominant pattern in the early postwar years. But during the early 1950s, as national politics swung against the left and the automobile companies struggled for economic survival, the centre of gravity shifted to enterprise unions involving both white- and blue-collar workers, a development which relegated the industry-wide federation to a residual role in collective bargaining.[11]

Mass production of automobiles posed new problems of job control for trade unions alongside the establishment of collective bargaining itself. In many countries, grievances about the impact of Fordism on working conditions and job security were as important as wages in the early unionization drives. The 1936 sitdown strikes at General Motors, for example, were sparked off by demands for an end to speed-up on the assembly lines. But by the late 1960s and early 1970s, observers in countries such as the United States and West Germany believed that the institutionalization of collective bargaining there had resulted in the sacrifice of these job-control aspirations to the pursuit of economic gains which did not threaten managerial prerogatives on the shop floor. In this light, radical critics of trade unions drew invidious contrasts with the situation in Britain and Italy, where powerful and autonomous workplace organizations appeared to exercise the direct controls over the production process so conspicuously absent at home.[12]

Recent research on the automobile industry, much of it contained in this volume, has tended to modify such stark contrasts between national systems of industrial relations in terms of the presence or absence of job control. In Britain, for example, shop stewards in many car factories during the 1950s and 1960s achieved a measure of control over manning, workloads and job definition that made them the envy of local militants in countries like the United States. But as we argue in chapter 4, job control under shop stewards was more limited and precarious than is commonly supposed. Controls over the production process did not form part of a wider union strategy but were tied instead to sectional bargaining over piecework prices, and there was little coordination even at the level of the individual factory, perpetuating wide differentials between shops and insecurity of earnings for the workforce as a whole. Such job controls were, moreover, rooted in British management's own past modifications of Fordism – its reliance on incentive systems rather than mechanization and tight supervision – and their exercise involved shop stewards' assuming considerable responsibilities for coordinating production to achieve high levels of output. When management strategies shifted away from piecework towards more direct administration of production during the 1970s, the weaknesses of union organization at the company level made it increasingly difficult for the stewards to defend the pattern of job control which had developed in the preceding period.

In Italy, by contrast, direct controls over the production process grew out of the success of a Fordist strategy rather than its limitations. During the 1950s and 1960s, Fiat management reorganized car production on Fordist lines and recruited vast numbers of southern migrants to fill the resulting unskilled jobs. It was these production-line workers who struck *en masse* in 1969-70, establishing a new system of factory councils based on elected shop stewards. Once in place, the factory councils used their new-found power not to push up the earnings of individual work groups as in Britain, but instead to impose strict controls over workloads, compress wage differentials, simplify job classifications and make layoffs close to impossible. In certain shops, as Contini shows in chapter 6, stewards began to experiment with a more cooperative style of shop-floor bargaining, but political rivalries and the shifting strategies of the national unions pushed workplace organization at Fiat away from any durable accommodation with management. As the economic and political climate began to change in the late 1970s, this confrontational line isolated the factory council from key sections of the Fiat workforce and left it vulnerable to a managerial offensive aimed at restoring productive flexibility. The failure of a company-wide strike against redundancies in 1980, because of widespread worker defections, resulted in a collapse of shop-floor organization as sudden as its emergence a decade earlier.

In the United States, we argue in chapter 4, the main constraints on managerial prerogatives came not from direct controls over manning and work organization as in Italy and Britain, but rather from contractually negotiated seniority rules and grievance procedures which governed the allocation of workers between jobs. While management was free to determine the initial job structure according to Fordist principles, the association of wage rates and job security rights with these job definitions then imposed substantial rigidities on the deployment of labour in the plant. In chapter 12, Katz shows that this has become a major problem for management in recent attempts at plant reorganization. The US industrial-relations system did not in itself preclude the decentralized bargaining over issues such as workloads which was central to job control in Britain, since production-standard grievances remained strikeable during the life of the contract. But as Lichtenstein demonstrates in chapter 5, UAW leaders' preoccupation with company-wide bargaining objectives – together with the centralization of corporate industrial relations policies and the growing political isolation of organized labour – left little room in practice for dynamic local bargaining over shop-floor issues.

Two more varieties of job control, rooted in varying management and union strategies, can be seen in the cases of West Germany and Japan. Detailed studies of workplace industrial relations in West German car factories show that while there are few constraints on managers' ability to allocate labour between jobs, they are much less free than their American or British counterparts to lay off workers in response to fluctuations in demand. As we have seen, West German works councils are legally prohibited from direct negotiations over wages or calling strikes; and sectional bargaining on British lines is further discouraged by the union's preoccupation with industry-wide objectives. But the works councils also have far-reaching statutory powers of codetermination in hiring, dismissals and overtime which they use systematically to protect the employment prospects of their core constituency in the factory. The result has been the development of long-term manpower policies in the enterprise – themselves consonant with the orientation of some German car firms towards specialized production and with public apprenticeship programmes –

which provide maximum security of employment in exchange for great flexibility in the deployment of labour within the enterprise.[13]

A similar trade-off between relative employment security and the flexible deployment of labour within the firm can also be seen in the case of Japan. While there is considerable controversy about the independence of Japanese enterprise unions – which often contain representatives of lower management in leading positions – Shimokawa in chapter 9 and Okayama in chapter 7 along with other recent scholars, suggest that these organizations can exercise considerable influence on company policy through an extensive system of consultation and consensus-building and through occasional alliances with factions of management. Thus at Nissan, where the enterprise union has been closely linked with key managers, union leaders have used their influence to impose greater restrictions on work intensity and automation than at Toyota, as well as to obstruct proposals for overseas production. Like German works councils, Japanese enterprise unions press corporate management to maintain maximum stability of employment for their core workforce; and they are also concerned to regulate the resulting inter-plant transfers so as to cushion their impact on individual workers, as in the case of the 'lending a hand' agreement described by Shimokawa in chapter 9. As the pace of industry expansion has slowed since the mid-1970s, union cooperation and consensus has been sustained by increasing stability of employment within the factory, secured through mobility of the core workforce between jobs rather than through the use of temporary and seasonal workers, who had previously played a larger part in responses to cyclical fluctuations. As we shall see in section III below, such mobility forms part of a flexible system of car production based on fluid job roles and broad worker training which marks a clear break with Fordist principles.[14]

National systems of industrial relations thus differ in the focus as much as the level of job control: direct controls over the production process in Britain and Italy; contractual seniority rules and job classifications in the United States; and broad employment guarantees in West Germany and Japan. These international variations in the focus of job control stem as much from differences in strategy as from differences in power: from differences in management's interpretation of Fordism and in the responses of unions once established. Each national pattern involves a complex balance of advantage and constraint for management and unions alike. But as the recent decline of shop-floor organization in Britain and Italy demonstrates, some forms of job control may prove less adaptable than others to the demands of new product and labour strategies.

III

For nearly three decades after the Second World War, both the American and European automobile industries remained faithful to the underlying principles of the Fordist model, with varying degrees of modification to accommodate more differentiated marketing strategies. But by the early 1970s a series of forces were at work within the world economy which would call this model into question more fundamentally than ever before. Throughout the Western economies, the postwar boom was losing momentum, with a small but visible slowdown in overall growth rates. Major national car markets were becoming saturated at existing income levels, and the proportion of replacement demand relative to sales of new models was rising. By the late 1960s, for example, replacement demand had reached 75–80 per cent of the US market with a motorization level of more than one car for every two people.[15]

These trends made it difficult to achieve continued economies of scale within national boundaries. Previously, trade between manufacturing countries had concentrated on the market segments furthest from the specialization of domestic producers, presenting little challenge to their product ranges, as in the case of small-car imports to the United States and exports of large luxury cars from Germany and Sweden to other European countries. But now slowly growing domestic demand and underutilization of capacity triggered off a scramble for exports resulting in direct head-to-head competition between mass producers in the core segments of each other's markets. In 1960, for example, cross-national trade between West European producers accounted for 20 per cent of total sales; by 1980 this figure had risen to 36 per cent. But while each of the major producers moved down this road, only the Japanese really succeeded in making a major impact across a wide range of foreign markets. By 1980 the Japanese had seized 23 per cent of the US market, 10 per cent of the European market and a 28 per cent share of world imports. Since no major manufacturer has been eliminated and all companies have invested massively in new production facilities, the resulting boost to overall capacity has exacerbated the struggle for market share. At the same time, however, the growing saturation of demand for basic transport has forced mass producers in each country to explore new forms of product differentiation in order to appeal to market segments increasingly sensitive to quality, technical innovation and the special attributes of products.

Superimposed on these structural trends were a number of external shocks which exacerbated the growing crisis of the Fordist model and brought it to a head in sudden and unexpected ways. Most dramatic were the oil shocks of 1974 and 1979 which sent petrol prices soaring and created widespread consumer alarm about the security of sources of supply. For the first time since the war, absolute levels of world demand fell off, declining by 16 per cent between 1973 and 1975. While car sales quickly recovered as oil prices fell back in real terms, they never returned to previous growth rates, and demand fell again by 12 per cent between 1979 and 1981. The oil shocks also had a major impact on the composition of demand within each market. Growing consumer anxiety about petrol consumption set off a headlong rush among producers to shift car designs in the direction of smaller, more fuel-efficient cars. This move towards 'downsizing' was most pronounced in the United States where imports of small cars rose sharply at the expense of domestically produced 'gas guzzlers'.

These broader trends in consumer awareness were given added bite by dramatic shifts in public policies. Governments everywhere set out to contain their dependence on imported energy sources by regulating the use and production of automobiles. Particularly important were the US Corporate Average Fuel Economy (CAFE) regulations which set mandatory fuel-consumption targets for domestic producers based on a weighted average of their product ranges and forced them to move towards a larger proportion of small cars. Alongside these interventions in many countries came the proliferation of regulations concerned with emissions controls and vehicle safety which gave a further impetus to product redesign.

To many observers, the events of the 1970s signalled the clear transformation of automobiles into a mature industry characterized by slow growth of demand for a well-defined and technologically stable product. The two oil shocks appeared to have accelerated this process by eroding the distinctiveness of national markets and promoting the convergence of international demand on a limited range of fuel-efficient cars. But viewed in the longer term, these assumptions about the development of international automobile markets proved ill founded. Firstly, the oil shocks of the seventies did not signal a once-and-for-all shift to higher oil prices. By the early 1980s the Organization of Petroleum Exporting Countries (OPEC) was struggling to maintain its cohesion and oil prices were falling again in real terms, as they had between the two shocks themselves. Secondly, the fears about the exhaustion of oil resources commonly voiced in the mid-seventies came to appear exaggerated as recession and energy conservation drastically reduced the fuel consumption of the developed countries. The real long-term consequence of the oil shocks proved to be a growing trend towards instability of raw material prices more generally, which, reinforced by the erratic fluctuations of exchange rates throughout the international economy, created major difficulties in forecasting demand and made large-scale investments and locational decisions increasingly uncertain.

Despite the worldwide pressures for greater fuel efficiency, moreover, the impetus to convergence of national markets proved less intense than had been expected. Economies in petrol consumption were secured across the whole spectrum of car sizes, and markets such as that of the United States remained distinctive in the share of larger cars in total demand. Within each national market, finally, competition came to centre increasingly on the multiplication of an ever-wider range of models and vehicle types and the introduction of new product features such as aerodynamic bodies, electronics and fuel injection, fragmenting demand into a larger number of less clearly defined segments. As Volpato shows in chapter 8, observers have accordingly come to see the international automobile industry as characterized by tendencies towards 'de-maturity' or indeed as a 'neo-infant industry' in which the definition of the product and the conditions of competition have once again become open questions.[16]

No one has done as much as the Japanese to push the world automobile industry towards 'de-maturity' and no one has benefited as much from the market trends associated with it. By 1982, Japan had become the world's biggest automobile producer, with an annual output of 6.9 million cars, 60 per cent exported. The Japanese had won a major stake in many Western car markets – 23 per cent in the US and 8.6 per cent in Europe – and their share would have been considerably higher had they not been forced to accept voluntary import quotas in many cases. To take the most extreme examples, Italy limits Japanese sales to 2,200 per year or less than 0.1 per cent of the domestic market and France to 2.7 per cent.[17]

The Japanese industry revived after the war as a low volume, high cost producer catering for a protected home market characterized by low incomes, poor roads and restricted demand. Japanese producers initially set out to emulate the Fordist model as far as possible. Some companies such as Nissan sought access to foreign technology and vehicle designs through joint ventures with Western companies such as Austin, employment of consultant engineers and imports of machinery. Others such as Toyota preferred to learn by doing rather than buy in ready-made equipment and designs, copying Western machines in their own workshops and adapting them to the smaller volumes demanded by the Japanese market. But in both cases, the Japanese struggle to catch up with their Western competitors through continuous rationalization and model upgrading gave rise to distinctive modifications of Fordist methods which would ultimately permit greater product diversity and productive flexibility.

As Shimokawa demonstrates in chapter 9, the Japanese pursued their dash for growth through the constant redesign of their manufacturing system and the establishment of new relationships between assemblers and suppliers and between managers and workers substantially different from those prevailing in Western car firms operating on Fordist principles. To offset the cost penalties of low-volume production, the Japanese reduced their dependence on special-purpose machinery by lowering minimum efficient scales of operation in each phase of the manufacturing process, replacing large machines with several small ones, attaching special jigs and fixtures to general-purpose equipment, perfecting quick die changes and machine set-ups, and assembling several different models on the same line. Similarly, to reduce the capital costs of rapid expansion, the Japanese cut down inventory and work-in-progress as far as possible. Rather than depending on large buffer stocks to ensure continuity of production, they developed 'kanban' systems whereby components were produced to order and delivered 'just-in-time' for the assembly process. 'Just-in-time' systems highlighted bottlenecks in production and helped to overcome the poor reputation of Japanese products in export markets by facilitating continuous quality control and defect prevention in place of the systems of inspection and rectification used by Western car firms.

To lessen their dependence on imported components and facilitate continuous upgrading of models and rationalization of production, the

Japanese assemblers deliberately stimulated the creation of networks of specialist suppliers clustered around the main factory, frequently spun off from their own organization. In contrast to prevailing Western practice of vertical integration, multiple sourcing and competitive contract tendering, the Japanese assemblers decentralized production as far as possible to component suppliers with whom they cultivated long-term relationships based on single sourcing and detailed collaboration on product engineering and technology transfer. After the defeat of the industrial unions in the early 1950s, the Japanese car manufacturers were also able to undertake a major restructuring of workplace relations as part of the broader changes in manufacturing practice. In return for considerable security of employment for their core labour force, the Japanese, as we have seen, created a highly flexible system of working practices based on widespread job rotation linked to broad worker training, a wage system that facilitated transfers between posts without constant renegotiation, and the devolution of responsibility for task assignment and quality control to supervisors and work groups. In the 1950s the Japanese enjoyed the advantage of wage levels well below those of Western producers, but by the 1970s earnings in the car assembly plants had begun to catch up with European standards and by the early 1980s had overtaken countries like Britain and Italy. As in Western countries, however, compensation levels in supplier firms remain substantially lower, and the Japanese continue to enjoy a relative cost advantage in this area because of their lower degree of vertical integration.

The Japanese innovations in car production began as a series of *ad hoc* modifications to Fordist practice designed to enable them to match Western standards of efficiency and quality in mass production as quickly as possible. But over time these innovations came to form the basis of a new system of production which could outpace Western car manufacturers in labour productivity, product quality and cost competitiveness whilst also permitting the production of a wider range of models and more flexible responses to market trends. With the main features of this system already in place, the Japanese automobile industry took off in the 1960s, pushed forward by high levels of investment and capacity utilization within a rapidly expanding domestic market and by the first wave of export sales. The oil shocks of the 1970s gave an added boost to the Japanese industry by cracking open the North American market and realigning demand in precisely those segments where they were strongest. As sales volumes soared, the Japanese were able to achieve dramatic advantages in cost competitiveness – as great as $2,000 per model over the Americans – while at the same time achieving higher standards of quality and reliability. This cost advantage, as a number of detailed studies show, is not the result of greater mechanization, nor can it be explained in any large measure by lower wages. Japanese companies' pioneering use of Computer Aided Design/Computer Aided Manufacturing (CAD/CAM) systems has allowed them to capitalize on their productive flexibility to speed up the introduction of new models and widen their product ranges, opening up a variety of specialist market niches. And by the mid-1980s, their growing financial and productive strength had enabled the Japanese to close the design gap with the Europeans and force the pace in technical innovation, leaving them poised to achieve competitive superiority across the entire product spectrum.

The crisis of the 1970s presented Western automobile manufacturers with three main strategic options which they pursued singly and in various combinations. Faced with changes in demand and new forms of international competition, Western car firms could seek to revivify the Fordist model through increased automation, decentralization of production to low wage areas abroad and reduction of manning and compensation levels at home; they could seek to emulate the Japanese by revamping their own manufacturing systems in the direction of increased flexibility and product diversity; or finally they could seek to insulate themselves from the effects of international trends through the pursuit of protection and joint ventures in their domestic markets.

In the late 1970s, the American producers in particular based their strategy on the diagnosis discussed earlier that international demand for cars was converging around a narrow range of models. They believed that the rise in oil prices necessitated a once and for all design shift towards smaller cars which would be even more standardized than their predecessors. This shift would revive the possibility of further economies of scale and cost reductions through the introduction of new forms of dedicated automation and the relocation of labour-intensive phases of production in low-wage areas abroad, a trend encouraged by the efforts of less developed countries to attract multinational direct investment. Costs in the remaining domestic production facilities could then be dramatically reduced by massive cutbacks in employment and pressure on the surviving workforce to accept lower wages and revised working practices. The most ambitious attempt to put this 'world car' strategy into practice was General Motors' J-Car, a small fuel-efficient model aimed to be built and sold world-wide, but Ford, too, sought economies of scale at a global level with its Escort-Lynx project, and European manufacturers such as Volkswagen began to step up their investments in Third World countries such as Mexico and Brazil. While most automobile companies trimmed their workforce, these cutbacks reached dramatic levels in the United States and the UK, where employment fell by more than 25 per cent between 1978 and 1981. The resulting unemployment, together with the threat of increased overseas production, gave the companies the opportunity to extract major concessions from the unions.

The world-car strategy quickly ran aground on a series of unforeseen problems. Rather than the expected convergence of national markets, as we have seen, world demand for cars entered a phase of progressive 'dematurity' and diversification. As Dombois shows in chapter 10, moreover, relocation in Mexico as in other Third World countries was no guarantee of low production costs: long supply lines, large inventories, poor quality control and unstable exchange rates more than offset the advantages of low wages. By the late 1970s, finally, political upheavals and labour militancy in countries like Brazil had begun to close the wage gap with domestic manufacturing facilities. With the increasing importance of tailoring production to precise segments of demand in individual national markets, even General Motors had been forced to retreat from its full-blooded world-car strategy by the early 1980s, though it continues to source certain components such as engines and minor mechanicals on a global basis.[18]

With the eclipse of the world-car strategy, automobile manufacturers in the United States as in Europe have turned increasingly towards efforts to emulate the achievements of the Japanese in product diversity and productive flexibility. As in the case of responses to Fordism in a previous era, however, reactions to the Japanese model have taken a variety of forms depending on the configurations of national markets, the political and institutional context and the strategic choices of the various actors concerned. And just as the lessons of Fordism proved ambiguous when the Europeans tried to appropriate them between the wars, so too the sources of Japanese success have been subject to countervailing and often contradictory interpretations by academics and Western car makers alike.[19]

Both in the United States and in Europe the 1980s have seen far-reaching renewal and restructuring of model ranges. As Volpato argues in chapter 8, in the United States, manufacturers' efforts have centred on large-scale entry into hitherto neglected market segments involving smaller vehicles and front-wheel drive, most notably in GM's proposed new Saturn project for the production of a wholly new American small car. In Europe, on the other hand, where vehicle designs were more advanced and model ranges wider, efforts centred initially on the rationalization and integration of unbalanced product lines through increased use of common components. But in both regions car manufacturers have become increasingly concerned to offer a wider variety of distinctive packages targetted at more narrowly defined market segments. The model replacement cycle has been accelerated, particularly through the use of CAD/CAM, and there has been a multiplication of engine types as well as an increasing emphasis on specialized products such as people carriers, off-road vehicles and high-performance saloons.

But both European and American automobile companies have concentrated their greatest attention on production, in order to narrow the Japanese cost advantage and introduce a larger measure of flexibility into the manufacturing process. Much of the effort and investment in this area has focused on the introduction of new forms of automation aimed at improved product quality and process efficiency rather than the elimination of direct labour *per se*. Whereas in the past automation had been associated with dedicated machines and extreme productive rigidity, technological developments such as reprogrammable robots have now made it possible to combine high levels of automation with increased flexibility. Such developments have accordingly reduced the importance of economies of scale in many parts of the manufacturing process, bringing the benefits of automation within the reach of specialist as well as mass producers. But the new technology also leaves considerable scope for managerial choice and some companies have gone further down this road than others. Fiat set a pioneering example with its Robogate system which allowed several different body types to be assembled on the same line, and as Jürgens, Dohse and Malsch show in chapter 11, German producers such as Volkswagen have largely followed this lead. Giant multinationals such as Ford of Europe have felt less need to move away from dedicated equipment because of their ability to achieve considerable flexibility through switching production between plants in different countries; while as Willman shows in chapter 13, British Leyland has turned increasingly towards flexible automation after its negative experience with rigid multiwelders installed on the Metro lines at end of the 1970s.

These changes in product and production strategies have driven car manufacturers to seek new relationships with their component suppliers. Pressures towards improved quality and lower costs along with the growing trend towards the use of common components across different models have led to the rationalization of component supply networks and the elimination of weaker companies. But Western automobile producers have also set out to imitate the Japanese *kanban* model by developing closer and more collaborative relationships with the suppliers who remain. Many companies have turned towards single sourcing and long-term contracts with a smaller number of suppliers whom they expect to take increasing responsibility for quality control, technical innovation and the reduction of inventory through frequent deliveries; and American automobile manufacturers in particular have pressed component firms to relocate around their main assembly plants. Even in the most advanced cases, however, these changes have tended to fall short of the Japanese example, since supply lines remain relatively long and manufacturers have found it difficult to resist the temptation to off-load the burdens of frequent deliveries onto their suppliers rather than helping them to develop genuine forms of 'just-in-time' production.

Efforts to imitate the Japanese example have also led European and American car manufacturers to seek far-reaching changes in shop-floor relationships and working practices. Growing product diversity and the shift away from rigid technologies creates pressures for more fluid job roles and more flexible deployment of labour within the factory. As Jürgens et al. in chapter 11, Katz in chapter 12, and Willman in chapter 13 all demonstrate, management on both sides of the Atlantic has pursued the goals of broader job classifications and the abolition of barriers to labour mobility. Widespread use of team working, the devolution of certain skilled tasks to production workers and the relaxation of demarcation lines on maintenance crews are all examples of this trend. But as in the case of automation, management retains considerable strategic choice in the development of working practices, and there remains great ambiguity about the implications of the Japanese example. In some cases, as Willman shows for Britain, management has been most concerned with the reassertion of its authority on the shop floor against the unions and the improvement of productivity through tighter discipline and more intensive working, with limited aims in the area of flexibility. In other cases, management has made increased flexibility of labour deployment a central priority, whether imposed unilaterally as in Italy or bargained with trade unions as in West Germany and the United States.

Where management has pursued increased flexibility of working practices as a central objective, the institutional context of industrial relations and trade-union strategies have strongly conditioned the outcome. In Italy, as we saw in section 2 above, the trade unions' political commitments and tactical rigidity made any durable accommodation with Fiat management impossible, and after its victory in the strike of 1980 the company swept away shop-floor controls and moved rapidly to introduce team working and job mobility. In West Germany, as Jürgens et al. describe in chapter 11, industrial unions and works councils concerned with job security have been quite prepared to collaborate with management in reorganizing work practices to enhance established patterns of flexible labour deployment, as in the case of the Lohndifferenzierungs-Tarifvertrag (LODI) agreement at Volkswagen which links wages to skill within broad job bands. Finally, in the United States, as Katz demonstrates in chapter 12, the UAW and its locals under intense pressure from management have moved slowly towards the relaxation of seniority rules and the widening of job classifications in exchange for greater job security, protection against outsourcing and the prospect of greater influence over business decisions. But in every case, the growing demands from management for increased productive flexibility are forcing the unions to rethink and revise job-control practices and bargaining strategies established in the heyday of Fordism.[20]

While Western car manufacturers have sought to emulate Japanese product, production and labour strategies, they have also sought to insulate themselves to some degree from the harsh winds of international competition through government protection and joint ventures with the Japanese themselves. Nearly every major car-producing nation maintains formal or informal restrictions on Japanese imports of varying intensity. In some markets such as France, Italy and Spain, Japanese cars are almost entirely excluded and in others such as Britain and the United States, domestic pressures have been mounting for some kind of local content legislation. At the same time, however, Western manufacturers have entered commercial tie-ups with Japanese automobile companies in hopes of learning to emulate their production methods, or, failing that, to gain a financial stake in Japanese success and keep intact their dealer networks by maintaining a full range of products. The Japanese, for their part, as Shimokawa observes in chapter 9, have responded to these barriers against their products by moving into direct foreign investment, either independently, as in the case of Honda and Nissan, or in collaboration with local manufacturers. The success or failure of these ventures, which are still in their early stages, will prove a major test of the transportability of the Japanese model outside its national base.[21]

By the 1970s the modified Fordist systems practised by American and European automobile manufacturers had become sluggish and internally contradictory. Their factories were bulging with inventory and work-in-progress; maintenance and work scheduling were a constant problem, resulting in frequent interruptions of production; and high-volume output was pursued at the expense of product quality. The diversity of models and options required for marketing stood in tension with the uniformity and standardization required for the efficient operation of a Fordist production system, and Western car manufacturers had become extremely vulnerable to any major disruption in the postwar growth pattern.

The Japanese set out initially to adapt Fordist systems to the requirements of an accelerated catching-up process, and some observers see their achievement as a quantum leap forward in the same direction. The Japanese, in this view, have brought out and eliminated certain key imperfections in the Fordist model, making it possible to combine product diversity with mass production on an unprecedented scale. In consequence, the gap they have opened up can now be closed by Western manufacturers through a straightforward process of organizational imitation and management reform without a fundamental reconsideration of established strategy and practice. Some automobile manufacturers appear to share this view, notably Ford, whose 'After Japan' programme concentrates on automation, inventory reduction and quality control with more limited shifts in personnel policies and relations with suppliers.[22]

Other observers, by contrast, see the Japanese innovations as a deeper challenge to the Fordist model which reverses its central principles and points towards the emergence of a qualitatively new system of production. This system, which can be termed 'flexible specialization' and has been observed across a wide range of industrial sectors, depends on the combination of increasingly flexible, general-purpose equipment and a skilled, adaptable labour force to manufacture an ever more diversified range of products for which economies of scale are becoming decreasingly important. Not only the Japanese but also some Western automobile manufacturers seem to be moving in this direction, notably the Germans and the Swedes, with their growing emphasis on multi-skilled work teams to exploit the full potential of flexible automation systems for the manufacture of a changing array of high quality products.[23]

Recent developments in the international automobile industry have undermined the foundations of the Fordist model as it developed in the postwar period. But many of the established features of automobile production can still be discerned, while the more recent innovations are susceptible to elaboration in different directions. CAD/CAM systems have reduced the lead time for the introduction of new models, facilitating the development of wider product ranges; but the increasing complexity of the product and the difficulties of integrating automobile subsystems experiencing different rates of innovation keeps research and development costs high and creates financial problems for small manufacturers. While there has been a qualitative expansion in the available range of vehicle types and models, the use of common components and subsystems has also become increasingly important in the generation of new variants. Flexible automation equipment and changes in job design have lowered minimum efficient scales of operation in many stages of component production and vehicle assembly, but substantial economies of scale still remain in the manufacture of major mechanicals such as engines and gearboxes, leading to growing reliance on joint ventures on the part of smaller producers. The new automation equipment can be used to decrease batch sizes and eliminate machine pacing for more broadly skilled workers, or can serve instead to move towards the ideal of a 'worker-less factory' through the integration of complex sequences of transfer machines. While overall skill levels have clearly been rising, it remains uncertain, finally, whether this tendency will be confined to the development of a wider range of interchangeability between semi-skilled jobs or will lead instead to the emergence of new job categories which more fundamentally erode the boundary between skilled and semi-skilled tasks. Current practice in automobile companies accordingly ranges from the reduction of rigidities in the manufacture of a broadly standardized product line to conscious efforts at building maximum flexibility into all aspects of an increasingly diversified production process.

The changed market conditions and new technologies of the 1970s and 1980s have brought with them shifts in competitive strategy and manufacturing practice which pose a fundamental challenge to the Fordist model. But as in the case of the emergence and diffusion of Fordism itself, the outcome of its crisis for the future of the automobile industry and its workers will be determined not by some intrinsic imperatives of markets and technology but rather by the strategic choices of corporate managements, trade unions and national governments.

NOTES

1   This account of Ford's innovations and the development of his competitive strategy draws on the following sources: A. D. Chandler, Jr. (ed.), *Giant Enterprise: Ford, General Motors and the Automobile Industry* (New York, 1964), pp. 23–95; D. Hounshell, *From the American System to Mass Production, 1800–1932* (Baltimore, 1984), pp. 217–63; S. Meyer III, *The Five Dollar Day: Labor Management and Social Control in the Ford Motor Company* (Albany, NY, 1981); *idem*, 'Mechanical Engineers and Automobile Workers: American Machine-Tool Technology and the "Transfer of Skill" from the 1900s through the 1930s', in N. Lichtenstein and S. Meyer (eds.), *The American Automobile Industry: A Social History* (Champaign-Urbana, Ill., forthcoming 1987); A. Nevins with F. E. Hill, *Ford: The Times, the Man, the Company* (New York, 1954); and C. F. Sabel, *Work and Politics* (Cambridge, 1982), pp. 32–3.
2   For an overview of the development of automobile production in Europe, see J. P. Bardou, J. J. Chanaron, P. Fridenson and J. M. Laux, *The Automobile*

Revolution (Chapel Hill, NC, 1982), pts. I–II. For a more detailed discussion of the German market, in which demand for automobiles was particularly constrained by social and institutional factors before the 1930s, see F. Blaich, 'The Development of the Distribution Sector in the German Car Industry', in A. Okochi and K. Shimokawa (eds.), *The Development of Mass Marketing* (Tokyo, 1982).

3   On plans for a 'people's car' during the late 1930s and their postwar realization, see Bardou et al., *The Automobile Revolution*, pp. 142–50, 172–88, 212–15. For German motorization under the Nazis and the Volkswagen project, see: Blaich, 'German Car Industry'; R. J. Overy, 'Transportation and Rearmament in the Third Reich', *Historical Journal* 16 (1973); and *idem*, 'Cars, Roads and Economic Recovery in Germany, 1932–8', *Economic History Review* 28 (1975).

4   This account of the transformation of the American market and the competing responses of Ford and General Motors draws on: Chandler, *Giant Enterprise*, pp. 95–178; Hounshell, *From the American System to Mass Production*, pp. 263–302; Meyer, 'Mechanical Engineers and Automobile Workers'; A. P. Sloan, *My Years with General Motors* (New York, 1964), esp. pp. 59–70, 148–68; H. F. Katz, *The Decline of Competition in the U.S. Automobile Industry, 1920–40* (New York, 1977); and M. J. Piore and C. F. Sabel, *The Second Industrial Divide* (New York, 1984), pp. 60–3.

5   For these developments in the American industry, see: Sloan, *My Years with General Motors*, esp. pp. 169–88, 238–47, 264–78; L. J. White, *The Automobile Industry since 1945* (Cambridge, Mich., 1971); C. E. Edwards, *The Dynamics of the United States Automobile Industry* (Columbia, South Carolina, 1965); B. Yates, *The Decline and Fall of the American Automobile Industry* (New York, 1983), esp. pp. 186–200; E. J. Toder, *Trade Policy and the US Automobile Industry* (New York, 1978); W. J. Abernathy, *The Productivity Dilemma: Roadblock to Innovation in the Automobile Industry* (Baltimore, 1978); E. Rothschild, *Paradise Lost: The Decline of the Auto-Industrial Age* (New York, 1973).

6   For this picture of postwar European developments, in addition to chapter 8, see: A. Altshuler, M. Anderson, D. Jones, D. Roos and J. Womack, *The Future of the Automobile* (London, 1985), esp. pp. 121–45; Bardou et al., *The Automobile Revolution*, pp. 172–209, D. T. Jones, *Maturity and Crisis in the European Car Industry: Structural Change and Public Policy* (Brighton, 1981); G. Maxcy, *The Multinational Motor Industry* (London, 1981), pp. 94–7.

7   For the debates over industrial unionism within the AFL, see: W. Galenson, *The CIO Challenge to the AFL* (Cambridge, Mich., 1960); and James O. Morris, *Conflict Within the AFL: A Study of Craft Versus Industrial Unionism, 1901–1938* (Ithaca, NY, 1958). For similar but more muted debates in Britain, see J. Hinton, *The First Shop Stewards' Movement* (London, 1973), pp. 275–337; and H. A. Clegg, *A History of British Trade Unions since 1889, vol. II: 1911–33* (Oxford, 1985), pp. 455–9.

8   See especially D. Brody, 'The Emergence of Mass-Production Unionism' and 'Reinterpreting the Labor History of the 1930s' in *Workers in Industrial America* (New York, 1980); and H. Harris, 'The Snares of Liberalism? Politicians, Bureaucrats, and the Shaping of Federal Labour Relations Policy in the United States, ca. 1915–47', in S. Tolliday and J. Zeitlin (eds.), *Shop Floor Bargaining and the State* (Cambridge, 1985).

9   Even in the United States, historians have recently argued that the AFL unions

showed greater organizational dynamism and flexibility than the polemics of the 1930s suggested: see C. Tomlins, 'AFL Unions in the 1930s: Their Performance in Historical Perspective', *Journal of American History* 64 (1979).

10 On the impact of the statutory framework on the relationship between industrial unions and works councils in the West German automobile industry, see W. Streeck, *Industrial Relations in West Germany: A Case Study of the Car Industry* (London, 1984), especially pp. 9–39; and E. Brumlop and U. Jürgens, 'Rationalisation and Industrial Relations in the West German Auto Industry: A Case Study of Volkswagen', in O. Jacobi et al. (eds.), *Technological Change, Rationalisation and Industrial Relations* (London, 1985); for the political conflicts surrounding its emergence in the late 1940s and early 1950s, see M. Nolan and C. F. Sabel, 'Class Conflict and the Social Democratic Reform Cycle in Germany', *Political Power and Social Theory* III (1982).

11 For parallel developments at Nissan, see M. Cusumano, *The Japanese Automobile Industry* (Cambridge, Mich., 1985), pp. 137–85.

12 For American views of Britain, see D. Brody, 'The Uses of Power I: The Industrial Battleground' in *Workers in Industrial America*; and N. Lichtenstein, 'Auto Worker Militancy and the Structure of Factory Life', *Journal of American History* 67, no. 2 (1980). For a West German view of Italy, see R. Zoll, 'Centralisation and Decentralisation as Tendencies of Union Organisational and Bargaining Policy', in C. Crouch and A. Pizzorno (eds.), *The Resurgence of Class Conflict in Western Europe Since 1968* (London, 1978), vol. II.

13 For an interpretation along these lines, see Streeck, *Industrial Relations in West Germany*; and for a detailed comparison with the United States, see C. Kohler and W. Sengenberger, 'Policies of Work Force Reduction and Labor Market Structures in the American and German Automobile Industry', paper presented to the conference of the International Working Party on Labour Market Segmentation, Modena, Italy, 7–11 September 1981; and *idem, Konjunktur und Personalanpassung: betriebliche Beschaftigungspolitik in der deutschen und amerikanischen Automobilindustrie* (Frankfurt, 1983).

14 For reviews of the recent literature on enterprise unionism and shop-floor practice in Japan, see: T. Shirai (ed.), *Contemporary Industrial Relations in Japan* (Madison, Wis., 1983), especially Shirai, 'A Theory of Enterprise Unionism' and K. Koike, 'Internal Labor Markets: Workers in Large Firms'; and 'Industrial Relations in Japan and the United States: How Different?', a symposium in Industrial Relations Research Association, *Papers and Proceedings of the 35th Annual Meeting* (Madison, Wis., 1982), especially K. Taira, 'Labor Productivity and Industrial Relations in the United States and Japan' and H. Shimada, 'Japan's Postwar Industrial Growth and Labor-Management Relations'; and R. E. Cole, *Work, Mobility and Participation* (Berkeley, 1979). For a comparison of enterprise unionism at Nissan and Toyota, see Cusumano, *The Japanese Automobile Industry*, pp. 174–9.

15 For the following account of changes in world demand for cars and the emergence of new forms of international competition during the 1970s, in addition to chapter 8 of this volume see: Althshuler et al., *The Future of the Automobile,* chs. 2 and 6; Piore and Sabel, *The Second Industrial Divide*, pp. 165–93; Jones, *Maturity and Crisis in the European Car Industry, passim;* Y. L. Doz, 'Shifts in International Competitiveness among Automobile Manufacturers', (unpublished paper presented to the 'America Challenged' conference, Hanover, NH, May 1982); D. H. Ginsburg and W.J. Abernathy

(ed.), *Government, Technology and the Future of the Automobile* (New York, 1980).

16   For the debate on maturity and 'de-maturity' in the international automobile industry, in addition to the works already cited see: G. Bloomfield, *The World Automotive Industry* (London, 1978); K. Bhaskar, *The Future of the World Automobile Industry* (London, 1980); P. Waymark, *The Car Industry* (London, 1983); L. T. Wells, 'The International Product Life Cycle and United States Regulation of the Automobile Industry', in Ginsburg and Abernathy, *Government, Technology and the Future of the Automobile*; Maxcy, *The Multinational Motor Industry*, pp. 159–78; Y. L. Doz, 'The Internationalisation of Manufacturing in the Automobile Industry: Some Recent Trends', *Social Science Information* 20, no. 6 (1981); and especially W. J. Abernathy, A. M. Kantrow and K. B. Clark, *Industrial Renaissance* (New York, 1983).

17   On the development and characteristics of the Japanese automobile industry, in addition to chapters 7 and 9 of this volume, see: Cusumano, *The Japanese Automobile Industry*; R. Schonberger, *Japanese Manufacturing Techniques* (New York, 1982); K. Shimokawa, 'The Structure of Japanese Auto Parts Industry and Its Contribution to Automotive Process Innovation', unpublished paper presented to the Massachusetts Institute of Technology Auto Program International Policy Forum, Hakone, Japan, 1982; D. Friedman, 'Beyond the Age of Ford: The Strategic Basis of the Japanese Success in Automobiles' in J. Zysman and L. Tyson (eds.), *American Industry in International Competition: Government Policies and Corporate Strategies* (Ithaca, NY, 1983); J. B. Rae, *Nissan/Datsun: The History of Nissan Motor Corporation in the USA, 1960–80* (New York, 1982); Abernathy et al., *Industrial Renaissance*, chs. 4–7; Piore and Sabel, *The Second Industrial Divide*, pp. 156–62 and 223–6; and Altshuler et al., *The Future of the Automobile*, pp. 146–64.

18   For the rise and fall of the world-car strategy, in addition to the works cited in note 16 above, see: R. B. Cohen, 'International Market Positions, International Investment Strategies and the Domestic Reorganization Plans of US Automakers', unpublished paper, New York Graduate School of Business, 1982; R. Jenkins, 'Internationalisation of Capital and the Semi-Industrialised Countries: The Case of the Motor Industry', unpublished paper presented to the Conference on Internationalisation and Industrialisation of the Periphery, Oaxtepec, Mexico, 1983; R. Kronish and K. S. Mericle (eds.), *The Political Economy of the Latin American Motor Vehicle Industry* (Cambridge, Mass., 1984); J. Humphrey, *Capitalist Control and Workers' Struggle in the Brazilian Auto Industry* (Princeton, NJ, 1982).

19   For competing interpretations of the impact of Japanese competition on Western automobile manufacturers' product and production strategies, in addition to the essays in this volume, see: Altshuler et al., *The Future of the Automobile*, pp. 77–105 and 164–80; Piore and Sabel, *The Second Industrial Divide*, chs 8–9 and 11, *passim*; H. C. Katz and C. F. Sabel, 'Industrial Relations and Industrial Adjustment in the Car Industry' *Industrial Relations* 24, no. 3 (1985); W. Streeck, 'Industrial Relations and Industrial Change in the Motor Industry: An International View', 1985 Leverhulme Lecture, Industrial Relations Research Unit, University of Warwick; K. Williams, J. Williams and C. Haslam, *The Breakdown of Austin-Rover* (Leamington Spa, forthcoming 1987), chs 3–4.

20   For recent developments in shop floor practice and industrial relations, in addition to the essays in this volume and the works already cited, see: Altshuler

et al., *The Future of the Automobile*, ch. 9; Katz and Sabel, 'Industrial Relations and Industrial Adjustment'; W. Streeck and A. Hoff (eds), *Workforce Restructuring, Manpower Management and Industrial Relations in the World Automobile Industry* (International Institute of Management (IIM), Berlin, 1983); Streeck (ed.), *Industrial Relations and Technical Change in the British, Italian and German Automobile Industry* (IIM, Berlin, 1985); *idem*, 'Industrial Relations and Industrial Change'; D. Marsden, T. Morris, P. Willman and S. Wood, *The Car Industry: Labour Relations and Industrial Adjustment* (London, 1985); S. Wood, 'Technological Change and the Cooperative Labour Strategy in the U.S. Auto Industry', paper presented to the European Group for Organizational Studies (EGOS) conference on 'Trade Unions, New Technology and Industrial Democracy', University of Warwick, 6–8 June 1986.

21 On protectionism, joint ventures and the internationalization of the Japanese industry, see: Altshuler et al., *The Future of the Automobile*, pp. 223–47 and 291–9; Y. L. Doz, 'International Industries, Multinational companies and Government Policies: The European Experience', unpublished paper presented to the IIM Conference on Multinational Corporation-Host Government Relationships in Developed Countries, Berlin, October 1980; *idem*, 'L'internationalisation de l'industrie automobile japonaise: potentiel et limites', *Cahiers IREP/Developement* no. 6 (1984); K. Shimokawa, 'New Developments in International Cooperation Within the Motor Industry', *The Wheel Extended* 13, no. 1 (1982); *idem*, 'Automobiles – Groping for Coexistence Rather Than International Rivalry', unpublished paper, Hosei University, Japan, 1984.

22 For interpretations in this direction, see: Williams et al., *The Breakdown of Austin-Rover*, ch. 3; and Wood, 'Technological Change and the Cooperative Labour Strategy'. For a senior management view from the Ford Motor Company, see the interview with James Bakken, Vice-President Operations Support Staff, Ford U.S. in *Automotive News* 28 February 1983.

23 For a fuller discussion of 'flexible specialization', see Piore and Sabel, *The Second Industrial Divide*; and C. Sabel and J. Zeitlin, 'Historical Alternatives to Mass Production: Politics, Markets and Technology in Nineteenth-Century Industrialization', *Past and Present* 108 (1985). Analyses of the automobile industry in these terms include Katz and Sabel, 'Industrial Relations and Industrial Adjustment'; and Streeck, 'Industrial Relations and Industrial Change', who also uses the term 'differentiated quality production'.

Part One
The Rise of Fordism

1

Management and Labour in Britain 1896-1939

Steven Tolliday

We want to construct some kind of machine that will last forever . . . We want the man who buys one of our cars never to have to buy another. We never make an improvement that renders any previous model obsolete.

Henry Ford, 1922[1]

Let me say at once that our success has not been achieved by what is commonly called 'mass production'. I prefer to spell 'mass' with an 'e'. So far mass production has meant merely *mess* production when applied to motor cars in this country.

William Morris, 1924[2]

By the early 1920s, the dramatic successes of Henry Ford's methods in the USA seemed to have defined a universal standard of practice for the mass production and marketing of automobiles. The methods of European manufacturers used before the First World War were rapidly outdated and many European producers believed that they had to emulate Ford to survive and prosper in the modern world. But some imitated the Fordist model more closely than others. In Britain, as the contrasting views quoted above suggest, leading mass producers like Morris departed from Ford's methods in important ways. Similarly, the dramatic rise of the United Auto Workers (UAW) in the USA and of the Conféderation Générale du Travail (CGT) in France in the 1930s suggested for a time that mass industrial unionism might be a uniquely appropriate trade-union counterpart to Fordism. In Britain, however, an untidy assortment of craft and general unions signally failed to make much of an impact on the motor firms.

The variety of ways in which Fordism was emulated or adapted in Europe raises important questions about the relationship between Fordist methods of mass production, the imperatives of different national markets and the importance of strategic decisions by management. The variety of union responses, in turn, throw up important questions about the relationship between union structures and effective union growth. The first part of this essay looks at how and why British producers adapted or departed from Fordist methods and what this implied for labour. The second part analyses how unions and workers reacted to the problems and opportunities they faced and attempts to explain their lack of success in coping with them.

FORDISM AND THE RISE OF MASS PRODUCTION IN BRITAIN

The emergence of Henry Ford's mass production methods for the manufacture of the Model T was predicated on what David Hounshell has described as 'an almost astrological alignment of circumstances'.[3] Ford's small corps of gifted mechanics in the workshops refined existing elements of the American tradition of repetition production, particularly in the fields of standardization and simplification of products, specialization of machine tools and interchangeability of parts. They allied these firstly to flow production and then to continuous motion in the form of the assembly line, building on a number of very recent developments in metallurgy and machine-tool design which made possible new levels of precision in manufacturing. But there were two further preconditions for the dramatic systematization of these developments. The first was Henry Ford's own overarching conception of how the pieces of the system fitted together. The second was the opportunity presented by a uniquely large and homogeneous market. The standardized Model T identified and tapped an enormous reservoir of demand based on Midwestern farmers needing cheap, tough, easy-to-repair cars for all roads. On this basis, Ford increased his output from 8,700 in 1906 to 34,000 in 1911, 300,000 in 1914 and to a peak level of 1.9 million in 1923.[4]

The core of this achievement was a series of technical solutions to the problems of dramatically increasing output and productivity in the absence of an adequate supply of skilled labour. But, as Stephen Meyer has shown, Ford was only able to realize the potential of the technology to the full by combining it with a distinctive labour strategy. Before the construction of the Highland Park plant in 1910, Ford's production was based on a series of craft shops within the plant: even after the new plant was commissioned, elements of this organization of production persisted.[5] But as the new methods were introduced, tasks were broken down and simplified, and a methodical study of work tasks and routines was applied to ensure that as far as possible all jobs were machine-paced and all needless movements eliminated. A vast influx of raw labour was brought into the plant to meet these new needs, primarily drawn from the ranks of newly arrived Southern and Eastern European immigrants in Detroit. By November 1914, 21 per cent of Ford's labour force was Polish, 16 per cent Russian, 6 per cent Rumanian, 5 per cent Italian and 5 per cent German. Many were from peasant backgrounds, few had any experience of industrial work, and many spoke no English.[6]

The immediate result was a situation of disabling anarchy and instability on the shop floor. In 1913, Ford experienced a labour turnover of 370 per cent; 71 per cent of these were so-called 'Five-day men' who simply quit after their first week without telling the company. Fatigue, sickness and 'Forditis' pushed up daily absentee rates as high as 10 per cent of the labour force. Carelessness, ignorance and lack of foresight proliferated breakdowns and undercut the new technology, and increases in overall productivity were disappointing. Ford was therefore obliged to devise new labour policies to complement his production system. These policies developed along two main axes. The first was the intensification of labour discipline using intense driving supervision and the enforcement of work norms on the labour force. The proportion of supervisors was dramatically increased from one per 53 workers in 1914 to one per 15 in 1917 and an army of clerical progress chasers were enlisted to control inventory and keep work-in-progress flowing smoothly through the factory. New hierarchies of foremanship were elaborated, in particular the use of so-called 'straw-bosses', driving disciplinarians who forced the pace of output and whose most essential qualification was to know the words for 'hurry up' in English, German, Polish and Italian. Secondly, parallel to this new coercive apparatus, Ford introduced a number of other reforms designed to stabilize and socialize the workforce, notably the 'Five-Dollar Day' and high wages and various attempts at wider social control through his Sociological Department. Between 1914 and 1917, these measures stabilized absenteeism and labour turnover and produced a renewed quantum leap in productivity. The welfare aspects of these measures proved to be relatively short-lived. In the early 1920s, with the labour force stabilized and relatively Americanized, Ford abandoned his welfarism and the priority accorded to the motivation of workers, leaving relatively high pay and strict, often repressive, supervision as the cornerstones of the system.[7]

The origins of Fordism, therefore, lay in a convulsive leap from craft to mass production. Once the system was established the main requirement at Highland Park and later at the giant River Rouge plant, was to run an insatiable machine-paced technology flat out. Enforced work norms, intense supervision and daily flat-rate payments were the most appropriate organizational forms. For most of the 1920s the product was unchanging and improvements were solely focused on refining the efficiency of the productive system. As the quotation at the head of this chapter suggests, 'changelessness' was part of both the technical logic of the system and of Ford's own ideology. The main emphasis was on continually cutting production costs. As Ford described it:

Our policy is to reduce the price, extend the operation, and improve the article. You will notice the reduction of price comes first. We have never considered any costs as fixed . . . One of the ways of discovering what a cost ought to be is to name a price so low as to force everybody in the place to the highest point of efficiency. The low price makes everyone dig for efficiency. We make more discoveries concerning manufacturing under this forced method than by any method of leisurely investigation.[8]

The limitations of this approach, however, were soon becoming increasingly apparent as Ford ate up his primary market during the 1920s. The Model T became outmoded in design and technical features, and the single-model policy was challenged by the new strategy of Alfred Sloan's

General Motors, focusing on product improvement and regular model changes. These developments resulted in a precipitate decline in Ford's sales in the late 1920s, and hounded by his dealers, Ford was forced to introduce a wholly new model to replace the Model T in 1928. Hounshell has recently described in detail how the rigidity of the production process made this a traumatic experience involving a long shutdown for the wholesale retooling of the plant and a major crisis for the company.[9] Following this Ford retreated somewhat from his philosophy of 'changelessness' and began to offer more models. The stern clarity of Ford's initial vision was relaxed a little, but the structure of the system was to remain intact until the Second World War and beyond.

Could the Fordist system be transposed to other national markets and circumstances? It has recently been argued, for instance, that it would have been both possible and rational for British manufacturers to imitate Ford's methods from the 1920s, and that their failure to do so was largely the result of resistance by organized labour, resulting in serious detrimental consequences for the long-term future of the British motor industry.[10] This essay takes a different view. The rest of this section argues that Ford's methods could only be successfully introduced in Britain in this period through extensive adaptation. This adaptation was required, however, not to deal with the problems of labour resistance but because of the peculiarities of the British product market. The form that the rise of mass production in the motor industry took exposed some serious weaknesses in the structure and organization of British unions, and the second part of this essay considers how they responded to these new challenges.

British market conditions made it unlikely that Ford's American methods could simply be reproduced there. In the first place, the UK market was a stark contrast to the expansive, egalitarian market of the USA. While Ford alone produced nearly two million cars in the United States in 1923, *total* UK car production was only 182,000 in 1929, reaching a prewar peak of 390,000 in 1937. No single firm sold more than 100,000 cars in any year before the war and no single model attained 70,000.[11] Not only was the market quantitatively smaller, it was also qualitatively different. The work of Maxcy and Silberston and Church and Miller has demonstrated that through the 1920s, the UK market was a restricted quasi-luxury one dominated by the well-off who bought family cars of medium size and price. In the late 1920s, this market was stagnating and sales almost stood still from 1925 to 1933. But the general recovery of middle-class incomes in the 1930s boosted sales to a new higher plateau in the mid-1930s. A whole new income layer was tapped by small but diverse and well-equipped cars. Competition was by model and design, not primarily price, and the diversity of the market precluded the firms with the leading mass-produced models from exerting or increasing their dominance in the overall car market. Thus, though Morris and Austin were able to build their combined market share up to 60 per cent in 1929, they retreated under pressure from several vigorous smaller firms in the 1930s and in 1938 took only 45 per cent of the market, with Ford, Vauxhall, Rootes and Standard all advancing to claim over 10 per cent of the market each.[12]

British mass production, therefore, in contrast to the USA, emerged from a long transition period of intermittently enlarging quantity-flow production. As Morris's disparaging comments on American-style mass production quoted at the head of the chapter suggest, the keynote of the market was quality and continuous improvement rather than quantity and price competition. Mere internal economies of scale could not guarantee market dominance and profitability depended primarily on bringing forward the right new models in an evolving market. The frontier of mechanization was, therefore, continuously shifting and rigorous machine-pacing was limited in its scope. Tasks were regularly reorganized and even in the most advanced flow systems of the 1920s and early 1930s, the separate operations at each stage still needed time and attention by individual workers for efficient completion. Firms therefore looked to adaptable payment systems with strong incentive elements to get the most out of their new machines and forms of work organization.

The more limited levels of output and different goals of production still made possible the adoption of many important elements of Fordist mass production. Even smaller relatively specialized firms like Humber or Rover utilized many of these techniques, such as special-purpose machine tools, the moving assembly line, work rationalization and the purchase of components from specialized outside suppliers. But these elements could be adopted gradually without launching a full-scale Fordist system. Indeed, it would have been counterproductive to pursue the inflexible indivisibilities of American-style Fordism. Many of Europe's leading automobile producers were seduced by the power and technocratic beauty of Ford's factories and sought to imitate them. But the conditions did not exist for them to transplant the integrated system of marketing, production and labour that characterized Ford in America. Ford himself, as we shall see, sailed close to disaster as a result of trying to graft its American strategy on to British conditions. In France and Italy, Berliet, Citroën and Agnelli (Fiat), in particular, were 'dazzled by the Ford spectacle' and nearly ruined themselves when their capital-intensive plants designed for single mass products could not cope with the upheavals resulting from demands for more varied and changing models.[13]

The history of Ford's determined attempts to transpose his methods intact to his British operations between 1911 and 1939 highlights the problems that Fordism faced in the context of other national markets. Only rather belated adaptation enabled a version of the system to survive.

Before the First World War, Ford enjoyed notable success with large-scale sales of the Model T in Britain. Ford established manufacturing operations in Manchester in 1911, bringing in engines and chassis from Detroit and manufacturing their own bodies, and by 1913 this was the largest car-producing factory in Europe. In that year Ford's Manchester factory produced 6,139 cars, compared with the next-best European producers,

Peugeot and Renault, with around 5,000 cars apiece, and the second largest British producer, Wolseley with about 3,000 cars.[14] In both France and the UK sales of cheap small cars stayed below 15 per cent of total sales before the war, and the emphasis was on larger, and generally more costly cars. Ford was able to penetrate the UK market dramatically by offering a similar-sized car at much lower prices. Most British producers concentrated on quality cars for this sector of the market, but Ford's vigorous marketing campaign was able to overcome resistance to 'cheap and nasty' American cars and uncover a potential market for rugged basic transportation in Britain, though the more nationalistic and elite French market remained resistant to the Model T.[15]

At the end of the war, innovations by Austin and Morris showed that the main competitive arena for cheap cars in Britain had shifted to the area of diverse and well-equipped small cars. Ford, however, stuck rigidly to their cheap and basic single Model T. The period from 1919–28 was the 'American era' in Ford of Britain. Detroit aimed to Americanize their British management, and after Percival Perry was sacked following a rift with Ford in 1919, they put in a series of generally short-lived Managing Directors from the United States under instructions to introduce a complete imitation of American products and methods. At times this went to absurd lengths. Until 1923, Henry Ford refused to allow the production of right-hand drive Model Ts for Britain on the grounds that if left-hand drives were good enough for America they were also good enough for Britain. Ford also slavishly pursued other American practices such as regular price cutting and, despite the fact that their prewar successes had been built on very different marketing methods, the establishment of an exclusive dealer network.[16]

Both of these practices had detrimental results, but more crucial was the refusal of Detroit until the late 1920s to listen to continued appeals from European engineers and managers for a new smaller car to replace the hefty and outdated Model T. By 1925, a visiting Detroit engineer noted that 'the entire Manchester organization are hoping that the company will give them a redesigned motor so that they can overcome the well-nigh impregnable sales resistance they now encounter.'[17] Yet Detroit refused to listen with the result that by the mid-1920s, Ford sales in Britain were collapsing utterly during a period of rapid expansion of overall auto sales. Between 1913 and 1929, Ford's share of the British market fell from 24 to 4 per cent. By 1926, their senior managers admitted that 'we have been defeated and licked in Britain'.[18]

Thus Ford's single-model product strategy proved quite inappropriate to Britain in the 1920s. It was accompanied by a parallel attempt by Detroit to introduce American-style methods of labour management into their British operations. In their early days at Manchester, Ford had encountered considerable problems with the craft unions in their body-making departments. In 1911–12, Percival Perry, the Managing Director, reported to Detroit that the Sheet Metal Workers' Union 'have almost broken my heart'[19] with their activities. As a result, in 1912, Detroit sent in one of their leading managers, Charles Sorenson, to bust the unions with a deliberate campaign of sacking unionists and wooing the remaining workers away from the unions with high wages and promises of job security. The result was that by April 1914, Perry could report to Henry Ford that 'the unionism which has always been cropping up heretofore has been absolutely broken up.' Sorenson himself noted on a return visit to Manchester that, even though there was no other employer in Manchester 'who is not obligated in some manner to labor organizations, I can also say that we are the only company in the vicinity who are absolutely free and independent and who are not having controversies any more with their men.'[20]

Manchester remained an almost union-free factory until it was closed after the opening of the big new green-field Dagenham plant in 1932. Ford established a high level of unilateral control over their workforce. One senior manager from this period recalled how, 'the men were treated like nothing . . . we hired and fired so rapidly that it was hard to keep track of what was going on.'[21] They aimed to keep out unions and maintain the pressure for maximum intensity of work from individual workers. The most dramatic manifestation of this policy was probably the work of the 'Yougos', a selected team from Detroit who toured the European plants in the mid 1920s sacking any 'surplus' labour they could spot. (Their name derived from their practice of patrolling departments and sacking people on the spot: 'O.K. You go, you go and you go!'[22]

Yet despite such high levels of authoritarian control, Ford were not able effectively to Americanize production methods at Manchester. Without high levels of demand and throughput, American methods created serious problems for local management, who were shackled on overall labour policies by Detroit. In order to adapt the functioning of the factory to local conditions they had to improvise whenever they could evade Detroit's supervision. For instance, they needed to adjust production to erratic levels of capacity utilization, deal with irregular supplies of parts of sometimes inadequate quality, to cope with frequent interruptions to production, or to solve accumulated problems of detailed engineering. Local management often believed that this required a more stable and integrated workforce than a hire-and-fire system allowed. Hence local management sometimes sought to keep their workforce together, to stabilize fluctuations in employment when sales fluctuated wildly and even to operate their own informal seniority system for workers. At the same time, they saw advantages in seeking a contented labour force through allowing self-help welfare activities in the factory or tolerating working practices such as smoking on the job or tea breaks.[23] These working practices existed only as long as management tolerated them. A Detroit inquisition in the winter of 1923 was scandalized by these practices and overrode the wishes of local management to get them scrapped. There was no visible resistance from the men to these changes and the Detroit team's diagnosis of the situation stressed the fact that the problems they observed in the factory were not the result of worker resistance but of the attitudes and practices of management and supervision.

They were scathing about the 'bunch of clowns' who managed their British operations and the 'stiff white collars' of supervision who refused to get their hands dirty and drive production. Periodically, Detroit decided to send someone 'to go over and fire the whole bunch', as they did in 1924, but the new management that they installed invariably slipped into similar attitudes.[24]

Henry and Edsel Ford's dogmatic attempts to replicate their American 'formula for success' in very different conditions frustrated and bemused many of their British managers. Their desire to implement a high-wages policy in Britain was a case in point. In the USA, high wages were linked to high output and high effort by strict job standards and supervision. But in the context of work organization at Manchester the link was more tenuous. In so far as high wages were part of their general European policy of paying 10–25 per cent above local wage rates to make unions unattractive, the policy had some logic: but at Manchester, the high-wage policy was fetishized and the link to high productivity was quite absent. By 1928, Ford wages were up to three times as high as those in neighbouring factories, and Henry and Edsel Ford regularly turned down appeals from British managers to be allowed to cut wages. When Perry returned as Managing Director in 1928, he severely criticized this practice and argued that, 'High wages are a sound investment on our part, but only up to the point where we can use high wages as an inducement to greater industry and efficiency, and I am convinced that we have passed that point . . . Our present rates are past even the limits of philanthropy.' Eventually, he got permission to hire new labour at reduced rates, though *not* to cut the wages of existing workers.[25]

1928 marked a big retreat by Ford from their policy of trying to Americanize their British operations, when Percival Perry was brought back as Managing Director after nine years in the wilderness with a newly enhanced degree of branch autonomy. Perry's first task was the introduction of the Model A to Europe. For the first time the European model, which had a smaller engine, differed significantly in design from its UK stablemate. But it remained essentially an American car. Ford cars remained distinctly bigger and more expensive than Austin or Morris, and the primacy of American methods continued to be demonstrated with the construction of the new works at Dagenham between 1927 and 1932, designed to be a one-tenth scale version of the River Rouge Plant in Detroit. However, by the early 1930s, Ford was beginning to allow each of its European operations to take on recognizably national characteristics, and this was confirmed for the UK by the introduction of their first real small European car, the Model Y, whose launch more or less coincided with the opening of Dagenham in 1932. Despite these national adaptations, Ford's system continued to experience serious difficulties in the 1930s. Even with the revival of sales associated with the Y and the later Popular, Ford were never able to generate the volume of sales necessary to run Dagenham at more than half its total capacity. They were only able to sustain this volume by slashing their prices – notably with their £100 car in 1935. But these tactics depressed profits too and the company went through the 1930s with a more or less constant cash crisis.[26] One consequence was an unrelenting drive to intensify labour and cut costs, together with a reversal of the previous high-wage policy. In April 1932, wages were cut by 10 per cent. The result was a spontaneous strike and the first stirrings of union activity in the plant. Ford acted quickly to nip this in the bud. Twenty years after his first union-busting mission to Manchester, Sorenson was again sent in to 'clean house' and again achieved the desired results. The unions were driven out of the plant and kept out till late in the Second World War, despite considerable efforts by the TUC and local Trades Councils to organize membership campaigns there in the late thirties. Dagenham in the 1930s had the reputation of a 'place of fear', with an extensive anti-union spy system, arbitrary layoffs and sackings, speed-ups and driving supervision. In the late 1930s, the company introduced rudimentary pensions and paid holidays, and began to let wage levels rise again – partly to forestall unionization attempts. But at no stage were there any incursions on Ford's managerial prerogatives.[27]

Thus the inflexibility of the Fordist system was softened at the edges and a limited amount of national adaptation was introduced. But its core remained poorly adapted to British circumstances and despite a partial recovery in the 1930s, Ford never really prospered before the Second World War. It was the British firms, Morris and Austin that devised the most effective product and labour strategies to respond to the growing and shifting market. Unlike Ford, they attached a much higher priority to quality and improvements in their models and looked for continuous improvements in the production process rather than seeking to establish a system with a fixed level of productivity. They avoided excessive capital intensity in order to maintain flexibility, both for model improvements and so that they could respond to the seasonal and cyclical fluctuations, which continued to mark the industry throughout this period, by layoffs and short-time working. In combination with this, they drove labour to intense efforts through tightly controlled piecework systems and took great pains to ensure that they retained a free hand continuously to rationalize the production process.

These practices can be clearly seen in the example of William Morris's factory at Cowley in Oxford. During the 1920s, Morris established a clear lead in the British industry. In the early 1920s, he annihilated competition by making high quality medium-sized cars at low prices. Between 1919 and 1928, the main Cowley plant was exclusively geared to the mass production of a single model, the 11.9 h.p. Cowley. In 1921 Morris made 3,000 cars: by 1925 this had risen to 55,000. Morris was fascinated by Ford's methods, and it might appear that this explosion of output provided a basis for imitating them. He did incorporate selected elements of Ford's methods into his factory, but he combined them with other practices to develop a distinctive system of his own. He had an assembly line of sorts at Cowley from 1914, with cars rolled along a track by hand to the next work station.

But he did not mechanize it and make it a *moving* assembly line until comparatively late, in 1933. He was willing to experiment with the most advanced forms of mechanization, notably the pioneer transfer machines introduced at his Coventry engine factory in 1923; but when it became apparent that this new technology was too rigid for his current requirements, he quickly abandoned it. Instead, he focused on continuous incremental improvements in productivity within his own factory, and by buying in a greater proportion of his components from outside suppliers than the more vertically integrated Ford, was able to concentrate his attention on perfecting his assembly operations without tying up large amounts of capital in component production.[28] Thus, even after the great leap forward of the early 1920s, Morris was able to keep the size of the workforce stable at 5,000–6,000, and yet continue to increase the output of cars per worker from 6 to 11.6 between 1924 and 1934. This figure compared extremely well with the British average of 6 cars per worker in 1935.[29]

Morris's methods of labour organization in the 1920s were explicitly Tayloristic, based on the subdivision of tasks and the timing and measurement of jobs. But Morris did not aim in the 1920s to eliminate handwork or labour inputs that required a significant degree of care and attention. This flowed from the product strategy. While engines and chassis were standardized and changes kept to a minimum, Morris continually made body-styling changes which were greatly facilitated by the continuing use of labour-intensive methods. One consequence was that when visitors from the Dodge Motor Company in Detroit visited Cowley in the mid-1920s, they found Cowley machinery 'more complicated' and less based on single-purpose operations than anywhere else in Europe.[30] Morris rationalized and mechanized where possible, but beyond a certain point kept the whole system moving primarily by the driving use of a piecework system. Morris himself provided a clear description of how this worked:

> We were turning out 425 cars per week on line assembling, but we wanted 500. We could have got it by putting men on overtime. Instead of taking the obvious course, the works manager went over the line and retimed all the stages. At several stages he found that he could speed-up by putting on additional men. Finally he decided to put on four extra men. Naturally the men already on the job grumbled. We said: 'All right, these men will not take part in the (group) bonus to start.' At the end of the fortnight we were getting 500 cars per week. The foremen actually came and asked the works manager to put the other men on bonus, since they did not think it fair they should be without their share.[31]

Almost complete non-unionism and high-pay levels facilitated the continuing manipulation of the payment system to keep levels of productivity high, and this situation continued to prevail through the 1930s, even while more of the factory became machine-paced.

The central role of piecework systems was a key feature of all the major British car firms in this period – even though their management differed in many ways. Only Rover flirted briefly with the idea of a day-wage system linked to direct control and task enforcement under a Bedaux system, but they rapidly abandoned the idea, partly because of the resistance of their workers, partly because they decided to stick to the production of quality cars rather than attempt to move into mass production, and partly because of the extreme hostility of the district and national Engineering Employers' Associations.[32] Apart from this, however, the major manufacturers were unanimous that Fordist systems of machine-pacing and day-rates were not applicable to British conditions. Even those who were once attracted by the Fordist model were forced to rethink their ideas. For instance, C. R. F. Engelbach, who was the head of production engineering at Austin through most of the 1920s, acknowledged in 1933 that:

A change has come over the spirit of our dreams of quick-time floor to floor production performances, accompanied by the spectacular removal at miraculous speeds of chunks of metal to the musical ticking of stop-watches . . . Rapid changes in fashion and ideas have slowed up the progress of special single operation machines. Continuous high production is too uncertain for special machines to be further developed. Designs have to be changeable at short notice . . . (and) at present there is no possible market likely to develop sufficiently that will lead to the extension of such specialised tool methods.[33]

Instead he, like most other manufacturers looked to flexibility achieved through the intensive deployment of labour governed by a piecework system. The key to productivity, therefore, as Engelbach argued elsewhere, was that earnings must be 'calculated literally on a scale which pays in units based on the amount of sweat given off by the workers. Nothing else is real.'[34]

As long as management were able to retain tight control of wage rates, manning levels and job standards, piecework was an ideal system to drive labour. In large part this depended on excluding union organization from the workplace. As Percy Keene, the head of the cost department at Austin noted in 1928: 'We definitely set out to manage as managers and the result is that we have no representation anywhere from the workers' side. No shop stewards, or shop committees, or anyone else wanting to interfere with management.'[35] Once unions became entrenched in the motor industry in the 1960s, they demonstrated how piecework systems could be 'captured' by the unions and used to great bargaining advantage. But, as we shall see in more detail in the next section, in the 1930s, the British car firms set themselves to keep out the unions and largely succeeded.

Until the late 1930s, the employers dominance of the shop floor was largely unchallenged. They paid high wages, but they also enforced a high pace of work, offered little job security and imposed arbitrary discipline. They used high proportions of youth labour on low rates of pay who were laid off as soon as they reached full rates of pay, and the regular seasonal summer layoffs were regularly used as an opportunity to get rid of union members or militant-minded workers simply by not rehiring them. In addition, short-time working or compulsory overtime were common. In many factories, workers would be laid off without pay for the rest of the day, or for several days, with little or no notice. New hirings and the allocation of jobs were largely at the discretion of powerful foremen, and outside the small craftsmen's shops there were almost no effective job controls over the manning of machines or the mobility of labour. It was only during the Second World War, in a vastly different environment for organizing and bargaining that this pattern was significantly disrupted.[36]

TRADE-UNION STRATEGIES AND SHOP-FLOOR BARGAINING

In the USA, Ford, followed closely by a number of competitors, seized the opportunity to transform the auto industry from craft to mass production in the space of a few hectic years. In Britain, the emergence of mass production was more gradual and was tailored to suit very different market circumstances. This contrast also had important implications for the development of trade-union structures and strategies. Some historians have argued, for instance, that patterns of workplace organization and job control characteristic of craftsmen in the older sectors of the economy persisted and shaped forms of organization in the new mass-production industries. Others have argued that there was a radical break from these traditions and that the emergence of shop stewards in the motor industry should be seen as a more or less spontaneous response to the requirements of shop-floor struggles which owed little to this prehistory.[37] As we shall see, there were major ruptures and discontinuities in the history of union development in the industry. Nevertheless, it appears that traditional forms and practices of union organization exercised an inescapable influence over the new forms that emerged, sometimes through a process of imitation, sometimes through a reaction against them and sometimes simply through perverse unintended consequences.

This section looks at the impact of union strategies and structures on the pattern of shop-floor organization that had developed in the industry by 1939. Employers did not always enjoy the freedom of action which they exerted during the spread of mass production. In the years before and immediately after the First World War, the unions had contested their dominance. But their overwhelming defeat in the early 1920s ended one phase of struggle and posed the need for different tactics and approaches to the problems of organizing the industry which, by and large, the unions were not equal to. The first subsection that follows discusses the unions' successes and failures in the first phase: the second subsection looks at their problems following the disasters of the early 1920s.

1896–1920

Even before the First World War, car production in Britain was not exclusively a craft industry. Particularly in the machine shops there was a considerable amount of repetition production, extensive use of jigs and fixtures and large numbers of dedicated machine tools. After the defeat of the unions in the 1897 lock-out, automobile employers had been able to introduce new machines fairly easily. But they introduced these modern tools not primarily to facilitate *quantity* of output, but because it was only with these modern tools that they could achieve the sort of high quality and precision machining needed for machining engines and related parts. Because of the variations in the product and short runs that remained prevalent, they needed to use these machines in a versatile way using the skills and adaptability of the workforce.[38]

It was not difficult for employers to introduce new machines, but workers did contest how these machines should be used once in place. In particular, they often refused to man several machines at once or restricted output through ca'canny or 'working without enthusiasm' to prevent intensification of effort. Nevertheless, as production runs got longer, it was easy for employers to slip from using skilled to semi-skilled workers simply by using the same machine tool in different ways. This facilitated the rapid rise of semi-skilled workers in the heart of the motor industry in Coventry between 1910 and 1914. By 1913, 45 per cent of Coventry engineering workers were categorized as semi-skilled against a national engineering average of 18 per cent. By 1914, the skilled engineer was being squeezed out of production work in the bigger motor firms and was largely confined to toolroom and maintenance work – though in bodymaking and trimming, skilled workers still remained predominant. As semi-skilled workers were eased in, employers frequently introduced piecework incentive systems to link wages to output and overcome problems of effort restriction. By 1913, 84 per cent of all fitters and turners in Coventry were on piecework, 48 per cent of them on the most sophisticated of these systems, Premium Bonus.[39]

The Amalgamated Society of Engineers (ASE), and most of the other smaller craft societies of the time, responded to these developments by attempting to extend to Coventry the tactics and principles that they were currently employing, with some success, in their rearguard action to defend their position in the heavy engineering sector in the North of England. They took their stand on the issue of the exclusive right of all-round apprentice-trained fitters and turners to be placed on machines capable of doing first-class or skilled work, and rejected any blurring of the distinction between skilled and unskilled work.[40] As George Ryder, the ASE's Organizing District Delegate (ODD) in Coventry put it in 1913:

We want to keep the succession going. We don't like the idea of a man being taken from the floor and being made a handyman . . . who will never be more than a half-inch mechanic during the whole of his days. We would like to eliminate the handyman altogether, if that were possible. We should like for the whole thing to be a matter of arrangement under the apprentice system.[41]

In the heavy engineering sector, the ASE were able to wage a tough defensive campaign around these issues, and in some parts of the motor trade away from Coventry they were able to make their claims stick. At the highest-quality end of the market, in firms like Belsize Motors in Manchester, Leyland in Lancashire and Argyll Motors at Alexandria near Glasgow, they were able to effectively regulate the manning of Potter and Johnston automatic lathes. At Crossley Motors in Manchester and at Coventry Chain, they were able to frustrate management's desire to introduce less-skilled labour on to Fay Automatics and turret lathes respectively.[42] In these cases, once an ASE man had got on to a machine, the union were able to ensure that it stayed rated as a skilled job. Several companies got themselves into difficulties by employing a skilled man on a machine at a skilled rate and finding themselves unable to change to a lower rate when they switched the machine to repetition work. Some firms even preferred to take the machines out of production rather than pay the full rate. The advice from the Engineering Employers' Federation (EEF) to its member firms was often against picking a head-on fight with the ASE on this issue at this time.[43]

However, dogged pursuit of craft regulation could also have disastrous results for the ASE. At the Mo-Car Company at Paisley in 1904 and at Humber at Beeston in 1905–6, ASE actions in pursuit of their claims resulted in lock-outs and exclusion.[44] At Humber, the ASE withdrew their members and declared the firm 'black', despite concern among the local ASE officials that they could not enforce this policy. Humber were delighted with the ASE's actions which, they realized, gave them a free hand to 'fill up with non-Society men'. Despite criticism from the EEF, they publicly declared themselves a non-union shop. As their Works Manager, Thomas Pullinger described it:

I have quite made up my mind after the way the ASE has treated me, never to have another one of their men working for me if I can possibly help it, and I shall use every means in my power to keep them out . . . I hope shortly to be in a position to know all the ASE men in this district and perhaps I shall be able to keep our shop free from their contamination.[45]

In this case the ASE's uncompromising pursuit of a 'closed' craft-union strategy backfired badly. Their prolonged picketing of the company proved futile and they were never able to re-establish themselves in the factory.

In Coventry, however, where there was no tradition of craft militancy, the ASE were much more willing to compromise and adapt their tactics. They made little attempt to control machine manning and accepted the greater use of semi-skilled workers and lower rates on particular machines, which nevertheless generally yielded high earnings. This pragmatic approach resulted in generally peaceable relations with the Coventry employers who, as a result, felt much less impetus to develop effective multi-employer organization than others elsewhere in the country. The Coventry District Engineering Employers' Association (CDEEA) was not formed until 1913. As the first Secretary of the Association described the position in 1913:

We have had no acute labour troubles in Coventry in the engineering trade, because this is an apparently modern addition to Coventry's industries and therefore the employers have not realised the necessity of combination like Northern employers. I suppose they live in the happy hope that as there never has been trouble, there never will be.[46]

This picture was, however, sharply redrawn in the years immediately preceding the outbreak of war by the emergence of the Workers' Union (WU), recruiting large numbers of the semi-skilled workers that the ASE and craft societies refused to admit. The WU founded its branch in Coventry in 1906. At first it did not aim to recruit engineering workers and wanted the ASE to open its ranks to the less skilled. But the ASE remained committed to its 'closed' strategy, partly on principle and partly because they believed that this category of workers were too unstable and inexperienced to be effectively organized. As the ASE's local organizer put it: 'They keep wandering into the . . . works and wandering out like the artistes at the Hippodrome, they come in and do a turn and bow to the public and get out.'[47] There was an element of truth in this analysis at the turn of the century, but two developments enabled the WU to make a big impact between 1910 and 1914. Firstly, Coventry's semi-skilled workers were acquiring an array of real skills in machining and assembly departments that gave them more bargaining power than mere labourers. Secondly, in a period of wider industrial and political turmoil, the WU were able to bring a new type of union growth to the industry. They pursued large-scale recruitment based on support for mass action and the political excitement of the Black Country strikes, or the sort of rolling wave of strikes and bargaining successes that they achieved at the Humber, Daimler and Coventry Ordnance Works in 1913. These successes brought them recognition from the CDEEA in 1913.[48]

These advances contained the seeds of an ideological and organizational challenge to the ASE. During 1913 the WU helped push the Coventry labourer's wage rate up to 71 per cent of the skilled ASE rate against a national average of 50 to 60 per cent.[49] The WU had an unprecedented commitment to growth and an unwillingness to accept a subordinate status to the ASE as an automatic assumption. Unlike the Gas Workers or the NAUL, the WU had no longstanding membership with interests to protect and could, therefore, take risks and go for an all-or-nothing strategy. At the same time, unlike these other general unions, they had not evolved as a labourers' union, specifically recruiting groups which stood in a traditionally hallowed relation of subordination to ASE craftsmen.[50]

The advent of war in 1914 followed by the postwar boom of 1919–20, appeared for a time to have dramatically realigned the positions and strategies of employers and rival unions. But in practice few of the new developments proved durable. The wartime shop-stewards movement in Coventry was less imbued with socialist rhetoric than those that developed in some of the other engineering centres and the lines of divide between 'official' and 'unofficial' action were more blurred. In consequence, some historians like Hinton and Friedman have tended to understate the extent to which it hindered employers' 'right to manage' during the war.[51] Lewchuk, however, has shown that at its high point at the end of the war it made significant incursions on managerial prerogatives, and, for a brief moment in 1919–20, seemed to be in a position to prevent the Coventry employers from introducing the sort of payment systems that they desired. However, he goes on to argue that the power of the unions in this period defeated moves by the employers towards 'a Ford-style industrial strategy' of machine-pacing and intense direct supervision of the labour process. The strength of labour forced employers to fall back on piecework systems which 'resulted in a sharing of management authority and a crude form of industrial democracy, since labour was allowed control over the pace of work'. These patterns, laid down in the early 1920s were, he argues, to structure management–labour relations in the industry until the early 1970s and were a major cause of the long-run decline of the industry.[52] This account is based on a serious misinterpretation of these developments. Firstly, as we have seen, British motor manufacturers had no great desire to push towards 'Fordist' systems for reasons to do with their product and their markets. Secondly, and partly in consequence, they found that piecework systems were much better suited to drive less rigid production systems than fixed day-rates, and their introduction had been a major objective of management in their attempts to secure tighter control of the workplace since the early years of the century. Thirdly, the apparent strength of labour was, as we shall see, partial and very short-lived and was to be followed by a period of defeats so serious that it is impossible to see the outcome of the events of these years as determining the long-term future of management–labour relations in the industry.

Similarly, impressive developments in union growth and organization and shifts in the strategies of different unions also proved to be false dawns. Rapid increases in membership, the emergence of all-grade union structures, and the acceptance of a new role for directly elected workplace representatives by the ASE seemed to herald the emergence of new directions in union development. But each of these changes was short-lived. The rapid inflation of union membership did not outlast the postwar boom. After a relatively harmonious start, the war exacerbated jurisdictional conflicts. And, though there appeared for a time to be a degree of convergence on organizational strategies, fundamental divisions were concealed rather than abolished.

The war brought a major shift in ASE attitudes to shop stewards. Before the War they had seen them simply as the appointed agents of the District Committee in the workshops, with strictly limited bargaining functions centred on the monitoring and enforcement of district rates, conditions and overtime agreements. They had, therefore, been consistently opposed to the direct election of stewards at the workplace. Until 1917 this remained very much their attitude and one that was shared by the other craft societies in the Coventry Engineering Joint Committee (CEJC), a local union coordinating committee of all the skilled unions in the district in which the ASE played the leading role. This changed at the peak of wartime agitation and militancy in 1917. Faced with the emergence of workshop committees and the threat of serious disruption of wartime production, the Ministry of Munitions twice exerted direct pressure on both unions and employers during major strikes at Hotchkiss and White and Poppe in Coventry to establish 'representative shop committees under trade union control'. These interventions precipitated a change in union policy.[53] Rather than try to override emergent shop-floor power, the CEJC reorganized itself to involve stewards as well as officials. Partly this aimed to exercise a greater measure of control over 'firebrands' on the shop floor by incorporating shop stewards into the official channels more fully: as one ASE official explicitly put it: 'The thing is far more sinister unofficial than official. That is our view.'[54] But it also seems that the ASE had come to recognize the importance of using the power of direct workplace representation. Between 1917 and 1919 (the dates of the two major national agreements on shop-steward recognition with the EEF), the ASE fought vigorously, and in part successfully, *against* limiting the role of shop stewards to a narrowly defined function under the heading of 'avoidance of disputes', and *for* specific protection for stewards against discharge or discrimination within the workplace.[55]

The CEJC, working in close liaison with the WU, also sought to generalize to district level the demand for all-grades shop stewards to be elected by all workers in a particular shop regardless of their union affiliation. Over the next two years, the ASE became the principal partisan of all-grade steward organization in Coventry. This appeared to be a still more radical move away from their earlier principles of district control and exclusive jurisdiction, and some commentators have seen it as representing a fundamental 'change of heart' in the ASE. In fact, however, it was rooted in the strategic calculations of the time and local circumstances rather than reflecting a conversion to new principles. Firstly, it should be noted that even within an 'all-grade' system, though an ASE steward could represent unskilled workers, there remained a provision that no unskilled man should represent an ASE man. Secondly, though the ASE in Coventry advocated this form of organization, it was never accepted by the ASE National Executive. In large part this was because the ASE in Coventry was clearly the most powerful force on the CEJC and could hope to dominate its workings. But when it came to National Conferences within the Engineering Procedure, the ASE could be and frequently was outvoted by coalitions of smaller craft unions. These factors left the way open for considerable back-tracking by the ASE/AEU on their approach to shop stewards during the interwar depression until, as we shall see, they underwent a further 'change of heart' in the late 1930s.[56]

Thus these shifts in jurisdictional and organizational tactics were more limited than they at first appear and do not mark a real convergence between the organizing strategies of craft and general unions. In fact, the alliance between skilled and semi-skilled workers became more and more uneasy as the war progressed. The ASE feared the rise of the WU. They refused to negotiate detailed demarcation agreements with the WU for fear that the latter's claims might be legitimized in grey areas, they refused to submit joint claims to employers and they usually insisted on separate conferences. The tensions burst out in 1918 when the WU refused to back the ASE's strike against the Reserved Occupations Act, when the ASE defended its members' exemption from military conscription. The legislation concerned created highly invidious comparisons between WU and ASE members who might be working on similar machines, but who might be 'reserved' or not, mainly depending on which of the unions they were in. The split was sharp. One WU leader described the attitude of the craft unions as 'mean little Toryism . . . one of the sinister features of the trade union movement which must be fought'.[57] In 1919, the WU removed from its rulebook its previously existing restrictions on the recruitment of craftsmen. By 1920, the antagonisms between craft and general unions in Coventry were as much, if not more, intractable than they had been in 1913.

1920–39

The strength and organization of the unions in the motor factories peaked at the end of the war. But it was very short-lived. By 1918, the tide had already turned against the unions; by 1919 their position was sliding, and the years 1920–22 saw something of a rout, culminating in the 1922 lock-out and leaving the union presence confined almost solely to craft shops. The postwar recession hit the Coventry firms, which concentrated on quality cars and luxury production, particularly hard. The bankruptcy of many small firms eliminated many strongholds of craft unionism. The firms that adapted best to the conditions of the 1920s and survived by moving over to small cars and large-scale production to cut prices, such as Morris and Austin, were situated away from the previously unionized factories in Coventry.

The most dramatic and direct consequence of the recession was the virtual annihilation of the Workers' Union by unemployment. In 1918 it was the largest union in Coventry. The union had 90,000 members in Coventry and Birmingham in 1920. By 1923 this had fallen to 15,000. They lost 50 per cent of their membership in the single year of 1921 alone. They exacerbated their already serious problems of decline by some serious errors in financial management and finally lost 90 per cent of their members in the 1920s. Their decimation effectively broke up union organization among semi-skilled motor workers.[58]

The Amalgamated Engineering Union (AEU), formed by an amalgamation of the ASE with several other craft societies in 1920, was also badly hit by the recession. Like the WU they compounded their own problems in the case of adversity. They attempted to retreat behind their defences as a group of skilled trades. Their defeat in the 1922 lock-out was a major contribution to their decline, but instead of minimizing the damage to their organization in the aftermath, they greatly intensified its impact by insisting on taking strict disciplinary action, including imposing heavy fines, on those who had returned to work early. Many left rather than pay the fines, and while nationally the AEU lost 30 per cent of its membership between 1920 and 1923, the Coventry AEU lost 57 per cent. At amalgamation in 1920, the Coventry AEU had 13,115 members. By 1925 this had fallen by almost 80 per cent to 3,035 and their membership continued to slip down to a low point of 2,415 in 1933.[59]

After the 1922 defeat, the AEU lost any effective presence in the workplace for a dozen years. They had no effective control over their remaining members who often accepted unauthorized deals with management. When Armstrong–Siddeley cut their wages in 1927, eight AEU branch secretaries were currently employed there. Yet the AEU heard nothing of what was going on until they received a semi-clandestine communication from a worker there.[60] They realized, as Lawrence Givens, the AEU District Secretary, put it: 'inside the shops you [the employers] have the economic power and can frighten the individual men.'[61] 'Mutuality' could be used against the workers because individuals could be more or less coerced into accepting jobs or prices. At Crossley Motors, for instance, when the AEU protested that a wage cut had been made under duress, the company got the workers to sign a document saying that the price was mutually agreed. The Works Committee Chairman neatly summarized the nature of this sort of bargaining:

It is quite easy for you to say you have had a mutual reduction, just the same as you might meet me with a revolver in your hand and say, 'I want your money or your life.' I might be mutually satisfied if I handed my money over and had saved my life, and you might be mutually satisfied that you had not another murder on your soul.[62]

The bargaining environment was harsh, but the AEU's retreat into craft defensiveness was an unproductive response. In so far as it emphasized issues of job control, such as machine-manning, overtime and the deployment of labour, it clashed with the central requirements of management in the industry at the time. There was probably more scope, however, for bargaining on the wages front among the newly recruited armies of unskilled labour, where, through piecework systems, management often payed low rates but allowed high earnings. The AEU's craft defensiveness, however, prevented them from linking themselves into these developments. Although they were formally an industrial union from 1920, nearly all their branches resisted the recruitment of semi-skilled workers. J. B. Jeffereys argued that the growth of the AEU's semi-skilled sections 5 and 5A after 1927 represented the transformation of the AEU into a true industrial union. But Claydon has shown that this is misleading. The figures in fact reflect many skilled workers opting to go into the semi-skilled sections because subscriptions were cheaper. Instead, despite the fact that semi-skilled workers were in a large majority in the industry, they remained a minority in Coventry AEU until 1937.[63]

Perhaps the central weakness in the recruitment strategies of the AEU in this period was the Coventry District Committee's insistence on recruiting only those earning the District Rate. Yet, in the motor industry, while most workers were employed on lower rates than engineers in the Northern engineering centres, they were usually getting much higher earnings through piecework and overtime. The Coventry District committee were more insistent on the district rate than the National Executive, and it was only under pressure from the latter in 1936, concerned with the threat of recruitment of semi-skilled workers by the Transport and General Workers' Union (TGWU), that the District Committee agreed to allow a wider framework of recruitment.[64] Its main concern was that a broader base in semi-skilled workers might weaken the position of those receiving skilled rates, particularly the toolmakers who dominated the District Committee. But this concern to protect the rights of the skilled was outdated in a changing industry, and the conservative and hierarchical vision on which it was based appealed almost solely to the rapidly shrinking body of skilled workers, making the AEU in the mid-1930s little more than a toolroom club in many works.

Similar internal weaknesses disabled the National Union of Vehicle Builders (NUVB) from responding to opportunities to organize semi-skilled workers from the late 1920s onwards. Before the war, vehicle builders had established strong organization in many craft shops, organizing woodworkers and trimmers in the high-class trade for landaulettes, phaetons, barouches, carriages and coaches. In 1919, however, as motor body-building employers began to organize themselves, the various coachbuilding and wheelwrights' societies banded together to form the NUVB. By 1920 they had 23,300 members. Though formally open to all grades, they were in fact an amalgamation of craftsmen. The NUVB were not locked out in 1922 and their membership held up much better than that of the AEU or WU in the 1920s. In 1922, the Coventry AEU had 8,971 members to the NUVB's 1,710: but by 1926 their advantage had been dramatically cut to 2,879 to 2,286.[65] In the late 1920s, the NUVB became for a while the largest union in Coventry. They thrived in the 1920s on the demand for bodymaking and trimming skills, particularly in the high-class trade and in commercial vehicles. Their relative health gave a new lease of life to their craft forms of organization and gave them encouragement that they might be able to continue to control entry to their preserves and exclude semi-skilled workers. Unlike the AEU, but like the Sheet Metal Workers unions (the most powerfully entrenched group of craft workers), the NUVB did not oppose piecework. They believed that they could control and use it. And in the early 1920s they did so effectively. Many of their members were attaining their high Coventry target of 3s. an hour or £7 per week in 1920.[66]

However, they were squeezed by the collapse of high-class work at the bottom of the depression in 1931–3 and the simultaneous rise of new techniques such as all-steel bodies and cellulose spray painting which eliminated many of their crafts. In London, where high-quality coach-building was particularly concentrated, almost all of their members were out of work in 1931.[67] Like the AEU, however, the NUVB's own policies also intensified their difficulties. In the late 1920s as unemployment rose, they sought to sustain their traditional friendly-society role by paying out relatively high levels of unemployment benefits to their members. But this could only be sustained by imposing unacceptably high levies on their shrinking membership in work and this drove many to leave the union. Their Coventry membership fell by 50 per cent between 1931 and 1933. The union finally escaped from this vicious circle only as an unintended consequence of its decision to open an Industrial Section for semi-skilled members. As with the AEU, most NUVB branches remained resistant to recruiting semi-skilled workers: but, as with the AEU's Sections 5 and 5A, it came to be used as an avenue whereby skilled workers could enter the union and yet avoid rather punitive levels of contributions. Once again, the apparent growth of a semi-skilled membership actually masked a more fundamental continuity. When, in 1936, the Executive forbade anyone who was qualified to join a skilled section of the NUVB from joining the Industrial Section, the proportion of members in that section tumbled from 56.7 per cent in 1933 to 9.6 per cent in 1938, a much more real indicator of the true position of the semi-skilled in the ranks of the NUVB.[68]

Thus despite appearances, the NUVB continued to shun semi-skilled workers and continued to concentrate on increasingly ineffective forms of craft control. For instance, when firms like Armstrong–Siddely or Harper Bean refused to pay NUVB rates in the early 1930s, they withdrew their members from the firm and instructed them to 'black' the companies. They were quickly replaced by non-unionists and the NUVB were excluded from the shops.[69] They refused to recruit on the basis of workplace struggles – as the TGWU were soon to do with at least partial success – because they feared that any such recruits would take the strike benefits but not prove the material of 'real trades unionists'. There was a germ of truth in their attitude. The union was badly stung by its experience in a 1935 strike at Carbodies in Coventry, when they recruited 129 members and paid out the comparatively large sum of £500 in dispute benefits, only to see all the new members leave within two years. Ted Buckle, their District Organizer, felt that they had been 'led up the garden path'. Thereafter he took up the unadventurous position that such workers were mere 'birds of passage' and not worth recruiting.[70] At the beginning of the Second World War, he was to come under severe criticism from his Head Office for his lack of organizing effort, which, the Executive Committee believed had allowed the TGWU to establish a presence in what might have been NUVB territory.[71]

The Transport and General Workers' Union (TGWU) entered the motor industry from 1929 when it took over the collapsed remnants of the Workers'

Union. In comparison to the AEU and NUVB, its attitude to recruitment was more positive and flexible, yet even so its efforts in the motor industry were relatively half-hearted. The union's leader, Ernest Bevin, was afraid to overstretch the resources of the union following a period of rapid expansion through amalgamations, and engineering was new and unfamiliar territory.[72] On the other hand, the union was ideologically committed to accepting into membership any group of workers who wished to join, and there was a significant degree of local autonomy for local officers to pursue their own priorities in expanding membership. Thus, when recruitment was virtually thrust upon them by explosive and spontaneous strikes at Rover in 1930, Lucas in 1932, Standard Motors and Pressed Steel in 1934, they did not reject the potential members as, in several of these cases, the AEU and NUVB did. At the Rover, for instance, the NUVB refused to recruit the striking female trimmers when they were approached, and the women turned instead to the TGWU. Following this, the NUVB changed its rules to allow them to recruit women to the union. But their attitude on this issue was almost wholly defensive, aiming to block such inroads into the motor trade by another union. As they explained their conference decision to their members: 'It is not anticipated that this will go beyond the motor car centres, but it will give us a control that now belongs to others.'[73]

The TGWU were willing to recruit these women, but where they did so, they remained ghettoized and little more than paper members. Most of the TGWU's membership in the motor industry at this time arose out of this sort of spontaneous struggle by women or other unskilled groups. But the TGWU were unwilling to build on such struggles, and they were often ready to settle disputes over the heads of their newly recruited members.[74] Often they failed to integrate such members and allowed them to drift away, as at Rover or Lucas. Elsewhere, at Pressed Steel in Oxford, where they made a quite exceptional breakthrough into large-scale recruitment following a mass strike by unorganized workers in 1934, they found themselves in a prolonged battle to control a workplace membership that was ready and willing to take matters into its own hands through aggressive local bargaining. A Negotiating Committee of shop stewards cut the TGWU District Committee out of plant negotiations and for three years conducted militant piecework bargaining and campaigns for closed shops in several departments. Their successes disturbed management and also threatened the equilibrium of the TGWU's broader commitment to respecting engineering procedure. From 1937, the TGWU put in a new District Secretary with instructions to push the stewards into more orderly bargaining. But he had little success and considerable animosity with the key stewards developed. When the company, supported by the regional employers' association, decided to use the downturn of trade in 1938 to sack the convener, the union defended him only half-heartedly. In the next few years, the TGWU came close to losing their position in the plant altogether as a move by some of the leading stewards to organize a mass defection to the AEU was only narrowly defeated.[75]

The rise of mass production and the new role of large numbers of semi-skilled workers posed enormous problems of adaptation for the unions. These difficulties were increased by major geographical shifts in the centre of gravity of the motor industry. Before the war it had been centred on Coventry where, over a 20-year period a core of experienced organization had grown up in relatively favourable circumstances. But between the war management moved into large-scale production at new locations such as Longbridge, Oxford, Luton and Dagenham. The new workforces generally had little experience of engineering and were composed of very high proportions of migrant workers. Dagenham, for example, was based almost entirely on a new labour force with a high proportion of workers from Manchester and Scotland. At Morris and Pressed Steel in Oxford by 1936, 46.7 per cent of the workers were migrants. The pattern was similar in the other motor centres. Large numbers of these migrants came in waves from the depressed areas: 21.5 per cent of all migrants to Coventry in 1937 and 11 per cent of all migrants to Oxford in 1936, were Welsh. But large numbers were also drawn in from smaller towns or the semi-rural hinterlands of new towns: 56.4 per cent of Oxford migrants in 1936 had come from the South West, London and the South East.[76]

It is hard to evaluate the impact of these migrants on the development of union organization in the industry. Some evidence suggests that these migrant workers brought with them important union traditions from historically well-organized sectors such as mining, steel or shipbuilding. Certainly, the prominence of Welsh migrants in the organization of Pressed Steel supports this view, especially in light of the fact that 40 per cent of the Oxford Welsh migrants came from a single district, Maesteg, and a striking 70 per cent of these from a single village, Pontycymmer.[77] Yet 'union traditions' cannot simply be imputed to whole geographical areas. The 'traditions' of Welsh mining communities at this time, for instance, were much shallower than is often supposed. Many migrants from Wales in the 1920s and 1930s came from families that had only settled in Wales during the boom years of 1890–1914 and who remained relatively mobile.[78] In addition, many of the migrants were young and lacking in work experience even where they came from families with trade-union backgrounds. Moreover, as Waller's recent work on the new Nottinghamshire coalfields of the interwar years shows, union traditions cannot be simply transplanted into radically different social and economic environments. Labour forces drawn from the highly unionized South Yorkshire coalfields could provide the basis for the militancy of the new Kent coalfield, but they could also provide the basis for an almost wholly non-union workforce in new towns in Nottinghamshire, often only a matter of 20 or 30 miles distant from the unionized coalfields.[79]

Migrants also encompassed a broad spectrum of potentially countervailing 'traditions', including agricultural workers and workers from the South East. Many unions alleged at the time that migrants undercut local wage rates and I have argued in another article that young workers, lacking in

experience and without any support networks to fall back on were vulnerable
and as likely to be passive as active as a whole.[80] Where local conditions
generated spontaneous action it seems that the presence of migrants with
union experience may have helped to channel and focus discontent in the
direction of unionization, but it is less likely that a high density of migrant
workers *per se* was particularly conducive to militant action or unionization.

The unions had failed to establish themselves in the motor industry before
the Second World War. None of the Big Six motor companies had any
substantial semi-skilled membership by that date, though there were pockets
of membership in some of the craft shops. The combination of managerial
hostility, high earnings, and insecurity of employment were serious barriers
to union growth. Unions like the AEU and NUVB concentrated on
defending their existing limited membership by traditional methods. These
often proved ineffective or counter productive. In particular, a job-control
focus impinged on the areas where employers were most intensely jealous
of their hard-won freedom of action. When the revival of union activity
came in the late 1930s, it centred on active piecework bargaining in the shops,
accepting the new 'rules of the game' but attempting to ameliorate some
of the harshest aspects of insecurity, discipline, working conditions and the
arbitrary fixing of job prices. When the TGWU began to show that they
could win some concessions in these areas, opportunities for more rapid
union development began to open up, and inter-union rivalry then acted
as a powerful spur to other unions to develop new approaches.

Part of the explanation of the slow and unimaginative responses of the
unions to the new challenges of the motor industry is to be found in the
structure of the unions. Their approaches were strongly conditioned by the
fact that the motor industry was on the periphery of their organizational
vision. The core of the NUVB lay in the woodworking trades, of the AEU
in skilled heavy engineering and of the TGWU in docks and transport. None
of them had the unionization of the motor industry as a major strategic
goal. But it would be wrong to argue that unionization failed simply because
of the inadequacy of the frameworks of craft and general unionism that
were available. In later years, as chapter 4 in this volume shows, the existing
unions showed that their craft or general origins were no barriers to creative
adaptation in organizing the postwar motor industry, and there is no
evidence to suggest that an industrial union for motor workers would have
been a radical and simple trigger for a breakthrough, even if this had been
a possibility.

The existing unions can be criticized for tactical and strategic failures,
but a comprehensive explanation of their inability to unionize a mass
production sector like motors must be pitched at a broader level. In
international comparative terms, mass unionization of a rapidly expanding
new industry required significant other social and political preconditions.
In the USA, unionization resulted only from an intense period of workplace
insurgency backed by sympathetic state legal regulation. In France it
emerged only out of the social and political turmoil of the Popular Front.[81]

It is probable that something on this scale would also have been necessary for a dramatic development of mass-production unionism in Britain. Something similar had occurred in the period of the emergence of 'new unionism' between 1889 and 1914, but the political context of the 1930s, with an entrenched National Government and a weakened Labour Party made this unlikely. In the absence of such external factors, the product and labour strategies of motor manufacturers provided poor soil for union growth and the unions themselves were unable even to make the most of their limited opportunities.

NOTES

1   Henry Ford, *My Life and Work* (New York, 1922), pp. 148–9.
2   W. R. Morris (Lord Nuffield), 'Policies that have built the Morris Business', *Journal of Industrial Economics* (1954), p. 195.
3   D. A. Hounshell, *From the American System to Mass Production, 1880–1932* (Baltimore, 1984), p. 335.
4   On the origins of Ford's system of mass production see; A. Nevins with F. E. Hill, *Ford, The Times, the Man, the Company* (New York, 1954); S. Meyer, *The Five Dollar Day: Labor Management and Social Control in the Ford Motor Company, 1908–21* (New York, 1981); A. D. Chandler Jr., *Giant Enterprise: Ford, General Motors and the Automobile Industry* (New York, 1964); Hounshell, *American System*, ch. 7.
5   Meyer, *Five Dollar Day*, pp. 25–34.
6   Ibid., pp. 72–80.
7   Ibid., pp. 80–165.
8   Ford, *Life and Work*, pp. 146–7.
9   Hounshell, *American System*, pp. 276–93.
10   W. Lewchuk, 'Fordism and British Motor Car Employers, 1896–1932', in H. Gospel and C. Littler, *Managerial Strategies and Industrial Relations* (London, 1983); *idem*, 'The role of the British government in the spread of scientific management and Fordism in the inter-war years'. *Journal of Economic History* XLIV, no. 2 (June 1984); *idem*, 'The British motor vehicle industry, 1896–1982: the roots of decline', in B. Elbaum and W. Lazonick (eds.), *The Decline of the British Economy* (Oxford, 1986).
11   G. Maxcy and A. Silberston, *The Motor Industry* (London, 1959).
12   R. Church and M. Miller, 'The Big Three: Competition, management and marketing in the British motor industry, 1922–39', in B. Supple (ed.), *Essays in British Business History* (London, 1977); *idem*, 'Motor Manufacturing', in D. Aldcroft and N. Buxton (eds.), *British Industry between the Wars* (London, 1979): Maxcy and Silberston, *Motor Industry*.
13   In addition to chapters 2 and 3 in this volume, see J. P. Bardou, J-J Chanaron, P. Fridenson and J. M. Laux, *The Automobile Revolution* (Chapel Hill, NC, 1982), pp. 91–139.
14   J. M. Laux, *In First Gear: The French Automobile Industry to 1914* (Liverpool, 1976), p. 199.
15   P. Fridenson, 'French automobile marketing, 1890–1979', in A. Okochi and K. Shimokawa (eds.), *Development of Mass Marketing: the Automobile and*

Retailing Industries (Proceedings of the 7th International Fuji Conference on Business History, Tokyo, 1980), pp. 127–43.

16 M. Wilkins and F. E. Hill, *American Business Abroad: Ford on Six Continents* (Detroit, 1964); R. Church, 'The marketing of automobiles in Britain and the U.S.A. before 1939', in Okochi and Shimokawa, *Development of Mass Marketing*.

17 'Report on foreign branches by W. S. Carnegie', n.d. 1925, Ford Archives, Detroit, Acc. 157, Box 266. I am grateful to the Ford Motor Company for permission to consult these archives.

18 E. Kanzler, quoted by Nevins and Hill, *Ford*, p. 410.

19 P. Perry to Henry Ford, 26 February 1913, Ford Archives Acc. 62, Box 59.

20 P. Perry to Henry Ford, 14 April 1914, Ford Archives Acc. 38, Box 52; C. E. Sorenson, Report to Henry Ford, 3 June 1914, Acc. 62, Box 59.

21 H. Mortimore, Sales Manager, Ford Ltd., interviewed by Mira Wilkins, 26 August 1960. I am grateful to Prof. Wilkins for allowing me to consult her interview typescripts.

22 Wilkins and Hill, *American Business Abroad*, pp. 155–7.

23 Reports from E. C. Kanzler, T. Gehle, and W. Klann on Manchester operations, 1923–4, in Select File (Ford Archives): and W. S. Carnegie, 'Report'.

24 Klann Reminiscences (Ford Archives) p. 141: Reports by Gehle and Klann, Winter 1923–4.

25 P. Perry to Edsel Ford, 7 August 1928 (Select File).

26 Wilkins and Hill, *American Business Abroad*, pp. 199–310: Church and Miller, 'Big Three', pp. 168–73.

27 Nina Fishman, 'Trade unionism at Dagenham, 1933–45', unpublished paper; C. E. Sorenson, 'Memorandum', 4 October 1933, Ford Archives, Acc. 572, Box 18: P. Perry, transcript of interview by Mira Wilkins, August 1960.

28 On Morris's methods see R. J. Overy, *William Morris, Viscount Nuffield* (London, 1976); P. W. S. Andrews and E. Brunner, *Life of Lord Nuffield: a Study in Enterprise and Benevolence* (Oxford, 1955); L. P. Jarman and R. I. Barraclough, *The Bullnose Morris* (London, 1965); R. C. Whiting, *The View from Cowley: The Impact of Industrialisation upon Oxford, 1918–39* (Oxford, 1983), pp. 29–53, 83–7; G. Lanning, C. Peaker, C. Webb and R. White (eds.), *Making Cars: A History of Car Making in Cowley by the People who Make the Cars* (London, 1985). The best sources for the technical side are H. K. Thomas, 'Fundamentals of cost reduction', *Proceedings of the Institute of Automobile Engineers* XVIII (1923–4), pp. 434–40; idem, 'Progressive Production', *The Motor*, 2 July 1934, pp. 955–6; A. A. Rowse, 'Thirty cars an hour at Cowley', *Motor Trader* XL (October 1927).

29 L. Rostas, *Comparative Productivity in British and American Industry* (Cambridge, 1948), p. 173.

30 G. S. Davison, *At the Wheel* (London, 1931), pp. 85–103.

31 Morris, 'Policies', p. 199.

32 S. Tolliday, 'Background Paper on the Rover Motor Co.', First Report to the ESRC, King's College, Cambridge, Research Centre, 1982; idem, 'Militancy and Organisation: Women workers and trades unions in the motor trades in the 1930s', *Oral History* 11, no. 2 (1983).

33 C. R. F. Engelbach, 'Presidential Address', *Proceedings of the Institute of Automobile Engineers* XXVIII (1933–4), p. 7; see also idem, 'Some notes on reorganising a works to increase production', *Proceedings of the Institute of Automobile Engineers* XXIX (1924–5), pp. 496–544.

34 C. R. F. Engelbach, Letter to the Editor, *Automobile Engineer*, February 1931, p. 42.

35 P. Keene, 'Production. A dream come true', *Proceedings of the Institute of Production Engineers*, 1928, p. 28.

36 On wartime and postwar developments see: S. Tolliday, 'Government, employers and shopfloor organisation in the British motor industry, 1939–69', in S. Tolliday and J. Zeitlin (eds.), *Shop Floor Bargaining and the State: Historical and Comparative Perspectives* (Cambridge, 1985).

37 J. Zeitlin, 'The emergence of shop steward organisation and job control in the British motor industry: a review essay', *History Workshop*, no. 10 (Autumn 1980); *idem*, 'Workplace militancy: a rejoinder', *History Workshop*, no. 16 (Autumn 1983); D. Lyddon, 'Workplace organisation in the British car industry', *History Workshop*, no. 15 (Spring 1983).

38 See in particular, W. Lewchuk, 'The economics of technical change: a case study of the British motor industry, 1896–1932' Cambridge Ph.D thesis. 1982; J. Zeitlin, 'Craft regulation and the division of labour: engineers and compositors in Britain, 1880–1914' Warwick Ph.D. thesis, 1981.

39 J. Hinton, *The First Shop Stewards Movement* (London, 1973), pp. 210–20: A. Friedman, *Industry and Labour: Class Struggle at Work and Monopoly Capitalism* (London, 1973), pp. 191–4; R. Hyman, *The Workers' Union* (London, 1971), pp. 160–80; E. Wigham, *The Power to Manage* (London, 1973).

40 EEF Archives, Machine Manning series M, especially files on disputes at Coventry Ordnance Works 1913 M(8)2, Coventry Chain Company 1913 M(9)22, Rees Roturbo 1912 M(9)20, Mo-Car Syndicate Ltd. 1913 M(9)7, and Crossley Bros. Ltd. 1914 M(9)27.

41 Local Conference between the ASE and the CDEEA, 28 February 1913, M(8)2.

42 EEF Files, Crossley Bros. Ltd. (Machine Manning) 1914 M(9)27, and Coventry Chain Co. (Machine Manning) 1913 M(9)22.

43 Ibid.

44 EEF File, Mo-Car Syndicate Ltd. (Paisley) 1914 M(9)7.

45 This account of the Humber affair is based on EEF Files on Humber in the Nottinghamshire and Coventry District Association series, E(1)12, E(1)14, P(5)31, P(5)8. For Pullinger's views see especially his correspondence with T. Biggart, January–February 1907, E(1)14.

46 EEF File, Coventry (CDEEA Membership) 1906 MM(1)79.

47 George Ryder at Local Conference between BDEEA and ASE, 9 September 1913, P(10)4.

48 Hyman, *Workers' Union*; EEF Files, Daimler (Freedom of Employment) 1913 E(1)27, Coventry Ordnance Works (Machine Manning) 1913 M(8)82, Humber (Piecework Prices) 1914 P(5)31.

49 Friedman, *Industry and Labour*, pp. 191–4.

50 Hyman, *Workers' Union*.

51 Hinton, *Shop Stewards*; Friedman, *Industry and Labour*.

52 Lewchuk, 'Fordism'; 'Roots of Decline'.

53 EEF Files. Hotchkiss (Shop Stewards Committee) 1917 S(4)6, Shop Stewards and Trade Unions, 1917 S(4)7, BSA (Shop Stewards and Works Committees) 1917 S(4)10, Shop Stewards (Conference with ASE) 1917 S(4)11, Shop Stewards and Works Committees 1918 S(4)12, Adjustment to prewar prices 1918 P(5)27. See especially A. Low (Secretary CDEEA) to EEF, 16 April 1917 S(4)6.

54 Local Conference between BDEEA and CEJC, 4 December 1917, S(4)10.

55 EEF Files S(4)10–14.

56   Ibid., and Lyddon, 'Workplace organisation'.
57   Hyman, *Workers' Union*, p. 122.
58   Ibid.
59   F. W. Carr, 'Engineering workers and the rise of labour in Coventry, 1914–39', Warwick Ph.D. thesis, 1978, pp. 278–80; T. J. Claydon, 'The development of trade unionism among British automobile and aircraft workers, 1914–46', Kent Ph.D. thesis, 1981 pp. 71–6.
60   Carr, 'Engineering workers', p. 279.
61   Local Conference on Armstrong–Siddely between CDEEA and AEU, 26 January 1927, P(5)126.
62   Mr Shaw (Works Committee Chairman) to Local Conference between Manchester District Engineering Employers' Association and AEU, 24 November 1921 on Crossley Motors, P(5)88.
63   J. B. Jefferys, *The Story of the Engineers* (London, 1946); Claydon, 'Development of trade unionism', p. 358.
64   AEU District Committee Minutes (Coventry), 5 March 1936.
65   Claydon, 'Development of trade unionism', pp. 363–5.
66   EEF Files, NUVB Piecework Agreement 1919, P(5)43.
67   *NUVB Journal*, 1931.
68   Claydon, 'Development of trade unionism', pp. 538–44.
69   EEF Files, Armstrong–Siddely Strike M(8)9, Harper Bean (Blacking) B(2)5.
70   NUVB Head Office Correspondence, E. Buckle to H. Halliwell, 26 January 1940.
71   Cf. Halliwell to Buckle, 25 June 1940.
72   A. Bullock, *The Life and Times of Ernest Bevin*, vol. 1 (London, 1960).
73   *NUVB Journal*, 1928–9.
74   Tolliday, 'Militancy and Organisation'.
75   This account is based on EEF Files, Pressed Steel Strikes 1936 S(5)17, Pressed Steel Strikes and Procedure 1938 P(12)72, and on interviews with Arthur Church, Harry Brown and Jack Thomas.
76   On migration to Oxford see: Whiting, *View from Cowley*, pp. 87–107: *A Survey of the Social Services in Oxford District*, vol. 1 (Oxford, 1938); G. Daniel, 'Some factors affecting the movement of labour', *Oxford Economic Papers*, 1940, pp. 165–7; *idem*, 'Labour migration and age composition', *Sociological Review* 31 (1939). On Coventry see R. Croucher, 'Communist politics and shop stewards in engineering, 1935–45', Warwick Ph.D. thesis, 1977, pp. 190–6; W. Lancaster, 'Who's a real Coventry kid? Migration into 20th Century Coventry', in B. Lancaster and T. Mason (eds.), *Life and Labour in a 20th Century City: the Case of Coventry* (Coventry, 1986); G. L. Marson, 'Coventry, a study in urban geography', Liverpool MA thesis, 1949.
77   Zeitlin, 'Rejoinder', p. 133.
78   G. Williams, 'From Grand Slam to Great Slump', *Welsh History Review 11*, no. 3 (June 1983).
79   R. J. Waller, *The Dukeries Transformed: the Social and Political Development of a 20th Century Coalfield* (Oxford, 1983).
80   Tolliday, 'Militancy and Organisation'.
81   On the USA see H. Harris, 'The snares of liberalism? Politicians, bureaucrats and the shaping of federal labor relations policy in the U.S.A. c. 1915–47', in Tolliday and Zeitlin (eds.), *Shop Floor Bargaining and the State* (Cambridge, 1985). On France see chapter 2 in this volume.

2

Management and Labour in France 1914–39

Sylvie Van de Casteele-Schweitzer

Between the two world wars, French industrialists learned how to mass-produce motor cars. This apprenticeship took place later than in the United States, where Henry Ford, in particular, served as a model. The orders generated by the First World War acted as an accelerator. Then in the 1920s and early 1930s, industrialists organized new factories without any sustained opposition from workers. Several factors have been put forward to explain this, including the split in the labour movement following the Russian Revolution, changes in the composition of the labour force, blindness towards the implications of the new systems of production, and a latent revolt which was to explode in the spring of 1936. None of these hypotheses should be set aside. However, as I shall argue, when studying the four major manufacturers (Marius Berliet, André Citroën, Robert Peugeot and Louis Renault) and their experience of rationalization, technological factors and a chronological break are particularly important.

But it would be reductive to represent – or even to symbolize – the scientific organization of work primarily in terms of the installation of the assembly line. This is only its final component. Vehicles could only be assembled after many other variables had been mastered. Companies have always been structured around three variables: space, machines and men. Scientific organization of work combined these and added a fourth: the mastery of time, following the model developed by F. W. Taylor. These four variables were not mastered in a day – nor even in ten years. The slowness of change in France can be explained by the evolution of employers' attitudes. In the ten years which followed the First World War, concern with the volume of cars to be manufactured took precedence over the time necessary to manufacture them, and only changed economic circumstances shifted the priorities of the employers. The slowness of change in the production process helps to explain the weakness of workers' resistance and with it the weakness of trade-union organization on the shop floor, which remained ephemeral until the strikes of the Popular Front period.

I

The First World War transformed motor-car manufacturers into 'cannon dealers' and had major consequences for industrial organization. The state provided orders and capital and virtually suppressed the competitive market, whilst the war forced changes both in production methods and in attitudes.

If it was a 'war of munitions', the First World War was also a 'war of motor vehicles' through their role in the victories of the French Army. One finds the 'Taxis of the Marne' in 1914 (Renault); the lorries of the 'Voie Sacrée' in 1917 (Berliet); and the tanks of the 1918 counter-offensive (particularly Renault). The motor car, which previously had had the status of a luxury object, was now proving its utilitarian qualities.

For industrialists, the war was also synonymous with the interventionist state. The latter made so many demands that it nearly did away with competition. It financed and absorbed enormous orders, and in exceptional cases, authorized large capital advances. The case of André Citroën was the most striking. In January 1915, he obtained a contract for shell production on the basis of a mere plan. He had no land, factories, machines or labour. Eight months later, the first shells emerged from his factory on the Quai de Javel in Paris. For these orders, however, the military authorities favoured industrialists from the Paris region, who were near to the decision-making centres. André Citroën knew Louis Loucheur, director of Artillery at the Ministry of War, and Louis Renault, another major figure, was influential in ministerial circles. Throughout the war he demonstrated a remarkable capacity for producing a wide and changing range of goods – the only other comparable case being that of Fiat in Turin. But the large provincial manufacturers also participated in this fantastic growth: Marius Berliet built his Monplaisir factories in the Lyon suburbs, whilst Robert Peugeot bought, extended and modernized at Montbeliard.[1]

Two important constraints dominated weapons manufacture: the capacity to organize mass production, often for new products (shells, tanks, etc.) and the need to use unskilled labour. Manufacturing methods hitherto little used in France were introduced, such as the regrouping of machines and work stations according to the order of manufacturing operations, and the simplification of production processes. Industrialists learnt how to integrate smelting, machining and assembly on a large scale. Whilst André Citroën had to come to terms with old industrial buildings, Marius Berliet built his 'integral factory'. He separated machining and assembly, built halls 130 metres long and invested in machine tools. But both made major investments in new equipment, much of it imported from the United States. War production demanded increased output, stable product quality, and a reduction in the number of skilled workers: new machine tools contributed to this change. Furthermore, since the factories employed a large proportion of women, the Ministry of Armaments required the installation of conveyors, especially in firms manufacturing heavy shells. This mechanization accelerated the establishment of new productive structures and the installation of the production line. But it did not lead immediately to the introduction of the continuous mechanical conveyor which formed the basis of the assembly line. In these immense war factories, parts continued to be handled manually.

The First World War thus promoted lasting changes in manufacturing practice. The entrepreneurs were driven to modify the organization of their factories, their production and their working methods. At the same time, their relationship with the workforce was also changing: the national consensus of the 'Union Sacrée' and the limited bargaining experience of the new recruits guaranteed social peace – at least until 1917.

Four entrepreneurs dominated the motor-car industry during these years: Marius Berliet, André Citroën, Robert Peugeot and Louis Renault. The subsequent development of the motor-car industry in France revolved around their stories. Two came from engineering backgrounds – Citroën (École Polytechnique) and Peugeot (École Centrale) – and two were mechanics – Berliet and Renault. But this difference in their careers does not correspond to the differences in their strategic choices. Berliet and Citroën were both unconditional advocates of large-scale rationalization and of the transfer of technology without any amendments. Their model was Henry Ford: for them, the civilian market for cars was thought to be as unlimited as military demand had been. As soon as peace was declared, they both announced that they were going to build 'the first French mass-produced motor car' at a rate of '100 models a day'.[2]

Although similar in their ambitions, they differed in their financial backing. Berliet was threatened with bankruptcy in 1922 and put under external financial controls. This failure reduced him to the rank of the medium manufacturers. At the same time, Citroën too was on the verge of ruin, having committed the same errors. But he had behind him his family and associates (the club of Diamond Cutters) who helped him to overcome this obstacle and become the number one French manufacturer. During this 1920–1 crisis, Peugeot, who was very cautious, renounced an expansionist strategy, and Renault opted for the same tactics, persisting in self-financing and 'peasant book-keeping'.[3] Thus Citroën alone succeeded in pursuing growth at any price. At the time of the Great Crash, he would make the same choice, but on that occasion the banks did not support him, preferring the prudent management of the Michelin family which took over the company in 1935.[4]

Between the two wars, Citroën, Renault and Peugeot were to confront each other in the same arena: the adoption of 'American methods' for high-volume production of motor cars. Before the First World War, France had already ceded to the United States her early primacy in motor-car production. The Americans progressed by leaps and bounds. Taylorism revolutionized conceptions of industrial organization and one manufacturer, Henry Ford, integrated it into his own plans. He designed, manufactured and marketed a single car by the millions – the Model T Ford fascinated other industrialists. Ford incarnated the scientific organization of work and became its major point of reference. His factories were visited, his industrial organization copied, and he served as a model in a thousand ways.

Ford said of his factories that they were a river nourished by streams. The sources of the river were the forges, the smelting and stamping shops; the streams were the assembly lines, and the river the final assembly. French manufacturers took this metaphor very much to heart. They also admired this model people, this 'young race, made up of all the most energetic elements of the old European races . . . should we hesitate to follow them, to make up our minds we only need to consider the material and moral results that these men have achieved.'[5] Berliet modelled himself most literally on America. Not only was his work area 'three times more vast than the Ford factories', but the factory's design inevitably recalled that of New York, with streets (A, B, C . . .) from east to west and avenues (1, 2, 3 . . .) from north to south.[6]

Whilst Berliet and Peugeot sent their engineers to visit Ford's factories, Citroën and Renault visited in person, and these visits were decisive for their industrial development. Following his first visit to Ford in 1912, Citroën was the first large private owner to manufacture a single weapon in a single calibre (shells of 75mm) during the war. After his second visit in 1923, he decided to adopt a single model of motor car, with a steel chassis, and to enlarge his firm whilst pushing for the integration of production. In 1931, he made his last visit, returning dazzled in spite of the depression, and entirely restructured his factory on the Quai de Javel (1933) in order to make it 'the most beautiful assembly line in Europe', more beautiful than Louis Renault's at Billancourt.[7] Louis Renault crossed the Atlantic twice, in 1911 and 1928. He visited 50 factories in one month on the second occasion, accompanied by the directors of his research and methods departments. On his return, he built his 'Ile Seguin' works for assembly-line production of his vehicles.[8]

The industrialists borrowed the layout of the factories they saw in the United States, the systems of organization and the machines. They admired Ford's single model and sought to impose it on the French market. Marius Berliet designed his new factory with the aim of manufacturing a single car (copied from the Dodge) and a single lorry, but he could not really follow this project through to its conclusion. André Citroën hesitated, producing one or two models in different periods, but his touring cars offered so many options (taxis, cabriolets, coupés) that this restricted product range lost its advantages. At Peugeot, as at Renault, management hesitated as well: though the model range was reduced immediately after the war, the firm soon turned back towards the diversification of production, no doubt as a result of the 1920-1 recession. Thus a director complained at Sochaux that 'the fear of not having the right model leads to the adoption of complicated programmes, even though the basic car remains the same: as soon as one can manufacture a comfortable, attractive model at a reasonable price, the demand is a sure thing.' This director left Peugeot to spend five years at Citroën.[9]

The manufacturers imported equipment as well as ideas. In 1919, Berliet completed the construction of a steel works ordered from the American group Carnegie. All the presses at the Montbeliard forge, copied from Ford, came from the United States, and the same was true of Citroën's works at Saint-Ouen, which also had large numbers of American machine tools. Although the quantity and quality of these imports is still not well known, we do know that everywhere they raised two problems. On the one hand, the United States had developed technologies which had not been mastered by French engineers, and the transfer of technology had to be supplemented by the establishment of American outposts (engineers, technicians) in French factories. On the other hand, these high-output machines, which had been conceived for the vast American market, generated tremendous over-capacity in France. At Citroën and Berliet in 1925, for example, the presses stamped enough in one hour to supply the daily production of the factory.[10]

But for an ambitious industrialist, the figures were eloquent. In 1917, the USA produced 1,746,000 cars, or three times more than in 1914 (548,000); between 1919 and 1923 its production grew again by 110 per cent though after 1924 the market became tighter and excess capacity began to appear. Even more spectacular figures encouraged men like Berliet and Citroën to imagine a glorious future for the French automobile industry: not only did France possess the second largest road network after the USA, but whereas in 1907 in France there had been one automobile for every 981 inhabitants and in the USA one for every 608, in 1913 the proportions stood at 1:318 and 1:77 respectively. In six years American progress had been staggering, and it continued during the following decade: one car for every 44 inhabitants in France in 1927 as opposed to 1:5.3 in the United States.[11] It was this image of American progress which set the horizons of French automobile producers.

Stimulated by war orders and fascinated by Ford's example, the four major French manufacturers imported at great cost. But it was not sufficient to look at and then to copy standardized production. It was also necessary simultaneously to bring into play the three important 'raw materials' required: space, machines and men. This is what the industrialists slowly learnt during the twenties. In the first stages, they concentrated on quantity, having grasped only the high-volume side of mass production.

II

With standardized production, industry entered into the era of the large scale – whether for space, output of machines or numbers of men. Furthermore, the difficulties were infinitely multiplied by the complexity of the motor cars, which demanded a synthesis of the latest technologies of all the applied sciences.

It was only by combining the physical and chemical properties of metals, by varying the dimensions of the components and by assembling and adjusting electromechanical equipment, that a sophisticated, finished object composed of 12,000 to 15,000 parts could be produced. One should therefore be wary of reducing rationalization to the assembly-line and the stopwatch, or of considering it merely from the point of view of the subdivision of tasks and the deskilling of labour.

The motor-car factories were perpetual building sites. Between 1919 and 1927, Citroën increased his working area fivefold (from 150 to 725,000 square metres). Renault expanded from 300 square metres in 1898 to 650,000 in 1934. But Berliet beat all records at Venissieux with 800,000 square metres in one block. The interior and exterior areas of the factories were always being changed to accommodate increased production. Shops needed to be adapted for the size of machines, as well as for stocking parts and material, and facilitating traffic management, handling, maintenance, the logical sequence of manufacture, and finally assembly. With experience, manufacturers realized that rationalization required virtually a clean sweep, and that buildings should be purpose-built. The design of jobs, distribution of skills and transfer of technology were inseparable, and were inscribed from the outset in the walls and the ground: 'When examining the design of a well-made plant, one should be able to reconstitute all the phases of production', proclaimed Ernest Mattern, an important engineer.[12]

With the establishment of high-volume manufacture, the workspace, the structure of workshops, interior outfitting of buildings, and the equipment of the work stations were all modified. There was a move from a rigid, closed space to a flexible, open one. Flexible, so that its organization could be modified at each change of production; open, since the production methods led to the disappearance of interior partitions. At the same time, the work station was closed in, so that the worker could avoid moving around and have everything close to hand.[13]

Mass production required simplification of models as well as standardization of components, but, above all, it needed the rigorous interchangeability of parts. Without this, assembly became impossible, as the workers all turned into fitters. At Citroën, 'the equipment was badly maintained and badly adjusted, the parts came out ill-formed from the presses and numerous alterations were then needed.'[14] At Berliet, management tried to deal with similar problems by forbidding workers to use files on the assembly line, but this was no substitute for the achievement of genuine interchangeability in component manufacture.

Technical uncertainties continued to reign in the workshop. As a government superintendant observed of her factory training: 'If I was never interrupted, everything would go all right. But, alas, the wheels break with disconcerting ease. If they don't break, they wear out . . . then, the belts get slack . . . Also sometimes the current fails and we're stuck for an hour with our arms crossed.'[15] In addition, each change of vehicle model led to a complete upheaval.

Uncertainties revealed themselves not only in everyday technical practice, but, of course, also in the third 'raw material' – labour. In the early years of this century, there could be no typical 'motor-car worker', in those immense factories encompassing all the different tasks of the engineering trades, from steel rolling to carriage building, from the design of engines and parts to the maintenance of buildings and machinery. The rationalization of work, with its redistribution of skills, also brought in new labour – from towns, the countryside and the colonies. Different generations of workers were henceforth to work alongside each other, some more traditional, others accommodating to the process of change.

During the period when the scientific organization of work was being established, it would be erroneous to speak of a systematic and accelerated deskilling of the workforce, although standardized production certainly led to the recruitment of labourers and the appearance of machinists. For some years the proportions remained in favour of skilled workers. It was war production (particularly shells) which led to a large majority of low-skilled and female labour (at Peugeot an average of 35 per cent were women, 25 per cent at Renault, 85.5 per cent working on shell assembly at Citroën).

The overall percentage of unskilled labour in a company does not, however, take into account the diversity of sectors which were unequally affected by the subdivision of tasks. Thus in parts manufacture, the first stage involved a narrowing of individual job assignments, the specialization of work stations and their reorganization into logical sequences – which was not synonymous with deskilling. The transference of workers' skills into the machine only came about gradually, with the extension and mastery of automation. On the other hand, the reduction of skill needed in the assembly workshops came from progress obtained in breaking down motions, the interchangeability of parts and reduction in the complexity of assembly – rather than from automation. In fact, manufacture and assembly were not the only activities of a factory. In 1927, at Citroën, only 64 per cent of the labour force was involved in these tasks (compared with 61 per cent at Renault ten years later). The rest of the workforce was employed in preparing, supervising and servicing the process of direct production, and their job assignments remained more fluid. For example, the Methods Time Study Department, which had hardly existed a few years previously, included 500 people, essentially skilled workers and engineers.[16]

Old skills were replaced by new ones, and industrialists were always complaining that training was not adapted to their new needs. They were all therefore compelled to create training schools which they organized in identical fashion. Classes mixed theory and practice for two to three years at three levels (skilled workers, foremen and future engineers). In the provinces, employees trained in this way usually stayed in the firm, but in Paris they felt less bound by the training acquired.

By allocating precise functions to each person, the scientific organization of work paved the way towards specialization, rather than systematic deskilling. The workers' perception of skills also varied. Stability, wage levels and status in the firm and society were all important, as well as the content of jobs. The highly skilled workers witnessed with bitterness the disappearance of their craft associations, but female and less-skilled male workers took a very different view. For them the status of waged worker had a positive connotation. Nor did all women experience work as oppressive. As a government factory superintendant observed: 'They are used to factory life and their love for it is greater because of their total lack of domestic education. The young woman worker who gets married never even thinks that she might stay at home. The former workers return to the factory once they have brought up their children, and not always because of necessity.'[17] The factory remained a means, for men and women, of participating in social life, and the large motor-car firm (even with its fatigues and ponderous hierarchy), was often chosen in preference to the small firm where the workday was longer, salaries lower and sexual discrimination more accentuated. Factories with scientific organization of work were not necessarily intolerably restrictive for workers, nor rejected by them overall.

Analysing worker opposition to the scientific organization of work is not a simple task. Attitudes were not clear-cut and were mostly not recorded in writing. Workers could complain about its daily effects without denying its socio-economic necessity. Although not clearly formulated, individuals perceived the arrival of mass consumption and felt the need to limit waste of all kinds that had occurred in the old-style factory (time, materials, skills, etc.). Rather than seeing a threat in the new factory, each individual sought a place in it. Firstly there was the fascination for techniques which liberated workers. 'You should see how they make the side-panels: in two minutes. Before, the same work took two hours,' explained a worker of the Citroën presses to a journalist from *l'Humanité*.[18] Mechanization trapped craft workers on their own ground; their entire value system encouraged them to admire productive efficiency. Furthermore, well-conceived rationalization could produce greater equity; to regularize the productive flow, work stations needed to be balanced and work equally distributed between the teams and individuals. Although unhealthy and exacting work remained, the arbitrary power of the boss was gradually restricted. Finally, remuneration was henceforward according to the quantity of work produced and the most skilful understood this well. Life in the workshops was not a continuous attempt to dawdle. As Georges Navel, observed of his time at Citroën and Berliet: 'teams become rivals in the work: fellow workers compete for the use of the moving bridges and the small pneumatic wheels which consume metal more quickly than the large files.'[19]

Of course, there remained resistance to work which favoured dexterity, diligence, regularity and nervous endurance. But this could hardly be compared with the work rules elaborated in the nineteenth century. In the new factory, the collectivity abdicated responsibility whilst the main resistance came from the individual. This was visible in the turnover of workers. Voluntary departures in 1928 at Citroën's forges and casting works equalled the entire workforce of the factory, and the same percentage applied to the Renault factories. On the other hand those in charge considered labour to be 'stable' in the provinces.

There were, of course, a variety of causes of labour turnover, which should not be conflated: seasonal layoffs initiated by management; the arbitrary power of the foreman, which the rationalizers were trying to curb during this period; and the many reasons of the workers themselves for voluntary departures, ranging from harsh discipline and working conditions, quarrels with supervisors and low wages to military service. Turnover might also have been related to skill levels. The most skilled – sure of finding work elsewhere – and the least skilled – who performed the most exhausting tasks – had the highest turnover rates. Restriction of output also existed, but there was a move away from open, generalized, slow-downs, organized by groups, towards individual resistance. Engineers strove to analyse it with the fine tooth-comb of chronometers, whilst recognizing that, 'one should admit that those working on an individual output level do limit their production, more often because they lack confidence in the rates conceded.'[20] Slow-downs took place when timings were being made (as a result they were conducted more and more secretly) and during production itself. At Citroën at least, however, documents showed that the timings included pause periods. In fact, resistance to the work rhythm set out by the Methods Department should be looked at from several angles; the technical tricks invented by the worker could earn him more money and/or rest time. In such cases an acceleration rather than a slow-down of production was involved.

Resignation was probably much more widespread than is usually believed. As Simone Weil wrote of her experiences in the Alsthom works in Paris in the late 1930s: 'Revolt is impossible, except in flashes. Firstly, against what? One is alone with one's work; one can only revolt against it. But if one felt irritated, one would work badly, and therefore starve.'[21] Strikes – which were rare – were organized around wage rates. Workers' demands shifted; it became legitimate and normal for earnings to be linked to individual output. Having been producers, workers acceded to the more ambiguous status of consumers, and laid their claim to a share in the increase of goods. In France, 1936 would witness the initial sharing out of the fruits of progress: increases in salaries, reduction of work time and paid holidays.

By 1936, however, the nature of rationalization had changed, having increased its influence over industrial management as a result of two major recessions. The first stemmed from Poincaré's monetary stabilization of 1927, which was followed by the Great Crash, which hit France in 1930–31. Industrialists had to cut production costs to remain competitive in foreign markets despite the stabilization of the Franc and the international collapse of prices, as well as to expand their domestic markets. In addition, a brief but intense upturn in the French economy in 1928–9 led to a shortage of skilled labour which pushed firms to use their existing plant more intensively. In 1930, Peugeot completed a profound restructuring of its production methods, and productivity increased by 50 per cent (90 per cent of its production now took place at Sochaux, compared to 60 per cent in 1928). Renault for his part built the 'Ile Seguin' plant, while Citroën, who had just made enormous investments in forges and foundries at Clichy, delayed restructuring at Javel. At the same time, all those who could not realize these essential investments were caught short by the crash: between 1929 and 1935 the number of French automobile manufacturers fell from 90 to 28. This restructuring expanded the so-called 'unproductive' services. After having stressed space and machines, industrialists discovered time – Taylor's time.

III

Like the war, economic recessions acted as an accelerator. The implementation of the scientific organization of work, however, had moved into new areas. 'We lack discipline . . . order . . . method . . . control,' the heads of departments at Renault were told in 1931.[22] These failures had to be remedied by Taylorist methods. Production norms would be established and enforced in practice. Departments would be set up to exercise this activity. The power of science was extended, a hierarchy established to measure time and new positions created to administer it. With measurement, science moved from the laboratories to the shop floor. Standardization depended on the precision of machining, but the latter was entirely dependent on the quality of materials used. The laboratories were entrusted with this control.

The knowledge – and hence the power – of the laboratories was enormous, giving them an ideological role. Through their mediation, science entered the factory and insinuated itself into people's minds. This ideology spilled over into new areas when science began to be applied to work organization by production engineers. Little by little, labour was perceived to be essentially similar to the objects of study of other sciences. The worker became an analysable object, his movements broken down and then counted, according to the universal unit – time. Everything contained within the factory became uniformly quantifiable and thus interchangeable: the strength, movement, wear and tear and output of both men and machines.

On the other hand, science claimed to suppress the arbitrary nature of individual choice. The new justice of the stopwatch, which measured each person's work on the same basis, was said to be neutral. Scientific knowledge transcended conflicts of interest since it expressed a natural and even biological hierarchy: 'the division of labour is natural . . . With man, each sense has its defined function and each one cooperates for the good of the whole which is the human body. What we can note in man also applies to companies.'[23] Science was thus a guiding light and an undeniable social arbiter. With inhuman impartiality it designed a place for everyone and kept everyone in their place.

At the same time, a new pyramid of authority was being constructed in the car firms. The new forms of production also transformed the position of the foreman. Foremen had always been the social and technical transmission belt between manufacturers and labour; they had decision-making powers in the definition and division of work. While they no longer fixed the price of parts, it was still possible to negotiate with them over payment of a job carried out too slowly and they were responsible for arranging overtime. They often recruited directly (or on recommendation) and could decide to make individual lay-offs. The foreman managed his portion of the workshop and his technical knowledge was too important to allow real control by his hierarchical superiors.

Having set up the work areas and machines, the rationalizers now became aware of the foremen's power. Its reduction took several forms: breaking down the foremen's control over individuals and reducing their technical knowledge by the deployment of new departments and the methodical study of work time. 'Functional' foremanship was circumscribed. From 1917, they followed Taylor's principles at Berliet: four heads of workshops shared what had previously been 'a single' responsibility. The administrator was responsible for the management of equipment and materials. The head of maintenance was in charge of the working of the machines. The inspector verified the quality and safety of work. The foreman controlled the execution of work and the training of new recruits. He thus had the undeniable authority of knowledge. On the other hand, the supervisors who harried suspected idlers were hated because they lacked knowledge-based legitimacy.

This organizational structure could remain purely formal for a long time. It was only in 1927 that Renault distinguished between foremen responsible for the preparation and quality of work and chargehands responsible for execution. At the same time, responsibilities of workshop heads were increased (work study, production scheduling, control of parts, supply of materials).[24] In 1928 at Panhard 'the foreman was a young man who looked severe and the appearance of his white overall caused all backs to stoop . . . We rarely saw him and we dealt on a continuous basis with the charge hand. The workshop head . . . very rarely came amongst the workers.'[25] Hierarchical relationships were in a complete state of flux and traditions were overturned. At Berliet 'foreman X . . . systematically refused to talk with the workers about service and forced them to go through the charge hand.'[26]

New skills, new responsibilities, but also new departments were established to administer the scientific organization of work. The Labour Department was to centralize and perfect recruitment and wages, whilst the Methods Department took on the retiming of work. The Labour Department, created in most firms around the middle of the twenties, had much wider functions than the Personnel Department (the head of which was usually a former army officer). It combined recruitment, transfers of personnel within the company, wages and layoffs. ('It has to be said in fact that too often layoffs were decided for futile and unjust motives and usually without appeal,' they explained at Citroën).[27] Departmental autonomy came to an end, for it was vital to regulate the size, skills and costs, of the labour force. This department was responsible for wages from two points of view: remuneration of the labour force, and scientific cost-accounting. In principle, modern wage systems, based on time, should have been introduced along with modern production methods, but different payment systems coexisted throughout the factories. There were daily rates, hourly rates, piecework, 'bonuses', the Rowan or Bedaux systems. These systems were frequently difficult to understand and caused perpetual conflicts with the labour force. Another consequence of these disparities was that without a unit of common measure, it was impossible to compare labour productivity in the different workshops. Some firms (including Citroën and Peugeot) therefore perfected a salary system which permitted a calculation of the professional value and activity rates of workshops. Thus, for the rationalizers themselves, production control was more important than any possibility of dividing the workforce by creating complex and confusing differences in individual earnings. The timing department was also given an accounting function, monitoring the relationship between hours of work and the number of cars coming off the lines. In addition, except at Berliet where pragmatism reigned, industrialists introduced psycho-technical selection of individuals for recruitment purposes.

The Methods Department, established at Peugeot in 1924 and Citroën in 1925, usually grew out of the Manufacturing Department. But the setting up of a department should not be misinterpreted. The break-up of work-stations was only introduced at the end of the 1920s. Until then, at Berliet, 'there were time-keepers, but the foreman arranged things with the workshop head. There was a stopwatch, but it wasn't the same as later on.'[28] In 1925 at Citroën, 'in the body methods department, there were joiners and saddlers, but no engineers.'[29] In 1928 at Peugeot, the methods department offices were 'virtually non-existent, times are established by the foremen . . . in the body shop, the production lines were used only for maintenance, most operations being carried out in fixed stations, without being subdivided.'[30]

Thus even when the Methods office did branch out to the principal departments, it only gave overall times to workshops and foremen, for example 15 hours for assembling a car. Then, empiricism and a step by step approach reigned; the commercial department would order a certain number of vehicles, for example 100. The multiplication of two figures gave the number of hours to be done (1,500 in this case) and the number of workers needed (150 for a 10-hour day). The car therefore was the determining unit of calculation. The arrival of the experts at the end of the twenties fundamentally changed the approach. The job was broken up and work stations timed individually, in minute detail, operation by operation. One no longer considered the car and the worker – only work in itself. Counting from then on was in time rather than in objects (and in minutes and seconds rather than in hours). Taylorism had become part of people's mentalities.

For a long time therefore, the French industrial outlook was determined by reasoning in volumes, and the number of objects to be manufactured, rather than reasoning in time and book-keeping. The wish to subdivide work was not determining. Above all the aim was to manufacture in quantity.

Structures of company organization were varied. From 1918, Berliet copied the system of the American firm Winchester and had six large departments: manufacture, research, preparation, job timing, production, inspection. Between the two wars, at Peugeot, the technical services had five important departments: information, creation of models, laboratory and various services, manufacturing, statistics. But these organizational structures were frequently purely formal and their efficiency depended on those directing the different departments. It would seem that a better point of reference for judging the efficiency of rationalization was the existence of analytical cost-accounting. This was practised daily, weekly and monthly and took into account all the variables of the scientific organization of work. It aimed at realizing profits whilst administering in one block wages and rejects, waste, the cost of raw materials and stocks; it also drew up charts.[31] There, again, it was no longer just a question of satisfying the order programme – 'The cars go out at whatever cost,' said a Citroën director in 1922 – since reasoning in numbers was overtaken by reasoning in time. Time became money.

Company welfare programmes need to be included among the "functional", "unproductive" services involved in rationalization. Their purpose was naturally to integrate the personnel and they took several forms: integration through leisure activity, through benefits, and through the cultivation of a collective identity by the company papers. All this was necessary to offset the negative consequences of scientific management and the large, anonymous factory by creating a new status for the wage-earner. Three phases can be distinguished in the development of company welfare policies during this period, corresponding to phases in the development of scientific management and its perception by managers and workers.

Just after the war, company practices were based on a nineteenth-century paternalism inspired by social catholicism and imposed on the workforce. The great arms firms thus developed a network of crèches, canteens, infirmaries, rest homes, cooperatives and other associations. During the 1920s, by contrast, these practices disappeared almost entirely, especially in Paris. The employers undoubtedly believed that the new organization of work would be sufficient to unite all the members of the enterprise: following Taylor, they believed in a factory peopled by free, self-interested workers whose relationship with the entrepreneur would be purely economic. This strategy seems to have failed, in part because of the low level of wages. Moreover, as the factories mushroomed in size, each workshop lost contact with the others and individuals became atomized; while the advancement of scientific management undermined the stability of the workforce and its concern with the job.

Management therefore began to look towards a better 'socialization' of the workforce, undertaking what would be called 'human relations' after

1945, a new stage of relations between workers and employers rooted at the same time in a nineteenth-century form of 'participation'. Automobile employers renewed their emphasis on integration through leisure activities – dressmaking for women, sport for men (at Berliet with the same linkage of theory and practice as in the vocational training schools) – as well as through the provision of benefits such as relief funds and social services. Factory supervisors clearly staked their claim to this latter function: 'technically and morally [it] allows the modern company to operate like a small artisanal workshop.'[32] At the same time, the company press, which inculcated an 'esprit maison', grew rapidly and underwent significant changes in its language: thus the *Bulletin des usines Peugeot*, founded in 1918, became in 1929 *Le Trait d'Union*; having previously been reserved for management, it was now distributed to all personnel.

These welfare programmes did not differ much in form from the paternalism of the nineteenth century, but their spirit was profoundly different, particularly when they are juxtaposed to the changing systems of wage payment. Systems of payment by the piece and then by time, replaced payment by the job which recognized workers' individuality and professional autonomy. As a system of production, scientific management was organized to stimulate the worker; even if its history shows the impossibility of eliminating individual worker initiative, its architects nonetheless pursued the ideal of the automaton relieved of all responsibility and motivated by the level of his wages.

The appearance of 'human relations' in the enterprise – with its accompanying programmes and later industrial sociologists – marked a new stage: the factory was henceforth seen as a social body which required the adhesion of all its members. Automobile employers began to implement this vision in the 1930s, but its crisis would come in 1936.

IV

The crisis of 1936 flowed from the delayed political repercussions of the new organization of work. Between 1880 and 1920, French industry had been the site of a conflict between skilled workers and employers for the control of work. Work rules, enforced by strikes and trade-union intervention, had been formulated in contrast to employers' norms.[33] However, in the motor-car industry there was nothing comparable until the middle of the 1930s. The labour force often had no bargaining experience and workers' organizations had been knocked off-balance by the new factory structures.

In 1921, the trade-union movement split between the Confédération Générale du Travail (CGT) and the Confédération Générale du Travail Unitaire (CGTU), and for 15 years was absent from large firms. Its reactions to the scientific organization of work, however, partly explain its attitudes in 1936. In fact the CGT and CGTU did not contest the bases of scientific organization of work – and hardly its consequences. The CGT firmly declared, particularly in *Standards* by H. Dubreuil, that rationalization was a source of progress, and it admired the United States. It supported productivism in its programme, calling for 'a maximum of production for a minimum of worktime'.[34] The CGT even accused employers of reticence in introducing the scientific organization of work.[35]

But the CGT had almost no influence in French automobile factories. Until 1936 the CGTU, too, had only a few hundred activists, but their role would become crucial between 1936 and 1938 (after the reunification of the unions which preceded the Popular Front, the CGTU faction was in a clear majority among the metalworkers), particularly because of the evolution of Communist discourse and practice during the 1920s and 1930s. Until the 'bolshevization' imposed by the Comintern in 1924, questions of enterprise management had been put off until 'after the revolution', and the Parti Communiste Français (PCF) showed little interest in everyday life and working conditions within the factories. The Party contested neither the ideas nor the symbols of rationalization, and *l'Humanité* even wrote that 'with the assembly line, the advance over older systems is undeniable; production is greatly accelerated and the workers do not complain' (February 1924).[36]

Even if there were disagreements among the Communists, it was only in 1927 that the debate over rationalization began to move on: a distinction was then drawn between capitalist and socialist countries, between 'bad' and 'good' rationalization, as in the case of Soviet electrification. But in any case scientific management was not rejected as a system of production, and the CGTU fought the effects and not the causes, demanding ways of regenerating the labour force (and reducing the working day, particularly for women): 'in order for workers to stand up to the fatigue, restore their forces and *continue to follow* the infernal speed of the machine, the line or the work team, it is essential that wages acquire greater purchasing power in relation to increased needs,' as the Fédération Unitaire des Metaux explained in 1929.[37] There was little criticism of deskilling and one finds few substantial analyses of new working methods nor real attacks against the 'ineluctable march of progress'. Redress for the workforce was sought in meteorological metaphors: scientific management was the rain, and the only solution was to 'open the umbrella' of trade-union protection against its consequences. Thus by the middle of the 1930s, the assembly line had entered the factories, without encountering the critical discourse of the Communist organizations. These analyses explain trade-union attitudes in 1936, and particularly the lack of support given to the formulation of union demands for job controls. Unions preferred to work for political rather than social goals, for joint committees of workers and employers and for arbitration in disputes. In this way, they linked up with previous efforts by the state to incorporate workers into 'the Nation'.

In 1936, the new motor-car factory was a favourable terrain for the birth of large-scale conflict, particularly due to the influence of the skilled workers.[38] From the First World War until then, social calm had reigned and worker activists had been persecuted and dwindled greatly in numbers. Nonetheless, they still played a certain role in the years before the Popular Front, particularly in connection with strikes which widened their experience and served as a model for the great explosion of May–June 1936.[39]

At Renault, between November 1931 and January 1932, a series of small disputes flared up which the Communists were unable to extend throughout the enterprise. Nevertheless they learned how to distribute widely their tracts and special pages of *l'Humanité*; the skilled workers and activists took the lead and formed strike committees, appointed shop delegates, held sit-down stoppages, and drew up lists of grievances. While this movement was itself unsuccessful, the PCF and the CGTU drew from it valuable lessons which they applied at Citroën in March–April 1933. This strike, now directed against wage cuts, lasted six weeks, including a month's lockout. It too was led by the skilled workers, with strong participation by the CGTU and PCF, who would derive important positive results from it: the nomination of a central strike committee of 120 members with representatives from all sectors of the factory, daily meetings, and the constant presence of union officials. After the strike, the CGTU had grown to over 1,000 members (as opposed to 100 previously) organized in 22 union sections, and the PCF had built up a number of factory cells. In this Citroën strike, the workers' organizations gained experience of responsibility: they negotiated directly with the Ministry of Labour, while the Communist deputies intervened in the National Assembly and the demands put forward by the strikers included those which would be granted in 1936 by the Matignon accords and new social legislation (except paid holidays).

In June 1936, the factories were occupied – in many cases briefly. Above all there was a massive increase in trade-union membership, which was unexpected and unique in the history of the French labour movement. Two Parisian firms, Renault and Citroën, stand out in this respect. In May 1936 there were about 100 trade-union members at Renault: a few months later there were at least 18,000, perhaps more. The movement was probably even stronger at Citroën. This explosion was also a political one (6,000 to 7,000 Communists at Renault) and allowed the French Communist Party to realize the 'bolshevization' advocated by the Communist International in 1924. Workers' organizations even took over company bodies, whether relating to welfare or sport. With the Popular Front, the workers' organizations thus achieved respectability through responsibility. Together with the state and the employers, they negotiated the Matignon agreements, and took part in drawing up collective agreements which inter alia recognized worker delegates. They sat on committees which settled disputes. They supported legislation for compulsory arbitration. They entered the era of legality and negotiation. Industrialists, taken by surprise and temporarily vanquished, remained conciliatory until the general strike of 30 November 1938 which was followed by a formidable purge.

Trade unions wanted a new bilateral relationship within the company. The workers, from their side, took up forgotten practices again. Although they voted in a body for the CGT when electing delegates, they became involved at workshop level in other ways. Following the factory occupations, the return to work took place on new bases, which were in no way covered by the workers' press. Thus, there were almost daily wildcat strikes at Renault. Workers struggled on all fronts: for the expulsion of reactionary and non-unionized workers and against overtime and unhealthy conditions. In the polishing shop, 'the slightest incident is used as a pretext, one strikes up the *Internationale*. Foremen were given 48 hours in which to join the CGT.'[40] However, resistance to work also took more radical forms. At Billancourt again, work rates went down by an average of 20 per cent. (Some teams stopped work when they considered that they had produced enough!) This went on until November 1938 when productive order was re-established within a week of firing the leaders. Punctuality and discipline also greatly decreased.[41] The atmosphere had changed in the workshops and employers were impotent when faced with this transformation. Trade-union representatives regularly called upon the labour force to be calm and disciplined; no doubt this opposition to certain forms of worker action partially explains the rapid fall in trade-union membership.

At the end of the thirties, French employers had discovered Taylor's time. Workers, on the other hand, had discovered the time for revolt, conviviality in the workshops and also leisure time – with the 40 hour-week and paid holidays. Neither side knew that, once again, would come the time of war.

Within an analysis of employers' policies and workers' practices, the introduction of mass-production methods therefore occupies a central place. A fundamental conflict was acted out at the intersection of two industrial eras. The initiative in the factories definitely changed hands. The age of technical virtuosity and workers' control came to an end, whilst the era of productive performance and employers' initiative began.

French employers seem to have had difficulty in adapting to the scientific organization of work, moving towards rationalization in two distinct stages. This difficulty was perhaps because the scientific organization of work hid its complexities under the appearance of rationality. Should one say, therefore, that industrialists rejected Taylorism, alarmed by its costs and social consequences, particularly the 1912 strike at Renault? That does not seem to have been the case. They failed, rather, to grasp its foundations and implications. They were mesmerized by the Fordist spectacle, and dazzled by the image of American productive efficiency. Blinded by its brightness, they did not want to see, at first, the other side of the picture – those unobtrusive, seemingly 'unproductive' services. Rather than shrinking from investment, they pushed for it – but in an incomplete way. It was only when forced to understand the interdependence between workshop organization and the general organization of the company that they were able to attain a level of productivity which would make possible mass production and consumption after the Second World War.

NOTES

1 G. Hatry, *Renault Usine de Guerre* (Paris, 1978); G. Déclas, 'Recherches sur les usines Berliet, 1914–46', (Paris I, mémoire de maîtrise, 1977); S. Van de Casteele-Schweitzer, 'André Citroën: l'aventurier de l'industrie' *L'histoire*, no. 56 (May 1983): D. Henri, 'La société anonyme des automobiles Peugeot de 1918 à 1930, histoire d'une strategie d'expansion', (Paris I, mémoire de Maîtrise, 1983).

2 A. Pinol, 'Travail, travailleurs et production aux usines Berliet, 1912–47', (Lyon II, mémoire de maîtrise, 1980), p. 101; S. Schweitzer, *Des engrenages à la chaîne, Citroën 1915–35* (Lyon, 1982), p. 14.

3 Henri, 'Peugeot', p. 38: P. Fridenson, *Histoire des usines Renault, naissance de la grande entreprise, 1898–1939* (Paris, 1972), p. 170.

4 J. L. Loubet, 'La Société Anonyme André Citroën, étude historique, 1924–68', (Paris X, thèse de troisième cycle, 1979).

5 Pinol, 'Usines Berliet', p. 40.

6 Déclas, 'Recherches sur les usines Berliet', p. 83: Pinol, 'Berliet', p. 65.

7 Schweitzer, *Des engrenages à la chaîne*, p. 45.

8 G. Hatry, *Louis Renault: patron absolu* (Paris, 1981), p. 225.

9 Y. Cohen, 'L'espace de l'organisateur: Ernest Mattern, 1906–39', *Le Mouvement Social*, no. 125 (1983); A. Moutet, 'Introduction de la production à la chaîne en France du début du XXème siècle à la grande crise en 1930', *Histoire, Economie et Société*, no. 1 (1983).

10 Pinol, 'Berliet'; Schweitzer, *Des engrenages à la chaîne*.

11 J. P. Bardou, J. J. Chanaron, P. Fridenson and J. M. Laux, *La Révolution Automobile* (Paris, 1977).

12 Cohen, 'Ernest Mattern'.

13 Pinol, 'Berliet'.

14 Schweitzer, *Des engrenages à la chaîne*, p. 70.

15 A. Fourcaut, *Femmes à l'usine en France dans l'entre-deux-guerres* (Paris, 1982), p. 96.

16 Fridenson, *Renault*; Schweitzer, *Des engrenages à la chaîne*.

17 Fourcaut, *Femmes à l'usine*, p. 24.

18 Schweitzer, *Des engrenages à la chaîne*, p. 32.

19 G. Navel, *Travaux*, (Paris, 1969), p. 110.

20 *Annual Report* of the Citroën works at Clichy (1927), cited in Schweitzer, *Des engrenages à la chaîne*, p. 83.

21 S. Weil, *La Condition ouvrière*, (Paris, 1974, 2nd edition), p. 68.

22 Fridenson, *Renault*, p. 195.

23 *Bulletin Citroën*, 1925.

24 Moutet, 'Introduction de la production à la chaîne'.

25 Fourcaut, *Femmes à l'usine*, p. 100.

26 P. Videlier, 'Banlieue sud: Venissieux entre les deux guerres', (Lyon II, thèse de 3ème cycle, 1982), p. 338.

27 Schweitzer, *Des engrenages à la chaîne*.

28 Pinol, 'Berliet', p. 167.

29 Schweitzer, *Des engrenages à la chaîne*, p. 72.

30 Y. Cohen, 'Quelques aspects de la pratique d'organisation de la production dans l'industrie automobile', *Cahiers du GERPISA*, no. 2 (1985).

31 See esp. Y. Cohen, 'Ernest Mattern, les automobiles Peugeot et le pays de Montbeliard avant et pendant la guerre de 1914 à 1918', (Besançon, thèse de 3ème cycle, 1981), pp. 298 and 333; Pinol, 'Berliet'.

32 Fourcaut, *Femmes à l'usine*, p. 201.

33 P. Fridenson, 'France, États-Unis: genèse de l'usine nouvelle', *Recherches*, no. 32/33 (1978).

34 A. Moutet, 'La première guerre mondiale et le taylorisme', Colloque international sur le taylorisme, Paris, May 1983.

35 G. Cross, 'Redefining workers' control: rationalisation, labor time and union politics in France, 1900–28', in J. Cronin and C. Sirianni (eds.), *Work, Community and Power: The Experience of Labor in Europe and America, 1900–25* (Philadelphia, 1983).

36 Schweitzer, *Des engrenages à la chaîne*, p. 156.

37 Schweitzer, *Des engrenages à la chaîne*, p. 120.

38 P. Fridenson, 'Automobile Workers in France and their work, 1914–83', in S. L. Kaplan and C. J. Koepp (eds), *Work in France* (Ithaca, 1985).

39 J. P. Depretto and S. van de Casteele-Schweitzer, *Le Communisme à l'usine: Vie ouvrière et mouvement ouvrier chez Renault, 1920–39* (Roubaix, 1984).

40 Depretto and van de Casteele-Schweitzer, *Le Communisme à l'usine*, p. 209.

41 M. Seidman, 'The birth of the weekend and the revolt against work: the workers of Paris region during the Popular Front, 1936–8', *French Historical Studies*, (1981).

3

Management strategies in the Italian car industry 1906–1945: Fiat and Alfa Romeo

Duccio Bigazzi

This article will examine labour-management strategies in two firms which are broadly representative of the Italian car industry – Fiat and Alfa Romeo. The output of Fiat, by far the largest firm in this sector, grew from 5.2 per cent of Italian car production in 1905 to a peak of 82.6 per cent in 1937 (see table 3.1 for statistical data) whereas Alfa Romeo is a good example of the other type of Italian car manufacturer, concentrating on high-quality production (such as sports and luxury vehicles). In this respect, Alfa Romeo was similar to other firms such as Lancia, Itala, Isotta Fraschini, etc.

The management strategies of these two firms had already begun to differ in the period just before the First World War when Fiat became very interested in American modernizing ideas and methods. In spite of the fact that Fiat was certainly one of the instigators of the press campaign against Ford's Model T, it was also one of the first European firms to attempt to imitate the production methods pioneered in Detroit.

In complete contrast to this was Alfa Romeo which was either unwilling or unable decisively to concentrate its production on car manufacturing until after the Second World War and instead expended time and resources on a variety of more or less profitable products such as munitions in the First World War, then railway stock and, from 1926 onwards, aircraft engines.

Market limits, financial problems and even management errors constrained Alfa Romeo's car output and, in 1923, the year in which its percentage of overall Italian car production was highest, its share was only 3.6 per cent. Drawing on experience making racing cars, Alfa concentrated on the manufacture of high quality products and, in the field of industrial relations, stress was placed on workers' skill, cooperation and loyalty to the firm.

While these contrasting strategies provide a broad framework for understanding the policies of the two firms, it is important to stress that, in the 40-year period under consideration here, there were also a number

Table 3.1   Output of Cars and Industrial Vehicles Fiat and Alfa Romeo 1900-39

Year	Fiat	Alfa Romeo	Total for Italy
1900	24		—
1901	73		300
1902	107		350
1903	135		1,308
1904	268		3,080
1905	461		8,870
1906	1,149		—
1907	1,420		—
1908	1,311		—
1909	1,848		—
1910	1,780	20	—
1911	2,631	80	5,280
1912	3,398	150	6,670
1913	3,251	205	6,760
1914	4,644	272	9,210
1915	7,646	205	15,420
1916	12,697	—	17,370
1917	19,184	—	25,280
1918	16,542	—	22,230
1919	12,591	—	17,900
1920	14,314	105	21,080
1921	10,326	} 182	15,230
1922	10,675		16,390
1923	15,162	829	22,820
1924	24,393	766	37,450
1925	39,720	1,110	49,400
1926	51,762	311	63,800
1927	47,513	504	54,300
1928	47,765	527	57,600
1929	46,187	876	55,100
1930	35,120	768	46,400
1931	19,382	492	28,400
1932	22,012	582	29,600
1933	32,227	408	41,700
1934	36,927	699	45,402
1935	37,355	302	50,493
1936	41,053	681	53,144
1937	64,157	1,121	77,708
1938	56,053	1,271	70,777
1939	55,701	934	68,907

Sources: Fiat: calculated from tables kept in Archivio del Centro Storico Fiat. Alfa Romeo: L. Fusi, *Le vetture Alfa Romeo dal 1910* (Milan, 1966) and production tables kept in Archivio del Centro di documentazione storica Alfa Romeo. Italy: Associazione nazionale fra industrie automobilistiche, *Automobile in cifre 1969* (Turin, 1970), p. 5.

of elements which ran counter to the main trend. First and foremost, the cultural climate within which Italian car managers operated was not so sharply divided as the initial description might suggest. In the case considered here there was even the actual transfer to Alfa of certain key members of the Fiat management such as the designer Vittorio Jano, in 1923, and the General Manager Ugo Gobbato in 1933. This meant that some very advanced aspects of rationalization were introduced at Alfa (especially from the late thirties) whilst, on the other hand, Fiat tempered its Fordism with a strongly paternalist outlook.

Furthermore, between the working classes of Milan (where Alfa was located) and Turin (Fiat), there were differences in historical development, composition and culture, and this meant that industrial conflict tended to take different forms. These factors frequently significantly influenced management decisions and sometimes obliged them to make decisions which were not necessarily the most logical in terms of the market situation or technological requirements.

For the sake of clarity, this article will deal separately with three themes, although these issues are, of course, clearly interrelated:

1   technology, work organization and the composition of the labour force
2   payment systems
3   industrial relations.

I

Up until the First World War, all Italian car manufacturers, whether large or small, used similar technology. From the 1880s, German management methods had been influential and consequently there had been a widespread use of German machine tools in the early Italian engineering industries (such as shipbuilding and the production of railway stock), but in the new-born car industry this was replaced by a strong interest in American management methods and technology.[1]

In the car factories which were visited in 1908–9 by an official of the US Department of Commerce,[2] no fewer than 70 per cent of the machine tools were American. This was very modern, technologically advanced machinery, bought in great haste and at a high price during the car boom between 1905 and 1907.

In this period, American machinery was seen as necessary, not because of a desire to introduce mass production, but rather for precision engineering, since even small-scale output required interchangeable parts, American machinery was, therefore, introduced in roughly similar proportions not only in the larger factories, such as Fiat (and in this period Isotta Fraschini and Itala), but also in the smaller ones such as Züst and Alfa itself (founded in 1906 as the Italian branch of the French Darracq).

As has been noted by other historians, in every country the rise of the automobile industry brought with it important modifications in the established production methods of engineering factories. In particular, general purpose machinery was largely replaced by specialized machinery, semi-automatic and automatic machines were introduced, the machine-shop workers lost their responsibility for the care and maintenance of tools and much of the assembly work, apart from the delicate final touches, became fairly repetitive.

Another aspect which has been less fully discussed, at least in the case of Italy, is the consequences of these changes for the position of skilled craftsmen and the composition of the labour force. Whilst the theory that during the years just before the First World War there was a sudden deskilling of factory work seems unfounded, on the other hand the image of the car worker of this period as generally versatile, open to technological innovation and with a strong work ethic, yet, at the same time, a political and a trade-union activist, seems contrived and romantic. This common description of car workers is, moreover, so vaguely anchored in concrete historical reference as to cover the whole period which goes from the foundation of the industry up to the early 1950s.[3]

In spite of certain recent publications which have presented some much more carefully thought-out ideas than previously for the Italian case,[4] there is, as yet, no one really convincing interpretation equivalent to Patrick Fridenson's study of the early car workers in France.[5] This article includes an extremely interesting description by the trade unionist A. Loyau of the shop-floor atmosphere in the prewar period:

In factories, frequently arguments break out for a host of different reasons, provoked by disagreements about the constant modification of the work process, especially when the bonus rates are being recalculated. There is a great deal of activity and energy and we live in a daily atmosphere of feverish excitement, struggle, and resistance which encourages the workers spontaneously to make demands.

I think that these comments are also applicable to the Italian situation and provide an explanation for many aspects of the contradictory image we have of the Italian car worker in the early twentieth century. These workers were, in fact, very different from the skilled nineteenth-century craftsmen. Once all-round general ability became irrelevant, specialized skills, linked not only to one particular type of machinery but increasingly even to the component being manufactured, grew more important. It was not simply by chance that the term 'specialized worker' (*operaio specializzato*) used in Italian labour contracts referred (in contrast to the French *ouvrier spécialisé*) to the most skilled workers. This ambiguously undervaluing term indirectly highlights the backwardness of Italian industrialization and the limited social and numerical weight of the skilled workforce in the late nineteenth century. The move from small workshops to large factories had happened too quickly for a proper legal or even linguistic recognition of the workers' new role.

From the contemporary viewpoint, the term *operaio specializzato* (first introduced in the early labour contracts for car workers) did, supposedly, adequately express the changes which had occurred in this period. Paralleling the increasingly limited nature of the work done by craftsmen in small shops (and also in 'general engineering' factories in the late nineteenth century) was the growing demand in the car industry for precision engineering which meant that workers needed to have a much higher standard of technical and general education than previously.

Most important of all, however, was the fact that the rapid introduction of the new technology was impossible, in this phase, without the active cooperation and participation of the workforce. This accounts for the traditional image of the energetic and alert car worker, found not only in socialist writings but also noted by the employers themselves. Agnelli himself commented that at Fiat 'a day seldom passed when some worker did not ask to be transferred to a new machine. Arguments were of no avail. Even when it was pointed out that the transfer would involve a reduction in pay, it made no difference with the men.'[6]

It seems clear, from this point of view, that there existed what David Montgomery has termed 'functional autonomy',[7] an informal mechanism which guaranteed the organizational functioning of the factory better than formal methods, through a close cooperation between the workers based on both technical knowledge and a real 'ethical code'.

Another extremely important aspect of the car industry was the fact that, more than in other sectors, there was a great deal of vertical mobility. Workers could win promotion on the shop floor to the status of foreman fairly quickly (although many preferred not to do this particular job), but even more enticing was the chance to become a test driver or even an actual racing driver. Others could aspire to leave the factory altogether by setting up a small repair or manufacturing workshop.

Like many of those who became overnight industrialists in the boom years of the car industry, many of the new car workers were raw and inexperienced. The majority of those who flocked to the car factories in this period were young and often without family ties, hoping to learn a trade quickly and willing to move frequently between different firms attracted by higher wages or a more interesting job.[8]

Fiat was the only firm where this situation began to change, possibly as a result of Agnelli's trips to the USA in 1906 and 1912, or, more probably, due to the fact that certain Italian engineers and managers had gained direct experience of American methods in the Fiat Motors plant in Poughkeepsie, New York.[9] Actual assembly lines were not, as yet, being introduced at Fiat but the innovations that were made seemed to be preparing for a flow layout and the old system of dividing up the shops according to the type of machine tools they contained was abandoned and replaced by a new division based on the specific parts or groups of parts being produced (such as engines, gears, rear axles, etc.). Internal discipline was tightened up, especially as regards absenteeism, lateness and mobility between shops.[10] Furthermore, an elaborate system of industrial accounting was introduced, which made it possible to analyse the cost of each individual work process, and a secretary was installed next to the foreman of every shop.[11]

These innovations only really got off the ground with the advent of the First World War. Whereas Fiat continued to concentrate on car production, the other firms, except for Lancia and Spa, manufactured a variety of products. Some of these, like aircraft engines (Isotta Fraschini, Bianchi, etc.), were related to car manufacture, but other, less delicate products were also made, such as shells. This product-diversification enabled Alfa to overcome its chronic difficulties and expand to become a large factory, with its workforce growing from 200–300 in 1914 to more than 4,000 by 1918.[12]

Fiat's growth was, however, even more impressive in this period. In spite of the fact that the firm had deliberately avoided an excessive expansion of the workforce, considered risky in view of the inevitable postwar demobilization,[13] the total number of workers grew from about 4,000 to over 40,000.[14] Vehicle output rose from 4,644 units in 1914 (mostly private cars) to 19,184 in 1917 (mostly military lorries).

The problems created by a qualitatively new scale of production compared with the prewar period, (by 1917 Fiat was producing 70–80 lorries per day and the record output was 176), led Fiat's management to develop a very ambitious project. In 1916, work began on the new Lingotto plant, modelled on the lines of Ford's Highland Park.[15]

Seven years (up until 1923) were necessary to complete the construction of the plant, entirely devoted to car production. Very different in design to the old Fiat Centro, the new factory had five floors, each 500 metres long. The engine and the body 'grew' from floor to floor in two separate areas of the building until they flowed together, on the fifth floor, for the final assembly line. From here each vehicle was sent up to the test track on the roof. The presses were located separately from the main building, whilst various metallurgical plants in the Turin area were reorganized and some new ones built.

The technological and social implications of the Lingotto project are inseparable. Optimistically productivist, the Fiat management's Fordism was quite explicit. The idea was to make an Italian copy of the American car factory where

unsuitable, incapable, lazy or slow workers have no place. They are automatically singled out and eliminated. The products are standard, each exactly the same as the next regardless of the varying levels of skill between one worker and the next. Even though he represents the intelligent part of the mechanism the worker himself is neither personal nor individual but collective and he is as interchangeable as the gear in a machine.[16]

The Turin factory councils had drawn up a plan for 'producers' self-government' based on workers' skills and the organizational ability of the industrial proletariat. Opposing this, there was now the equally radically new plan for an 'automatic factory', tailor-made for the 'common man, who had no special intelligence or particular qualities'.

In this respect, Fiat was an exception amongst Italian car firms. In spite of possessing such ample productive resources by the end of the war, Alfa Romeo failed to draw up a proper reconversion plan and wasted energy in a range of unrelated products (tractors, steam and electric railway engines, railway carriages, air compressors, etc.). Car production remained of only secondary importance and it was only with the sporting successes of 1923–5 and the problems which developed in the other engineering fields, that the firm decided to return to its original type of production. In contrast to Fiat and even certain other firms, however, prewar production methods were barely modified. The technical management did no more than invest in a little more modern machinery and roughly alter the layout of the shops, without actually creating a production line, as had already been done, for example, at Bianchi.[17]

The main innovation at Alfa, in this period, was the setting up, in the Portello plant, of a foundry shop specializing in light alloys and also a forge. These absorbed a great deal of the firm's financial resources and were frequently underutilized but did, at least, after considerable efforts, eventually come to guarantee the supply of high quality semi-finished products needed in the engineering shops.[18]

The firm was, in fact, counting on precisely this exceptionally high-quality type of production to escape from the financial problems that it faced after the easy years of the war. The labour-management strategy was also designed with this end in mind. During the whole of the 1920s, Alfa tried to attract skilled workers by paying them higher wages than the going rate in Milan and attempted to check the increased turnover which had characterized the initial postwar period.[19] Whereas Fiat had chosen to sack large numbers of skilled workers, seen as the least adaptable to the new production methods, concentrating instead on the recruitment of the semi-skilled, Alfa opted for a completely different strategy. (See Table 3.3.)

In addition to car production, hit by export problems during the revaluation of the lira, this firm won some orders for military aircraft engines. This enabled Alfa Romeo, under complete state control through the *Istituto di liquidazioni* from 1927 onwards, to survive the crisis years in spite of serious losses. In this situation, which enabled Alfa to continue to concentrate on high-quality production, the management was not really forced to cut costs or 'rationalize' production. This was made worse by the fact that the regime used Alfa Romeo for propaganda purposes. Mussolini himself declared that this firm manufactured 'the best possible Italian products'[20] and to demonstrate the extensive support for the regime amongst the workforce he turned up in 1930 at the factory gates without his escort in, of course, an Alfa sports car.[21] The firm enjoyed state protection, a mixed blessing since it also suffered from considerable state interference and was obliged to give in to the demands of the Fascist trade unions. This made it very difficult to impose redundancies or short-time

Table 3.2   Official Profits and Dividends Fiat and Alfa Romeo 1922–1939

Year	Fiat profits (millions of lire)	Alfa Romeo profits (millions of lire)	Fiat dividends (%)	Alfa Romeo dividends (%)
1922	19.1	− 5.1	7.50	—
1923	22.5	− 0.3	10	—
1924	26.4	3.8	11.25	5.50
1925	50.3	0.2	15	—
1926	66.6	− 0.1	15	—
1927	60.4	− 0.9	12.50	—
1928	61.3	0.7	12.50	6
1929	62.3	4.0	12.50	6
1930	40.9	3.1	9	4
1931	—	2.6	—	—
1932	—	0.6	5	—
1933	—	− 93.4	5	—
1934	24.2	− 1.7	5	—
1935	39.1	− 2.3	7.50	—
1936	41.3	4.3	7.50	—
1937	55.7	5.8	10	6
1938	43.7	5.2	10	6
1939	43.5	8.6	10	6

Source: Associazione italiane fra le società per azioni, *Notizie statistiche*, 1934 and 1940.

Table 3.3   Professional Grades of a Sample of 1094 Workers who Began Work at Alfa Romeo between 1915 and 1945 (%)

	1915–18	1918–25	1926–33	1933–40	1940–45
boys and apprentices	7	5.3	7.7	18.1	13.6
labourers	12.3	31.3	22.1	19.4	19.5
helpers and machine operators	33.5	18.5	10.6	14.9	36.8
skilled workers	37.9	38.7	47.1	37.5	16.2
services, maintenance, quality control	9.3	6.2	12.5	10.1	13.9

Source: taken directly from personal files for each worker kept in the personnel records of Alfa Romeo (Arese).

working like Fiat and the other firms in this sector. This meant that in 1932 the workforce exceeded 2,700, the highest level it had reached except in wartime.[22] The following year, however, Alfa went into crisis since the survival of such an unprofitable firm could not be justified during a prolonged slump. (See Table 3.2.)

During the reorganization of the state controlled firms run by the IRI (*Istituto per la Ricostuzione Industriale*), the definitive closure of Alfa was called for even more strongly than in the past and it was only due to a personal intervention by Mussolini himself, against the advice of the

Finance Minister and certain members of the Board of Directors, that production was allowed to continue.[23]

In December 1933, Ugo Gobbato was appointed Managing Director. Gobbato, a former Fiat director, had played an important role during the Lingotto project. After this, he had been responsible for the installation of Fiat plants in Germany, Spain and the Soviet Union.[24]

Gobbato quickly became aware of the extent of Alfa's technical and organizational problems ('generally low quality machinery', 'uncoordinated layout', 'materials being moved wrongly', 'non-existent cost accounting')[25] and therefore started a radical reorganization which was to take a number of years to complete.

First of all, after the failure of negotiations for the Italian licence to produce the Citroën 7HP, it was decided to concentrate on production for the aircraft industry together with lorries and buses. An attempt to draw up an agreement with Isotta Fraschini for the creation of a centre for aircraft production in Lombardy also came to nothing and after this Alfa had to finance the adaptation of its plant through the IRI.[26] Even more importantly, in this period, Alfa profited from rearmament for the Ethiopian war and the Spanish civil war. The workforce of 2,000 in 1934 swelled to 6,500 by 1937[27] (the firm claimed this figure up until 1945). The machinery was updated and added to and the various plants were totally reorganised 'to render the work cycles fairly consecutive, and the machinery was redistributed into lines so that the work processes could be done sequentially.'[28]

There were also important changes in the management of the labour force. The hierarchy was made more rigid and a set of extremely detailed 'factory norms' was drawn up, clearly defining each worker's responsibilities, aimed at drastically reducing the informality which predominated on the shop floor (foremen 'lending' workers to each other, unsupervised movements of workers around the shop floor etc.). Gobbato's overriding aim was, however, to raise productivity. Gradually the ratio between clerks and workers was altered and unproductive workers were replaced by more productive ones. There was a complete reorganization of time study, and new methods were introduced with the help of personnel drawn from the Italian branch of the Bedaux Company (Società Italiana Bedaux).

Responsibility for the calculation of times and bonus rates was taken away from the time-study engineers on the shop floor (who could easily be influenced by the workers) and given to a centralized Time Study Department. This made it easier to keep control of the bonus system which was being widely introduced (daily wages were abolished wherever possible) and it also made it possible to introduce a proper industrial accounting system for the first time.[29]

Alfa emerged greatly changed from this profound transformation. During the second half of the thirties and even more so during the war, the number of semi-skilled in the workforce grew, whereas the percentage of skilled workers fell. Central to Gobbato's plans was a project to assess the precise skills required at each specific phase of the productive cycle and, in 1942–3, this turned into a pioneering but unsuccessful attempt to introduce the job-evaluation methods which had been developed by the Bedaux company.[30]

It is important to remember, however, that in spite of this interest in rationalization, Alfa retained (and even expanded) its paternalist programme of welfare initiatives which had been characteristic of the firm in previous years. In this period, a range of welfare services were provided (some pre-existing and others newly set up) such as a canteen, a nursery, leisure and cultural facilities, etc. Social events, sporting activities and prize-giving ceremonies were organized and a factory newspaper was published to reinforce the 'Alfa Romeo spirit'. Gobbato's paternalist and conservative ideology is manifest in the following internal circular which stated that the worker must learn

that his labour did not simply give him the right to his wage packet but could ensure his own and his family's well-being and provide a foothold for his children, enabling them to work side by side with their parent, contributing to the family budget, so that eventually they could replace the parent at work and, with confidence, themselves found a new family which would, in turn, depend upon Alfa for its livelihood.[31]

At Fiat, on the other hand, the interwar period saw a series of abrupt policy reversals which had not been initially foreseen. Designed for a daily output of 300 vehicles, it proved impossible to maintain this level of production at Lingotto in spite of constant machinery updating and the introduction of the conveyor belt, which became definitively operational in 1925. Great fluctuations in demand and the decision to manufacture a varied range of models made it even more difficult fully to put into operation the new system of production. Other factors which contributed to this disappointing result were problems with the internal transport system, a lack of flexibility due to insufficient buffer stocks and, not least, the resistance of the workforce to the accelerated pace of work and the increased workload.

In 1926, these problems led Fiat's management to draw up a further rationalization plan, after a visit to the USA by a group of technical staff. The three main aspects of this plan were:

1 the centralized reorganization of time study;
2 a more efficient use of each worker's labour;
3 the replacement of the collective bonus system by individual piecework.[32]

This attempt to modify the purely 'automatic' function of the production line by increasing the control of the workforce through incentive systems and a rigid definition of tasks was carried even further with the introduction, in 1929, of the 'Bedaux system'.

Serious problems had already emerged at Lingotto when it was attempted to make the plant run at full capacity and now with the onset of the depression the 'stop watch factory' was slowed down by the insufficient and intermittent supply of materials to the production lines. Rejecting the idea of radically renewing its technology and plant (in contrast to many other large European firms which thereby obtained quite different results), Fiat coped with the depression mainly by drastically cutting labour costs. With the help of technical advisors from the Società Italiana Bedaux (set up in March 1927 by a group of important Italian industrialists including Agnelli himself),[33] Fiat was now armed with a 'scientific' basis for imposing its strategy of intensifying the workload, making working hours completely flexible, reducing the size of the workforce and levelling out wages.

It would, however, be wrong to see Fiat's use of the Bedaux system as an example of what *Lo Stato Operaio* (the theoretical journal of the clandestine Communist Party) condemned in 1932, as a 'poor man's rationalization', drawing an industrial parallel with the 'poor man's imperialism' of the Fascist economic policies.[34] The Bedaux system was, indeed, the cheapest and most efficient way of dealing with the problems of the depression but its introduction was, in fact, no more than the logical extension of the management's longstanding programme to Taylorize production, which had also involved significant technological changes.

Once the slump ended, moreover, Fiat returned to its interest in American ideas. If Highland Park had been the inspiration for Lingotto, River Rouge (and, more realistically, Dagenham) were the models for the new Mirafiori plant. Here, in contrast to Lingotto, the production lines were arranged on a single floor and laid out according to the needs of the final assembly.[35] The production lines of the individual components were spread along the sides of the main assembly line, resulting in a considerable reduction in the internal transport of materials and allowing the introduction of buffer stocks.

Although Mirafiori was equipped with the most modern machinery (far more efficient than the Lingotto plant despite constant updating), its most important characteristic was the avoidance of an overmechanized production line. For this reason overhead transport systems, and other innovations that might have made the productive cycle too rigid, were avoided and the aim instead became maximum flexibility. With the outbreak of war imminent it would not be too difficult to switch production from the 'Topolino' car to military trucks or even tanks.

II

This brief reconstruction of events in the two firms demonstrates the crucial importance during this period of incentive wage systems in management strategies. Taking the case of Fiat (far less is known about Alfa from this point of view) it is evident that the changes in payment systems correspond to different phases of the history of the firm as regards technology, organization and industrial relations.

In the years between the time when Fiat was only a small firm to the period of strikes and sit-ins known as the *biennio rosso* (1919–20) a straight piecework system was used, apart from various largely unsuccessful attempts to introduce the Rowan system, aimed at preventing workers from earning excessive bonuses at a time when the productive cycle was being constantly modified and time study methods were still very rudimentary.[36] In 1921, however, when the factory occupations ended and production gradually started at Lingotto, an agreement was signed by both management and unions introducing the collective bonus system for all car workers.[37] In this system bonus earnings were calculated according the difference between the 'standard hours' considered necessary for the production of a complete vehicle and the time effectively taken.

The unions saw this as the first step towards the creation of that hard-to-define 'workers control', which was, at the time, being shelved in parliament.[38] From Fiat's point of view, more concretely, this was a means of replacing the complex system of bonus rates (there were 25,000 different rates for the car section alone) with a much more simple and manageable method, especially in view of the imminent transfer from Fiat Centro to Lingotto, which would have entailed a complete revision of all the bonus rates and with it an explosion of shop-floor conflict. In this way, on the other hand, it became possible to give the workers a financial stake in the reorganization of the work process, to the point where they cooperated in 'sub-dividing tasks amongst themselves in a very rational and self-interested way. Without this help it would have been very difficult for the management to do this effectively especially in a fluctuating market situation.'[39] In other words, Fiat aimed to give direct responsibility to the workers themselves in the introduction of the new organization of the work process, whilst the altered power balance would enable a progressive generalized and negotiated reduction of bonus rates. This was precisely what happened soon after, when the 'standard hours' that had been agreed were cut, falling, for example, from 1326 in 1921 to 643 in 1924 for the '501' Model. In the same period the average wage fell from 3.74 lire to about 3 lire per hour.[40]

Once production lines were fully functioning, not only were there no moves to eliminate incentive systems (which had been described as 'out of date' by Fiat's General Manager Fornaca in 1922)[41] but the firm moved backwards towards individual piecework. After political defeat and the destruction of their unions with the rise of the Fascist Party, the workers of Lingotto, by now well used to the new work methods, returned to individual wage determination.

In 1927–8, there were further wage cuts. Added to the 'official' reductions of 10 per cent (August 1927) and 5 per cent (March 1928), there was the constant revision of the bonus rates by the Time Study Department. According to one Fascist trade unionist, the bonus rates had fallen by at least 30 per cent in little over a year.[42]

The Bedaux system which was being introduced at Lingotto from January 1929 onwards, further emphasized this tendency to individualize work and wage systems. Using this method of productivity measurement, however arbitrary in reality, the management were able to estimate the level of cutbacks in staff, hours and wages necessary in an unstable market situation which led to irregular production. The individual worker was, therefore, obliged 'spontaneously' to make the most of every single moment at work, not only to earn a wage sufficient to keep a whole family in a situation of widespread unemployment, but also because only a high number of 'Bedaux units' ensured safety from the threat of redundancy or layoff.

From this point of view the system was, indeed, effective. In the via Cuneo foundry, for example, (the only shop for which we have official figures) the workforce was cut from 516 in November 1929 to 465 in May 1931, whilst the 'Bedaux' output rose from an average of 53 Bedaux units (or 'B') to 72.5 Bedaux units.[43] The few wages statistics that are available are more surprising. After the first few years of the Bedaux system, which must have been very difficult for the Fiat workers (it was extremely hard to earn more than 60B and there were big reductions in working hours and also the wage cuts of 8 per cent in November 1930 and 10 per cent in February 1932), in the next few years it seems that the intensification of the work pace was paralleled by a slight rise in real wages relative to 1928.[44]

With the Bedaux system, Fiat had achieved complete freedom of manoeuvre in wages determination and was even able to ignore the guidelines laid down by the regime which, whilst generally agreeing to the industrialists' demands, was still affected by political and social pressures and frequently hindered by lengthy bureaucratic procedures.[45] The Secretary of the Fascist trade unions was forced to admit that, in factories where the Bedaux system was in use, labour contracts had effectively ceased to exist.

It is, however, probable that, given the economic recovery, the Fiat management was not particularly worried by the decision of the Central Corporate Committee, in November 1934, that incentive system rates would be henceforth subject to collective contracts.[46] In February 1935 the Bedaux system was 'abolished' at Fiat, to be replaced the following June by a full bonus system (i.e. a normal system calculated according to time). This 'abolition' was, however, purely nominal since the entire accounting and technical apparatus installed by the Bedaux engineers remained, and the same bonus rates and times as in previous years continued to be used. The only significant modification was that the percentage of bonus a worker could theoretically earn rose from 75 to 100 per cent; previously, the remaining 25 per cent had been seen as the foreman's share.[47] This change could not, however, have prevented Fiat's management from making use, when necessary, of all the means available (such as recalculating the times, altering the work cycle, etc.) to maintain the actual hourly percentages earned, at the previous level. Furthermore, with the 'full bonus' system the firm took away the compensation that had been paid previously to workers idled by material shortages as well as the extra payment given to those who were responsible for more than one machine. In the event, however, sizeable war orders and the recovery of the car market boosted profit margins enough to allow the firm to finance real productivity incentives, a strategy maintained even during the period of harsh repression of the unions after the Second World War.

This succession of different incentive systems reveals how far the management, from 1921 onwards, was able to impose the system most appropriate both to the needs of production and the state of relations with the workforce. The decision to replace one system by another was taken less for theoretical reasons than according to which specific method appeared to be most suitable at the time for raising productivity. The important factors were not simply the virtues and defects of the various types of incentive system, as described and graphically illustrated in contemporary manuals, but also tactical and strategic considerations, closely linked to the social context. Thus, agreements which were apparently favourable to the labour movement such as the introduction of the collective bonus system, paradoxically turned out, in practice, to be much less advantageous, regarding both wage levels and power relations, than other systems which it strongly opposed. As for the Bedaux system, it certainly meant an initial worsening of work conditions, yet in the long run it did not automatically mean a drop in real wages.

As we saw earlier, it was only after the First World War that Fiat – like other car firms such as Lancia[48] – began to consider the replacement of a piecework wage system with a fixed day-wage. This was never actually put into practice so it is impossible to tell with certainty whether a day-wage system would have yielded different results, either in terms of productivity or wage levels, than the bonus system. Certainly the various types of incentive system all gave the management a certain amount of freedom of manoeuvre and made it possible to disguise the progressive worsening of conditions. The choice of a bonus system was, however, linked, above all to the desire to make workers participate actively in the raising of productivity and the introduction of new work methods.

The successful example of Fiat seems to demonstrate the possibility of a painless introduction of Fordism in this period. Fiat was able to combine direct control of the productive process with an incentive system well suited to a workforce willing to experiment with new collective organization methods.

In contrast to the British case described by Lewchuck,[49] Fiat's management did not see any real contradiction between incentive systems and Fordism, or at least did not see the two as incompatible. Even once the new work methods were fully introduced, direct control seemed insufficient to guarantee an adequate productivity level and Fiat made use of, on the one hand, rigid incentive mechanisms and, on the other hand, the provisions of welfare services for workers and their families.

III

Two distinct phases can be identified in the industrial-relations strategies of Fiat and Alfa Romeo. The first ran from the origins of the industry until the great postwar conflicts, and the second from the rise of the Fascist regime until its fall.

In the first period, the managements of the various Turin car firms (Fiat being the most important) tended to accept collective bargaining with the workers' representatives in order to draw up a general set of rules governing wages and conditions. In Turin the engineering sector had scarcely existed previous to the growth of the car industry and the pool of skilled labour was very limited. It was, therefore, necessary to avoid competition between the different firms, ensuring a relatively low labour turnover and keeping conflicts within acceptable limits.

In return, the car industrialists were willing to offer conditions of work superior to those in other sectors, especially as regards hours and wage levels. This strategy did not, however, exclude disputes and there were, in fact, general car workers' strikes in 1908, 1912 and 1913 lasting up to several months.[50] These strikes were not, however, aimed at the destruction of the opponent and generally the 'rules of collective bargaining' were accepted. The main exception was the 1912 strike when the revolutionary syndicalists won control of the movement, breaking the traditional hegemony of the Italian Metalworkers' union, the FIOM.

The situation in Milan was very different. The car sector represented a far less important proportion of the overall engineering industry than in Turin and those few firms that did exist could choose from a much larger pool of labour.[51] Endemic unrest characterized the local labour movement and this soon led to a series of extremely serious general strikes and demonstrations (1898, 1904, 1907, etc.) According to Gramsci's well-known analysis, during the quieter periods the poorly-organized Milan labour movement tended to be controlled by the reformists whereas the revolutionary syndicalists took over in moments of tension.[52] This was precisely what happened in the car workers' strikes of 1907 and especially in the long general strike of 1913.[53]

The managements of Alfa and the other car firms demonstrated a willingness to make concessions about hours, wages, etc. but apart from these problems there was also the apparently insoluble dispute over the recognition of the workers' organization. The industrialists refused to negotiate with Corridoni and the other leaders of the syndicalist USI and explicitly aimed to bring about the collapse of this organization and the factory-based internal commissions linked to it.

The contrasting attitudes of the Turin and Milan industrialists became even more apparent during the war. In Turin, Fiat and the other car firms tended to give in to the workers' demands after only brief negotiations and in return benefited from the total absence of strikes and demonstrations during the disputes.[54] In Milan, on the other hand, the strength of the revolutionary syndicalists (especially at Alfa and Bianchi) drove the management of the car firms to take very uncompromising attitudes, and the resulting escalation of conflict became a source of great concern to the government's industrial mobilization committees. Of the Milan factories, Alfa had the most frequent stoppages, while the Bianchi workers went as far as to demonstrate on the city streets.[55]

A great deal has been written about the Turin factory councils and the role of Fiat workers in this movement.[56] For the purposes of our argument, however, we need only stress the fact that the militancy of 1919–20 reflected the various different and often contradictory tendencies in the workers' movement. On the one hand, the dominant ideology of the factory-council movement came from the skilled workers whose radical proposal for workers' control of the means of production was inspired by productivist values and a firm belief in technological and organizational progress. On the other hand, the semi-skilled and unskilled workers, a large proportion of the labour force in factories like Fiat, demonstrated their rejection of the factory hierarchy and the existing social order by frequent unrest and stoppages. The conflicts between these two groups must have been much greater than is suggested by the other hagiographic historiography of the period. These tensions were explicitly referred to by a worker correspondent in *Ordine Nuovo* in May 1921. After criticizing the elitist attitudes of those who saw themselves as the only '*real* workers, the only *authentic* professionals' the writer noted that 'As many will remember, it was during the occupation of the factories itself that this struggle between skilled workers and the semi-skilled machine operators became particularly acute, endangering worker solidarity and opening the door to police intervention.'[57]

On the other hand, Fiat's management found it hard to exploit these splits within the labour movement. The reorganization project which the firm was implementing at the time directly undermined the position of the skilled workers, encouraging them to patch up their differences with the rest of the workforce. This led to a direct conflict with the factory-council movement (founded in April 1920, continued in September 1920 with the occupation of the factories and ending with the mass layoffs of May 1921).[58] In the next few years, many of the politically active skilled workers emigrated to France or found work in small workshops;[59] with the opening of Lingotto, there was, for the first time, a mass influx of unskilled workers, new to the engineering industry, many of whom were immigrants from other regions, especially the Veneto.[60]

In Milan, the conflicts of the *biennio rosso* were, in many ways, simply an extension of the struggles of the previous period. Here the factory-council ideology was much less influential and strikes were more radical and violent. The most extreme cases of sabotage and obstructionism were at Alfa itself and it was here that the lock-out began which sparked off the occupation of the factories all over Italy. On this occasion the management was so intransigent that it appears even most other industrialists were amazed.[61]

In the following period, the Milan firm became, to use an expression frequently employed by workers writing in the left-wing press, a 'seaport':[62] the turnover of the workforce, whether skilled or unskilled was rapid. Research in the personnel records of the factory has, however, demonstrated that, in this period, it was rare for workers to be refused employment simply because they were political or trade-union militants.

The factory greatly needed skilled workers and therefore had to accept any that turned up at the factory gates. The 'purge' came later and this affected only those who continued their militant activity during the years of increasing Fascist repression.

In the Fascist period, the managements of the two factories continued to follow considerably different industrial-relations policies. Fiat gave its support to the regime but retained its autonomy from the government's economic policies and its attempts centrally to control the resolution of labour disputes. Fiat did not encourage the Fascist unions and developed, on the contrary, a paternalist policy of protecting its workers from Fascist interference. The welfare policy itself was administered, as far as possible, independently from the regime's initiatives.[63] Another important factor was the firm's campaign to defend 'Piedmontese industry' against the government's attempt to encourage the construction of new factories in central and southern Italy.[64]

Fiat's policy was not sufficient to prevent the outbreak of disputes and, in spite of the atmosphere of intimidation and heavy police surveillance in this period, there were even some strikes and stoppages in certain shops, especially in the first few years after the introduction of the Bedaux system. The violent and spontaneous nature of these strikes, mostly located on the vehicle-body assembly line, might suggest that there was widespread opposition to Fordism. It is, however, important not to underestimate the importance of other factors. The scarce and contradictory information that we do have suggests that an active part was played in these disputes by the Fascist trade unionists, who, since the management refused to recognize them as spokesmen for the workers, hoped to improve their bargaining power through this risky game.[65] Furthermore, during the economic crisis, the prestige of Fiat and Agnelli himself as 'job creators' was severely undermined.

At Alfa, on the other hand, the firm's problems led to a firstly partial and then complete, takeover by the state. The Fascist Party tried to make use of this opportunity to win control of the firm by infiltrating the management and also, by making use of the informal system of personal recommendations, to get in supporters even at the lowest levels of the factory hierarchy. The personnel records of the factory reveal that a large percentage of the *squadristi* (fascist activists) purged after the fall of the regime had started work in the firm as low-grade, unskilled workers but then had enjoyed rapid promotion to become foremen, guards, etc. The number of 'true fascists' was greater at Alfa than in the other Milanese factories, or at least this was the opinion of the workforce. The workers which I have so far interviewed remember an atmosphere of mutual suspicion in the factory where workers felt as though they were being secretly watched from all sides. It is, however, also important to take note of the fact that, at Alfa, the Fascist unions and Party were seen (and rightly so) by the workers as the sole supporters of the repeated salvage operations personally decided by Mussolini. It was not by chance that the only moment of real tension, up until the strikes of 1943, was in the period when the total closure of the firm was threatened (October–November 1933) and the real focus for attention during the dispute was the General Manager Orazi, seen as a Fiat man by the workforce. Apart from this, police records and oral testimonies reveal only a few (although sometimes very noticeable) demonstrations of discontent by individuals or small groups which were swiftly repressed or silenced by the police.

According to management figures, in 1930, 80 per cent of the workforce held Fascist trade union cards (compared with an average of only 15 per cent in Milan) and there were about 250 Fascist party members. The even more surprising (although probably also less reliable) figures for 1933 claimed that there were 1,000 Fascists and 150 *squadristi*.[66] This enabled the trade-union press to vaunt Alfa as an 'example of social collaboration in action'.[67] During the period when Gobbato was in control, attempts were made to reduce the heavy Fascist presence in the factory since it tended to lower productivity, aiming, as far as possible, at a neutral stance for the firm, but little actually changed and Alfa continued to be a stronghold of Fascism in Milan.

The same absence of strife also characterized other car firms such as Lancia and Bianchi. The Fascist unions contrasted the situation in these factories with the conflictual atmosphere at Fiat which they linked to differences in managerial strategies: 'latin' production methods versus Fiat's 'exotic' importations.[68]

Nevertheless, in a different social and political context, in the pre-Fascist period, high quality production had been accompanied by considerable industrial strife both at Alfa and the other firms in this sector. Furthermore, the introduction of Fordism has been proved historically (the case of Citroën is a good example) to be compatible, in the long run, with a low level of industrial conflict, even where political and trade-union freedom exists. It remains, therefore, far from proven that Fiat's choice of American production methods was the real reason for the more strife-ridden atmosphere of this firm compared with other Italian car manufacturers. Despite important recent research, our knowledge of industrial conflict and its sources in the Fascist period is still too rudimentary to allow well-founded generalization.

NOTES

1   For one example see Ing. Ernesto Breda, *Concorso ai premi al merito industriale indetto con Regio decreto del 4 agosto 1895, Memoriale e descrizione dello stabilimento* (Milan, 1896), and Società italiana Ernesto Breda, *Per la millesima locomotiva* (Milan, 1908).

2   US Department of Commerce and Labor, Bureau of Manufactures, *Machine Tool Trade in Germany, France, Switzerland, Italy and United Kingdom* (Washington DC, 1919), pp. 185–209; *idem, The Machine Tool Trade in Austro-Hungary, Denmark, Russia and Netherlands, With Supplementary Reports on Italy and France* (Washington DC, 1910), pp. 164–6.

3   For the first point of view see D. La Valle, *Le origini della classe operaia alla Fiat* (Milan, 1976), pp. 54–7) and 67–70, and A. Pepe, *Lotta di classe e crisi industriale in Italia, La svolta del 1913* (Milan, 1978), pp. 40–ff. and 50. The second point of view is common amongst historians with a sociological approach. Of especial interest are the comments in A. Accornero, *Il lavoro come ideologia* (Bologna, 1980), esp. pp. 97–102.

4   See especially S. Ortaggi, 'Cottimo e produttiva nel'industria italiana del primo Novencento', *Rivista di storia contemporanea*, no. 1, (1978); *idem*, 'Padronato e classe operaia a Torino negli anni 1906–11', *Revista di storia contemporanea*, no. 3, (1979). Also S. Musso, *Gli operai di Torino 1900–20* (Milan, 1980), pp. 57 and 145–8, and G. Berta, 'Dalla manifattura al sistema di fabbrica', *Storia d'Italia, Annali 1*, (1978), pp. 1095–106.

5   P. Fridenson, 'Les premiers ouvriers français de l'automobile (1890–1914)'. *Sociologie du Travail*, no. 3, (1979).

6   US Department of Commerce and Labor, *Machine Tool Trade in Germany*, p. 204.

7   D. Montgomery, *Workers Control in America* (Cambridge, 1979), p. 11.

8   See the interesting comments of A. Bondi, *Memorie di un questore (25 anni nella Polizia italiana)*, (Milan, second edition, 1913), p. 259.

9   V. Castronovo, *Giovanni Agnelli* (Turin, 1971), p. 62 ff.

10 Ortaggi, 'Padronato', pp. 362–3.

11 M. Gracco and T. Curcio, *Il segretario d'officina nelle sue mansioni, Parte 1: La mano d'opera* (Turin, 1916); see also S. Musso, 'L'operaio dell' auto a Torino', *Classe*, no. 14 (1977), pp. 119–20.

12 D. Bigazzi, '"I più turbolenti della città": la composizione operaia all' Alfa Romeo', in G. Procacci (ed.), *Stato e classe operaia in Italia durante la prima guerra mondiale* (Milan, 1983).

13 G. Fornaca, 'Note sulla situazione delle industrie automobilistiche italiane', reprinted in A. Pescarolo, *Riconversione industriale e composizione di classe, L'inchiesta sulle industrie metalmeccaniche* (Milan, 1979), p. 157.

14 Musso, *Gli operai*, p. 135.

15 M. Pozzetto, *La Fiat-Lingotto, Un'architettura torinese d'avanguardia* (Turin, 1975), and D. Bigazzi, 'Gli operai della catena di montaggio: la Fiat 1922–1943', in *Fondazione G. G. Feltrineli – Annali* (1979–80).

16 Unsigned report, which can be dated as 1919, headed 'Fiat. D. Relazione Tecnica', Archivio del Centro Storico Fiat (ACSF), Turin.

17 See the firm's publication, *L'Alfa Romeo* (Rome, 1932), and A. Lampignani, 'Sistemazione di lavorazione per produzione di automobili in esercizio effettivo presso la Società anonima E. Bianchi', in *L'industria meccanica* (August, 1928), pp. 501–26.

18 See especially the minutes of the Board of Directors meeting (MBD) of 26 April 1927 and 9 June 1930, kept in the Archivio del Centro di documentazione storica Alfa Romeo (ACDSAR).

19 MBD 19 March 1929. See especially the statistics in tables 3.2 and 3.3.

20 See the letter from G. Pesce and R. Bini, Fascist union representatives, to the Prefect of Milan, 8 November 1933, in Archivio di Stato Milano (ASM), fondo Prefettura (Pref), c. 712.

21 *L'Azione sindacale*, 30 May 1930 and ASM, Pref., c. 975.

22 See, for example, MBD, 6 November 1930, and letter from P. Capoferri to Prefect of Milan, 30 December 1930, in ASM, Pref., c. 712. Also see verbatim minutes of the Comitato direttivo dell'Istituto di Liquidazioni (VCDIL)

11 August 1932, Archvio storico IRI (AIRI), now kept in Archivio centrale dello stato (ACS).

23   Prefect's memorandum, 25 November 1933, in ASM, Pref., c. 712.

24   'Curriculum vitae Ing. Ugo Gobbato', 1940, in Archivio della Direzione generale dell'Alfa Romeo (ADGAR), b. 24, f. 368.

25   Handwritten memorandum by U. Gobbato, 28 June 1934, in ADGAR, b. 64, f. 43M.

26   See especially the documentation kept in AIRI, fasc. 'Alfa Romeo. 1933–40'.

27   *Ibid* 'Note sulla seduta di Consiglio 22 luglio 1937'.

28   Report by U. Gobbato to the Board of Directors, March 1936, in ADGAR, c. 96, f. 53.

29   'Note sui servizi amministrativi dell'Alfa Romeo', 20 July 1935, in AIRI, fasc. 'Alfa Romeo, 1933–40'.

30   D. Bigazzi, 'Organizzazione del lavoro e razionalizzazione nella crisi del fascismo 1942–1943', in *Studi Storici*, no. 2 (1978), pp. 378–80.

31   'Norma particolare dello Stabilimento di S. Martino', 18 April 1942, in ADGAR, c. 76, f. 55S.

32   'Relazione generale', 1926, in ACSF. There is a summary of this document in Bigazzi, 'Gli operai', p. 918 ff.

33   P. Fiorentini, 'Ristrutturazione capitalistica e sfruttamento operaio in Italia negli anni '20', in *Rivista storica del socialismo*, no. 30 (1967), pp. 148 ff.; G. Sapelli, *Organizzazione lavoro e innovazione industriale nell'Italia tra le due guerre* (Turin 1978), esp. p. 92 onwards.

34   M. Montagnana, 'L'organizzazione scientifica del lavoro in Italia, *Lo Stato operaio*, 1929, pp. 609–15.

35   Castronovo, *Agnelli*, pp. 47–50 and Bigazzi, 'Gli operai', p. 939 ff.

36   Ortaggi, 'Cottimo e produttivita', and Musso 'L'operaio dell'auto', pp. 120–1.

37   'Il cottimo collettivo applicato nelle officine "Fiat"', in Città di Torino, *Bollettino mensile dell'Ufficio del lavoro e della statistica*, no. 6 (1922), pp. 141–7.

38   P. Spriano, *L'occupazione delle fabbriche, Settembre 1920* (Turin, 1964), pp. 166–7.

39   U. Gobbato, *Organizzazione dei fattori della produzione*, (Turin, 2nd edition, 1932), p. 95.

40   Bigazzi, 'Gli operai', pp. 905–6.

41   Fornaca, 'Note sulla situazione', p. 170.

42   See *La Gazzetta del popolo*, 28 February 1923.

43   R. Monti, 'Economia della produzione e controllo dei prezzi di costo in fonderia' in *Congresso internazionale di fonderia, Milano, 12–27 settembre 1931, Memoria*. (Turin, 1932), p. 518.

44   Bigazzi, 'Gli operai', p. 929.

45   *Notiziario sindacale*, 30 November 1934.

46   G. Sapelli, *Fascismo, grande industria e sindacato, Il caso di Torino, 1929–35* (Milan, 1975), pp. 207–9.

47   See Bigazzi, 'Gli operai', pp. 937–8, and S. Musso, 'Americanismo e politica salariale alla Fiat tra le due guerre', *Classe*, no. 22 (December 1982, but actually published in 1984), p. 133. Pressurized by industrial action the Bedaux company also introduced this modification in various other countries, such as the United Kingdom – see C. R. Littler, *The Development of the Labour Process in Capitalist Societies* (London, 1982), p. 112.

48 M. Abrate, *La lotta sindacale nella industrializzazione in Italia, 1906–26* (Milan, 1966), p. 244.
49 W. Lewchuk, 'Fordism and British Motor Car Employers, 1896–1932', in H. F. Gospel and C. R. Littler (eds.), *Managerial Strategies and Industrial Relations* (London, 1983), p. 106.
50 See works of Musso, Ortaggi and Pepe cited above, and also P. Spriano, *Storia di Torino operaia e socialista* (Turin, 1972).
51 L. Davite, 'I lavoratori meccanici e metallurgici in Lombardia dall' Unità alla prima guerra mondiale', *Classe*, no. 5 (1972), pp. 333–434, and G. Paletta, 'Dinamiche occupazionali e sindacali nell'industria a Milano tra i censimenti del 1901 e del 1911', in *Economia e lavoro*, no. 4, (1982), pp. 91–104.
52 *L'Unità*, 21 February 1924.
53 Pepe, *Lotta di classe*, pp. 165 ff.
54 Spriano, *Storia di Torino*, pp. 348 ff., and Musso, 'Gli operai', pp. 172–3.
55 *L'Internazionale*, 7 October 1916, and Bigazzi, 'I più turbolenti'.
56 See the works of Abrate, Castronovo, Musso and Spriano cited above. See also, especially '1920, La grande speranza', special issue of *Il Ponte*, October 1970; C. Vallauri, *Il governo Giolitti e l'occupazione delle fabbriche (1920)* (Milan, 3rd edition 1974); G. Maione, *Il biennio rosso, Autonomia e spontaneità operaia nel 1919–20* (Bologna, 1975).
57 *L'Ordine nuovo*, 22 May 1921.
58 Castronovo, *Agnelli*, pp. 288 ff.
59 G. Comollo, 'Esperienza di un operaio comunista', in various authors, *I comunisti a Torino 1919–72* (Rome, 1973), p. 94.
60 *L'Unità* 25 July 1925 and 29 July 1925.
61 Spriano, *L'occupazione*, p. 51 ff., and Vallauri, *Il governo*, p. 26 ff.
62 *L'Unità*, 21 March 1924.
63 See Castronovo, *Agnelli*, esp. pp. 494–5 and 547–8; V. De Grazia, *Consenso e cultura di massa nell'Italia fascista, L'organizzazione del dopolavoro* (Rome–Bari, 1981), pp. 86–94.
64 L. Passerini, *Torino operaia e fascismo* (Rome–Bari, 1984) pp. 241 ff.
65 Sapelli, *Fascismo* pp. 116 ff.
66 See letter from the General Manager P. Gianferrari to the Prefect, 17 May 1930 in ASM, Pref., b. 975 and also the letter from the Fascist union representatives Pesce and Bini cited above.
67 *L'Azione sindacale*, 31 October 1931.
68 See, for example, *Il lavoro fascista*, 2 February 1932 and also the memorandum 'La situazione dell'industria automobilista torinese', 5 November 1931, in ACS, Ministero dell'Interno, Divisione Polizia Politica, b. 178.

Part Two
Industrial Relations in the
Age of Fordism

4

Shop-Floor Bargaining, Contract Unionism and Job Control: An Anglo-American Comparison

Steven Tolliday and Jonathan Zeitlin

I

International comparisons of industrial relations systems have historically carried a critical edge. Often foreign institutions are held up as a model by domestic advocates of reform; occasionally, a dominant power such as the United States attempts to export its own institutions as a formula for bringing political stability and industrial peace to its less fortunate allies. From the 19th century through the 1920s, the American Federation of Labor (AFL) and its sympathizers saw the voluntarist framework of British labour law as the template for the freedom from judicial intervention in collective bargaining which they hoped to obtain in the US; while in the 1930s and 1940s, the liberal arbitrators and labour economists who staffed the Federal labour relations agencies sought to promote the spread of the industry-wide bargaining procedures which they held responsible for Britain's contemporaneous record of industrial peace. Beginning in the 1950s, conversely, British politicians, lawyers and academics, alarmed at the growth of trade-union power and the proliferation of unofficial strikes, began to look with envy on the legally-regulated system of collective bargaining in the US. They believed it conducive to economic efficiency and orderly industrial relations, and the abortive Tory Industrial Relations Act of 1971 drew heavily on the American model.[1]

A similar perception of Anglo-American differences began to capture the imagination of radical critics dissatisfied with the apparent integration of American trade unions into the capitalist order during the 1960s and 1970s. From this perspective, the British labour scene seemed to embody much of what American radicals found lacking in the domestic trade-union movement. American unions, in this view, had lost by the 1950s most of the militant fire of their formative years. The pursuit of economic gains through the process of collective bargaining, it was argued, had led the unions to accept the hegemony of managerial authority in the workplace and largely to abandon the struggles for job control which had sparked their early organizing drives. In their quest for written contracts with employers, American unions had acquiesced in the elaboration of bureaucratic grievance procedures, capped in most cases by binding arbitration, which restricted shop-floor initiatives and rendered most forms of job action illegal during the life of the contract. Union officials were therefore obliged to assist management in imposing discipline and respect for procedure on their members, while the increasing centralization of bargaining and the consolidation of executive power had effectively excluded the rank and file from any substantive influence on union policy.[2]

British industrial relations appeared in this light to present an attractive contrast to conditions at home. In most industries, collective bargaining was highly decentralized, with negotiations conducted by shop stewards elected directly by the workforce and largely autonomous from national-union control. Collective agreements were not enforceable in the courts and there were few legal restraints on industrial action. The stewards were therefore free to take militant action in their struggles against management, using tactics such as slow-downs, overtime bans, and 'quickie' strikes; and the result was thought to be effective worker control over such key managerial functions as manning, workloads and the introduction of new technology. Thus to many American observers, the example of shop-floor bargaining in Britain seemed to signpost a road not taken by their own trade unions, one which might have bridged the gap between the organizations and their members and avoided the malaise which seemed to afflict the postwar American labour movement.[3]

In recent years, prominent American labour historians such as David Brody and Nelson Lichtenstein have drawn on this image of the British experience as a foil for their interpretation of the evolution of American industrial relations between the 1930s and the 1950s. In a pioneering essay on the domestication of American labour in the postwar period, Brody argues that the challenge to management control posed by unions at the end of the Second World War was ultimately contained by the employers, in part because of the development of a sophisticated managerial response, together with the underlying economism shared by workers and unions alike. Most crucial, however, was the emergence of the 'workplace rule of law', in the shape of written contracts, formal grievance procedures, and neutral arbitration which inhibited work groups from engaging in 'fractional bargaining', that is, from employing direct action in pursuit of their job-control objectives. 'In England, where union contracts did not penetrate down to the factory floor,' Brody observes, 'the shop stewards carved out a bargaining realm quite independently of the union structure. In America, fractional bargaining could not evolve into a comparable shop bargaining system. The workplace rule of law effectively forestalled the institutional-ization of shop-group activity.'[4]

In a stimulating study of workplace industrial relations in the automobile industry between 1937 and 1955, Nelson Lichtenstein goes further towards proposing the British model of shop-floor bargaining as an alternative option which was potentially available to American trade unionists in this period. Having traced the emergence of powerful networks of shop stewards who contested managerial prerogatives in a number of major auto manufacturing plants during the late 1930s and early 1940s, Lichtenstein goes on to suggest that,

The wartime struggle over factory discipline seemed to lay the basis for a decentralized system of postwar industrial relations in the auto industry that would incorporate both effective shop-floor bargaining over production standards and company-wide negotiation over pay and other benefits. This system would not have been different from that which in fact came to characterize large sections of British industry in the postwar era. There a militant, semi-autonomous shop stewards' movement won a central role in the life of the unions representing car workers. While the Amalgamated Union of Engineering Workers and other national organizations still negotiated periodic pay adjustments, these company-wide arrangements were little more than a platform from which stewards could legitimately seek to win improved conditions in direct confrontations with plant management.

In Lichtenstein's view, three factors explain the failure of these wartime struggles to establish a permanent role for shop-floor bargaining in the postwar auto industry. Powerful managements fought to regain control of the production process, assisted by bureaucratic grievance procedures which took shop-floor issues out of the stewards' hands and clamped down rigidly on unofficial strikes. The centralization of collective bargaining and of political authority within the United Autoworkers' union (UAW) further reduced the scope for shop-floor activity, as did the spread of automation, which eliminated many of the more combative occupational work groups in the factories.[5]

While this picture of Anglo-American differences has some real purchase on reality, particularly from the vantage point of the late 1960s and early 1970s, recent developments, contemporary and historiographical, on both sides of the Atlantic suggest that the contrast between workplace industrial relations in the two countries is overdrawn and misleading in important respects. In Britain, the onset of recession and monetarist economic policies have demonstrated the fragility of fragmented plant-based organizations, and many of the job controls won by stewards in better times have been rolled back by aggressive managements such as that at British Leyland.[6] Similarly, recent research on the history of industrial relations in the British auto industry shows that 100 per cent trade unionism, the construction of durable shop-steward organizations, and the erosion of managerial power in the workplace were only achieved in most of the major companies during the late 1950s and early 1960s. And even when shop stewards did achieve significant levels of job control, these were often applied in a flexible and cooperative manner except in periods of acute conflict.

On the American side, the resurgence of virulent and often successful employer anti-unionism even in companies with long histories of union organization casts doubt on the claim that the postwar system of collective bargaining placed no major constraints on management's freedom of action in the workplace. Michael Piore has argued, for example, that the seniority rules, job classifications and disciplinary procedures specified by most union contracts constitute a system of job definition and control which imposes substantial rigidities on the deployment of labor in the enterprise. During the period when Fordism and Taylorism were the central principles of efficient industrial organization, he suggests, these rules were acceptable and even advantageous to management. But rapid shifts in markets and technology have transformed them into major obstacles to the introduction of more flexible systems of work assignments needed to meet international competition, and contractual job controls have accordingly become a major stimulus to management's quest for a union-free environment.[7]

Piore's views are broadly confirmed by a comparative study of workforce reduction policies in the American and German automobile industries, which shows that American employers are much freer to lay off workers in response to short-term fluctuations in demand than their German counterparts, but much more constrained in the selection of which workers to lay off.[8] An even more striking finding is that of Bryn Jones's comparative study of the British and American aerospace industries which discovered that under favourable circumstances American unions are able to use the rights provided in their legally binding contracts to gain influence over manning on numerically controlled machine tools comparable to that established by British shop stewards through autonomous bargaining.[9]

These discoveries in the present find echoes in the rapidly growing literature on the emergence and development of American industrial unions. Many of these studies document the magnitude of the break marked by the coming of the Committee for Industrial Organization (CIO) with the arbitrary shop discipline and pervasive insecurity of the pre-union era; and even those writers most concerned to point out the eventual containment of the union challenge provide extensive evidence of the practical restrictions collective bargaining imposed on management's freedom of action in the workplace.

Our plan in the remainder of this chapter is as follows. In section 2, we present some results from recent research on the British motor industry which cast doubt on the received wisdom about shop-floor power in a major mass-production sector. In section 3 we draw on the recent historiography of the CIO, as well as on the older industrial relations literature, to suggest that the American system of collective bargaining placed greater constraints on managerial prerogatives in the automobile industry and other mass-production sectors than is generally supposed. While a comparison between the mass-production sectors in the two countries may understate Anglo-American differences arising from international variations in industrial structure, it is an appropriate focus for assessing the viability of British-style shop-floor bargaining in an American context. In the final section we return to the original contrast between the two countries to draw some tentative conclusions.[10]

II

The picture of shop-floor bargaining in the British motor industry used by Brody and Lichtenstein is based on a widespread but largely erroneous view.[11] This picture is that union organization established itself strongly in the motor industry by the end of the Second World War, taking advantage of the tightening conditions of wartime production. After the war, it is argued, employers were faced with almost insatiable demand and a shortage of labour and were prepared to concede high wages and a considerable measure of job control to powerful shop steward organizations in order to achieve continuous and expanding output. By the time that international competition began to intensify in the mid-1950s, employers had largely lost control of the shop floor and it is only during the current recession that they have been able to re-establish control over the entrenched shop stewards.

In fact, this picture is only accurate, with certain qualifications, for Standard Motors and the smaller motor companies in the Coventry area. But these firms produced less than a fifth of British car output during the postwar boom, and in the big producers the situation was very different. Employers maintained their prewar hostility to unions into the 1950s with considerable success. By 1956 Morris Motors was only 25 per cent unionized; Vauxhall was well below 50 per cent; Ford was in the same range and was notorious for its limitations on shop stewards; Austin fluctuated between 60–90 per cent unionization during most of the 1950s, but there too the shop-floor organization had made only very limited incursions on managerial authority during this period. In all of these firms, the consolidation of strong shop-floor organization occurs only in the late 1950s and early 1960s – and at Vauxhall it is arguable whether there has ever been a powerful shop-steward organization.[12]

It would be wrong to see these organizations as being built solely from the bottom up by autonomous oppositional action in the workplace. Shop-floor militants were able to build limited organization in face of managerial resistance in the 1940s and 1950s, but they were only able to consolidate it effectively when management moved away from confrontation and towards accommodation. The initial union breakthrough in the war period had much to do with the mitigation of employer hostility as a result of government policy, and the belated consolidation of organization in the late 1950s was closely associated with the refusal of government to back up employers who chose confrontation tactics.[13]

This is not to say that management exercised effective control over the workplace in the 1950s. Considerable informal bargaining took place on a day to day basis in the workplace, even where union organization was weak. Pressures for speedy output were urgent, labour was in short supply and the factories were characterized by a lack of investment in modern production facilities. In this situation, in firms with weakly elaborated managerial structures, shop-floor supervision had considerable autonomy and the leeway to make concessions and surrender cost control in order to get output and effort.[14] The result was an 'indulgency pattern' characterized by leniency and covering up for mistakes, side by side with hostility to unions and insistence on managerial prerogatives.[15] Management was actually prepared to pay high wages to keep unions out of the plant, and wages in weakly unionized firms moved forward at the same relative pace as those in the Coventry firms between 1948 and 1956, though the absolute gap was not narrowed substantially until after the unions entrenched themselves across all firms in the 1960s.[16] Managerial and supervisory discretion and slackness produced a creeping relaxation of custom and practice on the shop floor even without sustained union pressure. When union organization consolidated itself it was able to rigidify these practices and demand cash bargains for any relaxations of them.

Across the motor firms, a spectrum of job control developed depending particularly on the history of unionization, managerial strategies and the structure of wages systems. At the bottom end of the spectrum came firms like Ford and Vauxhall where day-wage structures denied stewards the opportunities of piecework bargaining and where management maintained a firmer control on the shop floor. From the 1930s, Ford at Dagenham sought to avoid any bargaining on the shop floor. Payment was on the basis of grading and day-rates and from 1944 these were negotiated solely with national union officials. Stewards received hardly any formal recognition and almost no facilities, and in the mid-1960s Ford still maintained an insistence that workloads were beyond the reach of negotiation. In the late 1950s and early 1960s this Ford system was put under pressure after Ford incorporated the adjacent Briggs Bodies factory and brought a powerfully organized piecework based shop-steward organization into the company with it. This was followed by a long and finally successful offensive to bring Briggs's conditions into line with those of Ford, the so-called 'harmonization' campaign. This produced the most sustained shop-floor challenge to Ford's right to manage, in the form of a running battle of constant short stoppages over workloads. But in 1963 Ford sacked the core of the stewards' organization; after that, resistance fell away. At Dagenham in the 1960s stewards were not consulted over speed-up, the company was able to move workers around the factory more or less at will, and individuals were pressurized by supervisors into accepting additional tasks on their jobs for the same money.[17]

In the mid-1960s the centre of shop-floor militancy within Ford shifted to their new plant at Halewood, near Liverpool. The degree of job control won by stewards there was significant, but a detailed study by Beynon has clearly demonstrated the underlying ambiguities and frailty of the stewards' bargaining position. Ford refused to negotiate over manning and individual workloads and rejected 'mutuality' in the timing of jobs and the allocation of work. Workloads were the site of a major struggle over job control. One central issue was resistence to the speeding up of the assembly line *during* shifts. By a campaign of unofficial walkouts, stewards won the right to hold the key that locked the line speeds during the shift. But the company still refused to negotiate about manning levels on the line, and when line speeds were increased they were often able to increase the manning less than proportionately.

Until the mid-1960s the foreman was able to decide unilaterally who was to work overtime and when, and only later did stewards begin to get this power out of the hands of the foreman and to apply a rota. On job timings it was only in the late 1960s that stewards won the right that Work Study should not *re*-time a job without a steward present, and the initial timings remained unilateral. On layoffs, those to be laid off were generally selected by the supervisors without consultation; only on the strongest sections were stewards able to get them selected by being pulled out of a hat instead. The controls that were established, as Beynon notes, 'did not involve a very radical challenge to management organization of the plant'. The struggle to control workloads was 'running flat out to stand still'. The shifts in the frontier of control that were obtained were won by periodic upsurges and frequently drifted back again afterwards.[18]

Apart from Ford and Vauxhall, however, all the other big motor firms worked on piecework, and it was within this wage system that shop stewards were able to exert their highest degree of control. The Donovan Commission focused on the loss of managerial control and the disorderly structures of industrial relations that had grown up under this system. But lack of management control was not the same thing as the existence of union control. Evidence to the Commission showed that the shop-steward system under piecework bargaining was fraught with inequity, lack of security, constant haggling and divisiveness. But it did provide stewards with enormous scope for bargaining and opportunities to show that union organization could deliver the goods in cash terms.[19] By the 1960s stewards were exerting real control over piecework prices, using their knowledge and sectional bargaining power to push up earnings and erode the predictability of wage costs for management.

This fragmentation of bargaining had consequences only partially satisfactory to stewards. One result of prolonged piecework bargaining was a wide and chaotic spread of differentials with neither managerial nor union rationality behind them. Workers in the same grade had widely different earnings, even in the *same* plant. It was common for a job to be highly rated within one plant's hierarchy of earnings but lowly rated in another. Jobs that were easy to rate-study were often on 'tight' prices and had below average earnings while jobs requiring no more skill or effort might have high earnings simply because they were hard to assess.[20] While differentials in the US auto industry had become highly compressed by the 1960s they remained very wide in Britain.[21] Moreover there was no tendency within the piecework system to change this; indeed, steward bargaining often sought to maintain those differentials even among semi-skilled workers, and workers on individual piecework were ready to tolerate surprisingly wide differentials between similar jobs.[22] The key factor that altered earnings was the frequency and vigour of collective bargaining, especially at the steward leadership level.[23] An immense amount turned on local interpretations of the 1931 National Engineering Agreement, whereby no changes could be made in piecework prices once a job had been assessed unless there was a change in 'means or methods of production'. In some departments this could be interpreted to limit severely the opportunities for renegotiation, whereas in others stewards were able to take advantage of it to demand complete renegotiation after very minor changes.[24]

In part, the high levels of strike activity in autos in the 1960s arose from the direct use of shop-floor muscle as a motor to increase wages. But strike activity is not a real indicator of union strength and control. Often short strikes were 'attention getters', a sign of cumbersome grievance procedures and inadequate management structures.[25] But in the mid and late 1960s they often arose from insecurity issues, such as loss of earnings arising from break-downs, faulty scheduling, shortages of components and layoffs.[26] Shop-steward organizations were at their weakest in mitigating such an unstable earnings environment and it was their weakness on these issues that gave management a particular leverage in introducing Measured Day Work (MDW) in the early 1970s, which increased pay stability as a trade-off against the loss of continuous bargaining rights.[27]

Thus stewards within the piecework framework were unable to challenge inequity and insecurity. They were also unable to develop broader strategic goals. Much of their bargaining advantage in the shops derived from astute manipulation of custom and practice. This, however, should not be be confused with unilateral regulation of conditions in the workshops. The rule of custom arose primarily in areas where managerial decisions had hitherto been absent. Its effects were partly random, since the implications of a particular decision were often unclear to both stewards and managers.[28] More importantly, the nature of such gains won through a policy of shop-floor opportunism meant that stewards could not think or act strategically. One result was the dissipation of the collective power of the workforce through frequent actions over somewhat tendentious grievances. The extreme decentralization of such bargaining exacerbated sectionalism and compartmentalism and could often foster internal antagonisms such as those which wracked Cowley in the late 1960s when actions by small sections often disrupted the work of others over issues that were not at all clear.[29] This lack of unity was rarely offset by effective company-wide Joint Shop Stewards Committees, which were often unable to overcome inter-union rivalries within multi-union companies, or to develop coherent policies. Over and above the factory level, steward combine organization remained skeletal throughout the 1960s.[30]

In certain areas where stewards did exercise job control it was often less oppositional and more cooperative with management than is often recognized. As a result, self-regulation within a piecework system was double-edged, for stewards played a quasi-supervisory role in work organization to ensure continuity of production, prevent bottlenecks and maximize production and hence earnings. Such expanded responsibilities soon posed a new set of problems which can be clearly seen at Standard Motors in the 1950s where this role developed furthest around the Standard 'large gang' system. Stewards exercised considerable control over the deployment of labour and manning levels. Under MDW this would be the essence of job control, but under payment by results it very much threw the ball into the trade union's court and was very ambiguous in its effects. There was a standing temptation to either de-man gangs and push up the intensity of effort so as to increase income or to discriminate against members of gangs, since, for instance, by having more members on lower grades within the gang, the proportion of the bonus taken by the higher grades was greatly raised. Once the system had been in motion for a few years these pressures created internal division and rivalry. Two or more gangs might both lay claim to a lucrative job, or one gang might conspire with management at the expense of another. In 1955 the firm decided to subcontract out the work done by women trimmers on Gang 13 unless they accepted a price at the level tendered by subcontractors. The Gang decided not to defend the women; instead they reached agreement with management to kick the women out and create a new women's gang, which would avoid the new low-priced job pulling down their earnings.[31] The line between job control and self-supervision was thin and under piecework stewards might choose to maximize output rather than strictly defend working conditions and rights.

The picture presented here seriously qualifies the commonplace notion of job control under shop stewards in the British motor industry. It developed in a much later historical period than is often suggested and even then required a significant degree of external assistance from the state and management. It was highly dependent on the bargaining opportunities of a particular payments system, and, largely because of the way shop-floor strategy was shaped by this context, it did little to curb inequities or insecurity. It was based on sectionalism, specific local conditions and the exploitation of loopholes. Stewards struggled to develop forms of coordination and more strategic control with little success. Even within piecework firms there was a considerable range of job control between the best-organized firms such as Standard Motors and the Coventry producers and a range of firms like Morris, Austin or Rover where shop-floor control remained significantly less developed.

III

Bearing in mind these findings on the slow development and limited achievements of shop steward organization in the British motor industry, to what extent did a more decentralized system of shop-floor bargaining represent a real historical option in American mass production industry?

A number of factors highlighted by recent historical treatments of the rise of the CIO – including those of Brody and Lichtenstein themselves – weighed heavily against this prospect.

The first is the sporadic and often highly sectional character of rank and file militancy. The most intense rank and file involvement in the upsurges of the 1930s appears to have come during the National Recovery Act strikes of 1933–4, which fizzled out quickly in the face of employer opposition and the ambivalence of the American Federation of Labor (AFL). During the formative years of the CIO itself, many mass production workers had little durable loyalty to the new unions, and after brief periods of mobilization would soon relapse into apathetic disinterest, leaving the union activists dangerously exposed to management reprisals.[32] Even after unionization, the rash of sitdowns, slowdowns, and 'quickie' strikes which hit the auto and rubber plants in the late 1930s proved extremely sectional and divisive, dissipating the collective power of the workforce in a succession of ill-timed stoppages which laid off large numbers of workers over the grievances of isolated work groups and threatened to provoke a devastating managerial counter-offensive.[33] Wartime wildcats raised similar problems for the unions, which manifested themselves in an extreme form in the 'hate strikes' against the promotion of black workers to more skilled jobs which erupted at Packard and other Detroit plants in 1943.[34] As in Britain, moreover, the proliferation of sectional bargaining would have produced large and persistent disparities of earnings and conditions among workers both within and between plants, which the egalitarian wage policies and opposition to piecework shared by most UAW activists explicitly sought to prevent.[35]

The unions' need to develop a more unified strategy was rendered more urgent by the vast power and resources of their opponents. Most of the giant corporations which dominated the mass-production industries had accepted collective bargaining only after bitter strikes or under intense pressure from government agencies. It seemed likely that they would try to rid themselves of union organization once the political and economic climate had changed; and it was evident that union strategies would have to be carefully calculated and coordinated if they were to have any assurance of survival. After the war, it was the enormous bargaining power and strategic capacities of corporations such as General Motors (GM) which forced the unions to accept management rights clauses and reductions in steward numbers; and only a relatively centralized bargaining strategy could prevent these companies from playing off one plant against another.[36] Finally, even in those auto firms where strong steward organizations did survive into the 1950s, the competitive pressure exerted by the industry leaders ultimately cut the ground out from under them, either through the firms' demise as at Packard and Studebaker or through the reassertion of managerial authority as at Chrysler.[37]

The overwhelming power of their business opponents was in turn the main reason for the CIO's dependence on support from government agencies.

As Brody and others have demonstrated, without the active support of the Federal government, the CIO organizing drive would probably have suffered the same fate which befell the 1919 steel strike; and the War Labor Board's backing was equally essential in forcing collective bargaining on the major holdout firms such as Ford, Goodyear, Westinghouse and Little Steel, which the CIO had been unable to subdue before the war.[38] An additional constraint was the resurgence of conservative forces in Congress from 1938 onwards, which gave CIO leaders ample reason to fear that a wave of uncontrolled wartime strikes would provoke harsh anti-labour legislation and administrative restrictions on union activity; indeed the Defence strikes of 1940–1 and the coal strikes of 1943 paved the way for the passage of the Smith–Connally Act, as the postwar reconstruction strike wave did for that of Taft–Hartley. From Lichtenstein's own account, it seems clear that the CIO leaders' commitment to the no-strike pledge in the later years of the war stemmed as much from their anxiety to avert a right-wing backlash and the threat of a 'labour draft', as from their social patriotism and their desire to reassert their control over the rank and file. Faced with powerful enemies in business and Congress, the CIO unions could not have gone it alone, as ambitious and opportunistic leaders such as Walter Reuther realized, and a majority of rank and filers who voted reaffirmed their support for the no-strike pledge in the UAW's March 1945 referendum.[39]

If the triumph of militant, autonomous shop-floor unionism was not a real possibility in postwar America, how far did the more centralized and contractual collective bargaining which actually prevailed place limits on management's freedom of action in the workplace? Most historians and industrial relations experts have emphasized management's success in containing and rolling back the union challenge to its control in the immediate postwar years. In the auto industry, for example, corporations such as GM and Ford resisted the UAW's attempts to intrude on their pricing policies and their strategies for responding to seasonal demand, fending off in the process demands for union participation in establishing production standards, job classification schemes, and disciplinary rules. More positively from their perspective, the auto giants extracted from the UAW sweeping declarations of management rights, significant reductions in the numbers and prerogatives of stewards and committeemen, as well as draconian powers to punish wildcat strikers. The National Labor Relations Board (NLRB) and Taft–Hartley further contributed to the re-establishment of managerial control by removing the protection of the Wagner Act from foremen and supervisors, whose nascent unions were quickly smashed. Developments in other mass-production industries followed a similar pattern, though few companies were as adept as GM in taking advantage of their revived bargaining power.[40]

While these developments marked a serious setback to the unions' broader ambitions and help to account for management's reconciliation to collective bargaining in most major companies, they should not obscure the magnitude of what had already been achieved by comparison to the pre-union era, or for that matter, to the situation in Britain even a decade later. The salient features of workers' experience in the pre-union auto factories, as in other mass-production industries such as rubber, steel and electrical goods, had been pervasive insecurity and subjection to arbitrary managerial discipline. Even where companies had themselves instituted seniority systems, management retained wide discretion in their administration, and even long-serving workers faced continual bullying from foremen and the threat of instantaneous dismissal.[41]

The seniority systems and disciplinary procedures won by unions in most plants by the 1940s marked a fundamental break with this regime. By 1950, seniority was well on its way to becoming the principal criterion for layoffs and recalls in most mass production industries, and in many cases it had made substantial inroads into transfer and promotion policies as well. In the rubber industry, layoffs were governed by strict seniority, which also applied to promotions where the worker was capable of learning the job within a reasonable period of time. In steel and autos, merit and ability still qualified seniority in layoffs and promotions, but arbitrators had ruled that the burden of proof for deviations fell on management. In the electrical industry, where seniority had become the main factor governing layoffs and recalls for 94 per cent of workers covered by Union of Electrical Workers (UE) contracts in 1947, Ronald Schatz observes that, 'The union seniority systems were less flexible than the pre-union company policies. They denied managers most of the freedom they had formerly enjoyed in issuing assignments to individual workers.'[42]

In most large companies, moreover, management was no longer free to discharge employees at will, but could ultimately be forced through the grievance procedure to justify its actions before a neutral arbitrator, demonstrating 'just cause' in the form of written rules, clear precedents, prior warnings and even-handed treatment of individuals; where any of these were absent, the arbitrator was likely to reverse or modify the penalty. By these contractual means, concluded Chamberlain in his 1947 study of conditions in the auto, steel, rubber, meatpacking, electrical and public utility sectors, unions 'have succeeded in sharing a very great measure of authority in the disciplinary control of employees'.[43]

Taken together, these limits on arbitrary discharge could have a profoundly subversive effect on shop-floor discipline. In the electrical industry, for example, Schatz reports that the coming of seniority and grievance procedures greatly eroded foremen's powers over individual workers. Whereas previously foremen could victimize those who crossed them, workers now felt sufficiently secure to challenge their authority on sensitive issues such as piecework times and prices, producing extensive wage drift. In each of the industries he studied, Chamberlain found that the union inroad in the disciplinary area had gone far beyond the provisions of the contract, but this clearly depended on effective shop-floor enforcement, and in the absence of detailed studies, it is difficult to say how far it persisted into the 1950s and 1960s.[44]

As collective bargaining became better established, seniority systems and grievance procedures were progressively elaborated and extended to new firms; and the constraints which they placed on management's freedom to allocate labour were if anything enhanced. In 1960, for example, Slichter, Healy and Livernash reported that, 'Many managements . . . are troubled by the inroads of the seniority criterion on the promotion of employees, and more particularly, they are convinced that seniority rules impair the flexibility of assignments needed for efficient operation.' The same was true of the classification systems and job descriptions which had become a standard feature of most union contracts during the preceding 20 years. 'Few companies', they observed, 'ever entered into these programs . . . with the thought that they would limit their right to assign work or that they would lead to unrest among employees concerning work assignments. Yet in a surprising number of cases these have been the consequences.'[45] Disciplinary procedures too continued to constrain managerial discretion: a study of 1,055 discharge cases between 1942 and 1955 showed that management's decision was sustained in only 41 per cent, the penalty reduced in 33.8 per cent and revoked entirely in 25.2 per cent, though there was some improvement between the late 1940s and the early 1950s.[46]

In some cases, unions had also managed to retain or acquire influence over important aspects of the production process. In the steel industry, for example, local rules concerning crew sizes and working conditions were protected by the national contract, and arbitrators had extended this protection to customary practices not recorded in the local contracts themselves. The steel companies' attempt to modify this clause was defeated in the protracted 1959 strike, though individual rules could be modified through technological change or bargaining with the locals.[47] In auto, the UAW had won substantial rest periods for assembly workers at the major companies, and the GM contracts specified that workers should be able to meet production standards while working at a 'normal pace', and the standards were supposed to vary with the model mix. In the last instance, production standards and health and safety issues were strikeable during the life of the contract, but only after the final step of the lengthy grievance procedure had been completed.[48]

In industries where certain issues were strikeable during the life of the contract, these could be used to put pressure on the companies over non-strikeable issues including managerial prerogatives not subject to mandatory bargaining under National Labor Relations Board rules. In the auto industry, for example, management at GM, Ford and Chrysler complained repeatedly throughout the 1950s that production standard and health and safety issues were used to force concessions over non-strikeable issues.[49] In the electrical industry, local unions took advantage of the collapse of national bargaining and the companies' resistance to arbitration to develop a highly successful strategy of using legal grievance strikes to harass management through short stoppages at well-timed moments. The locals could store up grievances which had passed through the procedure, enabling them to strike at any moment, or after 1970 with 24 hours' notice. It was these tactics, Bryn Jones argues, that enabled the unions to win control over new technology for skilled workers in the aerospace industry.[50] In the rubber industry, where 'fractional bargaining' was particularly well established, James Kuhn discovered that in many plants stewards and foremen were permitted to make 'mutual agreements' which modified the operation of the contract in particular shops.[51]

These last observations suggest that the 'workplace rule of law' was not in itself so severe a constraint on shop-floor struggles for job control as many historians have claimed. Why then did these not come to play a larger role in postwar American industrial relations? Part of the answer lies, of course, in the power of the corporations and their determination to clamp down on such developments, outside of exceptional cases such as General Electric.

But part of the answer also lies in the policies of the unions themselves. Sophisticated union leaders such as Walter Reuther were always careful to remain in touch with the mood of the rank and file and sought to incorporate demands over workplace issues such as production standards into their bargaining strategy to a limited extent. Less responsive leaders such as Sherman Dalrymple of the URW were unseated by rank and file revolts when they imposed harsh penalties on wildcat strikers. But for men like Reuther, these local grievances were always secondary to their larger concern with company-wide problems such as pensions and the guaranteed annual wage, as well as a potential threat to the effectiveness of central union control. The UAW therefore tended to press its locals to curtail their strikes over production standards to avoid interfering with national negotiations. From the 1960s onward, however, the International leaders responded to growing pressure from below by authorizing an increasing number of local strikes over shop-floor conditions – many during the life of the contract itself – which soon dwarfed wildcat stoppages in terms of man-hours lost in the industry as a whole.[52]

The contractual system of collective bargaining which emerged from the Second World War placed substantial constraints on management's freedom to deploy labour and to impose arbitrary discipline in the enterprise through the elaboration of seniority systems, grievance procedures, and binding arbitration. But it also left a certain amount of space for shop-floor struggles over job control which was not fully utilized because of the centralizing ambitions of both management and unions. In this limited sense, workplace industrial relations in postwar America might indeed have been different, though they could never have conformed to the imaginary model of shop-steward power in Britain.

IV

Reflecting on the British labour scene in 1920, the American economist Carter Goodrich observed that the 'greater or less degree' of control is at once impossible to measure and less illuminating than 'the nature and policy of the union exercising it.'[53] Subsequent commentators on the 'frontier of control', however, have tended to regard it as a straightforward index of the shop-floor balance of power between labour and management, ranking national systems of industrial relations along a single scale by the level of job control they allow the workforce.

A detailed historical examination of the British and American automobile industries – a classic case in point – undermines both such national stereotypes and the conception of job control which underlies them. On the British side, as we have seen, trade unions and shop-steward organization were weakly established for much of the postwar period, while even in their heyday during the late 1960s and 1970s, job controls remained partial and defensive and were often applied in a flexible and cooperative manner except in periods of acute conflict. In both countries, however, when unions established themselves in the workplace they placed significant constraints on management's freedom of action, through contractual seniority rules and grievance procedures which enhanced workers' security in the US and through more decentralized bargaining over manning, workloads and piecework prices in Britain. These differences in the focus of job control reflect the very different histories of industrial relations in the two countries; but each system entails a complex blend of power and constraint for both unions and management whose precise implications depend in large measure on the bargaining strategies of the contending parties themselves. And never is this scope for choice more important than in a period of economic and political upheaval like the present.

NOTES

1   Conservative businessmen and politicians dissatisfied with the Wagner Act also looked favourably on the restrictive provisions of the British Trade Disputes Act of 1927. For information on American perceptions of British industrial relations in this period, see Howell Harris, 'The Snares of Liberalism? Politicians, Bureaucrats and the Shaping of Federal Labour Relations Policy in the United States, ca. 1915–47', in Steven Tolliday and Jonathan Zeitlin (eds.), *Shop Floor Bargaining and the State: Historical and Contemporary Perspectives* (Cambridge, 1985). For the influence of the American model on the drafters of the Industrial Relations Act, see Michael Moran, *The Politics of Industrial Relations: The Origins, Life and Death of the 1971 Industrial Relations Act* (London, 1977); and for a British study of industrial relations in the automobile industry which contrasted American arrangements favourably with the prevailing pattern in the UK, see H. A. Turner, Garfield Clack and Geoffrey Roberts, *Labour Relations in the Motor Industry* (London, 1967), ch. 10.

2   For representative interpretations of American labour history in these terms, see Stanley Aronowitz, *False Promises: The Shaping of American Working Class Consciousness* (New York, 1973); and Jeremy Brecher, *Strike!* (San Francisco, 1972).

3	Another important contrast between the two labour movements concerned their relation to politics. Much of the discontent of American radicals with the trade unions stemmed from the latter's support for the Vietnam War and close ties with the Democratic Party. British trade unions, on the other hand, had thrown their weight behind a Labour Party committed to a socialist constitution, while many shop stewards were open supporters of the Communist Party or small far-left groups. For a good picture of perceptions of British labour on the American left in the early 1970s, see the special issue of *Radical America* on 'Class Struggle in Britain', vol. 8, no. 5 (1974).

4	David Brody, 'The Uses of Power I: The Industrial Battleground', in his *Workers in Industrial America: Essays on the Twentieth Century Struggle* (New York, 1980), pp. 172–214; the quotation is from p. 206.

5	Nelson Lichtenstein, 'Auto Worker Militancy and the Structure of Factory Life, 1937–55', *Journal of American History* 67, no. 2, (September, 1980), pp. 335–53; the quotation is from p. 348. Lichtenstein shows that at Studebaker and Packard, the steward system remained intact until the companies' collapse in the late 1950s, as it did at Chrysler to a substantial extent until the 1957–8 recession; ibid., p. 359; cf. also his 'Life at the Rouge: A Cycle of Workers' Control', in Charles Stephenson and Robert Asher (eds.), *Life and Labor: Dimensions of Working-Class History,* (forthcoming); Steve Jefferys, *Management and Managed: The Movement of Managerial Authority and Workplace Legitimacy in the Chrysler Corporation Since 1933*, (forthcoming, Cambridge University Press); and Robert M. MacDonald, *Collective Bargaining in the Automobile Industry*, (New Haven, 1963), chs 6–7.

In his study of the CIO during the Second World War, Lichtenstein assigns the principal weight in the emergence of contract unionism to the formal grievance procedures and provisions for union security imposed by the War Labor Board, and to the CIO leaders' willingness to support the no-strike pledge as a result of their political alliance with the Roosevelt administration and their pursuit of power over the rank and file within the unions themselves. In his conclusions, he returns to the British example: 'In contrast to Great Britain, where the post-war prosperity and growth of unionism gave rise to an increasingly confident stratum of shop steward militants, in America the rigidity of the collective bargaining process thwarted the emergence of an independent cadre that could give continuous leadership to the episodic conflict that still unfolded in the workplace.' Nelson Lichtenstein, *Labor's War at Home: The CIO in World War II* (Cambridge, 1982), pp. 243–4.

6	For an account of recent developments at British Leyland, see chapter 13. For evidence that British shop-steward organization has held up better outside the nationalized sector, see Michael Rose and Bryn Jones, 'Managerial Strategy and Trade Union Response in Plant-Level Reorganisation of Work', in D. Knights, H. Willmott and D. Collinson (eds.), *Job Redesign: Organisation and Control of the Labour Process* (London, 1985); and Eric Batstone, *Working Order: Workplace Industrial Relations over Two Decades*, (Oxford, 1984).

7	Piore takes as his point of departure the elaborate internal job structures established by union contracts negotiated at the plant level. 'The union imposes on this structure a set of negotiated wages, actually specifying how much an employer must pay for *each* job . . . a set of "job security" provisions which determine how these jobs are distributed among the workers; and a set of disciplinary standards which limit, in the light of each worker's own particular work requirements, what obligations he or she has to the employer and how a failure to meet those obligations will be sanctioned.' Most interpretations of American industrial relations emphasize management's freedom to define the initial job structure. But as Piore points out, 'what is often missed in such discussions is that the jobs must nonetheless be defined, the jobs stabilized over a period long enough that they have real meaning, and the employer accept the wages, worker allocation and disciplinary procedures which his job definitions imply.' Michael J. Piore, 'American Labor and the Industrial Crisis', *Challenge*, March–April 1982, pp. 8–9. See also Piore and Charles F. Sabel, *The Second Industrial Divide: Possibilities of Prosperity* (New York, 1984), pp. 111–32, 240–6; and the discussion in Thomas Kochan (ed.), *Challenges and Choices Facing American Labor* (Cambridge, Mass., 1985).

8   Christoph Köhler and Werner Sengenberger, 'Policies of Work Force Reduction and Labor Market Structures in the American and German Automobile Industry', paper presented to the conference of the International Working Party on Labour Market Segmentation, Modena, Italy, 7–11 September 1981; and their *Konjunktur und Personalanpassung: betriebliche Beschaftigungspolitik in der deutschen und amerikanischen Automobilindustrie* (Frankfurt am Main, 1983). A detailed study of current trends in the US auto industry which supports this view and that of Piore is Harry C. Katz, *Shifting Gears: Changing Labor Relations in the U.S. Automobile Industry* (Cambridge, Mass., 1985).

9   Bryn Jones, 'Controlling Production on the Shop Floor: The Role of State Administration and Regulation in the British and American Aerospace Industries', in Tolliday and Zeitlin, *Shop Floor Bargaining and the State*.

10 For a comparative study which highlights the importance of industrial structure in explaining differences in Anglo-American industrial relations, see Bernard Elbaum and Frank Wilkinson, 'Industrial Relations and Uneven Development: A Comparative Study of the American and British Steel Industries', *Cambridge Journal of Economics* III, no. 3 (1979). The limited existing research on industrial relations in other British mass-production sectors suggests a broadly similar pattern to that of the automobile industry: cf. on electrical engineering, Ronald Dore, *British Factory–Japanese Factory* (London, 1973); and on rubber, Ian Maitland, *The Causes of Industrial Disorder: A Comparison of a British and a German Factory*, (London, 1983).

11 For this view see: Jonathan Zeitlin, 'The Emergence of Shop Steward Organization and Job Control in the British Car Industry: A Review Essay', *History Workshop Journal*, no. 10 (autumn 1980), pp. 122–3; Andrew L. Friedman, *Industry and Labour* (London, 1977), ch. 14; Richard Hyman and Tony Eiger, 'Job Controls, the Employers' Offensive and Alternative Strategies', *Capital and Class*, no. 15 (autumn 1981), pp. 133–4; Peter J. S. Dunnett, *The Decline of the British Motor Industry: The Effects of Government Policy, 1949–79* (London, 1980), esp. pp. 52–5, 82–5 and 108–14; Richard Price, 'Rethinking Labour History: The Importance of Work' in James E. Cronin and Jonathan Schneer (eds.), *Social Conflict and the Political Order in Modern Britain* (London, 1982), p. 196; Keith Middlemas, *Politics in Industrial Society* (London: André Deutsch, 1979), p. 400.

12 Figures on union density derive from work in progress funded by Kings' College Research Centre Cambridge and the Economic and Social Research Council. For the weakness of unions at Vauxhall even in the 1960s see J. H. Goldthorpe,

et al., *The Affluent Worker: Industrial Attitudes and Behavior* (Cambridge 1968).

13   These points are argued fully in Steven Tolliday, 'Government, Employers and Shop Floor Organisation in the British Motor Industry, 1939–69', in Tolliday and Zeitlin, *Shop Floor Bargaining and the State*.

14   On weaknesses of managerial structures, see Richard J. Overy, *William Morris, Viscount Nuffield* (London, 1976), esp. pp. 60–6; Roy Church, *Herbert Austin. The British Motor Car Industry to 1941* (London, 1979), pp. 157–68.

15   For the 'indulgency pattern' generally, see Alvin Gouldner, *Patterns of Industrial Bureaucracy* (Glencoe, Illinois, 1954), p. 177.

16   Based on information from Engineering Employers' Federation wage data cited in Tolliday, 'Government, Employers and Shop Floor Organisation'.

17   A good account of this is given by Ernie Stanton who was a NUVB steward at Ford in the early 1960s, in Ernie Stanton, *What Happened at Fords*, Solidarity Pamphlet no. 26, 1967. On the wider background of industrial relations at Ford, see Henry Friedmann and Sandor Meredeen, *The Dynamics of Industrial Conflict: Lessons from Ford* (London, 1980); Huw Beynon, *Working for Ford* (Harmondsworth 1973). On the 'harmonisation issue' see *Report of a Court of Inquiry* (Cameron Report), Cmd. 131, HMSO, 1957; and *Report of a Court of Inquiry* (Jack Report), Cmd. 1949, HMSO, 1963.

18   Beynon, *Working for Ford*, chs 5–7.

19   Minutes of Evidence to Royal Commission on Trade Unions and Employers Associations (Donovan Commission), HMSO, 1965–8, and RC Report, 1968, Cmnd. 3623.

20   Turner, Clack and Roberts, *Labour Relations in the Motor Industry*, ch. 5. The classic example of the hard-to-time job is that of grinder, where an experienced worker can raise an impressive shower of sparks while barely touching the metal and thus run rings around the rate-fixer.

21   In 1963 in the USA three-fifths of production workers earned between $2.70 and $2.90, a range of less than 8 per cent; MacDonald, *Collective Bargaining in the Automobile Industry*, pp. 84–88. To encompass a comparable proportion of British auto workers a range of more than 50 per cent would be required: Turner, Clack and Roberts, *Labour Relations in the Motor Industry*, ch. 10.

22   William A. Brown, *Piecework Bargaining* (London, 1973), pp. 51–60. At Standard Motors which was the best organized auto plant in the 1950s, the 'large gang' system had the closure of differentials as one of its major initial aims. In practice it failed to maintain the initial narrowing of relativities. Price-fixing developed on a ratchet system. When a new job came in, the demand was for the price to yield the average earnings of existing work. Then, once the gang got the hang of the job and improved efficiency the earnings moved ahead. But some sections might not get a new job for several years and gangs working on the oldest vintages had the lowest earnings and those on the newest the most. Once a new job came in it was very often possible to leap-frog to the top of the wages hierarchy. In the meantime, however, despite union bargaining strength, wide inequalities were tolerated for long periods. In contrast to the relatively stable relativities on individual piecework at Austin Motor Co., the Standard gang system had very erratic fluctuations. See Steven Tolliday, 'High Tide and After: Coventry Engineering Workers and Shop Floor Bargaining, 1945–80', in Tony Mason and Bill Lancaster (eds), *Life and Labour in a Twentieth Century City: The Experience of Coventry* (Coventry, 1986).

23 Eric Batstone, Ian Boraston and Steven Frankel, *Shop Stewards in Action*, (Oxford, 1977), pp. 234–5.
24 Brown, *Piecework Bargaining*, p. 90; for comparable analyses of the wage structure irrationalities created by piecework bargaining in the electrical engineering and rubber industries, see Dore, *British Factory–Japanese Factory*, pp. 76–94; and Maitland, *The Causes of Industrial Disorder*, pp. 74–91.
25 For an example from a Coventry motor firm, see G. Clack, *Industrial Relations in a British Car Factory* (Cambridge, 1967), pp. 61–3.
26 Turner, Clack and Roberts, *Labour Relations in the Motor Industry*, ch. 4. See also 14th Report of Select Committee on National Expenditure, 1975, ch. 9. This was particularly the case at Morris Motors, Cowley. See interviews with Tom Richardson, Industrial Relations Manager at Cowley, 1965–8 and with Alan Thornett, former TGWU Deputy Senior Steward at Cowley, November 1982. Transcripts in the possession of the authors.
27 Interviews with David Buckle, TGWU District Secretary for Oxford Area, and Bill Roche, TGWU Covenor Cowley Body Plant, 1982.
28 Brown, *Piecework Bargaining*, esp. pp. 142–53.
29 For a classic example of this in the early 1970s see S. Johns *Victimisation at Cowley* (Oxford, 1974). For cases in the late 1960s see the Les Gurl Papers at the Modern Records Centre, Warwick University.
30 Shirley W. Lerner and John Bescoby, 'Shop Steward Combine Committees in the British Engineering Industry', *British Journal of Industrial Relations*, 1966. On the problems of the BMC Combine Committee, see the papers of Les Gurl, the former Secretary of the Combine Committee, MRC, Warwick.
31 The Standard system has been described, and somewhat idealized by Seymour Melman, *Decision-making and Productivity*, (Oxford, 1957), and D. Rayton, *Shop Floor Democracy in Action* (Nottingham, 1977). See also A. Friedman, *Industry and Labour*, ch. 14. For a critical discussion of the situation at Standard see S. Tolliday, 'High Tide and After'.
32 On the sporadic character of rank and file militancy and the weak commitment of workers to the unions during the 1930s, see Brody, *Workers in Industrial America*, pp. 134–5; Lichtenstein, *Labor's War at Home*, pp. 9–14; Ray Boryczka, 'Seasons of Discontent: Auto Union Factionalism and the Motor Products Strike of 1935–36', *Michigan History* 61, no. 1 (1977); and Robert H. Zieger, 'The Limits of Militancy: Organizing Paper Workers, 1933–35', *Journal of American History* 63, 3 (1976).
33 Lichtenstein, *Labor's War at Home* pp. 14–17; Ray Boryczka, 'Militancy and Factionalism in the United Auto Workers' Union, 1937–41', *The Maryland Historian* 8 (autumn, 1977). Thus Lichtenstein writes, 'Uncoordinated and unpredictable – at least to top union officials – these strikes made it difficult for the union as a whole to formulate a general strategy toward management. They proved immediately advantageous to workers who were strategically located in the production process, but they could destroy solidarity among the larger group, especially when a strike in one department produced a layoff in another. Finally, these strikes threatened the union's entire relationship with the company. They undermined the managerial incentive to continue recognizing the union, and during the 1937 recession, when the union stood on the defensive, they were used by management as occasions to eliminate shop floor militants.' Ibid., p. 15.
34 Ibid., pp. 121–7.

35   On wage drift and shifts in relativities generated by piecework bargaining at
     Studebaker, see MacDonald, *Collective Bargaining in the Automobile Industry*,
     pp. 123–5; on the UAW's egalitarian wage policy and its opposition to
     piecework, see ibid., pp. 90, 105–33, 148–59, 206–36.
36   Howell Harris, *The Right to Manage: Industrial Relations Policies of American
     Business in the 1940s* (Madison, Wisconsin, 1982); Brody, *Workers in Industrial
     America*, pp. 183–8; Lichtenstein, *Labor's War at Home*, pp. 219–30.
37   MacDonald, *Collective Bargaining in the Automobile Industry*, pp. 259–84,
     317–29, 346–67.
38   'The Emergency of Mass Production Unionism', in Brody, *Workers in Industrial
     America*, pp. 82–110; Harris, 'The Snares of Liberalism?'.
39   Lichtenstein, *Labor's War at Home*, pp. 47–51, 56–63, 95–6, 157–71, 182–202.
     On the central role of Congressional conservatism, see Richard Polenberg, 'The
     Decline of the New Deal, 1937–40', and David Brody, 'The New Deal and World
     War II', both in John Braeman, Robert H. Bremner, and David Brody (eds.),
     The New Deal: Volume One, The National Level (Columbus, Ohio, 1975). Cf.
     also Harris, "The Snares of Liberalism", p. 183, who argues that ' "responsible
     unionism" *paid off*. During the war, unions observing the no-strike pledge,
     not pressing the full weight of their bargaining power, obtained insti-
     tutional security of income and membership, a recognized status in the plant
     or firm, liberalized fringe benefits, some extensions of joint consultation and
     bargaining, and arbitration-terminated grievance systems which denied employer
     demands for unilateral authority at the same time as they confined unions and
     their members within the language of contract and time-consuming, legalistic
     procedures. It is not self-evident that "irresponsible unionism" would have
     secured more than this, given the willingness and ability of Congress and the
     administration to strike at non-complying unions in a variety of harmful ways.'
40   Brody, *Workers in Industrial America*, pp. 173–95; Harris, *The Right to
     Manage*, pp. 67–89, 139–58; Lichtenstein, *Labor's War at Home*, pp. 221–31,
     241–5; *idem*, 'Auto Worker Militancy'.
41   On pre-union conditions in the auto plants, see Roger Keeran, *The Communist
     Party and the Auto Workers Unions* (Bloomington, Illinois, 1980), pp. 28–59;
     and Frank Marquart, *An Autoworker's Journal: The UAW from Crusade to
     One-Party Union*, (University Park, Pennsylvania, 1975), pp. 6–39. On the
     electrical industry, see the excellent study by Ronald Schatz, *Electrical Workers:
     A History of Labor at General Electric and Westinghouse, 1923–1960*
     (Champaign, Ill., 1983). The references in this chapter are to his 1977 University
     of Pittsburgh Ph.D. thesis, esp. pp. 67–9, 77–87, 120–2 and 134–6.
42   Neil W. Chamberlain, *The Union Challenge to Management Control*, (New
     York, 1948), pp. 78, 81, 270 and 281; Schatz, *Eletrical Workers*, pp. 127–33;
     the quotation is from pp. 131–2. Seniority had also become an important factor
     in promotions at GE and Westinghouse, though here aggressive local bargaining
     was needed to enforce contractual provisions.
43   Chamberlain, *The Union Challenge to Management Control*, pp. 79–80, 270–1,
     292–3, 309–10; the quotation is from pp. 79–80.
44   Schatz, *Electrical Workers*, pp. 133–9. Foremen also lost the right to assign
     overtime, though they retained some power over piecework allocation and some
     influence over promotion. For Chamberlain's findings on the informal extension
     of union powers in the disciplinary area, see the passages cited in note 41 above.
45   Sumner Slichter, James J. Healy and E. Robert Livernash, *The Impact of*

Collective Bargaining on Management (Washington DC, 1960), pp. 106–9, 139–41, 252–3; the quotations are from pp. 140 and 252, respectively. The authors also found that in many cases seniority had become a constraint on managerial discipline and even in some instances on management's right to subcontract work, as a result of decisions by arbitrators. As one industrial relations director told them. 'It's bad enough to be saddled with the seniority rules we know about, but now we find seniority can be used to support almost any kind of restriction the union dreams up.' Ibid., p. 141. For a more critical view of seniority in the late 1960s, see Richard Herding, *Job Control and Union Structure* (Rotterdam, 1972), pp. 17–28, 145–57; and for contemporary evidence of the constraints placed by seniority rules on the deployment of labour in the auto industry, see Katz, *Shifting Gears.*

46   Slichter, et al., *The Impact of Collective Bargaining on Management*, p. 657; cf. also Orme W. Phelps, *Discipline and Discharge in the Unionized Firm* (Berkeley, 1959), esp. pp. 138–40. While these figures show that management was especially successful in dismissing workers for 'incompetency and/or inefficiency', a more recent case study of a Ford engine plant shows that charges such as 'careless workmanship' or 'excessive scrap' had higher than average rates of redress: Carl Gersuny, *Punishment and Redress in a Modern Factory* (Lexington, Mass., 1973), p. 43.

47   Brody, *Workers in Industrial America*, pp. 195–6; Herding, *Job Control and Union Structure*, pp. 31–4, 133–9; Jack Stieber, 'The Work Rules Issue in the Basic Steel Industry', *Monthly Labor Review* 85, 3 (1962).

48   Herding, *Job Control and Union Structure* pp. 28–30, 124–32 for an account which emphasizes the weight of bureaucratic delays and pressure from the international in curbing production-standard strikes.

49   MacDonald, *Collective Bargaining in the Automobile Industry*, pp. 316, 325–6, 337–8; cf. also Slichter, et al., *The Impact of Collective Bargaining on Management*, pp. 673–74 and 758. In the 1950s, Ford charged that, 'Since 1949 not a single negotiation of an authorized strike notice has been restricted to the so-called strikeable issue. In almost every instance the strikeable issue has been insignificant in the negotiations which we have been forced to undertake with the union to avoid an actual walk-out or to end the walk-out which has already taken place.' Quoted in MacDonald, *Collective Bargaining in the Automobile Industry*, pp. 337–8.

50   James W. Kuhn, 'Electrical Products', in G. G. Somers (ed.), *Collective Bargaining: The Contemporary American Experience*, (Madison, Wisc., 1980), pp. 251–61; Jones, 'Controlling Production on the Shop Floor'.

51   James W. Kuhn, *Bargaining in Grievance Settlement* (New York, 1961), esp. pp. 174–6.

52   For gains made in contract clauses and grievance procedures dealing with production standards in the auto industry during the 1950s and 1960s, see Herding, *Job Control and Union Structure* p. 29. For evidence of the calculated flexibility of Reuther and his associates in incorporating demands from below into their own program, see Jack. W. Skeels, *The Development of Political Stability Within the United Auto Workers Union* (Wisconsin Ph.D. thesis, 1957), pp. 334 ff.; Jack Stieber, *Governing the UAW* (New York, 1962), pp. 153–5; William Serrin, *The Company and the Union* (New York, 1973), *passim* (on the treatment of the '30 and out' demand during the 1970 GM negotiations); and Lichtenstein, *Labor's War at Home*, pp. 146–57, 194–7,

214–15, and 221–9. On the wildcat strike issue and the dismissal of Dalrymple in 1945, see ibid., pp. 197–201; and for the UAW's changing line on local strikes, see the discussion in chapter 5 of this volume.

53 Carter L. Goodrich, *The Frontier of Control: A Study in British Workshop Politics* (1st edition, 1920; rev. edition, London, 1975), pp. 253, 260.

5

Reutherism on the Shop Floor: Union Strategy and Shop-Floor Conflict in the USA 1946–70

Nelson Lichtenstein

In recent years the stable system of labour relations that emerged during the early postwar era has again become an important subject of political and scholarly debate in the United States. While an earlier generation of economists and social scientists often found in the system of pattern bargaining and orderly industrial jurisprudence a bulwark of pluralist democracy and progressive economic advance, contemporary observers have been far more critical. According to the more recent analysis, the 'labour–capital accord' which emerged after the Second World War laid the basis for a crisis-free quarter century of union–management relations, but it also provided the framework for the rigid, hierarchical system of industrial relations that eventually undermined the competitiveness and creativity of the nation's core industrial firms at the same time that it stymied the labour movement's once hopeful effort to refashion industrial America along more genuinely democratic lines.[1]

This study of the United Auto Workers (UAW) examines the part played by the union itself in building this postwar settlement, a process which reflected the dynamic relationship that has existed between the social ideology of the UAW leadership, the collective bargaining strategy it pursued and the character of shop-floor struggle in the core firms of the industry. The essay first argues that the conservative political stalemate that descended upon national politics in the late 1940s subverted the UAW's bold early effort to use the tools of collective bargaining as a lever by which to restructure management of the auto industry and expand the welfare state. The focus of the union's collective bargaining programme was thereafter increasingly restricted. The UAW built a system of pattern bargaining that won large economic benefits for union members and pioneered in the creation of a private 'welfare state' for workers in heavy industry, but this system simultaneously eroded the possibility that the union would serve as the vanguard of social reconstruction so genuinely desired by its leading personality. As we shall see, the burden of this failure would fall with increasing force at the level of shop-floor unionism where the endemic conflict fought by UAW local unions on production standards and other workplace issues could not be resolved within a collective-bargaining framework which largely subordinated this struggle to the maintenance of a stable, patterned system of bargaining with the major corporations of the industry. The net effect was an erosion of the union's internal democratic structures and the persistence of a systemic tension between the goals of local union bargaining and that of the International. This meant that in the early 1980s, when the shop-floor work regime became the central focus of managerial efforts to restructure production, the UAW had no coordinated or effective strategy with which to meet this challenge.

THE VANGUARD IN AMERICA

When Walter Reuther and his 'caucus' consolidated their control of the UAW leadership in late 1947, the union stood at a critical juncture in its history. For the first time in more than a decade the union faced neither a depression economy, wartime regulation nor bitter internal factionalism. It had fully organized all the major firms in the auto industry, and with the postwar models finally coming off the assembly line, the economic leverage of the million-member UAW was sufficient to make labour relations the chief problem confronting the rich and powerful corporations with which the union bargained. Now in command of the UAW, the 40-year old ex-socialist was already widely known for his ambition and social imagination, as well as his capacity for tough political infighting. More than any other unionist of his time, Reuther represented that meeting of organized power and social vision so rare in the history of American labour. 'We are the vanguard in America,' he told the union convention that had given him full control of the UAW, 'We are the architects of the future.'[2]

Reuther's bold assertion encapsulated a distinctive trade-union outlook. As a sort of ideology of modern liberalism, 'Reutherism' came to combine the tactical approach of traditional business unionism with the political economy of liberal Keynesianism and the social vision of Western European social democracy. Throughout the 1940s and even well into the 1950s, the UAW sought to use the tools of collective bargaining as a lever that could shift the balance of forces in the political economy and open wide the welfare state. The UAW would lead progressive forces in the fight against economic insecurity by 'transforming a formless, anarchic economy into a rational industrial society'.[3]

Reutherism's early, radical programme of structural transformation sought to align the union's social and industrial goals with the larger political currents that characterized the late New Deal era. Reuther rose to national prominence in 1940 and 1941 by linking a bold UAW assault on the traditional prerogatives of the auto corporations with President Franklin Roosevelt's ambitious call for the production of 50,000 military aircraft a year. His famous '500 planes a day' plan would accelerate aircraft production by a state-sponsored rationalization of production throughout the entire auto/aircraft industry. Winning wide support among old New Dealers and social-planning liberals, the Reuther Plan was ultimately delayed and then defeated by an automobile industry both hostile to social experimentation and increasingly well represented within the offices of the government's wartime production agencies.[4]

The Reuther plan nevertheless cast a long shadow, for it contained hallmarks of the strategic approach so characteristic of 1940s Reutherism: an assault on management's traditional power made in the name of social and economic efficiency, an appeal for public support in the larger liberal interest, and an effort to shift power relations within the structure of industry and politics, usually by means of a tripartite governmental entity empowered to plan for whole sections of the economy. Thus, toward the end of the war Reuther proposed a Peace Production Board that would preside over the reconversion of defence plants to ensure the mass production of railroad cars and working-class housing in the postwar era. The Board would establish a central research clearing house, increase product diversification (build a small people's car), end seasonality of production and set up 'technical commando units' composed of engineers, draughtsmen and tool and die workers that would eliminate production bottlenecks and increase efficiency in marginal firms.[5]

The redistributive and Keynesian orientation of Reutherite social unionism became evident during the UAW's dramatic 113-day strike against General Motors in the winter of 1945–6. Reflecting the contemporary fear that a postwar economic collapse might come if working-class incomes were not sustained at their wartime levels, Reuther and the UAW put forward the novel demand that industry pace setter General Motors raise wages by some 30 per cent without increasing the price of its product. Like the 500 planes a day plan of 1940, the GM strike programme also made a strong appeal to the public interest, this time not so much in terms of rationalized production and democratic control, but as part of the emerging Keynesian consensus that a substantial boost in mass purchasing power would be necessary to avoid a postwar depression. Thus Reuther and his supporters consciously politicized the GM strike by challenging managerial control of product pricing and by emphasizing the stake the consuming public had in the victory of the autoworkers. These UAW demands raised, if only implicitly, fundamental issues over the control of the political economy.[6]

REUTHERISM AND AMERICAN POLITICS

The GM strike represented the apogee of the UAW's effort to make a radical transformation in its bargaining relationships with the large automakers. Thereafter Reutherism lost much of its politically imaginative quality. It tied its fate more closely to that of the industry and increasingly subordinated the endemic shop-floor struggle over working conditions and production standards to the UAW's national bargaining programme. As a union political–economic strategy, Reutherism moved from a demand for structural changes in the management of the auto industry, and by implication in the political economy as a whole, to negotiation of an increasingly privatized welfare programme that left unchallenged essential power relationships in the industry. In this shift, Reutherite collective bargaining paralleled the social and intellectual path taken by modern liberalism itself. Just as postwar liberalism gradually reduced its commitment to national planning and eschewed issues of social and economic control, so too did Reutherite social unionism abandon the quest for labour participation in running the automobile industry. And just as liberalism increasingly came to define itself as largely concerned with the maintenance of economic growth and an expansion of the welfare state, so too did the UAW redefine its mission in these terms as well.[7]

This constriction of the Reutherite social vision was predicated upon two characteristics of the postwar political economy. First, the postwar automobile industry was prosperous enough to accommodate the UAW on strictly business–union terms. In the years after the Second World War, the American automobile corporations dominated a continental market and held a rate of productivity growth which outstripped that of most other industrial sectors. Within little more than a decade, General Motors and the Ford Motor Company built scores of new plants, almost doubled their respective capacities and increased their workforces by about 30 per cent. Chrysler and the independent producers, like Packard, Studebaker and American Motors were not so self-reliant, but their weakness merely heightened the importance of the pattern-setting collective bargaining exercise in which the UAW and the Big Two engaged.[8]

Second, American politics shifted to the right in the immediate postwar era. The Republican capture of Congress in 1946, the subsequent passage of the Taft–Hartley Act and the defeat of most Fair Deal welfare state initiatives after 1948 all limited the possibility that union leaders like Walter Reuther could forge a postwar link between union bargaining strategy and government economic policy. Meanwhile, the industrial union movement's opposition to the third-party campaign of Henry Wallace and the defeat or expulsion of the Communists from within its own ranks had the practical effect of robbing these new unions of their oppositional character and welding them ever more closely to the Democratic Party. Thus Walter Reuther, who in earlier years had often spoken of the need for labour to form its own party, abandoned this perspective after the 1948 elections, even as a political threat to be held in reserve.[9]

The defensive political posture adopted by the union movement, in turn enhanced the apparent appeal of a more traditional brand of private sector collective bargaining. For example, the conservative victory in the 1946 congressional elections had a dramatic impact on Reuther's own thinking. In a radio debate of May 1946, well before the elections, Reuther told his audience that rhetoric about a 'government-controlled economy' was a big-business scare tactic. The real question, he said, is '*how much* government control and for whose benefit'. But in the wake of the massive Republican victory of November 1946, Reuther made a rhetorical about-face, now urging 'free labor' and 'free management' to join in solving their problems, or as the UAW President put it in another context, 'I'd rather negotiate with General Motors than with the government . . . General Motors has no army.'[10]

'THE TREATY OF DETROIT'

This retreat to a more privatized conception of what labour could accomplish meant that UAW leaders were forced to make agreements with employers on far narrower and less favourable economic terrain. Reuther therefore proved receptive to the far-reaching proposals offered by General Motors in 1948. GM had long sought the containment of UAW power, and to achieve this end it was willing to make substantial economic accommodation to the new Reuther leadership. The Corporation realized that disruptive strikes and contentious annual wage negotiations, especially if couched as part of a broader offensive against corporate power, merely served to embitter shop-floor labour relations and hamper the company's long-range planning. GM sought to dampen the impact of the postwar inflationary surge, negotiate multi-year contracts and assure management of a free hand in rebuilding its automotive empire. GM therefore offered the UAW a contract which included two pillars of the postwar social order: first an automatic cost of living adjustment keyed to the general price index, and second, a 2 per cent 'annual improvement factor' wage increase designed to reflect, if only partially, the still larger annual rise in GM productivity.[11]

Two years later GM offered an even richer package: a $100-a-month pension, an improved cost of living adjustment, a more substantial annual improvement factor and an unprecedented five-year contract, all of which would make predictable GM labour costs during the Corporation's mammoth expansion programme of the early 1950s. Unlike the Reuther 500 planes a day plan or even the left-Keynesian GM strike programme of 1945-6, this collective-bargaining compact was pacesetting precisely because it did not threaten structural change within the industry. *Fortune Magazine* declared the 1950 UAW–GM contract the 'Treaty of Detroit' because of its promise of social peace and confirmation of managerial initiative. 'GM may have paid a billion for peace' declared the magazine, 'but it got a bargain. General Motors has regained control over one of the crucial management functions . . . long range scheduling of production, model changes, and tool and plant investment.'[12]

The Treaty of Detroit had a profound, long-range impact on the internal structure of the UAW and the character of auto-industry industrial relations. It symbolized and helped consolidate the stable and relatively centralized bargaining structure which would characterize the auto industry for the next quarter century. There were two reasons for this, the first political, the second structural. Before 1950 annual contract renegotiations had helped sustain and channel political debate and union consciousness at the local level; the end of the annual contract round, along with the simultaneous and not unrelated elimination of internal union factionalism, helped subordinate local union initiative to that of the International and reduce the level of social and political awareness among rank and file workers. Throughout the 1950s many union radicals, who had once given larger meaning to local union politics, were either co-opted onto the International union staff or politically isolated by the sophisticated mobilization of the union's considerable organizational strength.[13] As an institution, the UAW increasingly came to resemble a combination political machine and welfare bureaucracy which 'serviced' the membership and 'policed' the national contract. Conventions were made biennial rather than yearly, and while UAW membership grew but 30 per cent, the staff nearly doubled within the next seven years.[14]

Second, the 1950 contract put the UAW in an ambiguous relationship with regard to local union efforts to maintain satisfactory working conditions and resist management 'speed-up' efforts. National leaders of the UAW increasingly focused their attention on those elements of the effort bargain which could be most easily quantified and monetized, generally wage and fringe-benefit improvements in the national contract. Those chronic, daily conflicts involving production standards, management prerogatives, work assignments and the like were not ignored, but from a leadership perspective they took a necessarily subordinate place in the bargaining agenda. Moreover, since the five-year contract provided management with an unprecedented degree of certainty about wage costs, it literally forced these companies to look at how they might increase productivity. This would be especially important for firms like Chrysler and Studebaker, whose relative labour costs were much higher than at GM. The contract's annual improvement factor clause was predicated upon a steady and uniform reduction in unit labour costs, not all of which might be won through technological innovation. In summing up the impact of the UAW–GM contract, the respected labour economist Frederick Harbison concluded, 'This kind of collective bargaining calls for intelligent trading rather than table-pounding, for diplomacy rather than belligerency, and for internal union discipline rather than grass roots rank and file activity.'[15]

PENSION POLITICS

The impact of this new bargaining environment can be seen by examining the relative difficulty involved in the negotiation of two pioneering innovations on the UAW agenda; first pensions, then the Guaranteed Annual Wage. Union demands for company funded pensions became important during the late 1940s, largely because of the failure of an increasingly conservative Congress to raise social security benefits during that inflationary era. The pension demand was first raised at the Ford Motor Company in 1947, where an ageing workforce, the oldest in the industry, and a new management, sensitive to social issues, seemed to provide the best circumstance for winning such a contractual innovation. Reflecting an older style of highly politicized, decentralized bargaining, the pension demand was championed by leaders of the giant UAW Ford Local at River Rouge, and by Ford Department Director Richard Leonard. The 60,000-member local was a centre of opposition to Reuther's still tentative leadership of the UAW, while Leonard was an important factional opponent.[16]

Though a pension-plan victory would have aided anti-Reuther forces in the UAW, their quest was complicated by Ford's simultaneous demand for assurances against wildcat strikes, and by the elimination of the informal paid lunch period which had taken root in many Rouge shops. Moreover, there was much controversy over the technical requirements of the pension plan, and much confusion within the ranks of Ford Local 600 as to the actual cost of the plan in equivalent cents per hour. As a consequence, union and company agreed to an unusual referendum vote on the issue, in which workers turned down the plan by a three to one margin.[17]

Two years later the Reuther leadership of the UAW took command of pension negotiations at Ford. Success in securing such a pension was essential to bring the UAW abreast of other major unions like the Miners and the Steelworkers, who had company funded pensions high on their agenda, set the pattern for the rest of the automobile industry, and also aid Reuther in finally building a real base of support at the Rouge. But his pension programme was again held hostage to more pressing local issues. The course of events surrounding Local 600's famous 'speed-up strike' of May 1949 provides a spectacular example of the very real conflict that could develop between a local's determination to resist management's shop-floor offensive and the larger bargaining strategy of the national union to which it belonged.

In late 1948 the Ford Motor Company swung into mass production of its first postwar model. Under enormous pressure to increase output for a car-starved public, Ford engineers determined to tighten production standards in all their facilities, but especially at the Rouge, the heart of the company's manufacturing and assembly operations. In the 'B' building assembly plant, management authorized foremen to increase the line speed above their own time-study 'standard' to make up for those minutes when routine breakdowns had halted the conveyor. UAW Local 600 denounced this policy in early 1949 and opened a fruitless series of negotiations to modify it. The issue became a central one in the politically powerful local. Following an impressive strike vote, the UAW International authorized the work stoppage, and in the first complete shutdown since 1941, 62,000 struck the Rouge for some 24 days in May 1949.[18]

Although the UAW had authorized the strike, Reuther was reluctant to make the strike a full-scale showdown with Ford, because a lengthy stoppage would disrupt his efforts to secure from the company the long-sought pension plan. During the negotiations Ford managers complained bitterly that wildcat strikes and other forms of disruptive shop-floor activity threatened to undermine good-faith bargaining at the highest levels. In turn, Reuther told Ford executives: 'Have you ever thought that to get control the leadership must fight to get the machinery necessary for control.'[19] He was therefore amenable when Ford executives agreed that the issue go before a special arbitration panel empowered to determine if temporary increases in the line speed were detrimental to worker health and safety. This postponed the issue for several weeks, took the International off the hook, and allowed the union to get on with what Reuther considered his central task: renegotiation and improvement of the national agreement. When more than a month later the panel promulgated a decision, the award proved anticlimatic and largely ineffective at resolving the central issue that had touched off the strike.[20]

THE GUARANTEED ANNUAL WAGE

By way of contrast, the UAW campaign to win the Guaranteed Annual Wage (GAW) in the mid-1950s reveals quite graphically the transformation that had taken place in the theory and practice of Reutherite social unionism. Union pioneers had long demanded the annual wage as a way to reduce cyclical unemployment and dignify the labour of hourly paid blue-collar workers. In the immediate postwar era serious discussion of the annual wage was near the top of the union policy agenda. A War Labor Board commission reported that guaranteed annual wage systems could work if they were coordinated with state unemployment insurance, while Reuther, in a characteristically radical vein, argued that a tripartite auto-industry council could eliminate seasonal employment changes by enforcing a sliding scale of auto prices designed to even out demand throughout the year. The UAW set up a task force as early as 1950 to prepare a collectively bargained annual-wage proposal while the Ford Motor Company, the UAW's key negotiating partner on this issue, began work on its own proposals. Unlike the pension campaign, there was little confusion or divided counsel on the union or company side. Sumner Slichter, the noted Harvard economist, would later declare the elaborate and well publicized struggle over GAW the 'classic' set of collective bargaining negotiations in the postwar era.[21]

The UAW's 1955 annual wage proposals were prototypical of the union leadership's mid-century strategy of incremental social advance, the 'foot in the door' approach to contract innovation, now substituted for the bolder approach of the mid-1940s, which had seen collective bargaining as a device for transforming management behaviour or as a lever to win structural changes in the political economy. The initial 1955 version of the Guaranteed Annual Wage was rather like the Holy Roman Empire, neither guaranteed, annual nor a wage. It was best described by its new name: Supplemental Unemployment Benefits (SUB). Finally to bring the 1955 SUB up to 95 per cent of straight-time take-home pay for 52 weeks of idleness required four contract renegotiations over more than 12 years. Moreover, the SUB agreement represented a management commitment of money, not of production policy. Ford and other auto makers agreed to set up a fund from which a supplementary unemployment benefit would be paid to guarantee laid-off workers a total, with unemployment insurance, of a proportion of their straight-time after-tax pay. The corporation would pay into the reserve fund only so long as it was below a certain figure. The UAW had hoped that these financial incentives would 'compel the industry, by imposing penalties for instability, to schedule steady employment for its workers', but the big auto companies ran their plants pretty much as before, and whatever incentive the corporations might have had for avoiding layoffs and keeping the reserve fund full evaporated when the UAW later dipped into this kitty for additional contract benefits like severance pay, Christmas bonuses and short-work-week supplements. In the end GAW came to represent not the stable work schedule demanded by the union but a sort of company-financed insurance policy.[22]

Finally, the big push for GAW in 1955 was almost entirely a leadership initiative. During the sustained auto boom of the mid-1950s, fully employed auto workers could see little immediate need for an annual wage, while from the leadership's perspective, the boom made GAW easier to achieve because the initial expense of this benefit would be relatively low. To the extent that popular interest in a particular collective bargaining initiative did exist in the mid-1950s, it lay in another direction. Secondary union leaders overwhelmingly opposed another five-year contract because they found it an inflexible and debilitating framework in a period of rapid economic and technological change. Moreover, many argued that employment stability could best be achieved through the depression-era UAW demand for 30 hours work for 40 hours pay. Adroit at accommodating pressure from below, the UAW's top leadership thereafter reduced most contracts to but three years' duration, and although they began planning an effort to gradually phase in the 30-hour week, the sharp recession of 1957–8 threw the union onto the defensive, ending the possibility of progress on this front.[23]

NATIONAL BARGAINING AND SHOP-FLOOR PROBLEMS

If Reutherism had reached a mature stability in these years, the 1955 contract settlement also ushered in the start of an era in which the divergent interests of the national UAW and the shop floor became increasingly manifest. Reuther probably recognized this problem, if only inadvertently, when he spoke before the National Ford Council in the midst of the GAW talks. After outlining the union's future goals: higher wages, better medical and hospital care, more secure pensions, the UAW president concluded, 'And then, in addition to these national things, there are local problems that are close to the Ford workers' daily needs. We have to work on those, and we shouldn't permit the local things to get lost in the shuffle.'[24]

That local problems had in fact been short-changed became apparent immediately after Ford signed its 1955 contract. On June 7, the same day that Detroit newspapers reported the GAW breakthrough, 114,000 of 140,000 Ford workers stopped work in 89 plants and parts depots. The *Detroit Free Press*, perhaps somewhat bewildered, hailed these strikes as the 'revolt of the victors', and reported that about 75 per cent of the Rouge plant negotiating committee was dissatisfied with the new contract. Actually, these stoppages, while technically unauthorized, were led by elected local leaders and coincided, more or less, with the deadline set for the UAW's authorized strike that the last-minute national settlement averted. These stoppages were not protests against the GAW, but were directed at specific plant-level issues that had been left unresolved. Of most importance were the grievances of skilled maintenance and tool and die workers who felt apprenticeship standards in decline and lines of demarcation under attack. Moreover, since they had been fully employed for more than a decade SUB was of little use: they were most aggrieved by the wage differential that existed between them and AFL craftsmen or the non-union skilled trades in Michigan job shops.[25] Although the stoppages lasted but a few days, these strikes set an important precedent; from this point on, local issue bargaining would become of increasing importance, and no national UAW contract would be settled without a series of local work stoppages over plant issues.

In recent years some scholars have argued that such bargaining over local issues was an important part of the process by which unions like the UAW were able to win a substantial degree of 'job control' at the shop-floor level, largely through the negotiation of an elaborate system of job classifications and seniority bumping rights that limited management authority and strengthened traditional shop practices.[26] Indeed, such work rules existed, and were expanded by local unions whenever possible. But the union effort to control the shop-floor work environment was clearly on the defensive in the postwar era; and work rules were less the product of union power than a consequence of its defeat.

In the UAW's early years a vigorous shop steward system, backed by the occasional use of extra-contractual collective action, had defended a system of shop-floor 'mutuality' which challenged managerial hierarchies and made plastic the division of authority in the shop. At the apogee of union influence, stewards often held an informal veto over management selection of foremen, the determination of job assignments, the pace of production. But this system was subversive of the industrial-relations structure being built in the early postwar era. Denounced by corporate management, deplored by the new generation of government mediators and academy-based arbitrators, and finally renounced by UAW officials, this steward-centred shop-floor system was gradually eroded (first at GM and then at Ford and Chrysler) and superseded by a more formal grievance procedure and an increasingly elaborate set of guidelines designed to define both the extent and the limits of management authority at the shop-floor level.[27]

Auto management's offensive outlook on this issue is clearly reflected in the assessment of Ford labour-relations officer John DeMotte, who reported that some of the least publicized but most arduous conflict during the Corporation's 1955 bargaining round came in its dealings with newly elected local negotiating committees.

Their solution to most of the things they are unhappy about in the shop is the simple one of eliminating by contract most of management's rights to exercise its discretion or to take unilateral action. They would substitute for these management rights, either rigid rules or a requirement of union consent. They are at a loss to understand how their predecessors could have been cajoled out of providing this obvious remedy in past negotiations. And they are determined not to be similarly hoodwinked. But, in a very real sense, it is necessary in each set of our contract negotiations to argue out all over again the vital necessity for preserving those areas of management flexibility and discretion which are basic to the effective and efficient conduct of our business, and to the continued vitality of the automotive industry.[28]

The multi-year contracts that came to characterize collective bargaining in the 1950s exacerbated this conflict. Local issues piled up as technology, management policy and employment levels changed. The core of local-issue bargaining involved the physical working conditions of the plant (lockers, heat, toilets, cleanliness, parking lots) safety and health (gloves, coveralls, air pollution, grease removal, lighting) and general plant administration (scheduling, posting of vacancies, private telephone calls, payment times). Seemingly minor demands were often intimately connected with the larger issues of wages, hours of work and the distribution of authority in the plant. Thus a dispute about the location of a parking lot might, in fact, involve the total length of the work day. The removal of air pollution might require that an entire production facility face reorganization, while a change in job posting procedures often became a bitter contest over management's desire to promote out-of-line seniority.[29] For example, during the 1964 contract talks, GM Ternstedt Local 326 in Flint put more than 121 local issues on the table. It took 51 meetings and more than a month's time to discuss, withdraw, resolve or compromise the Local's demands.[30] The number of local grievances left unresolved at General Motors increased substantially throughout this era, rising from 11,600 a year in 1958 to over 39,000 annually in 1970. 'It used to be that you faced up to the boss every year and told him what you thought and what your problems were and you fought to an agreement,' reported a former auto worker, but 'under the three year contracts, you'd wind up with a table full. In no way could you resolve them all. And when the economic settlement came along, the local issues were shoved under the rug.'[31]

THE 'SPEED-UP' ISSUE AND LOCAL STRIKES

In the automobile industry, conflict over the pace of work – production-standards disputes – were the most chronic of local union grievances, and the issue which created the most tension between rank and file workers and higher-level union officials. The auto union had been founded in opposition to management's authority to 'speed up' production, and indeed much evidence suggests that, in many UAW-organized shops, the union did win a degree of control over the work quota. The situation at Ford was typical. In the early 1940s, Ford's recognition of the UAW touched off a virtual revolution on the shop floor. Workers ignored petty shop rules that regulated smoking, eating and talking, unpopular foremen were forced out of their departments, production standards were set only after checking with the department committeeman. UAW Ford contract language reflected the shop-floor reality. The original 1941 agreement contained no mention of production standards, while the second contract signed a year later merely set forth the principle of a 'fair day's work for a fair day's pay'.[32]

In the immediate postwar era, Ford's new management team was determined to win back substantial control of the production process from union committeemen and informal shop groups that held it hostage. The 1946 contract contained the first specific clause giving management the right to determine, maintain and enforce work standards. The Ford Motor Company could now fire any employee who refused to meet established standards or who 'participate[d] in any plan to control or limit the amount or speed of production'.[33] Ford local unions, like those in other UAW-organized shops, had the right to strike over such issues once they had won International Executive Board authorization, but as the 1949 'speed-up' strike at the Rouge demonstrated, the disruptive impact such stoppages might have on national contract negotiations meant that in the future local strikes would be subordinated to the International's larger bargaining strategy.

The production-standard problem remained an issue which the UAW could neither ignore nor solve. At every UAW convention, the leadership put forward a lengthy resolution declaring, among other things, that 'the fight against speed up must be spearheaded at the plant level . . . The fight to protect the workers . . . requires that the members and the local union leadership be forever vigilant, disciplined in the use of the machinery provided in our agreements and prepared to carry just grievances to the picket line when peaceful negotiations fail.'[34] But the UAW bargained with the most powerful corporations in the world, Walter Reuther reminded his membership time and again. 'This requires central direction in terms of timing and strategy and tactics, and if we dilute this central direction that is built around authorization of strikes . . . You dissipate the power of the union at the bargaining table.'[35]

The degree of control UAW leaders exercised over the local strike weapon was made graphically manifest during two episodes that took place during the decade of the 1950s. In 1951 and 1952 Reuther and other leaders of the UAW found the five-year contract they had so recently signed a growing embarrassment. The Cost of Living Adjustment (COLA) formula did not fully compensate for Korean war inflation, but of more importance was the simple unpopularity of the long-term contract among many of Reuther's own partisans. In early 1952 therefore, Reuther demanded that GM and Ford reopen the master contract on the grounds that such agreements were 'living documents' that must reflect changed economic conditions. When the companies refused, the UAW authorized a series of strikes over production standards. The most important of these came at Ford's foundry at Canton, Ohio, later dubbed the 'Canton Can Opener' because of the key role this crippling stoppage played in forcing Ford to finally reopen the company-wide master contract and accede to union demands for an across-the-board wage increase.[36]

Five years later, during the recession of 1957–8, the union clamped down hard on local strikes. Until production picked up and the new model year abated, the UAW vowed to 'rock and roll' with plant supervision by keeping the workforce on the job despite the expiration of the old contract and the union's inability to sign another. The International adopted this restrictive policy for two reasons. First, it wished to avoid dissipation of union strength to make credible a strike threat when master contracts were renegotiated in the fall of 1958. Second, the UAW was not unaware of the pressures under which those auto companies in competition with highly efficient GM now did business. Chrysler, for example, had seen its market share fall by 50 per cent during the 1950s, and a new management group was determined that the company would not go the way of Kaiser-Frazer or Studebaker-Packard. Hiring industrial engineers from both Ford and GM, Chrysler completely re-evaluated its work standards at the start of the 1957 model year. Despite intense opposition from the company's big Detroit locals, Chrysler cut back the power of the well-established steward system, tightened up on production standards and eliminated 20,000 jobs over the next two years.[37]

Since Reuther and other UAW leaders were extremely reluctant to break the national wage pattern to aid Chrysler, they undertook the more subtle task of allowing the company greater latitude in revising its work standards, plant rules and seniority classification system.[38] Chrysler locals demanded authorization to initiate production-standard strikes, but the International insisted that they postpone any action until the economic package had been signed. Such a policy required organizational fortitude and political skill. 'I have never been under greater pressure than I was in that period, 'admitted UAW Secretary-Treasurer Emil Mazey, 'It was a painful process to explain to them [the locals] the policy of the organization.'[39]

GRIEVANCE BARGAINING

The decline of the informal system of shop-floor 'mutuality' and the rise of what David Brody has termed the 'workplace rule of law' put the UAW cadre – its committeemen and local officers – under tremendous pressure. When work stoppages, slowdowns or other infractions of workplace legality occurred these union representatives were often reduced to the status of contract policemen who could be severely penalized themselves if they failed to take vigorous action to end extra-contractual violations of the established work order. Meanwhile, shop disputes reduced to writing took between two and three months to work their way up the grievance ladder.[40] 'Time and time again management does things that I know it has a right to do under the contract,' reported one Chrysler union official in the early 1950s, 'but the men don't know it. If I explain to them that the company has the right under four or five rulings made previously they get sore at me.' As a consequence, politically savvy committeemen 'become demagogues. They tend to fake on all this stuff. They write grievances when they know they shouldn't, the art of buck passing is developed to the nth degree.'[41]

Indeed grievance bargaining in UAW organized shops accelerated dramatically from the late 1950s onward. In part this represented an index of the bureaucratic routinization that increasingly governed shop-floor industrial relations in the decades after 1950, especially that which reflected the codification of the management prerogatives outlined above. 'Management moves and the union grieves' became the well-worn cliché to describe this relationship.[42] The annual model change and the daily variation in body mix kept work assignments, manning schedules and production technology in relatively constant flux. The fight against speed-up was a Sisyphean struggle. As one Ford local reported in 1961, 'We had some 350 production standard disputes . . . settled to the satisfaction of the parties, but we found that in a number of cases after the disputes were settled, management would change the method, operation and in some cases the work assignment of the employees. As a result of these changes other standard disputes developed, and we found ourselves going back thru [sic] the same occurrences.'[43]

But grievance bargaining is also a social phenomenon in its own right, an important index of shop-floor tensions, part of the trench warfare of the class conflict in the unionized workplace. As Sidney Lens once put it, the grievance procedure is an 'opportunity for realignment of forces, for fencing and minor skirmishes, for strengthening of positions.'[44] At the Ford Motor Company, to take but one example, the proportion of grievances over the issue of 'foreman working' rose fourfold between 1950 and 1964. It was the first or second most numerous grievance in the early 1960s. The Ford–UAW contract provided that under certain circumstances these management representatives could work, so a high proportion of these grievances were found to be without merit. Yet the very act of filing such a grievance registered a general complaint by the worker against the foreman, thus providing a partial index of the esteem in which the former held the latter.[45]

At General Motors, the sheer volume of grievance activity also increased enormously, about tenfold between 1947 and 1980, although the size of the UAW-represented workforce grew but 30 per cent. The number of grievances filed first rose sharply in the 1950s, especially during the latter years of the five-year contract, and then again during the long industry boom extending from 1960 to 1973 (Table 5.1). Although grievance activity declined during the industry's periodic recessions, the general rate of grievance handling per GM employee marched steadily upward throughout the postwar era. Increasingly, these disputes were resolved at the lowest step of the grievance procedure, the level of foreman–worker interaction; the proportion of grievances resolved by the UAW's local bargaining committees and the plant management, or by higher-level union officials and the corporate personnel department has declined rather dramatically since the early 1950s.[46]

Table 5.1   Grievance Rate per 100 Employees General Motors

Year	Rate	Year	Rate	Year	Rate
1947	12.8	1958	27	1970	52.8
1950	14.9	1961	31.7	1973	71.9
1954	22.6	1964	42	1976	61.3
1955	26.2	1967	53.8	1979	69

Source: data courtesy Craig Zabala.

These patterns demonstrate the high level of shop-floor tension that has existed throughout at least the latter half of the postwar era. Demographic changes in the automobile industry workforce – the concentration of blacks in urban factories and the influx of young workers influenced by the social and political currents of the 1960s – have often been given great weight in explaining the rise of rank and file militancy. But in fact the unionized workforce was relatively stable in the 1960s. As of 1967 more than 65 per cent were UAW veterans with ten or more years' experience. The growing shop-floor dissidence of that era was in fact symptomatic of the larger and longer-range phenomenon which Reutherite social unionism failed to address.

This was evident in two UAW membership surveys which Walter Reuther himself authorized in 1961 and 1967. In general, auto workers held a strongly favourable impression of the UAW and they backed the union's then-current efforts to secure better retirement and SUB benefits and greater protection against layoffs and short work weeks. They valued the International as a wage-setting and welfare institution, although a remarkably high proportion of UAW members were unclear as to the actual composition of their fringe-benefit package. However, when it came to an assessment of the union on the local level, workers were far more critical. While two-thirds of all production workers held a favourable impression of the UAW International, only about half thought the same of their local union or their shop committeemen, a rating somewhat lower in 1967 than 1961. When asked if they thought their committeeman was a 'stand up guy who protects the workers', only about 16 per cent answered in the affirmative in 1967, down from 26 per cent six years earlier. Workers approved of strikes over workloads and local issues to a greater degree than over the national contract, but they were also more likely to think the handling of such strikes 'only fair' or 'poor'.[47]

THE END OF REUTHERISM

Beginning in the late 1950s, collective bargaining in the automobile industry began a subtle shift which focused it somewhat less on the national contract and somewhat more on local working conditions. In part this represented the end of the era in which Reuther could produce one dramatic contract innovation after another, and in part it represented an accommodation by key UAW officials to the increasingly well-voiced demands generated from below. The companies favoured local bargaining as well; they wanted to negotiate important issues involving automation, manning schedules and health and safety on a plant-by-plant basis so as to sever as much as possible the link between shop-floor problems and national wage and benefit issues. But none of this represented a devolution of centralized union control, at least not on issues considered vital to the UAW–Big Three relationship. Local strikes still had to be authorized by the International and local agreements had to be ratified at that level as well and were to last the full term of the national agreement.

In the 1960s the UAW authorized an increasing number of local strikes over shop conditions. These were of two sorts, those which took place in the wake of each master contract settlement, and those which were authorized during the term of the contract itself. While the former could involve demands over virtually any question, the latter were almost exclusively concerned with production standards and health and safety issues. In part such strikes, especially those over a build-up of production-standard grievances, were a substitute for the job actions and local wildcats which had dominated plant-level strike activity as late as the mid-1950s. Ford, and especially Chrysler, took advantage of the 1957–8 recession to crack down heavily on these work stoppages, but even GM, which had always maintained a reputation for tight labour discipline, saw a reduction in unauthorized strike activity after the late 1950s. Meanwhile, authorized local strikes at GM, which had hardly been noticeable before 1956, increased moderately up to the mid-1960s and substantially thereafter. Total man-hours lost in these local strikes far exceeded time lost in the still sizeable number of wildcat stoppages in the industry.

Table 5.2   Local strikes–Yearly Average

	Chrysler		Ford		General Motors	
	Wildcat	Authorized	Wildcat	Authorized	Wildcat	Authorized
1937–40	56.2	.5	—	—	—	—
1941–5	144.8	0	151.5	0	71	.2
1946–50	100.8	.5	63	2	25.6	.2
1951–5	157.6	.2	86.3	1.7	43.8	.4
1956–60	241	1.8	—	—	22.4	4
1961–5	15	1.8	—	—	18.4	4.6
1966–70	58.4	2.4	—	—	28	10
1971–5	49.4	3.8	—	—	16	9
1976–8	45.7	8.3	—	—	8.7	7

Note: Despite the unavailability of Ford data, the situation there mirrored that at GM and Chrysler. Although the company complained in 1955 that the number of unauthorized strikes was 30 times the level at GM, a decade later Ford reported its problems with such stoppages greatly diminished. Ford Motor Company, 'Collective Bargaining Review and Proposals', July 16 1964, in box 18, Bannon Collection.

Sources: Chrysler Corporation, Strikes and Manhours Lost (US Locations); and General Motors, Annual Work Stoppage Totals, Summary Report (US Operations), both courtesy Sean Flaherty, Department of Economics, Franklin and Marshall College. Ford data from 'Study on Work Stoppages', box 'Ford Department', Bannon Collection, Archives of Labor History, Wayne State University.

The massive set of 1964 strikes at GM are illustrative of the new focus in auto industry bargaining. With the return of high levels of automobile production in the early 1960s work-load problems were a burning issue. In 1963 more than a third of the top officials in the UAW production locals had been denied re-election in campaigns that turned on this grievance. 'Work Standards – this is the high point – what we get from the company here is what makes or breaks you in this job,' reported one Flint local official. Characterizing GM as a 'huge, dehumanized production machine', Reuther and GM Department Director Leonard Woodcock began a campaign denouncing the industry's 'gold-plated sweatshops' while championing demands for 'dignity and humanity on the job'.[48] General Motors was recognized as the greatest offender, and in the contract negotiations of 1964 the UAW pressed this issue strongly. GM negotiators thought all the talk of improving local working conditions could readily be boiled down to a five-hour increase in the grievance handling time of the nearly 1,800 union committeemen at the corporation. When GM vice-president Louis Seaton offered such an increase at the 11th hour of the contract talks, Reuther eagerly accepted, thinking it sufficient to assuage local leaders and avert a strike. But both the UAW and GM had miscalculated. Unresolved local issues were of such magnitude that an 11-member negotiating team from the GM locals felt it essential to turn down the contract. The UAW was forced to call a week-long company-wide strike, and although all national contract issues were soon easily cleared up, GM was effectively shut down for an additional 31 days until the bulk of the UAW–GM locals had signed separate local agreements.[49]

Except for prolonged strikes in key plants, the UAW held somewhat aloof from these local disputes, allowing each union to 'slug it out' with management. In fact, the International often had little direct knowledge of the issues involved in many of these post-settlement stoppages. Usually, these local strikes ended in piecemeal fashion, with only the most recalcitrant local leaderships pushed to settlement by the International. 'Politically, the line of least resistance of international officials is to let local militants learn the lessons of reality the hard way,' commented Ford labour-relations official Malcolm Denise with some insight.[50] Thus after the conclusion of the GM local strikes in 1964, Walter Reuther declared that 'No strike in the history of our union . . . and in the history of the American labor movement has yielded the kind of meaningful results . . . as this strike.' But Louis Seaton, GM's vice-president for personnel, replied that as far as he could tell, no major breakthroughs had been made in local bargaining. 'We haven't agreed to anything that is going to impair our responsibility to our shareholders to run an efficient business . . . and that's what this strike has been about.'[51]

Until the late 1970s, automobile-industry industrial relations remained relatively stable, but at least two characteristics of the 1964 bargaining round contained a hint of the difficulties which would engulf the union during the more unfavourable environment a decade later. First, the UAW no longer sought to forge an intimate link between the political process, collective bargaining and structural reform within the auto industry. The union programme was essentially one of incremental economic advance, especially if it involved expansion of the private welfare regime which the union had pioneered in the late 1940s. The union's leaders proved increasingly reluctant to conduct lengthy, company-wide strikes against any of the Big Three auto makers, unless, as in the case of GM in 1970, a stoppage was necessary to maintain such a pillar of the postwar union–management relationship as the uncapped cost-of-living adjustment. Second, the modest increase in plant-level militancy engendered by the civil rights movement and the high-employment work environment of the late 1960s and early 1970s left remarkably little institutional legacy. Despite the well-publicized interest in the 'humanization' of working conditions, no system of shop-floor power sharing returned to even the most well-organized locals, nor did the UAW national leadership develop a coordinated strategy for meeting this challenge. Thus, such nationally publicized strikes of the early 1970s as those at GM's Lordstown and Norwood assembly plants were at best standoffs for the locals involved, as were the 1973 series of Chrysler walkouts that the UAW itself encouraged as an alternative to a company-wide strike.[52]

Given this background it is not surprising that the UAW had few resources, institutional or ideological, with which to meet the drastically more adverse economic scene of the last five years. Although much of the contemporary discussion of industry-labour relations echoes early Reutherite concern with job security and worker participation in management decision making, the invocation in the 1980s of the social rhetoric of the 1940s serves largely to obscure the crucial differences between the two periods. Because of its contemporary weakness and timidity, the UAW's historic effort to use the tools of collective bargaining as a means to restructure the auto industry has been turned on its head, and it is the auto companies who now use the changing character of the industry as a lever to dismantle such long-standing fruits of UAW power as wage standardization and pattern bargaining. Meanwhile, at the local level, the endemic conflict fought by workers on production standards and other shop-floor issues has become increasingly manifest, but these chronic problems are largely unresolvable within a collective bargaining framework which has long subordinated this struggle. The threat of plant closures and outsourcing during the 1980–2 recession has thus given the renewed interest in shop-floor issues, in work rules, worker–foremen relationships and the quality of work life, a managerially oriented character far different than it had in the years when the balance of power was not tipped so decisively against auto workers and their union.

NOTES

1 Of the older school see Derek C. Bok and John T. Dunlop, *Labor and the American Community* (New York, 1970); scholars who emphasize the degree to which the current system of industrial relations has impaired efficiency and innovation include Harry Katz, *Shifting Gears: Changing Labor Relations in the US Automobile Industry* (Boston, 1985); Michael Piore and Charles F. Sabel, *The Second Industrial Divide: Possibilities for Prosperity* (New York, 1984); Samuel Bowles, David M. Gordon and Thomas E. Weisskopf, *Beyond the Waste Land: a Democratic Alternative to Economic Decline* (Garden City, 1983). The last two chapters in historian David Brody's influential synthesis, *Workers in Industrial America: Essays in the 20th Century Struggle* (Oxford, 1980), pp. 173–257, provide the best overall discussion of the decline in postwar labour's economic and political fortunes.

2 United Automobile Workers, *Proceedings of the Eleventh Constitutional Convention*, November 9–14 1947, p. 8.

3 Victor G. Reuther, 'Look Forward Labor', *Common Sense* 14 (1945), p. 9; Reuther's career is briefly sketched in John Barnard, *Walter Reuther and the Rise of the Auto Workers* (New York, 1983) and Nelson Lichtenstein, 'Walter Reuther and the Rise of Labor-Liberalism', in Melvyn Dubofsky and Warren Van Tine (eds.), *American Labor Leaders* (Champaign, Illinois, 1986).

4 David Brody, 'The New Deal in World War II', in John Braeman et al., *The New Deal: the National Level* (Columbus, Ohio, 1975), pp. 281–6.

5 Victor Reuther, *The Brothers Reuther and the Story of the UAW* (Boston, 1976), 247–8; Stephen Amberg, 'Alternatives to Fordism: Autoworkers in the Postwar Settlement', paper delivered at the Social Science History Association, Washington DC, October 1983.

140   *Industrial Relations in the Age of Fordism*

6   Barton Bernstein, 'Walter Reuther and the General Motors Strike of 1945–46', *Michigan History* 49 (September 1965), pp. 260–77; and Nelson Lichtenstein, *Labor's War at Home: the CIO in World War II* (Cambridge, 1982), pp. 221–6.
7   For a good discussion of the changing character of the liberal economic agenda, see Alan Wolfe, *America's Impasse: the Rise and Fall of the Politics of Growth* (Boston, 1981), pp. 13–79.
8   Robert M. Macdonald, *Collective Bargaining in the Automobile Industry: A Study in Wage Structure and Competitive Relations* (New Haven, 1963), pp. 258–306; Emma Rothschild, *Paradise Lost: the Decline of the Auto-Industrial Age* (New York, 1973), pp. 41–3.
9   Alonzo Hamby, *Beyond the New Deal: Harry S. Truman and American Liberalism* (New York, 1973), pp. 293–351; Mary Sperling McAuliffe, *Crisis on the Left: Cold War Politics and American Liberals, 1947–54* (Columbia, Missouri, 1978), pp. 3–74; and Mike Davis, 'The Barren Marriage of American Labour and the Democratic Party', *New Left Review*, 124 (November–December 1980), pp. 68–84.
10 'Are We Moving Toward a Government Controlled Economy?', May 30 1946 and UAW Press Release, December 7 1946, in box 542, Walter Reuther Collection, Archives of Labor History, Wayne State University (unless otherwise noted this is also the archive for all other cited documents); Lester Velie, *Labor U.S.A.* (New York, 1958) p. 64.
11 For studies of GM labour policy, see Howell Harris, *The Right to Manage: Industrial Relations Policies of American Business in the 1940s* (Madison, Wisconsin, 1982), pp. 139–43); and Kathyanne El-Messidi, 'Sure Principles Midst Uncertainties: the Story of the 1948 GM–UAW Contract' (University of Oklahoma Ph.D. thesis, 1976), pp. 80–139.
12 Barnard, *Walter Reuther*, p. 143.
13 Author's interview with John (Whitley) Sarri, 10 October 1982, Dearborn, Mich.; Harvey Swados, 'The UAW – Over the Top or Over the Hill?', *Dissent* 10 (1963), pp. 321–43; Frank Marquart, *An Auto Worker's Journal* (University Park, Pennsylvania, 1975), pp. 144–54.
14 Seth Wigderson, 'The UAW in the 1950s: Development of a Service Union', paper prepared for the Southern Labor History Conference, September 1982, pp. 12–13; Jack Steiber, *Governing the UAW* (New York, 1962), pp. 34–7.
15 Frederick H. Harbison, 'The General Motors–United Auto Workers Agreement of 1950', *Journal of Political Economy* 58 (1950), pp. 397–411.
16 Benjamin M. Selekman et al., *Problems in Labor Relations* (New York, 1950), pp. 298–309; 'Leonard Strike Power in Pension Talks', *Wage Earner*, 8 August 1947.
17 Minutes, National Ford Council Meeting, 28 July 1947, pp. 2–37, and 'Pensions – Elimination of Company Security Clause', both in box 5, Bert Matthews Collection; 'Leonard Strike Power in Pension Talks', *Wage Earner*, 8 August 1947; 'Ford Workers Couldn't Afford Pension', *Wage Earner* 26 September 1947.
18 Ford Motor Company, 'Executive Communication', 4 March 1948, in box 12, UAW Research Department Collection; Al Commons, 'The 1949 Ford Strike – Beginning of an Era', unpublished seminar paper, History Department, Wayne State University; 'Ford Provoked Strike: Reuther Faces Hard Test', *Labor Action*, 5 May 1949; see also Selekman, *Problems in Labor Relations*, pp. 323–59.

19 Ford Motor Company, 'Study on Work Stoppages (1955)', 5, in box 'Ford Department', Bannon Collection.

20 FMC and UAW-CIO, 'Arbitration Award', in 'FMC box', Bannon Collection; Local 600 leaflet, 'Strike Betrayal', in UAW Local 600 vertical file. The arbitration panel ruled that Ford had no right to run its lines faster than 100 per cent of 'standard' at any time, but the decision did nothing to resolve the long-range problem because the 'speed-up' issue had always been one involving not only line speed, but also work assignments, manning schedules, production mix and the evaluation of new technology.

21 Paul Sultan, *Labor Economics* (New York, 1957), pp. 263–7; 'Reuther to Seek Annual Wage through an Industry Council', *Wage Earner*, 29 March 1946; author's interview with Nat Weinberg, former director UAW Research Department, 11 November 1982, Washington DC.

22 Frank Cormier and William J. Eaton, *Reuther* (Englewood Cliffs, 1970), p. 328; Brody, *Workers in Twentieth Century America*, pp. 193–4.

23 Author's interviews with Walter Dorosh, former president, UAW Local 600, 21 October 1982, Dearborn; Malcolm Denise, former vice-president, labour relations, Ford Motor Company, 21 October 1982, Detroit; Weinberg interview; 'Report–Nat Ganley–July 1955' in box 1, Nat Ganley Collection (ALHUA).

24 Proceedings of Special Meeting, National Ford Council, May 9, 1955, Detroit, 44, in box 'Ford Motor Company', Bannon Collection.

25 'Revolt of the Victors', *Detroit Free Press*, 8 June 1955; 'Skilled Workers Spur Attack on UAW', *Wall Street Journal*, 18 April 1958; Carol Isen interview with Joseph Dunnebeck, former skilled-trades oppositionalist, 15 October 1982, Detroit; Dorosh interview.

26 Chapter 4 in this volume; Sabel and Piore, *The Second Industrial Divide*, pp. 111–32; Katz, *Shifting Gears*.

27 Nelson Lichtenstein, 'Auto Worker Militancy and the Structure of Factory Life, 1937–1955', *Journal of American History* 67 (September 1980), pp. 335–53; Brody, *Workers in Industrial America*, 204–9; and Steve Jefferys, *Management and Managed: the Movement of Managerial Authority and Workplace Legitimacy in the Chrysler Corporation since 1933* (Cambridge, 1987), esp. ch. 7.

28 John DeMotte, 'The 1955 Ford–UAW Contract', *Addresses on Industrial Relations*, Bulletin no. 24, (Ann Arbor, 1956), p. 2.

29 Richard Herding, *Job Control and Union Structure* (Rotterdam, 1972), p. 144.

30 UAW Local 326, 'Minutes of Special Management–Shop Committee', in box U-4, UAW–GM Collection.

31 B. J. Widick, (ed.), *Auto Work and its Discontents* (Baltimore, 1976), p. 9; Bureau of National Affairs, 'Significant Changes in Local Issue Bargaining Noted in Auto and Steel', *Daily Labor Report*, 18 December 1973, p. 4.

32 'Production Standards: Chronological Review of Contract Language', in box 17, Bannon Collection; Sarri interview.

33 'Production Standards: Chronological Review . . .'

34 UAW, *Proceedings of the Fourteenth Constitutional Convention*, 8–12 April 1953, p. 318.

35 UAW, *Proceedings of the Eighteenth Constitutional Convention*, 4–10 May 1962, p. 519.

36 Ford Motor Company, 'Study on Work Stoppages', pp. 19–21, in box 'Ford Department', Bannon Collection; Weinberg interview.

37 Macdonald, *Collective Bargaining in the Automobile Industry*, pp. 317–25; Jefferys, *Management and Managed*, esp. ch. 8; B. J. Widick, 'The Limitations of Unionism', *Dissent* 6 (1959), pp. 446–53.

38 UAW, 'Report of Walter Reuther', submitted to the *Seventeenth Constitutional Convention*, 9–16 October 1959, pp. 18–23; Maurice D. Kilbridge, 'The Effort Bargain in Industrial Society', *Journal of Business* 33 (1960), pp. 10–20. Some evidence exists that the UAW actually favoured Chrysler's effort to make its work standards compatible with those at GM and Ford. When news of this arrangement became public, Reuther was, of course, forced to deny it.

39 UAW, *Proceedings*, 1962, p. 522.

40 George Heliker, 'Grievance Arbitration in the Automobile Industry: A Comparative Analysis of its History and Results in the Big Three' (University of Michigan Ph.D. thesis 1954), pp. 339–51; Brody, *Workers in Industrial America*, pp. 200–10.

41 George Heliker interview with B. J. Widik, 6 March 1954, in Ernest Frank Hill Papers, Henry Ford Museum, Dearborn. On this point, Heliker, a strong proponent of the routinization of shop-floor bargaining agreed with Widick: 'If in addition to doing his job as an administrator and upholder of the agreement, he also has ambitions as a union politician, his assignment requires the skill and self control of a tight rope walker. Small wonder that it is often difficult to persuade the most competent men to accept the position.' Heliker, 'Grievance Arbitration', p. 343.

42 As quoted in Lloyd Ulman, 'Connective Bargaining and Competitive Bargaining', *Scottish Journal of Political Economy* 21 (June 1974), p. 99.

43 M. A. Williams, UAW Local 560, to Tom Bladen and Jeff Washington, National Ford Department, 24 July 1964, in box 17, Bannon Collection.

44 Sidney Lens, 'The Meaning of the Grievance Procedure', *Harvard Business Review* 26 (1948), p. 720. See also Craig Zabala, 'Collective Bargaining at UAW Local 645, General Motors Assembly Division, Van Nuys, California, 1976–1981' University of California Los Angeles Ph.D. thesis, 1983, for an extended argument that workers effectively use both the grievance machinery and unofficial job actions (sabotage, slowdowns, etc.) as part of their bargaining relationship with management.

45 Ford Motor Company, 'Collective Bargaining Review and Proposals', 16 July 1964, p. 21, in box 18, Bannon Collection.

46 Zabala, 'Collective Bargaining at UAW Local 645', pp. 123–5, 348–57.

47 Oliver Quayle and Co., 'A Study in Depth of the Rank and File of the UAW: May 1967', in box 147, Walter Reuther Collection (ALHUA); Louis Harris and Associates, 'The Mandate of the UAW Rank and File for Contract Negotiations in 1961', in box 10, Bannon Collection.

48 Gene Roberts, 'Officials Ousted in Many States', *Detroit Free Press*, 28 July 1963; 'UAW Target: Tedium on the Line', *Detroit Free Press*, 21 June 1964; Norman Miller, 'Auto Union Ferment', *Wall Street Journal*, 24 September 1964.

49 Norman Miller, 'Surprise Strike', *Wall Street Journal*, 5 October 1964; B. J. Widick, 'GM Strike: Prototype for More Conflict', *Nation* 16 November 1964, pp. 349–52; UAW News Release, 'Transcript of Remarks of UAW President Walter Reuther', 5 October 1964, in box 49, Leonard Woodcock Collection.

50 Norman Miller, 'What Was Won in GM Strike', *Wall Street Journal*, 3 November 1964; Jack Crellin, 'Local Differences Block Ford Return to Work', *Detroit News*, 13 October 1961; Ford Motor Company, 'Remarks by

Malcolm Denise, vice president – labor relations, before the 13th Annual Union–Management Conference', Notre Dame University, 27 February 1965, p. 20, in box 'Ford Department', Bannon Collection.
51 Miller, 'What Was Won'.
52 Jefferys, *Management and Managed*, ch. 10.

6

The Rise and Fall of Shop-Floor
Bargaining at Fiat 1945–1980
Giovanni Contini

Fiat has always played a crucial role in the history of Italian industrial relations. In the 1920s, the occupation of the factories, which immediately preceded the Fascist seizure of power, was centred on the Fiat plants. In 1943 the anti-Fascist strikes at Fiat marked the first mass struggle against the Fascist regime in Italy. After the war, Fiat was the leading stronghold of the Works-Council (*Consigli di Gestione*) Movement. Again in 1955, the defeat of the CGIL (Confederazione Generale Italiana del Lavoro, the Communist and Socialist union) at Fiat, opened a general period of weakness for the whole working-class movement in Italy. The same is true for the re-emergence of industrial conflict at Fiat at the end of the 1960s and for its sudden and dramatic collapse at the end of the 1970s: in both cases, developments in Fiat were considered, and actually were, paradigmatic for what would happen more broadly elsewhere. This chapter is mainly concerned with the events of the past 15 years: the rise of shop floor bargaining in the late 1960s, and its demise in Fiat in the late 1970s. Schematizing considerably, one could say that two main explanations of this process have been proposed: the first sees the defeat of trade unionism at Fiat in the 1950s, its strength in the 1970s and the final crisis as a mere reflection in the factory microcosm of external political events: the weakness of the left in the fifties and early sixties, its growth in the sixties and seventies, and its crisis in the late seventies. The second explanation, instead, stresses technical change as the main cause of this same trajectory. The rationalization wave of the fifties is seen as the cause of the unions' sudden defeat: there was a dramatic shift in the composition of the labour force, as the number of unskilled workers increased rapidly, and the strategies of the unions and left-wing parties, which had been aimed at 'skilled workers', suddenly became obsolete. Only when the process was completed, had 'touched bottom', as Panzieri, an influential new-left theorist, put it, could the new class composition give rise to a new strategy, now directly and immediately revolutionary. When this was defeated in 1980, technological determinism again provides an explanation: the workers lost because of the growing automation of the production process. The rules of the game were transformed, and the ground was cut out from under the existing 'class composition', presumably to 'touch bottom' once again.

If the first explanation is misleading, taken by itself, the second is wholly unconvincing. Technology is presented as an independent force, against which the labour movement can only choose between confrontation or capitulation. In my view an explanation of the rise and fall of shop-floor bargaining would need to consider a number of variables, without presuming one to be determinant. Thus technological change would be only one of the elements which shape the changing context within which the various actors make their decisions: it may constrain their options, but some margin for choice necessarily remains.

My aim in this chapter is to reconstruct the successive strategies and choices adopted by the main actors – trade unions, shop stewards, managers and workers – together with the changing context in which they made their decisions. The body of the chapter consists of three main sections. First, I give a brief account of industrial relations in Fiat from the end of the Second World War to the struggles of 1969 (the so-called 'hot autumn') emphasizing three elements, neglected by previous studies of the period, which are crucial in explaining the re-emergence of industrial conflict at Fiat in the late sixties: the peculiarity of the Turinese labour movement, the shift of Fiat's top management towards a more 'enlightened' personnel policy and the distinctive culture of the southern migrants who flocked into the main Fiat plants in the sixties and early seventies.

The second section deals with the ambiguous and contradictory phase of industrial relations at Fiat between 1973 and 1977. In this period, I will argue, a number of different outcomes were possible: for the first time a more open management found in the unions a bargaining partner also more open to the institutionalization of shop-floor bargaining. For some years a network of agreements was organized, particularly in certain shops. The role of the Communist Party in this process was crucial: in 1975 and 1976 this party made substantial electoral gains, and launched a new strategy – the historic compromise aimed at forming a governing coalition with the Christian Democrats. Following this strategy, the Communists pushed for a more conciliatory line in the factories; and the energy crisis of 1974 also pushed the unions in the same direction.

The third section focuses on the crisis of industrial relations at Fiat since 1977, and examines its various causes. The radicalization of the former Catholic union in Fiat (FIM – Federazione Italiana Metalmeccanici), together with the resumption of product demand and hiring at Fiat in 1977 undermined the Communists' claims that cooperation with management was needed to overcome the crisis of the enterprise. The emergence of a new, aggressive style of militancy aggravated the pre-existing tensions between unions and workers, while the appearance of terrorism increasingly paralysed union organization within the factory, and cut the shop stewards off from the deeper concerns of their constituents. At the same time, Fiat management, too, changed its attitude towards the unions, whom they saw as increasingly unreliable bargaining partners. In conclusion I will examine the confrontation of autumn 1980, in which Fiat management was unexpectedly able to sack 24,000 workers and dramatically to reduce the unions' strength at one stroke. The research is based on a combination of the available documentary sources and interviews with workers, stewards, foremen and managers.

THE EMERGENCE OF SHOP-FLOOR BARGAINING

Industrial relations in Fiat from the fifties to the late sixties

In the 1940s the labour movement had built up several different forms of representation at Fiat. There were works councils (*Consigli di Gestione*), whose aim was the improvement of the firm's productivity, with 50 per cent worker representation. There was the *Commissione Interna*, an electoral structure composed of representatives of the three main trade unions, the FIOM (Federazione Impiegati Operai Metallurgici – the metalworkers' section of the CGIL, the Communist and Socialist trade-union confederation) the FIM and the UILM (Unione Italiana dei Lavoratori Metalmeccanici), linked respectively to the Catholic and Social Democratic union organizations, which had split off from the CGIL in 1948. There were also unofficial *Commissari di Reparto*, who, though unrecognized by management, performed the role of shop stewards in plant bargaining.

From 1948 to 1955, industrial relations became more and more conflictual. The cold war, the expulsion of the Communists from the government, the political split in the labour movement: all these events made themselves felt in the factory. Structures like the *Consigli di Gestione*, based on collaboration between workers and management, were the first to enter into crisis.[1] Later, the left-wing parties organized a huge number of political strikes, undermining their support from the workers in the longer term. In the early fifties, moreover, Fiat began to transform the production process, for which the left was quite unprepared, since they were still expecting a general collapse of capitalism; and their defensive struggle against 'speed-up' was ultimately unsuccessful.[2] From the 1940s, Fiat workers' wages began to rise well above the Turinese average, to nearly double by the mid-fifties. Finally, the management embarked from 1953 on a direct attack against the highly political FIOM, whose militants were called 'the wreckers' and were victimized. In 1955, FIOM lost the elections for the *Commissione Interna*: its votes fell from 32,000 to 18,000 and for the next eight years Fiat workers abstained from strike activity. Despite Fiat's participation in the 1963 national contract strikes, in the following five years the workers resumed their usual passivity, though some bargaining was going on in certain shops.[3]

The 1969 strikes were thus effectively the first in 15 years. It was only then, according to my interviews, that the climate of the factory changed dramatically, despite the experiences of 1963. In a few months, the Fiat plants were literally paralysed by 'chequerboard' or rolling strikes in strategic departments, and shop stewards were elected, apparently autonomously. Job control rose from nothing to its apogee in a few months, and in the following years the workers managed to maintain their power and to consolidate it. In accounting for the emergence of shop-floor bargaining, I will focus on three main aspects of the situation in the 1960s which paved the way for the developments after 1969: the specific features of the Turinese labour movement, the culture and attitudes of the new migrants from the south and the changing strategies of Fiat's management.

The peculiarities of the Turinese labour movement

As we have already noted, the left-wing organizations in Turin, and particularly in Fiat, had lost their position on the shop floor by the mid-fifties, and so were forced to form their picture of Fiat workers from general statistical data on levels of earnings, employment and technological change. From 1956, well-known politicians within the Socialist Party began to develop a new strategy, based mainly on the idea that political bodies in the factory rather than the parties were to become the crucial element of the socialist transition. Although defeated in the Socialist Party itself, this line persisted elsewhere: Panzieri, former deputy editor of the Socialist journal *Mondo Operaio*, moved to Turin at the end of the fifties. Interestingly enough, immediately after the defeat in Fiat, Turinese unionists had played an important role in a discussion which proposed shop-floor bargaining as the sole way of overcoming the crisis.[4]

As Vittorio Rieser has recently pointed out, *Quaderni Rossi*, the journal that Panzieri founded in Turin, and which was usually seen and studied as the theoretical precursor of many extraparliamentary groups in the sixties and seventies, was really part of a broader intellectual and political debate in Turin during the late fifties and early sixties.[5]

Turinese left-wing organizations had been studying and discussing intensively the 'neocapitalist factory', which in Turin meant Fiat. They were conducting several inquiries[6] but without real success in the short run: Fiat workers remained somehow inaccessible. It is not surprising then that Fiat's ability to increase productivity and integrate the workers at the same time became for many years a central problem for the unions and for the parties; in this situation, Panzieri's ideas fell on extremely fertile ground. In his seminal essay in *Quaderni Rossi*, technological development itself was seen as deeply marked by its capitalist character, and put forward as the main battlefield of the class struggle for 'workers' control in a revolutionary perspective'. In the same number, Garavini, a leading Communist in the Turinese CGIL and Vittorio Foa, a socialist militant, were arguing very strongly in the same direction.[7]

This line, which in Turin crossed the borders between different organizations, was aimed to counter the new positive attitude within the

Italian labour movement towards technological development. Its longstanding view of the Italian industrial system as 'malthusian' or technologically stagnant had been suddenly abandoned in the mid-fifties, and a new, benevolent and uncritical attitude emerged instead: capitalist development was expected to produce in the short run a contradiction between the forces and relations of production. On the left, and particularly in Turin, the two positions somehow fused into what can be called the theory of 'class composition': capitalist development itself was supposed to create an increasingly unskilled workforce willing to undergo a process of revolutionary class struggle.

The intellectual background of the extreme left and its organizational and propagandistic efforts proved of cardinal importance for the development of industrial conflict in Turin. Particularly important was the split in the Socialist Party, the PSI, which produced a new left group, the PSIUP (Partito Socialista Italiana di Unità Proletaria) in 1964: in Turin the PSIUP managed to capture all the socialist workers' representatives despite its modest electoral success; the following years the PSIUP managed to set up a very militant structure within the factory, whose main target was the creation of the *Consigli Operai*, workers' councils, a political trade-union organization. Last but not least, the Catholic union in Fiat had suffered in 1958 a split of its right wing, which later formed a company union known as SIDA (Sindacato Italiano dell'Automobile). That split was particularly serious in Fiat, where CISL passed from being a relatively important and collaborative union to a small group with little influence. As a consequence, in the following years the CISL collaboration with CGIL was particularly precocious and in Turin it was particularly prepared to share the militant and conflictual approach of CGIL in hopes of rebuilding its organization. If we now look at the end of the decade, we find many different organizations with different political ideologies and different aims, all pushing in a similar direction: workers' control of the organization of the work. It is also very noticeable that the programme of 'workers control' had a peculiar feature among the PSIUP and the 'workerist' faction of the student movement which was to become *Lotta Continua* and *Potere Operaio*: the organizations were proposing it, but denying their involvement at the same time, since only 'workers' could be the protagonists of such demands.

Finally, it is very important to note that both the unions and the political organizations tended to ignore the cultural, political and ethnic features of the new working class; at the beginning of the migratory stream some Socialist and Communist MPs proposed that the Turinese labour movement should organize the migrants as migrants. But this proposal was immediately dismissed: it seemed a sort of left-wing racism, particularly dangerous because of the newly-formed MARP (Movimento Autonomista Regione Piemonte), a Turinese nativist group, and the risk of building up two distinct, ethnically and politically divided, organizations. Moreover, this proposal was particularly repugnant to political forces who saw the workers as mainly defined by their relation to the factory and to the organization of work rather than their socio-cultural origins.

The new migrants

In 1969 Fiat was forced for the first time to hire an enormous number of new workers, mainly from the south, without being able to select them, as usual, according to political criteria. Some of the new recruits (in total about 20,000) had worked in West Germany, where they had experience of the union within the factory. When they entered Fiat they looked actively for the unions, and they were extremely disappointed when they did not find them. Even more important, some of them were quite educated, with several years of secondary school, and were forced to migrate because of the absence of jobs in their villages in the south. When they arrived at Fiat, they were often sent to the assembly lines of Mirafiori and Rivalta, where there were few possibilities of promotion. Unlike the workers who worked in other shops, the assembly-line workers could very rarely get beyond the 'third category' (semi-skilled production worker). As the foremen pointed out in their interviews, they were condemned to 'die in the third category'.[8] Moreover, in Fiat careers were possible mainly for Piedmontese workers, because the local dialect and the fact of being part of the northern culture was (in part still is) a very important element in opportunities for promotion to foreman or supervisor.[9] The lower management was often less well educated, however, than the new blue collar workers;[10] and their prerogatives were not particularly impressive, from a technical point of view. As even the most sympathetic recent studies show, lower management had largely lost any functional autonomy and remained principally responsible for controlling and directing other people's work.[11]

The most recent migrants thus rejected the strategy of some of their predecessors in the 1950s and early 1960s, who had assimilated into Turinese culture in order to win a career. By the end of the decade, this kind of transformation seemed an excessive humiliation, considering the limited success of the previous migrants' efforts: very few of them were in fact foremen and supervisors; their disguise had failed since lower management still reproduced itself according to strict ethnic criteria. Moreover, both educated and uneducated new workers experienced very difficult working conditions. All the foremen and supervisors I interviewed declared unanimously that 'make-up' work and 'stretch-outs' made the work on the assembly lines particularly hard: workers were obliged to make up for lost production, when the assembly line stopped for technical reasons; and output levels had to be maintained, even if fewer workers were present.[12]

Finally, outside the factory the migrants found, if possible, worse problems: housing difficulties, lack of schools for the children, poor transport and shopping facilities and overcrowding.[13] Fiat's wages had lost much of their previous edge, a major disappointment for the large numbers of migrants who came hoping to save money and to invest it in their villages, as the first generation of migrants had done.

These were the workers who participated in the struggles from 1968 onward, those the foremen and supervisors called 'the dregs', 'wankers', as compared with the previous migrants, 'real workers' and 'good citizens'.[14] These newcomers, experiencing very bad working and living conditions, the same for everybody, and a common exclusion on ethnic grounds, were particularly receptive to the left-wing parties' and unions' propaganda focused on job control and egalitarian demands.

Democratic modernization: Fiat management's new strategy

When Valletta, the architect of the mass-production revolution in Fiat and of the victimization of the unions since the fifties, retired, the firm was a gigantic monolith whose central direction still had to take virtually all the most important decisions. A process of bureaucratization was already developing in a firm which was much more product-oriented than market-oriented. The new management set out to decentralize Fiat, devolving functional responsibility and dismantling the rigid hierarchical structure, whereby 'between an assembly line worker and Valletta there were no less than fourteen levels of authority.'[15]

The policy of blind repression of the FIOM and FIM militants was also abandoned, or at least relaxed: already before 1969 the pressure on the union militants fell considerably. In 1967 Gianni Agnelli wrote two important articles stressing the central importance of the large firm as the main interpreter of the general interest, proposing a new social contract between institutions (firms, unions and parties), in order to replace the previous social contract between individuals, which had proved unsuccessful.[16] From 1967–8 CI members were allowed for the first time to move around in the plant,[17] and Fiat started to put up a noticeboard on which the daily piecework figures were to be displayed to the workers in accordance with the famous agreement of 1955[18] which had never before been put into effect. From 1969 Agnelli quickly replaced the old class of top managers, the authoritatian 'cavalieri' drawn from the ranks of foremen and supervisors,[19] with new recruits from the universities. But if this change happened at the top, the line management on the shop floor remained the same, and the workers were ruled according to the traditional authoritarian criteria.

From the 'hot autumn' to 'permanent conflict' 1969–70

As we have seen, the ideological development of the Turinese labour movement, the experience of the new migrants, and the shift in Fiat's personnel policy were all paving the way for the strike wave. At the same time, political and legal changes and a tight labour market were both pushing in the same direction.

For the first time the migrants participated in internal strikes on 2 December 1968 and 9 April 1969, protesting because the police had killed workers involved in demonstrations in the south. In the spring of 1969 strikes started which seemed to be independent of the unions. The next autumn, the struggles continued, and shop stewards were elected. The stewards were the expression of the *gruppo omogeneo di produzione*, the work group, and they were first recognized by Fiat, then progressively incorporated into the unions, while those political forces which had pushed for total autonomy of the working class from the organizations started to decline.[20] In 1970 the stewards were recognized by the Communist Party,[21] and, more important, they were powerfully supported by the new labour code, which allowed the unions to have representatives within the factories and which protected them against victimization.[22]

Political initiatives played a central role in the strike wave from its inception. Although small, the PSIUP seems to have been extremely influential, particularly in some sections of Fiat.[23] But even the unions, particularly the left-wing ones, were very active indeed, at least from the hot autumn onwards, when they succeeded in incorporating progressively and in a flexible way the newly formed structures of the shop stewards.

This is not surprising: when the new shop stewards had to shift from confrontation to bargaining, they soon needed the help of the old militants, who possessed what my interviewees called the 'historical memory of Fiat'. In other words, they knew the language of bargaining, and were therefore able to understand the technical sides of the previous agreements and of the new ones.[24]

This is the reason why that process which Sabel describes happened so quickly, namely the convergence of the old, weak unions and the new militants of southern origin. The process was a double one: not only did the newcomers assimilate the language of the existing political organizations, but they changed it in the process of assimilating it. The 'struggle that prefigures its objective', so common in those years, very closely recalls the struggles in the south, such as the occupation of the land after the Second World War. The same is true for the egalitarian wage claims. As a final consequence, the left wing of the Turinese labour movement, already very influential, as we have seen, fed on this process, becoming dominant locally for several years.[25]

Contradictions in Fiat's management strategy likewise played a central role in the emergence of a strong shop-steward organization in the plants. While 'make-up work' and 'stretch-outs' remained as bad as in the early sixties, and the foremen maintained their authoritarian attitude towards the workforce,[26] the victimization and control of the unions was weakened.

The workers were still exasperated by their working conditions, but for the first time they had effective trade unions behind them, anxious to settle the scores of 15 years' political discrimination. When the strikes erupted Fiat wavered between a 'tough' line, locking out the workers in the shops affected indirectly by the chequerboard strikes, which pushed the latter towards militancy of their own,[27] and an opposed 'soft' line. In this second approach, top management recognized workers' representatives and negotiated directly with them, by-passing the foremen among whom they provoked an identity crisis; as a consequence, the latter were less inclined to perform their role in the traditional authoritarian way.[28] The top management were then facing the shop stewards, and they would discover in the following years how difficult it would be to deal with this new bargaining partner committed to 'permanent conflict'. The new labour code, moreover, not only protected shop steward organization where it had sprung up spontaneously, but also independently tended to encourage its formation in other shops.[29]

The golden age of shop-floor bargaining in Fiat 1970–73

The assembly-lines agreement of July 1971 can be taken as paradigmatic of this phase in Fiat, constituting one of the few agreements that the unions were able to obtain on topics like the organization of work: only in Olivetti did they obtain a similar agreement,[30] but a survey conducted by the end of the decade shows that *formal* shop-floor agreements had by then become very rare.[31] In Fiat, and at Mirafiori, this remained the only agreement in the body shops; in the machine shops, on the contrary, it marked the first step in a much richer bargaining development. Many more agreements were signed in 1975 and again towards the end of the decade. As a result of the 1971 agreement 'piece rate committees' were instituted, 60 for all Fiat's plants in Italy, which were allowed to discuss the new piecework times for some months after their introduction.[32] The times, beginning in 1970, were based on job analysis rather than shop-floor observation. Moreover, a commission was instituted charged with the restructuring of the lines and discussion about the new lines to be set up. On the assembly lines the breaks were improved (40 minutes instead of ten, to be allocated according to the decision of the work group), and actual working time was pushed down to 88–84 per cent of the day, from 92–95 per cent in the early 1960s.[33] The shop stewards I interviewed considered the agreement a real milestone, which changed the landscape for years.[34] Finally, Fiat pledged itself to collaborate with the unions to eliminate all those operations which endangered the workers' health, marking a break with the unions' previous policy of exchanging dangerous working conditions for more money, and the starting point of what would prove the most successful area of shop-floor bargaining in the future.[35]

A first consequence of this agreement was the further marginalization of those positions among the stewards promoting a purely conflictual attitude toward top management, recognizing neither a bargaining ground nor bargining structures. But the real result of the agreement was a gigantic collective project of restructuring, which involved shop stewards, experts of the 'committees', foremen and top managers. Without any doubt the most successful area was the one related to the unhealthy shops such as the paint shops,[36] but other sections were also deeply involved. Some lines were restructured as a result of the bargaining process,[37] sometimes the off-track work which had been reduced in the 1960s[38] was expanded again.[39]

The different shops performed this task in very different ways. In the body shop, for instance, where the majority of the workers were recently arrived southerners, the shop stewards tended to rely on their accumulated strength, considering the agreement as a sort of outpost in a bargaining process still seen as a battle;[40] in the machine shops, instead, the shop stewards' council (largely dominated by the Communist Party) developed a quite different style of bargaining. They tried to beat the Job Analysis Office at its own game: for three years the stewards collected information about every single operation, restudying it according to the time-and-motion schedules, and they organized archives. The experts of the committee then engaged the top management in exhaustive technical discussions, demonstrating often that the rate fixers were incompetent. When the managers gave the task to external rate fixers, the stewards were able to compare the two results to invalidate both. More generally, they were able to profit from the gap which had now emerged between the top management and the foremen. While the latter were displaced from the bargaining process, the managers found themselves in a difficult position, because they did not know how the shops actually worked. The foremen, for their part, could not understand why the managers did not consult them.[41]

The line of the committee and the shop stewards proved more defensive than they themselves realized, as was becoming clear in those shops faced with major technological innovation. In the paint shops, for instance, the transformation meant a precocious automation of the cycle. Where the transformation had consisted of a series of detailed changes the stewards had managed to keep their control,[42] but in the paint shop they were unable to control major new developments.[43] But for the moment the experience of the paint shop remained quite isolated, and workers experienced a substantial advance of job control, a marked reduction in the speed of the assembly line, and the elimination of unhealthy jobs.[44] In the national agreement of mid-1973, accompanied in Fiat by the occupation of the Mirafiori plant – white- and blue-collar workers obtained an integrated system of grading and wage differentials, the *inquadramento unico* which represented a real revolution in Italian factories where status differences between blue- and white-collar jobs had been traditionally very strong.

A LESS CONFLICTUAL UNION?

The oil crisis: workers' mobility or union rigidity?

From 1974 to 1978 a series of contradictory events suggest that many different outcomes were still possible for industrial relations in Fiat. The previous period, as we saw, witnessed an irresistible growth of shop-floor power, and each new development seemed to reinforce that general trend. By contrast, the period from 1979 to the present seems to point in just the opposite direction, with Fiat launching an aggressive and successful attack against the unions and their power to an extent unbelievable only a few years, or months, before. It would be wrong, however, to consider the intervening period as a teleological progress towards the final outcome, as unfortunately both the union officials in their writings[45] and the shop stewards I interviewed tend to do. They described Fiat's top management formulating long-term Machiavellian strategies, with clear goals planned several years ahead, which always informed their day-by-day bargaining activity. But it is hardly surprising if the people involved in a series of events with dramatic points of departure and conclusion tend later to emphasize in their accounts of the period only the beginning and the end, while tending to compress, if not to suppress, each ambiguous moment in between when several outcomes might have been possible.

The new phase in Fiat's industrial relations was inaugurated by the oil crisis of 1974 and its dramatic consequences for automobile demand. As a first consequence, labour recruitment in Fiat was blocked. Since the firm had always experienced an extremely high percentage of voluntary separations, the labour force decreased very quickly. Between May 1973 and May 1974 employment in the machine shops of Mirafiori fell from 16,904 to 15,901. In the body shop, it fell from 18,390 to 17,718. Two years later, Mirafiori as a whole had fallen from 45,000 workers to 37,000 and Rivalta from 18,000 to 13,000.[46] Despite the dramatic decrease in the number of workers there is no reason to believe that the unions were weakened proportionally.[47] The decision to stop hiring could be taken unilaterally by Fiat's management; they still had to negotiate with the unions over the movement of workers to meet the daily necessities of production.

At first the demand for internal mobility seemed to have taken the unions by surprise, and the work groups from which the shop stewards were elected entered a period of crisis. But soon the unions managed to organize strikes against mobility,[48] and finally claimed control over it. The line of those who proposed a frontal resistance to mobility remained a minority position[49] in the Turinese United Metalworkers' Federation (FLM). Already in 1975 two agreements stated that the unions were to be given advance information about the productive situation in the different sections, and the related needs for worker mobility.[50]

Despite the difficulties it produced, mobility as such does not seem to have undermined the structure of the 'work groups' because the shop stewards managed to control it (far too much, the stewards say today). Besides, even the figures produced by those who think that mobility quickly destroyed the unions' strength show the opposite. In Mirafiori's machine shops, which supposedly suffered the heaviest blow, only 6 per cent of workers were transferred.[51] Fiat had to ask in 1977 for six Saturdays of overtime on the line which produced the model 127, specifically because the unions refused to allow sufficient mobility.[52]

In fact, mobility seems to have been seen by the unions as a means to reopen the bargaining on work organization, which had become harder as a result of the crisis. The 'quality of work' initiatives of Fiat, namely the 'assembly islands' in Cassino and Rivalta, whose purpose was to meet the unions' claims for 'job enrichment', had been quickly abandoned as uneconomical.[53] Now, the unions tried to revive the bargaining on this point in a minor key, using mobility for job enlargement, upgrading workers able to move from one job to another, and demanding a corresponding wage improvement. In 1978 a survey aimed at discovering the results of bargaining on work organization discovered that 60 per cent of the changes had involved job enlargement (rotation and recomposition of tasks), while job enrichment was only 18 per cent of the total, the restructuring of the workplace 20 per cent and automation 5 per cent.[54]

If the increase in mobility did not mean the destruction of the 'work group', and if the stewards managed to win control over it, its results did not prove particularly satisfactory for the workforce. Both stewards and foremen told me that the workers were quite disappointed by the job enlargement experiences, which were particularly poor in comparison with the great hopes for the transformation of the quality of work in the endless discussions at the beginning of the decade. Only at the end of the 1970s in some shops did the stewards elaborate a project for the recomposition of production and maintenance tasks within a single group,[55] and later the unions took up that demand for Fiat workers as a whole. But both at a company and at a shop-floor level these demands met a rigid refusal from Fiat.[56]

Communist power and inter-union rivalry

The struggle over work organization and wages only represents one side of the workers' mobilization in Fiat. Political demands had always played an important role, starting with the first successful strike in 1968 for pension-scheme improvements, to the strikes organized in 1970 for structural social reforms. As a matter of fact, politics always constituted one of the deepest motivations of the majority of the stewards, and that can be seen not only in their involvement in general political struggles, but also in their struggles for job control and job enrichment. The main political force in the factory councils at Fiat, the Communist Party (PCI) moved away quite soon from a rigid application of job-control practices. In 1975 and 1976 the PCI gained an unexpected success at the polls. Just when bargaining within the factory was encountering its first difficulties, the PCI's share of the vote rose to 36 per cent. These gains strengthened the appeal of its strategy of directing the power which arose from social struggles into the political arena.

As we have seen, the PCI had been much less influential at the beginning of the new cycle of struggles, when the small left-wing party, the PSIUP, the students' movement and the unions had really promoted and led the mobilization. But now the Party began to regain its ascendancy in the unions. A recent survey of the political commitment of CGIL militants in Piedmont shows that 89 per cent belong to the Communist Party[57] and although we do not have a specific survey on Fiat, it seems likely that the figures are similar to those for the region as a whole. Quite soon, however, in 1973 the PCI developed the line of the 'historical compromise', the formation of a government *together* with the Christian Democratic Party. In order to achieve that target, the PCI had to recover its control over the social movements, most notably the unions. At the same time, the oil crisis itself pushed the unions towards a more cooperative line and the old Communist productivism gave a political and theoretical justification for moderating demands and promoting the productivity of the firm. In 1976 the Communist line for industrial workers pushed even more in this direction: they were asked not to put forward new wages claims and to collaborate in overcoming their firms' crisis.

Even if this strategy was called 'the line of sacrifices', it did not imply a complete surrender to management. It meant instead a period in which the more open attitude of management met a quite receptive bargaining partner. In the previous years the top managers had set up, although with many difficulties, a much larger organization of lower personnel managers and they had more than doubled the number of foremen and supervisors,[58] in order to decentralize the bargaining process. Specialists in personnel management were hired in order to help the foremen in the more technically demanding aspects of the bargaining process, and the pursuit of a soft line seemed if not enormously successful, quite reasonable. The bargaining over mobility was part of this process, but thousands of agreements were signed, particularly in sections like the machine shops which were more interested in obtaining formal agreements than in committing themselves to a relationship of pure force. Not surprisingly, the vast majority of the machine shops' stewards' council was controlled by the PCI.[59]

THE DEMISE OF SHOP-FLOOR BARGAINING AT FIAT

The onset of the crisis: the new recruitment of 1977

The Communist line entered into a period of progressive crisis as a combined result of two main factors: the upturn in demand for Fiat cars, which became evident in 1977 when Fiat started to hire again[60] and the radicalization of the FIM, the union which had been created in the forties as a right-wing split from the CGIL, but which in Turin and among metalworkers particularly had by the sixties become a very left-wing and conflict-oriented union.

In the same election (1976) in which the PCI won its major success, the extraparliamentary groups were badly defeated and never recovered. Many of their militants joined FIM, and managed to acquire important positions within the union. FIM was, as one militant puts it, 'a house with wide open doors and windows' and it increased both its strength and its leftist orientation. The new recruitment by Fiat strengthened its line, because it was now more and more apparent that the 'sacrifice policy' could mean very little in a firm which had recovered from its previous crisis. It appeared that that policy had suddenly become grounded more in the electoral, instrumental needs of the Communist Party, than in the workers' interests. Besides, as we have seen, the line of 'responsible bargaining' had encountered several difficulties. It was more successful when it had had to deal with simple reorganization of the existing technology, such as mobility of labour or the modification of assembly lines, but was less successful in dealing with substantial changes in the technology itself. The component of the labour movement which decided to follow the already familiar path of rigidity, conflict and relationships based on force, then had an increasingly easy task. In doing so, they pushed management toward a more belligerent strategy and undermined still further the already embattled 'responsible' line.

The first episode which is considered by many of the stewards I interviewed as a paradigm of the new relations between unions and management occurred in the autumn of 1977. As we noted earlier, Fiat asked for six Saturdays of overtime, because the line of model 127 was particularly behind schedule. But the unions refused and pickets were organized. For the first time, a substantial number of workers, and not the traditional 'blacklegs', tried to force their way through the pickets. Some evidence suggests that it was the local metalworkers' union federation, the FLM, who pushed for the hard line, against the advice of several stewards. In the local FLM the FIM were very influential, while the FIOM representatives were also more radical than most of the rank and file, who were more directly influenced by the Communist Party.[61]

The new workers of 1977-80: passivity and radicalism

Between 1977 and early 1980, Fiat hired a total of 20,000 new workers. By law, it was obliged to hire people from the Labour Exchange lists, and its right to choose its own manpower was thus reduced. The majority of the new workers were women and young people, coming often from the secondary schools of Turin. In the first case, that meant that, for the first time, the Fiat lower management was facing a completely new problem: the foremen did not consider the women as ordinary workers, and they insisted on allocating them only in a restricted range of jobs, refusing to give them the traditional 'male' ones. They then remained for some time relatively underemployed.[62] The young workers, on the other hand, helped to aggravate the crisis of the unions in the plant. Unlike the previous generation of new workers with a background of migration, they expressed a very negative feeling both toward their jobs and toward the unions, who could not understand them from their side either. The migrants who entered Fiat in the sixties and early seventies, in fact, had considered the factory as a social centre, where they met their friends, and where they had developed their political and trade-union militancy. The new workers found the jobs, despite the bargaining of the previous years, 'awful' and 'inhuman'.[63] Their social life was external to the factory, and had been developing during their school years, and they had known nothing comparable to the experience of migration. They looked aggressive and detached at the same time: 'they were different [from us] about the jobs, about everything: they didn't care! They weren't like us, already old Fiat workers . . . they behaved as if they were in command, they were more self-confident. I had been there for eleven years and I was still unconfident, you see . . .'[64] They became a perfect seed-bed for the newly formed 'Autonomia', an extremely aggressive and violent organization which emerged after the defeat of the old extraparliamentary groups and whose relation with the union officials inside the factory was no longer based on friendly polemics as had been the case with previous extreme-left groups. Now, as one official described it, 'in many of them you could see the hatred against us, which actually meant hatred against certain kinds of workers' struggles, which they . . . really, hated. You were the enemy, then . . .'[65]

It is quite interesting to note that evidence from both foremen and stewards gives a very similar picture of the late 1970s. Demand for cars was very erratic, activating and deactivating different sections of the works, but now the rigidity of the unions towards internal mobility prevented the management from shifting workers rapidly enough, from the sectors where production stagnated to ones which suddenly had to produce a much higher volume of output. Fiat was then forced to hire, but found it difficult to employ the new workers properly. Of course, to see in the unions' rigidity the main, if not the sole, cause of the new hirings, as a FIOM official I interviewed claimed, is perhaps excessive. In fact Fiat hired because it expected to repeat the exploits of the sixties, not realizing that the market had become less predictable. No serious research had been done for the new models, so that the new cars were already old when they were launched, and remained largely unsuccessful.[66] The unions' rigidity, nevertheless, was also important and therefore was liable to become the scapegoat for others' mistakes in management and in marketing.

On a second point the evidence both from the foremen and from the stewards' perspectives coincides. In the late seventies, there was a growing gulf between the tough strike tactics which the unions were proposing, and a growing number of 'moderate' workers. As one union official described it, 'from 1968 to 1980 we never really conquered . . . [them] . . . we never looked back; we were like a bulldozer: we went on, crashing over everything, we didn't care if we were leaving broken pieces behind. And in fact terrorism too played its role, and at the end we were forced to realize that the workers we had left behind were . . . were a lot.'[67] Even the ones who participated in the struggles, were very angry about strike tactics. Foremen and supervisors, for instance, were forced to lead an internal demonstration, carrying a red banner in their hands.[68] Machines were damaged: 'For

God's sake, why did that machine have to be overturned? What's the point of that?'[69] At first the reaction of the workers was not an open rebellion against the unions. They were more fed up and they did not agree, becoming as a consequence less militant and more passive. Instead of joining the demonstration, they preferred to play cards, and the women crocheted. But then, sometimes, 'small squads came, armed with clubs, they threw bolts. [The other workers] were upset, they were forced to run away . . . some people were also wounded: they arrived, switched off the light . . .'[70] This evidence, which came from the foremen, is supported by similar, if less highly coloured stories from the stewards.[71]

Terrorism at Fiat

Terrorism at Fiat began in the first half of the seventies, but only after 1977 did it become a major problem in the factory. When the main extraparliamentary groups went into crisis, not all the militants decided to join the unions. Some recruits to the terrorist organizations even came from the PCI when the Party began clearly to seek a compromise with the Christian Democrats, abandoning its previous strategy of 'structural reforms'. These discontented Communists and ultra-left militants secretly joined the terrorist organizations, above all the Red Brigades and *Prima Linea* (Front Line), the latter largely formed by former militants of Lotta Continua after its dissolution in 1976.

The common strategy of the terrorist organizations within the factories seems to have been to defend by force workers' gains in the factory, attacking both the technical structures and the so-called 'capitalist articulation of command within the plant', namely the foremen, supervisors and managers. In so doing, they were hoping to recruit more militants and to be able to enlarge their organization. They repeated the *form* of the most violent and radical actions typical of the seventies, such as the internal demonstration and the picket, but they were now outside their original context and this had serious consequences. The foremen, as I said, had often suffered a sort of symbolic persecution. Now, instead, their possessions were destroyed (cars, houses), and they themselves were wounded or even killed. Likewise, attacks on a grand scale were organized against Fiat's plants: assembly lines and stockrooms were burnt with magnesium.[72] Again, the terrorists thought that they were expressing the attitude to sabotage which they thought was typical of the new working class. They particularly attacked those foremen and those managers most open to a dialogue with the unions,[73] and the stewards whose position was clearly against terrorism and who wanted to pursue bargaining based on compromise. Finally, even those workers who showed passive behaviour towards the struggle became the butt of small-scale terrorism: their clothes were burnt in their lockers, their cars were damaged.[74]

The effects of the terrorist campaign in Fiat were quite different from those the terrorists had expected, though certainly devasting. For the less politicized workers who were already disappointed in the unions, the distinctions between unions, 'Autonomia' and terrorists began to blur, and they became hostile to all three. The unions were literally paralysed for more than three years, as the uninterrupted initiatives of the terrorists forced them into a reactive role. Strikes against the attacks and the murders became the dominant initiative, while the discussion about technical changes in Fiat and about the problems of bargaining over work organization were left on one side. To discuss those topics, on the other hand, became difficult for another reason. The attacks and the murders often depended on information which could only have come from within the unions themselves. As a consequence, mutual suspicion made discussions even more difficult. The managers and foremen had already begun to lose confidence in the unions' capacity to follow a consistent bargaining strategy and now the terrorist attacks introduced a new source of tension and a further reason to withdraw from any collaboration.

1980: the crisis of trade unionism at Fiat

In the autumn of 1977, as we saw, the unions had organized pickets against the management's demands for overtime work. A few months later, the union staged a second strike for supplements to the national agreement concluded only the previous year, which alienated the company management still further. In 1978 the unions launched their 'EUR line', a dramatic change in their national strategy named after the Roman suburb where the policy was first presented: the proposals that the PCI had been putting forward since 1973 were now accepted by the unions as a whole. The EUR line meant a formal commitment from the unions to recentralize the decision-making process at the top of their organizations, and to place sharp limits on shop-floor bargaining. But at precisely the same time the Fiat stewards launched a company-wide dispute about shift working.[75]

At the beginning of 1979 the government, which the PCI supported, fell, giving renewed vigour to those who preferred to rely on direct action rather than agreements. During the strikes for the national agreement in July 1979, strike tactics became tougher than ever: not only was a total blockade organized inside the factory, but even traffic outside was stopped, producing a lasting resentment among Turin's inhabitants against Fiat workers.[76] More important, immediately after the holidays, in September, a wildcat strike began in the paint shops. There, the cabins had been automated, and the managers wanted to cancel the rest-breaks as laid down in the internal agreement. Autonomia managed to get control over the struggle, and the strikes lasted two weeks, provoking great resentment among the workers on the assembly lines in Mirafiori whose output was blocked by the paint-shop dispute. The workers said 'what is this nonsense right after the contract?'[77]

In October Fiat decided suddenly to fire 61 workers: the victims were carefully chosen, some of them were terrorists (as later evidence proved) some were left-wing members of the unions, and some ordinary stewards. A solidarity strike was organized, but it failed twice. In Fiat, the majority of the workers said 'Fiat is right': they personally knew many of the workers fired: 'I do not want to strike to defend Tom, Dick and Harry, who were bullying me . . .'[78] 'But I personally know this one, I saw him doing that with a foreman, I saw him near that machine, doing such and such . . . the other ones will be the same.'[79] But apparently only Fiat proved able to draw the proper conclusions from the failure of these strikes.

Once the PCI-supported government fell in early 1979 the Party's ability to restrain the demands of the shop stewards and local unions became weaker. Amendola, a leading figure in the PCI, attacked the lack of democracy of the workers' assemblies in the plants, which did not use secret ballots, were easily manipulated and tended to alienate the sympathy of the majority of the workers.[80]

The contrast between the unions' position in Fiat and that of the Communist Party was clearly evident by the beginning of 1980. The PCI organized a conference in January where the main point of the discussion was the crisis of the international automobile industry, and the crisis of Fiat within it. (Fiat, interestingly enough, was still hiring, and did not yet acknowledge any crisis.) The PCI saw the main problem as how to make Fiat productive and competitive again, rather than how to overcome the assembly line and how to bargain over the organization of work, the points which the Fiat combine committee[81] had proposed as the central issues facing the unions. The more aggressive line, traditionally very powerful in Turin, was victorious. As a representative of that line later pointed out, the combine committee 'aimed at using the problems posed by the crisis and the post-crisis period to push forward class conflict and shift the power equilibrium within the factory' through the creation of 'embryonic forms of workers' control over the process of restructuring production'.[82]

But a sociological survey, conducted on the basis of a very large sample in January 1980, showed that the workers were only mildly interested in such problems. Only the reduction of unhealthy work was a popular theme, while improvement of the quality of work was not particularly appealing (of interest to only 9.7 per cent). From the same survey a finding emerged which would later cause a sensation: 45 per cent of the workers said that collaboration with the employers was necessary, and 30 per cent that it might be possible. Moreover, the majority said that West Germany was among the countries where the workers were treated better than in Italy.[83]

Meanwhile the crisis in Fiat became very serious indeed. The car section had acquired a separate balance sheet for the first time in 1979 and the losses were quite impressive: 97 billion lira in 1979, 130 the following year.[84] The market was declining sharply: Fiat, in September 1980, expected its sales to decline by some half a million cars over the following year and a half. Part of the responsibility for this was attributed to the nine million strike hours in 1979, which reduced the supply when the demand was still rising.[85] Facing a crisis of this magnitude, even the new experimental automatic lines were to be abandoned, since Fiat thought at that point that they were too expensive and too rigid. The most recent robotic system (Robogate, 1978) celebrated until a few months before, was now said to be six times more expensive than a traditional assembly line, and to take up four times more space.[86]

Fiat's main aim became to sack large numbers of workers and to recover its control over the workforce.

In July, Umberto Agnelli was replaced by Cesare Romiti, a managerial hawk from the accounting division of Fiat. Immediately after the holidays, Fiat proposed to place 24,000 workers in *Cassa Integrazione*, the state-financed temporary unemployment fund. The unions rejected this outright and broke off negotiations; at that point Fiat declared its intention to *sack* 15,000 workers, beginning on 6 October. At the end of September, after a series of unsuccessful meetings between union and Fiat managers and a series of strikes, solidarity strikes and demonstrations, the government collapsed for a variety of reasons. Alarmed by the power vacuum, Fiat then proposed to return to its original proposal: 24,000 in *Cassa Integrazione*, and only for three months.

But the unions refused, and hardened their strike tactics instead. They decided to blockade Fiat, beginning on 3 October. Three days later Fiat sent letters of dismissal to the 24,000 workers, and from that point these workers began to be paid by the *Cassa Integrazione*. Those workers on strike who were still employed by Fiat, however, were now losing their wages entirely. Fiat, suffering from an overproduction crisis, was not particularly worried by the strike: its stocks were still full of cars, and it could save large sums on wages.[87] Finally on 14 October the foremen and supervisors, who had tried several times to break through the pickets in the previous days, organized a demonstration, which proved amazingly successful: from 25,000 to 40,000 people, and among them many blue-collar workers as well, demonstrated silently in Turin against the unions' policy. That very night an agreement was signed which represented a real defeat: 24,000 workers in CI and not for three months, but for three years. They would not be reintroduced into the factory until June 1983. In fact in 1985 they had still not been re-employed.

The agreement met fierce resistance from the more militant workers and produced terrible disappointment, and a collapse of confidence in the unions. Although the stewards' structure was not dismantled, many of the work-group leaders not directly linked to the unions were sacked. In some cases the unions survived, but without their informal organization in the shop; in others the latter survived while the steward was sacked, or transferred. As one steward pointed out, 'in some places they left the water and took away the fish, elsewhere they left the fish and drained the water.'[88] In the following years only a small minority of the Fiat workforce was involved in strikes. The more militant and conflict-oriented wing of the unions (FIM, for instance) suffered the most severe crisis, while a clear analysis of the defeat did not occur. Instead, quite mythical interpretations of what had happened flourished: Fiat was supposed to have hired the 20,000 workers from 1977 to 1980 in order to prepare its revenge; again, Fiat was supposed to have completely organized the demonstration of the 40,000 and so on.

It is interesting, though, that in those shops where the stewards had managed in previous years to set up a formalized process of internal bargaining, there have recently been new agreements, such as that dealing with the LAM (*Linea Asincrona Montaggio Motori*) in the machine shop, where electrically controlled trailers are used on engine assembly.

CONCLUSIONS

In this chapter I have emphasized the central influence of political discourse, organizations and events in shaping the history of industrial relations at Fiat since the late 1960s. But this centrality of politics is not confined to the 1960s and 1970s. As we have seen, it was already present in the labour upsurge of the 1940s and the employers' reaction of the 1950s. In fact, its origins can be traced back to the *biennio rosso* of 1919–20, when Fiat was the most important factory in Italy occupied by the workers, and to the subsequent Fascist reaction.

Industrial relations in Fiat, then, presents, in an exaggerated form, the distinctive pattern of Italian industrial relations more broadly: a series of dramatic strike waves, followed by an opposite reaction by the employers; and every swing of the pendulum reconfirms the pattern, as the momentary losers plan their future revenge. The memory of defeat and the desire for vengeance are stored up by the unions and parties outside the factory, as well as by the firm's top management, ready to be brought back to the shop floor when conditions change.

Most recently, Fiat's management has turned its massive automation projects against the unions' previous strength in the plant, and has used a technology which would in theory allow an increase in worker responsibility to centralize information and decision-making instead. On the other side, an important strand within the labour movement is developing an interpretation of the 1980s in terms of capitalist plot and repression. Though this line is stronger among union officials outside the factory than among working shop stewards, it seems unlikely that this pattern of politicized, conflictual industrial relations at Fiat will be broken in the foreseeable future.

NOTES

1 L. Lanzardo, *Classe operaia e partito comunista alla Fiat* (Turin, 1971), pp. 529–92.
2 G. Contini, 'Le lotte operaie contro il taglio dei tempi e la svolta nella politica rivendicativa della Fiom (1955–1956)', *Classe* 16 (December 1978).

3   R. Gianotti, *Lotte e organizzazione di classe alla Fiat (1948–1970)* (Bari, 1970), pp. 233–48.
4   V. Foa, 'La struttura della paga ieri ed oggi', *Rassegna Sindacale*, 31 December 1955; S. Garavini, 'Bisogna contrattare la produzione', *Rassegna Sindacale*, 31 January 1956.
5   V. Rieser, 'L'inchiesta operaia come strumento di analisi e di lotta', in E. Benenati (ed.), *Cultura e sindacato a Torino sul finire degli anni '50* (Cuneo, 1981).
6   The first and most famous inquiry, was: G. Carocci, 'Inchiesta alla Fiat', *Nuovi Argomenti*, March–June 1958.
7   R. Panzieri, 'Sull'uso politico delle macchine nel neocapitalismo'; V. Foa, 'Lotte operaie nello sviluppo capitalistico'; S. Garavini, 'Salario e rivendicazioni di potere', all in *Quaderni Rossi* 1 (reprinted, Milan, 1970).
8   First interview with a group of Fiat foreman, 5 July 1983.
9   A. Baldissera, 'Alle origini della politica della diseguaglianza nell' Italia degli anni '80: la marcia dei quarantamila', *Quaderni di Sociologia*, 31, no. 1 (1984); E. Deaglio, *La Fiat com'è* (Milan, 1975), p. 58.
10 Interview with F. Celestini, worker in Fiat Mirafiori press shop, 6 September 1983; interview with N. Laterza, former worker in Fiat Mirafiori body shop, 11 May 1983; interview with Dr A. Eustache, former personnel manager in Fiat, 8 July 1983.
11 B. Bottiglieri, 'I capi intermedi nella grande industria meccanica torinese', unpublished paper, May 1983, p. 23.
12 First interview with a group of Fiat foremen.
13 G. Fofi, *L'immigrazione meridionale a Torino* (Milan, 1976), p. 305. This point is confirmed in interviews with N. Laterza; G. Alasia, former militant of the Italian Socialist Party and then of the Italian Socialist Party of Proletarian Unity (PSIUP), 24 May 1983; L. Azzolina, worker and shop steward in Fiat Mirafiori body shop, 22 September 1983; M. Hernis, former worker and shop steward in Fiat Mirafiori, now union official (FIOM), 21 September 1983; F. Zagaria, former worker in Fiat Mirafiori 9 May 1983; P. De Stefani, worker and shop steward (FIM) in Fiat Mirafiori mechanic shop, 14 September (1982).
14 The difference between the two migratory streams is stressed in my first and in my second (5 July 1983) interviews with two groups of Fiat foremen.
15 V. Comito, *La Fiat tra crisi e ristrutturazione* (Rome, 1982), p. 59.
16 G. Agnelli, 'Le prospettive della produzione e lo sviluppo tecnologico italiano ed europeo', *Mondo Economico* 1 April 1967. G. Agnelli, 'Potere politico ed impresa economica per lo sviluppo della società italiana', *Mondo Economico*, 24 June 1967.
17 Interview with M. Hernis, a Communist worker from Sicily who was a member of the *Commissione Interna* in the 1960s.
18 The agreement is reproduced in G. Mafodda and R. Pigollo, 'La contestazione dell'organizzazione del lavoro attraverso l'esperienza di un delegato' (thesis, Università di Torino, 1978–9). In an interview with G. Frasca, worker in Fiat Mirafiori, 21 September 1983, it was reported that a foreman exclaimed 'What?! They put the notice boards *there*?' and a second said, 'Don't worry they [the workers] don't understand anything.'
19 A. Dina, 'Fiat: i 35 giorni e dopo', *Classe* 19 (June 1981), p. 31.
20 On the early crisis of 'Lotta Continua', the major extraparliamentary group, in its relations with Fiat workers, see L. Bobbio, *Lotta Continua* (Rome, 1977) pp. 59 ff.

21 M. Burnier, Fiat: *Conseils ouvriers et syndicat* (Paris, 1980), pp. 235–7.
22 G. Contini, 'Politics, Law and Shop Floor Bargaining in Postwar Italy', in
    S. Tolliday and J. Zeitlin (eds.), *Shop Floor bargaining and the State*
    (Cambridge, 1985).
23 A. Dina, 'Un'esperienza di movimento politico di massa: le lotte interne alla
    Fiat (fine 1968–giugno 1969)', *Classe* 2 (1970); Gruppi di lavoro del PSIUP
    torinese (eds.), *Per un movimento politico di massa* (Turin, 1969).
24 Interviews with M. Hernis; F. Albergoni, former worker in Fiat, 26 May 1983;
    G. Alasia; L. Azzolina; P. De Stefani; C. Cosi, worker and shop steward in
    Fiat Mirafiori mechanic shop, 7 July 1983.
25 C. Sabel, *Work and Politics*, (Cambridge, 1982) pp. 145–67.
26 Interview with M. Hernis; see also note 12.
27 First interview with foremen.
28 On the crisis of the foremen at the beginning of the seventies, see Deaglio, *La
    Fiat*, pp. 59–61; Bottiglieri, 'I capi intermedi' pp. 58 ff. (he argues that a crucial
    cause of the foremen's crisis was the fact that in the seventies they lost the power
    of giving out bonuses directly to their workers). The foremen that I interviewed
    gave me abundant information about their crisis during the seventies; other
    information came from workers and managers.
29 Contini, 'Politics, Law and Shop Floor Bargaining'.
30 I. Regalia, M. Regini and E. Reyneri, 'Labour Conflicts and Industrial Relations
    in Italy', in C. Crouch and A. Pizzorno (eds.), *The Resurgence of Class Conflict
    in Western Europe since 1968* (London, 1978), vol. I, p. 130.
31 F. Chiaromonte (ed.), *La contrattazione aziendale dell'organizzazione del lavoro
    1976–79* (Rome, 1981).
32 The agreement of July was published by FIM-FIOM-UILM: *Fiat, Testo
    dell'accordo luglio 1971* (Turin, 1971).
33 Interview with U. Monzeglio, worker in Fiat Mirafiori and now national official
    of FIOM, 21 September 1983.
34 Mafodda and Pigollo, 'La contestazione', p. 362.
35 Moreover, 16,000 workers were promoted to a higher category; job enrichment
    and job enlargement were envisaged, in terms of job improvement (if possible)
    and in terms of rotation.
36 A. Milanaccio and L. Ricolfi, *Lotte operaie e ambiente di lavoro* (Turin, 1976).
37 A. Palazzo, 'La contestazione dell'organizzazione del lavoro a Mirafiori
    (1972–1975)' (thesis, Università di Torino, 1978–9), pp. 81 ff.
38 First interview with Fiat foremen.
39 Interview with U. Monzeglio.
40 Interviews with C. Cosi, P. De Stefani, N. Laterza and F. Celestini.
41 Palazzo, 'La contestazione', p. 23.
42 Ibid.
43 Milanaccio and Ricolfi, *Lotte operaie*, pp. 95–9.
44 The success in these areas (particularly the second) is recognized even by those
    scholars who stressed in their research the gulf between the unions'
    representatives in the plants and the rank and file. See, for instance, Burnier,
    Fiat, pp. 201–3.
45 M. Rollier, 'Mutamenti nell'organizzasione del lavoro negli anni '70: Fiat',
    Rassegna Sindacale 64–5 (1980). Even Comito, in *Fiat*, follows this pattern,
    pp. 234–44 basing himself on the introductory document for the national
    conference of Fiat Communists held in January 1980.
46 Deaglio, *La Fiat*, pp. 90–1; Burnier, *Fiat*, p. 249.

47 Part of the literature on this topic is unreliable. E. Deaglio, in *La Fiat*, talks about the persecution of the workers, but in fact from his book the workers he is talking about seem to have been, more precisely, very well-known militants of Deaglio's own group, 'Lotta Continua' (p. 72); the same seems true, though in a much less open way, for A. Bulgarelli's statements in *Crisi e mobilità' operaia* (Milan, 1978).

48 Bulgarelli, *Crisi*, p. 112.

49 Ibid.

50 In 1977 the agreement, which at first concerned only the Mirafiori body shop, Spa Stura and Rivalta, was extended to Fiat as a whole: ibid., p. 130.

51 Ibid., p. 102.

52 Ibid., p. 133.

53 Comito, *La Fiat* pp. 237–8.

54 Quoted in A. Dina, 'Crisi Fiat: si discute il nuovo modo di lavorare negli anni '80', *Classe* 18 (December 1980) p. 32.

55 Particularly in the press shop, where the shop stewards tried to set up an 'integrated work group': interview with G. Gino 8 July 1983, and with F. Celestini.

56 Rollier, 'Mutamenti'; Dina, 'Crisi', p. 33.

57 IRES-CGIL (ed.), 'Ricerca su consigli di fabbrica e delegati', (xerox, Turin, 1983), ch. 2, p. 14.

58 Deaglio, *La Fiat*, p. 59. The difficulty of reshaping the existing personnel to fit it into this new task emerges from my interview with Dr Eustache.

59 Interview with C. Cosi.

60 A. Becchi and S. Negrelli, 'Personnel Planning and Industrial Relations. Fiat: Case Study of Italy's Auto Industry', in W. Streek and A. Hoff (eds.), *Workforce Restructuring, Manpower Management and Industrial Relations in the World Automobile Industry* (Berlin, 1983).

61 It is interesting to note that in 1977 the unions were confronting the problem of unemployment as a major one, particularly youth unemployment. There was a quite strong campaign in the media, the unions being accused of defending only the strong sector of the labour force.

62 Interview with Dr A. Eustache; A. Pesce, 'La difficile utopia del possibile', *Inchiesta* 48 (November–December 1980), p. 12.

63 ISFOL/ Regione Piemonte and Cooperativa Matraia (eds.), *Caratteristiche e comportamenti degli operai Fiat in mobilità* (Rome, 1983), p. 123.

64 Ibid.

65 Interview with L. Azzolina.

66 Comito, *La Fiat*, pp. 220–31; Becchi and Negrelli, *Personnel*.

67 Interview with L. Azzolina.

68 Interview with N. Laterza. Second interview with Fiat foremen.

69 Interview with L. Azzolina.

70 Second interview with foremen.

71 Interviews with M. Hernis and with F. Zagaria.

72 Burnier, *Fiat*, p. 257.

73 Interviews with C. Cosi and with U. Monzeglio.

74 Second interview with Fiat foremen.

75 Interview with U. Monzeglio.

76 Interviews with U. Monzeglio and with A. Giallara, workers at Fiat Mirafiori, 23 September 1983); see also G. Bocca, *I signori dello sciopero* (Cles, 1982) p. 72.

77 Interviews with U. Monzeglio and with M. Hernis; see also Bocca, *I signori*, pp. 71–3.
78 Interview with U. Monzeglio.
79 Interview with L. Azzolina.
80 Quoted in Bocca, *I signori*, pp. 71–3.
81 Pesce, 'La difficile', p. 7.
82 Ibid.
83 A. Accornero, A. Baldissera and S. Scamuzzi, 'Ricerca di massa sulla condizione operaia alla Fiat: primi risultati', *Bollettino CESPE* 2 (February 1980).
84 Comito, *La Fiat*, p. 226.
85 See the statements of Fiat's top management, 10 September 1980 in *Bollettino Mensile di documentazione – Federazione CGIL-CISL-UIL Piemonte* 36 (December 1980), pp. 26–7.
86 Dina, 'Crisi Fiat', p. 35.
87 D. Gambetta, 'The Fiat Strike: Turin, September–October 1980', unpublished paper, Cambridge, April 1981.
88 Interview with G. Giulio.

7

Industrial Relations in the Japanese Automobile Industry 1945-70: the Case of Toyota

Reiko Okayama

The Japanese automobile industry dates back to the early 1900s. At that time it was unable to produce automobiles commercially, partly because of the technical incompetence of the industry and its suppliers and partly because of unfavourable market conditions. The First World War and the great earthquake of 1923 gave some momentum to the development of the industry, but it was foreign manufacturers such as GM and Ford who grasped those opportunities. In 1933 1,000 cars were produced domestically while 36,000 were imported.

The government was concerned about the backwardness of the industry, which, they thought, would aggravate the balance of payments, impede the development of the engineering industry and hamper the military security of the nation. On the outbreak of the Manchurian War in 1931 the government hastened to promote the development of the industry. Under a law that came into effect in 1936, automobile manufacturers were required to be Japanese corporations and to have a licence from the government. The government intended to enhance the competitiveness of the domestic automobile industry by concentrating production in a few big firms. Toyota and Nissan, and some years later, Isuzu, were granted this privilege.

In 1939 the production of domestic manufacturers rose above 30,000 units while the number of imported cars decreased drastically to zero. This occurred because the government raised tax rates on imported parts by up to 60 per cent and on cars by up to 70 per cent of the value, and also because the government put a considerable degree of restrictions on knock-down production by foreign manufacturers. During the war, the Japanese car firms were busily employed and in 1940 total production, mostly trucks for the army, reached over 50,000 units. The Japanese automobile industry thus established itself as one heavily concentrated on truck production.[1]

After defeat in the Second World War, the industry began a new era and shifted its course from military to civilian production and towards a highly competitive market. Since its foundation in 1937, Toyota had been interested in making mass-produced small-sized passenger cars. Immediately after the surrender of Japan it was hard to imagine that the Japanese automobile industry would develop into one of the most competitive in the world. Even in 1950, the Governor of the Bank of Japan remarked that it would be absurd for Japan to build passenger cars itself. Japan should buy American cars which were cheap and of better quality as it was now the age of the international division of labour.[2] Yet in one generation the Japanese industry became the world leader. How did they manage to achieve such success in this short period of time? This article will focus on Toyota and try to clarify this question in relation to the development of its industrial-relations and labour-management techniques from 1945 to 1970, paying special attention to the company's market and technological conditions.

The period will be divided into three phases: 1945–50, the 1950s and the 1960s. Each stage is characterized by different conditions of markets and technology. These two interrelated factors were crucial in some of the key managerial decisions about labour management. At the same time, the technology of the production process would play a decisive part in determining the character of the labour force that was required. Accordingly I will pay special attention to Toyota's market and technological conditions and the structure of the market.

The following analysis starts with the period 1945–50 and considers the relationship between labour and management in the period immediately after the war. First it considers the industrial strife of 1950 which proved to be a turning point in the history of postwar industrial relations at Toyota. Then it focuses on the technological innovations in the 1950s and their impact on work and shop-floor practices. Finally it examines aspects of the mass-production system established in the 1960s to shed light on the managerial techniques which fostered the integration of the workforce into the business bureaucracy. Some concluding comments will follow concerning the contemporary system of human resources management at Toyota.

1945–50: BUSINESS TURMOIL AND INDUSTRIAL RELATIONS

In the midst of the general collapse immediately after the war, some automobile manufacturers showed considerable foresight. At a meeting of management at the Toyota Motor Co., one senior executive remarked as early as 16 August 1945, the day following unconditional surrender, that the company had to resume production as a civilian industry and that the future would lie in business overseas. In October of the same year, Kiichiro Toyoda, the president of the firm said, 'we are going to have a free market economy and there will be fierce competition in both the domestic and overseas markets. We shall have to cope with these new conditions. Japanese auto makers have been accustomed to a protective environment since their infancy, and this has dramatically reduced their competitiveness.' He also suggested that they produce a limited range of cars; that machines and facilities should be specialized and that mass production should be introduced.[3] Despite this, the company was confronted with a discouraging and harsh environment. In September 1945 the General Headquarters of the Allied Forces (GHQ) allowed Japanese automobile makers to produce 1,500 trucks a month to ease shortages and assist internal transportation. But the production of passenger cars was prohibited until June 1947, and until October 1949, annual production was restricted to 300 cars. Commercial vehicles were in very short supply due to the seizure of motor-vehicles for munitions purposes during the war. At the end of 1945 there were only 5,808 trucks left for commercial use and 14,875 horse/ox-drawn carriages and man-pulled carts.[4]

Furthermore, management in the automobile industry was severely restricted by a series of regulations set up by the Occupation forces. Toyota was luckier than other automobile manufacturers, such as Nissan, in that although the main factory of Toyota was designated to pay reparations in June 1946, it was released almost at once in August 1946 because of its slight involvement in war production. Nevertheless, management at Toyota was still under strict control from April 1946 to April 1951. During this period it needed permission from the Finance minister to start new ventures, invest in new machinery, issue stocks, declare dividends and so on.[5] They also suffered from a vicious inflationary spiral and, as time went by, a shortage of capital, raw materials, parts and components due to price increases and an economic run-down in related industries.

However, with the development of the cold war and an increased realization that severe restrictions on Japanese industries had caused only economic chaos, which would make Japan a burden to US taxpayers, the Occupation redirected its policies at the beginning of 1948 to make Japan stand on its own feet. Against the background of this shift, automobile industrialists in October 1948, after a year of pressure, obtained a promise from the government that priority would be given to auto production in the allocation of resources. At the same time the government set out a five-year recovery plan for the automobile industry, beginning in 1949 with the intention that all motor vehicles supplied during the period concerned should be produced domestically.[6] Also in 1949 the GHQ abolished the restriction on the production of passenger cars.

But just as the industry appeared to be moving towards reconstruction, it was hard hit by the deflationary policies of 1949 introduced by Dodge, the American special envoy responsible for the direction of the Japanese economy, in an attempt to counter the spiralling postwar inflation. The automobile industry was thrown into confusion again and all firms fell into a critical condition. Toyota, one of the biggest, faced impending bankruptcy at the end of 1949, and in the following months of early 1950 they experienced a period of intense industrial strife. For the first time in its history the company was confronted by organized labour. This conflict was a turning point in Toyota's industrial relations and shaped the future system of labour relations in the company. The next section considers the birth of a labour union at Toyota and the events of 1950.

AN ALL-GRADES UNION

In the early days of the Occupation, trade unionism was actively encouraged as part of a 'democratization process'. Organized labour was encouraged to counterbalance the power of management. A directive from the Supreme Commander of the Allied Powers (SCAP) concerning democratization was issued to the Japanese government on 11 October 1945 and the Trade Union Law was promptly enacted on 22 December and came into force on 1 March 1946. For the first time since the country's industrialization, Japanese workers had the legal right to organize, to engage in collective bargaining and to strike. Partly encouraged by this support from the Occupation, partly intoxicated by liberation from the rigours of war, and partly driven by the desperation of a defeated country, and above all, by the shortage of food and spiralling inflation, labour organization spread like wildfire. Even in the short and chaotic period from the day of the surrender to the end of 1945, some 380,000 workers became union members. One year later, the membership had risen to nearly 5 million, and the number of unions had reached 17,266. By June 1948, at the end of the 'reform' era which was introduced by changes in Occupation policy towards the trade-union movement, there existed 33,900 unions and their membership had leaped to 6,533,954.[7] Toyota workers were also involved with this hurried unionization.

On 15 August 1945 the Toyota Motor Company had 11,000 employees at the Koromo plant, the main factory, including the mobilized workers, who were disbanded immediately after Japan's surrender. In a state of confusion about the future of the automobile industry and in response to SCAP's first directive on 2 September that the armed forces should be dismantled and all munitions production stopped, the company decided on 15 September to cut the workforce by half and made an appeal to the employees for voluntary retirement. Owing to deep anxiety about the firm's future, there were only 3,700 workers left in October, 800 fewer than the management had planned at first.[8] It was these employees who organized a labour union in Toyota on 19 January 1946.

According to the memoirs of a senior official at the time, the management had observed a move towards unionization among their blue-collar workers immediately after the war. The management felt extremely uneasy that the proposed union might only consist of blue-collar workers, and they were seriously alarmed at the threat of the emergence of a 'class-struggle' oriented union. Therefore, taking advantage of a move among the white-collar employees towards unionization, the management held several talks with some engineers, managerial staff and clerks who sympathized with the fears of the management and asked them to try to persuade the blue-collar workers to construct an all-grades union.[9]

However, the blue-collar workers were proud of being skilled workers who built cars with their own hands and they were suspicious of the white-collar employees because of differences and distinctions between them in socio-economic conditions. There were harsh, heated arguments and discussions over the rules and officers of the proposed union, but finally the negotiators from both sides agreed upon one union organization, named the Koromo Labour Union of Toyota Motor Company. All employees were entitled to join except for the senior management.[10] It seems natural that the organization should be based on the enterprise, since up to that time the majority of them had no experience of the trade-union movement and there was no inheritable legacy of other types of trade unions upon which they might otherwise have modelled themselves. Another important factor was the significance that the workers attached to the company's 'internal labour market', which recruited juveniles as future key workers and provided training in the company, a promotion ladder, security of employment and company welfare facilities.

Shortly after its establishment, Toyota had set up a company training school for their locally recruited apprentices.[11] Like other big employers at that time, Toyota adopted this policy in order to develop their future key workers through their own educational system. Bargaining about employment and working conditions had always been on a company basis and it was only in the workplace that workers identified a need for solidarity to protect their common interests. As one Toyota worker put it, 'No one had any doubt that the proposed union should consist only of his fellow workers in the plant.'[12]

Why did the blue-collar workers prefer an all-grades organization? The *Sanpo* organization during the war may have had some influence on the adoption of this form of organization. The *Sanpo* movement started in 1938 to raise efficiency and promote cooperation under the guidance and control of the government. Each firm was forced to establish an institution called *Sanpo* inside the company, headed by the President and including all employees, the first time blue- and white-collar workers had been brought together in the same organization. After the war, it was the senior blue-collar workers, especially *kumicho* (under-foremen) and *hancho* (heads of work groups) who took a lead in the formation of an all-grades union, and overcame the opposition of the rank and file workers to being in the same organization as the *shokuin* (the white-collar employees). On 19 January 1946, the Koromo union held its opening ceremony amidst tremendous enthusiasm. The leadership of the union was assumed by junior managers or supervisors and an effort was made to reflect a balance of white- and blue-collar representation in the union hierarchy.[13]

The policy of the Toyota union immediately after the war was a curious mixture of confrontation and cooperation with management. This in some ways reflected the atmosphere and orientation of the contemporary labour movement. On the one hand, driven by hardships and the shortage of necessities, the union's prime objectives were increases in production and the reconstruction of industry so that their members could get better conditions. The idea of industrial reconstruction was a pervasive ideology which influenced postwar labour circles in varying degrees. On the other hand, unions insisted on having their say in business management by building up 'joint councils' in the firms, driven by a spirit of democracy and egalitarianism.

The Toyota union, too, proposed to management in March 1946 that the union and management should set up a central works council, consisting of senior executives and senior union officers, in order to promote the development of the industry. The proposal was accepted and from April 1946 to April 1950, when there was the industrial trouble, the council members met 125 times and dealt not only with matters concerning working and employment conditions but also production and personnel management.[14] The union also demanded other changes, notably an end to discrimination between the *shokuin* and the *koin* (the blue-collar workers) and the narrowing of pay differentials between them. Work groups were allowed to express their opinions about the *kumicho*. Finally a committee composed of shop stewards and supervisors was established on the shop floor to assess and settle pay increases for individual workers. However, these new, and radical measures to give a voice to rank and file workers were short-lived. The employers soon began to recover their right to manage.[15]

Although nearly all postwar Japanese labour unions started as enterprise unions, they soon began to develop industry-wide federations so as to avoid the weaknesses of enterprise-based unions in collective bargaining. In this way, the All-Japan Automobile Workers Union (AJAWU or the Federation) took shape in April 1947 initiated by some big unions such as those of Toyota and Nissan, and comprising 108 affiliated enterprise unions with a membership of 44,817 in the automobile and related industries.[16]

The AJAWU demanded industry-wide collective bargaining with the automobile employers. In reality, however, they could not ever establish hegemony over the affiliated unions. Plant or company-wide bargaining continued, with each union putting forward its own claims locally for security of employment, a seniority wage system and welfare facilities. As time went on, the leadership of the Federation became increasingly politicized and began to call for a united front of industrial workers in order to establish a democratic government instead of the established capitalist one.

Even so, the moves of the Toyota union were influenced by the militancy of AJAWU. In the late 1940s, leadership of the union was in the hands of some enthusiastic engineers, managerial staff and clerks who devoted themselves to the idea of the reconstruction of the company. However, at the same time, some active unionists were sympathetic to the Federation's militancy, including some communists, most of whom were young, and they exerted considerable influence among the rank and file.[17] Thus the power structure of the union was not monolithic. But even these radicals had an affinity to the idea of the reconstruction of the industry and of the company as a means to obtain better conditions. Until the late 1940s, the behaviour of the union was tolerated by management because management itself was dismayed by the socio-economic upheavals of the time. They badly needed their employees' help in the reconstruction of the company.

However, from early 1948, the tide began to change in favour of management. As the preceding section described, the Occupation's policy towards Japanese industry and the Japanese labour movement was redirected towards fostering a revival of capitalism in the economy. Encouraged by this shift in the business environment, and in part alarmed at the considerable influx of foreign-made cars into the domestic market through the Occupation forces, Toyota management started to implement their rationalization programme to reduce costs and raise productivity. Machinery and facilities were repaired and modernized by government loans that amounted by the end of 1948 to ¥427 million. (From 1949 to 1971 the conversion rate of the Yen was ¥360 to the dollar.) A wage system based on payment by results was forced into the machine shop. A general staff section was established at the top tier of management to help senior executives coordinate departmental activities.[18]

At the same time, management was careful to maintain the cooperation of the union in the reconstruction of the company. In October 1948 a business rationalization committee was set up including some union officials. In January 1949 the management proposed to the union that middle managers such as section managers should be excluded from membership of the union. Management appear to have become confident that they could deal with the union without the agency of these middle managers. Moreover, the union membership of section managers had become an obstacle for higher management in their pursuit of rationalization. The union, however, rejected these proposals because they had reaped many advantages from the knowledge of their white-collar members in matters of day to day management.[19]

The rationalization plan caused a lot of friction and conflict on the shop floor because it intensified labour effort and also broke down the traditional shop culture. However, management proceeded with their plan and succeeded in maintaining the union's cooperation. It was at this moment that they encountered the drastic economic changes resulting from Dodge's deflationary policy. The general recession that followed resulted in a major confrontation at Toyota in 1950.

THE INDUSTRIAL STRUGGLES OF 1950–3

At the time of the government's reconstruction plan for the automobile industry in October 1948, automobile manufacturers were optimistic about the future. Toyota drew up a five-year plan based on small-sized passenger-car production. But the plan was doomed to fail because of the business upheavals of the following year.

In November 1948 the GHQ proclaimed that the economy should be stabilized and that loans and subsidies which might impose a heavy burden on public finances would be forbidden. Toyota was not slow to respond to this shift and set up a business-rationalization committee consisting of senior management executives and representatives from the union to enhance efficiency and cut costs to the minimum. The company was badly short of working capital by September 1949, and had only ¥200 million in cash, even though they had sold ¥350 million worth of cars. In the recession which followed the implementation of the Dodge line, wages and salaries were not always paid regularly and on 23 December the management and the union in a meeting of the central works council agreed to the proposal from the rationalization committee that there should be a ten per cent cut in the wage bill until April 1950 but that there should be no redundancies at all.

Nevertheless, the situation went from bad to worse. A bank consortium, which had rescued the company with a loan of ¥188 million at the end of the year, demanded that the company should undertake thoroughgoing remedies, including the separation of sales from production. They wanted a new sales company to be established, and wanted surplus employees to be dismissed. The company resisted but eventually had to give in to this final demand. On 22 April they presented a reconstruction plan to the union. The average monthly production target was to be 940 units. About 1,600 workers (20.3 per cent of all employees) were to be made redundant. There was also to be a ten per cent reduction in average wages and salaries for the survivors. The union, since its establishment, had cooperated in every effort by the management to revive the industry and now the workers felt deceived. There was a spate of disturbances. There were walk-outs, shop rallies, union meetings and supervisors were heckled. Production dropped sharply to 304 units in May, compared to 992 units in March, and the price of stock tumbled. Amidst this turmoil Kiichiro Toyoda, the president, Kazuo Kumabe, the vice-president, and Kohachiro Nishimura, a managing director, resigned on 5 June. The new management made a desperate appeal to the employees for help and asked them to accept the proposed reconstruction plan. In the end, this plea was successful, mainly because of the great concern about the future of the company felt by the employees, particularly those who had benefited from special training inside the company. This feeling was intensified by the resignation of the top three executives and also by the fact that other automobile manufacturers had intensified competition following the removal of controls on automobile production and distribution by GHQ in the autumn of 1949. On 10 June the union accepted the proposal of the management and the two months of strife ended. About 1,700 individuals left the company and nearly 6,000 remained.[20]

Those discharged included all Communists and many activists.[21] A few months later, Japanese labour circles experienced a 'red purge' that was ordered by GHQ because of the Korean War. However, nobody was discharged in Toyota for being an alleged Communist at that time. The redundancy of 1,700 individuals had already enabled management to get rid of those who were standing in their way.

Even so, after the 1950 dispute, labour relations remained difficult. Management remained hostile to the union, which they believed was influenced by radical 'outside' unionism through AJAWU. AJAWU swung left as part of a broader trend within the labour movement immediately after the formation of *Sohyo* (General Council of Trade Unions of Japan) in July 1952. The establishment of this body was supported by GHQ as part of their policy of promoting 'true' democratic labour unions. The Toyota union also began to make some renewed radical moves under the leadership of AJAWU. In May 1953, AJAWU instructed its affiliated unions to demand wage claims based on years of job experience and the cost of living.

Following this instruction, the Toyota union, together with the Nissan and Isuzu unions, made a demand for wage increases as well as for bonus payments equivalent to two months' wages. Management's reply was that this was a time for increased cooperation and effort towards producing Japan's first passenger cars, and not the time to demand such pay increases. The union stopped work on 11 June at the assembly works and carried out shop rallies, walk-outs and heckling of the plant director till 5 August, when the strike ended in the defeat of the union. It appears that the apprentice workers played an important role in encouraging workers to return to work.

Management made no concessions, reaffirmed their managerial prerogatives and rejected all claims from 'militant' unions to widen the functions of collective bargaining beyond the boundaries of each firm.[22]

Alongside their unyielding stand, management also took new steps to get the workforce to identify personally with the company. In 1952, two newly appointed personnel officers had begun to try to improve labour relations but had encountered deep hostility from the workers. Although baffled and perplexed at first, these two personnel officers approached some key workers who had long since graduated from the company training school and finished their apprenticeships. The personnel officers talked to them every evening after work in informal groups of former classmates from the school. The officers argued that harmonious employer–employee relationships and mutual understanding were an indispensable prerequisite for the company's survival. If things continued as they were, the company's future would be jeopardized.

Gradually they won over groups of workers. The workers began to participate in discussions and management encouraged them to make up small groups based on school careers, birthplaces, managerial positions, sex, interests, etc.[23] These human-relations techniques and communications systems contributed to fostering the integration of the workforce into the company's goals.

Meanwhile, the failure of the industrial disputes of 1953 doomed AJAWU to dissolution. In the early summer of 1953, the Federation's strategies provoked open or skeptical criticism by the affiliated unions. At a meeting of the Federation, a Toyota union delegate openly attacked the Federation by saying that it was the wrong policy to put workers against management by disruptive activities at the workplace.[24] Before long, the Toyota and

Isuzu unions gave in, although the Nissan union fought on bitterly until mid-September. The united front of the three unions had been broken, and finally the Federation was dissolved in December 1954. This dissolution paved the way for a further development of the enterprise-based industrial relations of the industry. Soon after the dissolution of AJAWU, the Toyota union established their own federation in conjunction with the labour unions which organized regular employees in Toyota's related companies.[25]

This action by the Toyota union started a new trend. They shifted course towards harmony and stability in industrial relations. They now believed that improved conditions for union members inside, as well as outside, the factory were linked inseparably to the company's growth. Furthermore they realized that the growth of the company, and hence improved employment conditions, depended upon increased productivity.

TECHNICAL INNOVATION AND WORKPLACE INDUSTRIAL RELATIONS

From 1950, the Korean War set off a long wave of rising demand and rising profits. The reinvestment of these profits, the associated technical innovation, and, from the mid-1950s, harmonious industrial relations provided the foundations for Toyota to move into mass production. During the war period, increases in production could never keep pace with rapidly growing demand. By March 1951, the company was producing 1,542 trucks per month, although its monthly production capacity was supposed to be 1,200 units. By September 1951 the profits were ¥733 million, and from March 1951 the company resumed dividend payments of 20 per cent which had been stopped since 1944. They were also able to invest ¥350 million in the company in September 1951, whereas before the outbreak of the Korean War they had had a deficit of ¥129 million.[26]

Thus the Korean War was a panacea for the depressed economy. After the Peace Treaty of 1952, however, the automobile manufacturers found themselves facing severe competition from the increased influx of foreign passenger cars into Japan. The auto makers particularly feared European competitors, whose product strategies, like their own, were based on small-sized cars.[27] Some Japanese automobile companies scrambled for licences from European automobile makers so that they could close their technological lag and compete with foreign imports. Toyota, however, chose to make their own passenger cars after some abortive negotiations with Ford.[28] In both cases colossal sums of money were invested during the fifties to update equipment. As a result the 1950s was a remarkable period of technical innovation, preparing the way for the advent of mass-production systems in the sixties. These innovations, and the new production and labour-management techniques which accompanied them, transformed the shop floor.

Meanwhile, during the Korean War, two senior executives of the company, Eiji Toyoda and Shoichi Saito, made independent tours of the

United States between July 1950 and January 1951. They looked at automobile technologies, business management techniques, and market conditions around the country, and in particular studied Ford, in Detroit. On their return home, the company introduced a five-year rationalization plan of production facilities to update its equipment, largely by importing modern machinery from abroad, and to enlarge the scale of production to cope with the anticipated intense competition. The company aimed at the production of 3,000 units per month at the initial stage of the plan, without any increase in personnel. The management also invested heavily to realize their long cherished idea of full commercial production of a small-sized passenger car. Thus the Toyopet Crown, the first Japanese mass-produced passenger car was put on the market in January 1955. It was immediately popular and production rose sharply from 1956.[29]

In the period of this five-year plan, the company's total investment amounted to ¥5,936 million. In the following five years, until 1960, they invested a further sum of ¥18,901 million in plant and equipment. In September 1959, the Motomachi plant, the first factory geared to the mass production of passenger cars, started business.

Because of the new investment in modern machines high productivity was achieved and output doubled in only three years between 1956 and 1959, from 5,000 units per month to more than 10,500 units.[30] Thus it was in the fifties that the company established a firm foundation which enabled it to make astonishing strides in mass production in the sixties. This step-up in production in the latter half of the fifties was also helped by rapid economic growth. A catch-phrase in vogue in 1956 was 'This is no longer the postwar period. The period of hunger has gone.' GNP between 1954 and 1958 increased at an average rate of 7.8 per cent per year. The swift economic growth led to the rapid spread of motorization, promoted brisk business activity in road transportation and ushered in a rise in all types of consumer demand.

With the introduction of technologically advanced equipment during the fifties in many shops, first in the machine shops, and then in the casting and forging shops,[31] considerable changes occurred in the workplace. In the early fifties, automatic specialized machine tools were substituted for all-purpose machine tools in the machine shops. This renewal of machinery brought about a further division of labour and each man's task became simpler; experienced, versatile skilled workers became semi-skilled machine operators. Moreover, these machine operators worked a large variety of machine tools installed in the line according to the product. By 1953 one operator was able to manipulate at least ten different machine tools. This system had its origins as early as August 1948 when management reorganized the machine shop. They changed the layout of machine tools from an arrangement by process to an arrangement by product. Although most workers objected to this system which was called *tadaisu-mochi* or 'operating a lot of machines', management succeeded in introducing it into the machine shops. The substitution of the new machinery in the fifties accelerated the division of labour, and intensified the development of *tadaisu-mochi*.

While new casting equipment introduced into the foundry, in the first half of the fifties, increased productivity and reduced the workforce by 30 per cent, the manual dexterity of skilled men was still needed in these production processes. But from the mid-1950s, the advent of automatic operating equipment such as the shell-mode precision casting method, removed the need for the manual dexterity of these skilled workers, and similar changes resulted from automation in the forging shop where hammer men were displaced by press machines.

Thus the mechanical innovations of the late 1950s brought about the simplification of work, increased the division of labour and made obsolete many versatile skills that had hitherto qualified as leading jobs on the shop floor. Most production jobs no longer needed a long training period.

Along with this modernization of production processes, the management also rationalized labour and production management. Since the early 1950s, management was attempting to establish standard times for machine operations through time and motion studies.[32] Early attempts along these lines had been made as early as November 1948 in some places in the machine shop. In the early 1950s, white-collar employees assigned to the shop floor were given a much wider range of functions in the fields of labour and production management, and at the same time, senior foremen (*kocho*) and under foremen (*kumicho*) on production were restricted to monitoring and instructing the men working in the production processes. In some shops such as the foundry, the senior foremen, who used to be skilled workers themselves, were now selected from all the foremen, irrespective of their skills. Until 1953–4 the foremen and the heads of work groups (*hancho*) had been assigned by the plant superintendent, but they now came to be appointed by head office. A strong move towards centralization in personnel management was under way.[33]

INTERNALIZATION IN PERSONNEL MANAGEMENT AND INDUSTRIAL RELATIONS

After Toyota produced 10,000 units in December 1959, output continued to rise steadily. In October 1963 it amounted to 30,000 units and in November 1967, when the company celebrated its thirtieth anniversary, monthly output had surpassed 80,000 units. The next year it rose to 100,000 units and in the early 1970s it leapt to 200,000 units.[34] (See table 7.1) Toyota made successive huge investments in new factories equipped with the latest technology, mainly specializing in the newly developed small-sized passenger car.[35] This expansion inevitably resulted in a number of new labour problems, particularly in regard to large-scale recruitment and training, and the induction of the new labour force into Toyota's business culture and philosophy.

In the first half of the 1950s, the total workforce in Toyota remained close to 5,000 workers. However the number of employees increased

Table 7.1   Employment, Output and Profits at the Toyota Motor Company 1945–70

Year	Employment White-collar	Blue-collar	Total	Output (Units)	Operating profit (¥1,000)
1945	1,411	7,360	8,771	3,275	1,667
1946	1,233	5,230	6,463	5,821	37,594
1947	1,378	4,967	6,345	3,922	
1948	1,444	5,037	6,481	6,703	129,225
1949	1,573	5,884	7,457	10,824	
1950	1,717	5,350	7,067	11,706	16,934
1951	1,304	4,011	5,315	14,228	1,202,931
1952	1,285	3,943	5,228	14,106	1,572,443
1953	1,316	3,975	5,291	16,496	1,906,999
1954	1,318	3,931	5,249	22,713	2,165,280
1955	1,310	3,852	5,162	22,145	1,535,543
1956	1,278	3,783	5,061	27,261	3,513,506
1957	1,368	4,536	5,904	42,482	5,196,752
1958	1,384	4,567	5,951	39,959	5,226,965
1959	1,573	5,486	7,059	52,016	9,173,623
1960	1,789	8,161	9,950	81,475	11,421,451
1961	2,102	9,861	11,963	108,163	15,061,131
1962	2,442	11,000	13,442	113,382	17,884,910
1963	2,746	13,253	15,999	165,165	25,977,593
1964	3,285	17,653	20,938	210,543	39,910,463
1965	4,275	18,320	22,595	240,498	27,368,146
1966	5,020	20,560	25,580	308,098	32,489,888
1967	5,541	24,644	30,185	445,969	49,192,239
1968	6,039	28,039	34,078	572,187	55,193,025
1969	6,588	30,101	36,689	771,911	76,613,474
1970	7,167	33,198	40,365	847,830	77,984,848

Source: annual company reports.

gradually from the late 1950s and multiplied several times by the late 1960s. In 1961 the total workforce exceeded 10,000 employees and in 1964 surpassed 20,000: by 1967 it had jumped to 30,000 and by 1970 it had exceeded 40,000 (see table 7.1). Since that time, the number of employees has fluctuated but not risen significantly. Where did these huge numbers of workers come from?

Until the end of the 1950s, Japan still had an ample labour surplus, particularly in the form of those underemployed in agriculture. Until the late fifties Toyota was able to recruit its workforce from its local labour market. In this period the company only recruited small numbers of apprentices, numbering about 40 junior-high-school leavers each year, and was cautious about an increase in personnel partly because of their bitter memories of the 1950 strife and partly because of their uneasiness about the prospects for the industry.[36] We can see this also in their determination to rationalize and reduce costs with investment in labour-saving machinery. The company's first five-year rationalization programme of 1951 planned for no increase in employees.

However, at the onset of the sixties the labour market became tight, particularly for junior-high-school leavers, owing to the rapid development of heavy and chemical industrialization. Japanese businesses were faced, for the first time since their industrialization, with the problem of a shortage of school leavers. If we look at the three years of 1959-61 the working population in all industries increased by 3.5 million, and the number of regular employees in non-agricultural industries rose by 60 per cent.[37] The economic boom as well as the increase in enrolled students in higher education also contributed to this tight situation in the labour market. From 1960 onwards automobile makers had to struggle to find workers because of this tight situation in the labour market.

Toyota, like other leading automobile manufacturers, started to recruit temporary workers in 1956 to meet the rise in production in the latter half of the fifties. They recruited 233 in early 1956 and the figure had increased to 1,721 people in 1959, when the Motomachi plant started operations.[38] From then on every year until the early seventies, thousands of temporary workers were recruited. On the other hand, during this period, far fewer school leavers were recruited because of the shortage of their supply. Toyota could use temporary workers as a buffer against fluctuation in demand because they could easily dismiss them at the termination of their contract, which was usually of two months duration although it was renewable at the discretion of the employer. In addition, since the temporary workers were not union members they could not enjoy the same conditions of employment as union members did.

However, it is interesting to note that the ratio of regular workers to the total workforce in the sixties increased rather swiftly, in spite of this large-scale recruitment of temporary and seasonal workers. At first, the proportion of regular workers to the total workforce fell in the late 1950s, reflecting the company's recruitment policy. In 1961 the ratio had fallen to a low of 43.2 per cent, but from 1962 onwards the trend was reversed. The ratio continued to rise steadily and reached 87 per cent in 1973, or 96 per cent when the number of trainees was added. Regular workers in 1961 number some 3,850 persons, whereas by 1973 they amounted to 27,000 persons.

The temporary workers recruited in the sixties formed the major source of regular workers. In 1959, 45 temporary workers were promoted to regular workers, based on the company's modified policy of recruitment. Temporary workers, after a year's diligent service, might be promoted to regular workers on the company's recommendation. This policy, the management said, was adopted in order to encourage temporary workers to look forward to future prosperity and to enhance their morale. From the mid-sixties onwards temporary workers promoted through this system increased steadily and more than half of those recruited each year became regular workers. Over a period of years this implied that practically all temporary workers were eventually enrolled as regular workers, except for those who left the company voluntarily before or at the end of their contract term, or those who were extremely bad at work.[39] In this way, temporary workers were no longer used as a cushion against economic fluctuations. At the same time, the labour market of Toyota extended from local to nation-wide. in the fifties the company was able to recruit its temporary workers, like its apprentices, from the local market, mainly Aichi prefecture. But in the sixties many of the temporary workers came from Hokkaido, Tohoku and Kyushu.[40]

Furthermore, from 1963, the company began to take on some local peasants as seasonal workers while they had no work to do on their farms. Before long, the employment of seasonal workers increased gradually and these workers came to be drawn not only from peasants but also from various other kinds of occupations. Thus, in place of temporary workers, seasonal workers came to act as the buffer against business fluctuations.

At the same time, in 1961 the company began to recruit some honourably discharged men from the Self-Defence Force, first as temporary workers and later, impressed mostly by their industrious work, as regular workers. In addition in 1962 the management started to employ high-school leavers as blue-collar workers, because of the shortage of junior-high-school leaver applicants. However, it proved difficult to recruit them and difficult to keep them. As a result, the management began to increase the number of juvenile workers taken on as trainees and, in the late sixties their number doubled from that of the early sixties.

Thus during the sixties the company recruited their employees from diverse sources, driven by the pressing need for manpower to operate mass-production equipment. This rapidly increased and heterogeneous workforce needed to be integrated into the company's organization.

In 1966 the company conducted a sophisticated employee consultation programme, called the 'Personal Touch Movement', to promote mutual understanding and communication and hence good human relations at the workplace. Under this programme, some diligent workers of good character, who were in their early twenties, were assigned as 'senior workers' to help the newcomers from high school and teenagers settle in their own shops in the minimum amount of time. These 'senior workers' were required to take a ten-hour Workmanship Training Course and they were also expected to develop their leadership potential through their assigned duties as 'senior workers'. At the same time, the management encouraged employees to hold meetings in each workplace and talk about issues which were common in individual work groups. These meetings were headed by workers below the rank of under-foremen. Sometimes supervisors such as senior foremen, foremen and under-foremen joined the meetings to have lively discussions with their men.[41]

At the same time, along with these techniques based on a human-relations approach, the management tried to reform payment and promotion systems. During the postwar industrial turmoil the union had stuck to the seniority principle and claimed wage increases based on the cost of living. After the 1950 events, however, management was in a strong position. In June 1951 it abolished the payment system based on seniority, and instead, introduced a basic wage system based on grades representing competence in the tasks allocated to workers. In the 1953 disputes, the management turned down the union's wage claims and attacked a sliding-scale system that the union had also insisted on. It also successfully introduced a personnel assessment system and established the no-work/no-pay principle.

However, it took some time for the management to introduce more systematic measures to rationalize labour-management practices such as wage payments, promotion, training and so on. Finally, in 1969, the *shokuso seido*, or qualification grade system of employees was introduced.[42] Under this system, every individual worker was ranked through assessment by management, and given a specific grade representing a qualification for specific positions. Now the employee was to be paid corresponding to the grade he was ranked in, irrespective of the job he performed, although within the same grade there existed some wage differentials based on performance assessment. Although this system was completed in 1969, wage payments based on worker qualifications had been made since 1964, when the union had finally agreed to the management's proposal.

The qualifications in this system began with the common job grade, in which all newcomers were placed. This grade itself was divided into three classes, the top one for college graduates and the bottom for blue-collar workers – high-school leavers, ex-Self Defence Force men and those who had been promoted from temporary workers. The highest grade for blue-collar workers was senior foreman, a lower managerial position corresponding to the grade of *kakaricho*, or subsection manager in the office. There were five grades for blue-collar workers in 1969 but in the mid-seventies another two grades were added in order to give more incentives to promotion. An additional grade was added below foreman for those who had sufficient competence to be a foreman but were assigned as under-foremen, and the other grade added above the common job grade, for those who showed fine leadership comparable to that of an under-foreman, although they were not assigned as under-foremen.

It is interesting to note that this grading system was ushered in after trials of various job evaluation techniques which the management found inconsistent with the development of *tanoko*, or 'multi-functional' workers.[43] As we have noted, multi-functional workers who can cope with a wide range of different jobs, and hence move from job to job inside or between workshops, had been an important feature at Toyota since 1948. Beginning in the machine shops, these practices had spread into other shops such as the foundry, the paintshop and so on. Versatility to deal with many jobs was developed by on-the-job training so that workers could be transferred easily inside or between the work processes. As for the worker himself, he could have a chance to climb up the promotion ladder step by step, and improve his ability to cope with many jobs, through internal mobility within the enterprise he worked for. The skill-grade system of employees established in 1969, therefore, was the structure most appropriate for the internal labour market which was now entrenched in the company.

The foreman played a key role in this system.[44] He was placed in charge of implementing educational programmes to develop multi-functional workers and he had to break up the work process for which he was responsible and assign tasks to the individuals under his direct supervision. According to the number of trained men he would need in a certain period for each job, he formulated training plans, with due consideration for their competence and seniority. Through these training schemes, it was the foreman who could ascertain how many had achieved his training targets and also what stage of development each worker had attained. Therefore, when asked by the Personnel Department about the transfer of workers to other shops or factories, so as to meet production fluctuations, the foremen were in a strong position to judge who should be moved and the Personnel Department simply monitored whether the foreman's choice was appropriate or not. This considerably enhanced the responsibility of foremen and it should be remembered that they, as well as senior foremen and under-foremen, were organized into the same union as the rank and file workers. Moreover, these supervisors played a leading part in the union's activities. A great number of shop stewards were foremen. We can see here the dual role these supervisors carried out, both as union representatives and as lower level management.

The shop stewards were expected to draw up various kinds of demands and grievances from their men and convey them to the shop-steward committees, and in order to do this, the stewards held meetings at the shops once a month to discuss such issues as wage increases, manning, working conditions, etc. A shop steward committee was composed of the shop stewards who represented workers in the ratio of 15 to 1 and it was chaired by the senior shop steward.[45]

In the 1960s, management established a joint-consultation system. As early as 1951 management proposed to the union that the Central Works Council should be abolished because its function would hamper managerial prerogatives. The union initially refused, but finally agreed in 1959. Thus the Labour and Management Joint Council replaced the old Works Council. Under the new council, five special committees were established covering production, health and safety, employee welfare, wages and personnel management. Three tiers of consultation bodies were also established at the levels of shop, plant and enterprise.[46]

Senior shop stewards and ordinary shop stewards were the members of the Joint Council at the shop level, along with a union branch officer. These shop-level meetings were generally held once a month to discuss shop-floor grievances with management. Above the shop level, there was a joint conference at plant level which generally met four times a year, involving the plant superintendent and departmental managers with senior union officers and senior shop stewards. The aim of these two conferences was to discuss a wide range of issues regarding business policies, administrative matters and also employment conditions, though not necessarily to come to any agreements.

At the enterprise level, this consultation system was used by the company not only as a channel for management to inform and consult with the union but also for negotiating terms and conditions of employment. On matters such as recruitment, transfers, wages, working hours and the application of collective agreements, decisions at the Central Labour and Management Council were reached by consensus. The difference between consultation and bargaining tended to be blurred.

CONCLUSION

The ambiguities of Japanese collective bargaining raise difficult issues from a western point of view. Is this sort of union a true union? The enterprise union *is* a bona fide union in that it has tried to and succeeded in maintaining and promoting its members' interests without company support, financial or otherwise, even though it is at times susceptible to employer interference and pressure. But it can be clearly distinguished from craft or industrial unionism. Firstly, formalized job control at the workplace, such as the seniority system in the USA, is negligible. On the other hand, employment security rights of regular employees are defended to the last. Employment security is taken for granted as a vested right of regular workers and a long-established practice. Secondly, it is only the interests of regular workers that the union will try to improve because temporary and seasonal workers are not union members. Finally, in the internal labour market system, with its institutionalized arrangements, which Ronald Dore has called 'welfare corporatism'[47] employees' interests depend crucially on the prospects and prosperity of the company for which they work. Consequently a union tends to pursue strategies on the basis that economic betterment of union members will be attained only through the growth of the company and hence of the industry in which its members are employed. At the same time, these union strategies are strongly supported by the members' identification with the company. In addition, under fierce market competition, the union tends to choose strategies of cooperation with management so as to improve productivity and win the race.

The shift of the union from conflict towards cooperation in the 1950s was not due simply to the defeat of the union in the industrial strife of the early 1950s. In this period of growing competition and technological change, the great majority of the rank and file came to see their interest as being identical with that of the company in the battle for the new expanding market. In addition, the massive increase in unorganized labour, resulting from the influx of temporary workers in the late 1950s, considerably weakened the bargaining power of the union. Furthermore, the temporary workers who were promoted to permanent status in the 1960s were selected for their loyalty and inclination to climb the organizational ladder of the company.

The picture of industrial relations at Toyota depicted in this article, however, does not mean that the whole workforce at Toyota identified their own interests with the company, although most of them seem to have accepted their working milieu. In *Japan in the Passing Lane*,[48] Satoshi Kamata, a freelance journalist, describes his experiences when he joined Toyota as a seasonal worker for a six-month contract in September 1972. He severely criticizes the alienated factory life at Toyota, the barracks-like discipline for seasonal workers, and the union's inactivity in defending its members at the workplace. He described the picture from the vantage point of the most unprotected and segregated worker, and showed the problems that arose when Toyota was recruiting a new mass labour force to cope with the new demands of mass production. This policy of introducing massive numbers of new workers led to a high rate of labour turnover. A former personnel executive at Toyota has said that as many as 10 per cent of regular employees left the company each year in the late 1960s.[49] Faced with this problem, Toyota developed new policies and stopped recruiting both seasonal and temporary workers in 1974. Later they reopened recruitment to meet fluctuations in demand, but, in general, the situation that Kamata described was soon to disappear.

NOTES

I would like to thank the following people for their comments and advice during the writing of this article: Professors T. Shirai and Y. Kuwabara, Mrs Olive Checkland, Dr H. Gospel, Mr A. Lawrence, the editors of this book and the participants at the Coventry Conference, June 1984.
    The following notes cover the main sources for this article. Some words of explanation may be helpful for Western readers. Very few Japanese firms, unlike their Western counterparts, maintain archives for research purposes. Instead, a considerable number of Japanese firms have thorough company histories, which are suitable for academic study. Similarly, most labour unions have published their own histories. Therefore, both sides of Toyota have published very extensive history books, which, along with some official publications as well as many secondary materials, have been useful sources of information for this paper. Some of them are particularly worth mentioning. First, on technological innovation during the fifties at Toyota, there is a comprehensive survey carried out by the Nihon Jinbun Kagaku-kai in 1959: *Gijutsu Kakushin no Shakaiteki Eikyo* (*The Social Impact of Technological Innovation*) (Tokyo, 1963). On the work and life of Toyota workers, sociologists at Ritsumeikan University in Kyoto have recently devoted their energy to studying them, including interviews with Toyota workers. The results of their research have been published in the journal *Atarashii Shakaigaku no Tameni* (*For New Sociology*). Finally, an oral history (referred to below as 'Yamamoto interview') by a former personnel officer at Toyota, Keimei Yamamoto, is informative on the personnel management strategies and practices during the period discussed here. He has talked to Hirohide Tanaka, a labour economist, about his experiences at Toyota, in an article 'Nihon-teki Koyokanko o Kitzuita Hitotachi' ('The Japanese Style of Management and the People who Contributed to the Establishment of the

System'), in *Nihon Rodo Kyokai Zassi*, the monthly journal of the Japan Institute of Labour, vol. 24, nos. 7, 8 and 9.

1   For the development of the prewar Japanese automobile industry, see Soji Yamamoto, *Jidosha (Automobiles)* (1938); *idem, Asu no Jidosha (Automobiles in the Future)* (1939); Masahisa Ozaki, *Nihon Jidosha Kogyo Ron (The Japanese Automobile Industry)* (1941); Seiji Nakamura, *Nihon Jidosha Kogyo Hattenshi Ron (The Development of the Japanese Automobile Industry)*, (1953); Shoji Okumura, 'Jidosha Kogyo no Hatten Dankai to Kozo', in *Gendai Nippon Sangyo Koza* ('The Development Stages and Structures of the Japanese Automobile Industry', in *A Series of Modern Japanese Industries,*) vol. 5, (1960); Kazuo Tomiyama, *Nihon no Jidosha Sangyo (The Japanese Automobile Industry)*, (1973).
2   Quoted in *Nihon Keizai Shinbun*, 13 April 1950.
3   Toyota Motor Company, *Toyota Jidosha 30-nenshi (Thirty Years of the Toyota Motor Company)* (Toyota City, 1967), pp. 234, 237–8.
4   Shogo Amatani, *Nihon Jidosha Kogyo no Shiteki Tenkai (Historical Development of the Japanese Automobile Industry)*, p. 83; Shoji Okumura, *Jidosha (Automobiles)*, (1954), pp. 202–4.
5   *Thirty Years of Toyota*, pp. 256–61.
6   Ibid., pp. 283–4.
7   *Year-Book of Labour Statistics and Research*, (1948).
8   Toyota Motor Company, *Toyota Jidosha 20-nenshi (Twenty Years of the Toyota Motor Company)* (Toyota City, 1958), p. 222; *Thirty Years of Toyota*, p. 240.
9   Yamamoto interview, p. 51; T. Kumagai and I. Saga, *Nissan Sogi* (The 1953 Strife at Nissan) (Yokohama, 1983), p. 326.
10 *Thirty Years of Toyota*, p. 262. At that time, section managers had union memberships in most enterprise unions.
11 *Twenty Years of Toyota*, p. 213.
12 Quoted from Tomihisa Suzuki, 'Sengo-10-nenkan no Toyota Roshikankei no Tenkai' ('Toyota's Industrial Relations 1945–55'), in *Atarashi Shakaigaku no Tameni* (For New Sociology), September 1983, p. 38.
13 Toyota Labour Union, *20-Nen no Ayumi, (Twenty Years of the Toyota Union)* (Toyota City, 1966), p. 6. For the birth of the union, see ibid., pp. 66–7, and also Yamamoto interview,, p. 52.
14 Toyota Labour Union, *Kagiri naki Zenshin-30 nen no Ayumi (Thirty years of the Toyota Union)* (Toyota City, 1976), p. 2; *Thirty years of Toyota*, pp. 262–3, 298.
15 Suzuki, 'Toyota's Industrial Relations, 1945–55', p. 41.
16 Toyota Labour Union, *Kumiai Soritsu 10-shunen Kinenshi (Ten Years of the Toyota Union)* (Toyota City, 1956), pp. 67–9. Japan Ministry of Labour, *Shiryo Rodo Undoshi, Showa 22-nen (Documentary History of the Labour Movement, 1947)*, (1952), p. 643.
17 With the development of rationalization in 1948, the pressure on the union officials from activists increased and, in April 1949, the union executives called an 11-hour strike strongly influenced by AJAWU, which thoroughly disappointed the management.
18 *Thirty Years of Toyota*, pp. 270–1.
19 It was in 1956 that the union finally agreed to this proposal.

20   For the circumstances of the 1950 strife, see *Twenty Years of Toyota*, pp. 304–13; *Thirty Years of Toyota*, pp. 292–313; *Ten Years of the Toyota Union*, pp. 73–6; *Twenty Years of the Toyota Union*, pp. 21–33.

21   *Ten Years of the Toyota Union*, pp. 77; *Twenty Years of the Toyota Union*, pp. 35.

22   For the 1953 strife, see *Twenty Years of Toyota*, pp. 447–8; *Thirty Years of Toyota*, pp. 416–17; *Ten Years of the Toyota Union*, pp. 86–7, 89–92; *Twenty Years of the Toyota Union*, pp. 56–61; Yamamoto interview, pp. 41–2.

23   Yamamoto interview, pp. 41–2.

24   Kumagai and Saga, *The 1953 Strife at Nissan*, pp. 232–3.

25   At the meeting of AJAWU in December 1954, 93 unions, including those of Toyota and Isuzu, cast votes for the dissolution of AJAWU, whereas 25 unions, including those of Nissan and smaller-sized companies, voted against it. See *Twenty Years of the Toyota Union*, pp. 66–7. For the establishment of the federation of Toyota unions, see *Ten Years of the Toyota Union*, p. 91.

26   *Thirty Years of Toyota*, pp. 326.

27   Ibid., p. 349. The tax on imported cars at that time was 40 per cent of the value but they were still competitive with comparable Japanese cars: e.g. Morris, 1000cc, ¥955,000; VW, 1200cc, ¥740,000; Austin A40, 1200cc, ¥1,150,000; whereas a Toyopet SF, 1000cc cost ¥1,100,000. (*Automobile Year-Book*, 1953, 1954).

28   *Thirty Years of Toyota*, pp. 345–8. The description in *Twenty Years of Toyota* concerning this matter (pp. 374–5) would give a false impression.

29   See *Thirty Years of Toyota*, pp. 333, 342, 846. Also, Nihon Jinbun Kagaku-kai, *The Social Impact of Technological Innovation*, p. 20.

30   *Thirty Years of Toyota*, pp. 342, 852.

31   For technological changes in the fifties, see, *Twenty Years of Toyota*, pp. 409–20; *Thirty Years of Toyota*, pp. 332–42, 398–414.

32   Nihon Jinbun Kagaku-kai, *The Social Impact of Technological Innovation*, pp. 88–90, 93; *Twenty Years of Toyota*, p. 417.

33   Yamamoto interview, pp. 26–7.

34   Toyota Motor Company, *Toyota no Ayumi* (*The Development of Toyota in its Forty Years*) (Toyota City, 1978), p. 536.

35   During the mid-sixties to the early seventies, Toyota built specialized plants one after another for small passenger cars, engines and other parts: Kamigo (1965, engines, transmissions), Takaoka (1966, cars), Miyoshi (1968, chassis parts), Tsutsumi (1970, cars) and Myochi (1973, engine parts, chassis parts).

36   Yamamoto interview, p. 66.

37   Ministry of Labour, Division of Labour Statistics and Research, *Labour Force Survey* and *Monthly Labour Survey*, 1961.

38   Toyota Motor Company, *30-Nenshi Bekkan* (Supplement to *Thirty Years of Toyota*) (Toyota City, 1975) p. 534.

39   Large-scale recruitment of temporary workers until the early seventies was not unique to Toyota. The regular workers in the leading automobile companies increased from 24,868 in 1955 to 31,006 in late 1960, while temporary workers increased from 1,212 to 15,640. Similarly, promotion of temporary workers to regular workers was also common in Toyota owing to the tightness of the labour market. For the promotion system of Toyota, see Yamamoto interview, p. 68.

40   Kiyoshi Yamamoto, *Nihon Rodoshijyo no Kozo* (*Structure of the Japanese*

Labour Market) , (1967), pp. 232–95. Chiki Kozo Kenkyo kai, 'Shiryō Aichi-ken niokeru Jidōsha oyobi Dōkanren Kogyō no Rōdōshijyō to Toyota Jidōsha Kogyō no Koyōkanri' ('Toyota's Employment Policies and Labour Market in Aichi Prefecture'), *Bulletin of Nihon Fukushi Daigaku*, no. 45, pp. 114–15.

41 For the PT movement, see Yamamoto interview, pp. 43–4.
42 For the Shokusō Seido, see the explanation in Yamamoto interview, pp. 33–7.
43 Yamamoto interview, pp. 33–4.
44 For the role of foremen in developing multi-functional workers and in labour management at the workplace, see, Yamamoto interview, pp. 28–33.
45 For the functions of shop stewards and their committees at the workplace see, Yoshio Okumura, 'Toyota Jikō Rōdō-Kumiai no Shokuba-Soshiki' ('The Workplace Organization of the Toyota Labour Union'), *Atarashi Shakaigaku no tameni (For New Sociology)*, no. 30 (September 1983), pp. 24–33.
46 Toyota Motor Company, *Toyota Motor Corporation: Company Report*, January 1984.
47 Ronald Dore, *British Factory – Japanese Factory* (Berkeley, 1973).
48 Satoshi Kamata, *Japan in the Passing Lane*, (London, 1982).
49 Yamamoto interview, p. 71.

Part Three
Beyond Fordism?

8

The Automobile Industry in Transition: Product Market Changes and Firm Strategies in the 1970s and 1980s

Giuseppe Volpato

PROBLEMS

During the last ten years the international car industry has been going through a very complex process of change. This will continue, but we can already say that the phase of greatest uncertainty is past. This does not mean that either the individual car companies or the industry as a whole have resolved the problems that arose with the 1973 oil crisis, but simply that the nature of these problems is now understood. They may be set out as follows.

1   As far as demand is concerned, the car is, and will remain until the end of the century, the main means of personal transport. So the survival of the sector, which in certain quarters looked threatened, is no longer in doubt. In highly motorized countries the crisis undoubtedly lowered the point of market saturation, and demand has become more cyclical because of the prevalence of replacement demand over that for first purchases.[1]

In the less developed countries the fall-off in demand is tied exclusively to the low growth rate in real *per capita* incomes. More favourable economic conditions would cause demand to rise towards sustained growth rates.[2]

Beyond this, car owners' preferences have not become spartan, nor even modest in regard to car features. Buying and running costs remain important, but the clientele increasingly show preferences for quality and well-designed cars within particular price segments. The problems that the car companies have to face in this area arise from the need to speed up model renewal, improve product technology and enlarge the range of cars produced. This philosophy can be seen in the preparation of numerous versions of a single model, two to three levels of specification and many different engine types (petrol, diesel, injection and turbo) and in the creation of new market segments. Moreover, car manufacturers are tending to develop new and highly specialized models such as mini-vans, mini pick-up trucks and four-wheel-drive vehicles. This is a case of cars being produced not in great numbers, but for niches of the market where there is low competition.

2   In terms of competition, it is clear that the car industry can no longer be considered as a mature sector. The extraordinary competitive capacity shown by the Japanese car companies is stimulating a profound renewal process in the whole sector in both the United States and in Europe. This process in the sector is based on innovations in the product, the manufacturing system and the materials. From this point of view the industry is better classified as a 'neo-infant' industry than as a 'mature' industry.[3] One of the characteristic aspects of this process of 'dematuration'[4] comes from its role as sponsor industry for advanced technologies such as automation and robotics. Both directly and indirectly, many car companies have gone into the production of machine tools and robots to the point that no company producing particularly sophisticated machine tools can think of development without sponsorship from a car company.

The extent of the problems of competitive reorganization can be seen from the unprecedented levels of investment that the car companies have had to undertake in this industrial renewal operation.

3   The internationalization of markets is bound to continue. But, unlike the past, it can no longer be based either on the export of finished cars nor on small production operations in sheltered markets. Internationalization today means running an integrated system of exchange between many productive units and many markets. New problems arise from the need to manage, in an integrated way, a logistical system of production and supply on an international scale.

4   In process technology the aim of all the companies is *automation*. This is because automation permits greater flexibility and a high level of productivity. The previous orientation was towards Taylorist policies, but these have not proved adequate for a new phase in which the number of versions of any one model is continually on the increase and where demand shows accentuated cyclical variations. The automation of welding, painting and machining, apart from reducing dangerous and dirty work, allows a considerable gain in productivity.

Here the problem arises from perfecting a new, unfamiliar and costly technology and from the need to control the contraction of employment levels brought about by this kind of innovation.

5   In the car components industry, the need to innovate and produce new devices is worth noting. These are generally of an electronic type and used to raise the efficiency and reliability of engines, brakes, suspensions, etc.

Evolution here involves, to a massive extent, new relations between the car makers and the components suppliers.

The problem here is the need to reorganize logistical functions. This has been neglected by many car companies in the past, when their policies favoured low-cost components instead of quality ones. The companies also need to increase the scale economies of production as far as possible, consistent with the enlargement of the product line.

6   Finally, one area in which many companies have to modernize extensively is that of management. Up to the 1970s, both in Europe and in the United States, a situation prevailed that White called 'room for all'.[5] This caused a sharp drop in managerial dynamism and created very little urge to grasp new opportunities for rationalization. This delay still exists.

In this case, the problem is one of regaining innovative tension in management, as is required in an industry which is going through a renewed phase of 'infant' development.

STRATEGIES

If you ask, 'What is the strategic area where your effort of rationalization and innovation is most highly concentrated?' any car-industry executive invariably answers, 'Every area of business is of strategic importance for us. We are involved on the whole operational front, from finance to marketing, from buying to production, with the objective of improving products and reducing costs.' The answer is one that seems almost to be taken for granted, if only because there is no executive who would want to give the impression that, in this firm, any stone is left unturned in increasing its productivity. But it *is* true that the American and European car companies have involved themselves in a broad-based policy of reorganization. There are two main reasons for such a broad approach.

The most obvious but perhaps less important has to do with the fact that the economic and energy crisis of the second half of the seventies has changed the place of the automobile in the structure of consumer goods. During the fifties and sixties the average price of cars showed a drop in real terms. It is significant to note that in Europe at the beginning of the seventies, the replacement of a medium-sized car cost the same as an average hi-fi or a colour television, once the value of the one traded-in was taken into consideration. After 1973 the steep rise in car prices and running costs gave the automobile a different position in consumer budgets. The vertiginous increase in petrol prices orientated consumers towards relatively highly priced cars which were more economical and more reliable. High reliability and low maintenance costs are aspects which are increasingly held in consideration in designing cars. Therefore the need to introduce new product features led to major reorganization throughout the companies.

The most important stimulus towards a rationalization of the complete range of operations, however, comes from the poor competitiveness of the American and European automobile industries, in relation to the Japanese.

This lack of dynamism stems from the convergence of a long period of sustained demand and a stable framework of oligopolistic competition. The only exception to this 'brakes-on' state of competition in the fifties and sixties was the Japanese car industry which found itself in a highly competitive national environment, and profited from an industrial culture pervaded by a high business *esprit de corps*.[6]

In order to show the most important differences in strategic behaviour between American, European and Japanese car companies more clearly, it is necessary to put forward some rather schematic distinctions.

The American car industry

In the case of the American car industry the fundamental problem raised by the oil crisis was the need for a radical renewal of the range of models (product design) and raised productivity in the car plants (process technology). Stagnation in demand and its subsequent orientation towards low-consumption, high-reliability cars on the one hand, and the massive commercial penetration of Japanese and European cars on the other, dictated that priority be given to changes in vehicle design and production processes.[7]

The introduction of these essential radical changes were seriously delayed in the American car companies. At first, the reorganization programmes of the 'Big Three' were more concerned with the requirements of the CAFE energy-saving standards than responding to foreign competition. Only General Motors put their down-sizing policy into action right away, starting with model-year 1977, while Ford, perhaps because they already had more compact vehicles, did not make an immediate start on a similar project. Neither did Chrysler, which had great difficulties in making the investments necessary for down-sizing. In this situation the effect produced by the second oil shock was explosive. The average price of petrol went from 69 American cents in January 1979 to 105.2 in December of the same year. But it was above all the supply difficulties that scared drivers, who turned *en masse* to low-consumption cars. This caught the American car manufacturers unprepared, with a very limited production of compact cars. They found themselves having to close down numerous car plants making standard-sized models, while also working at full speed on the assembly of compact and sub-compact vehicles. The volume of production, however, was not sufficient to satisfy the demand, which turned to Japanese and European supply.

This development exposed further problems. The American companies believed their problems derived from the nature of the product and not from technology or productivity, and they focused their attention on car redesign. This, on the contrary, was only one aspect of poor American competitiveness. It was not enough just to produce economy cars, you had to be able to make them at remunerative prices. This result could have been achieved only through a wide-ranging reorganization of the production process which, for the most part, was still based on obsolete plants which were too inflexible for modern market conditions.

The problem of the American companies, then, was the recovery of adequate productivity levels, and a new technological and commercial image.[8] One of the major causes of the success of Japanese cars was the diffusion of an image of technical excellence and qualitative accuracy. Many market surveys have shown a decidedly favourable attitude among American consumers towards Japanese cars, which they judge to be better finished and more reliable. It is therefore obvious that a recovery in competitiveness by the American car companies had to be directed into setting up more modern plants and more flexible procedures.

In 1981, a Department of Transportation document stressed that,

The transition to front wheel drive and smaller engines will require replacing most of the manufacturing system in the plants which produce major machined components. As new equipment is introduced it is more likely to reflect the major advances in machining, assembly and testing technology which have been developed since the equipment being replaced was first installed. The result is likely to be far more widespread use of automated testing and assembly techniques and much higher manufacturing productivity.[9]

The European car industry

In Europe, the national car industries have developed along lines which are very different to the American and Japanese ones. The production of cars often had a semi-craft organization of processes up to the end of the forties. The reasons for this are:

a   smaller dimensions of national markets separated by strict customs barriers
b   lower income level of European consumers
c   high petrol prices.

All of these have kept the car as an elite commodity for a long time. This resulted in a competitive structure in which a large number of car manufacturers sought to carve themselves a niche in the market by means of a highly differentiated product range, i.e. the so-called *petites collections*.[10] This different market philosophy is reproduced in the organization of parts supply, with more attention being paid to the engineering side than to more general aspects of productivity. Substantially, in the European car companies, each new model was planned and built as an independent project and not strictly integrated into the business system as a whole. The very slowness in renewing models, in both engines and body-work compared to the American model-year policy (one has only to think of the Volkswagen 'Beetle', the Renault R4 and the Citroën 2CV) favoured separate planning for each model. This scant attention to the benefits of standardization over the entire range of products is even more amazing if one considers that as a result the opportunities for exploiting scale economies – already limited compared to those enjoyed by the American Big Three – were further reduced.[11]

The stable and continuous growth in demand in all European markets from after the Second World War, permitted and covered up a level of inefficiency not tolerated in other industries.

The need for overall reorganization became apparent with the formation of the Common Market and the reduction of customs tariffs, completed in 1968. But, given the rigidity in such a vast and complex sector, reorganization turned out to be very slow indeed, and the crisis of 1973 caught the European car industry still in a state of transition.[12]

A sharp drop in demand and the progressive entry of Japanese competition imposed a strategic line of reorganization on the firms operating in Europe. This was substantially different to the one that was given priority in the American firms. From a strictly technological point of view the European makers could boast levels of excellence in their individual products which were close to the new requirements for energy-saving. But even though their products are *technically* competitive with Japanese models, numerous inefficiencies had a negative impact on costs and the commercial organization of production.

This aspect becomes obvious if one considers the structure of the product line and the level of components standardization shown by the European car companies in the mid-seventies. Fiat and Audi, for example, were working in segment 'F' (large vehicles) with volumes of production below 2,000 units compared to Mercedes' level of 300,000.[13] Citroën was present in the first three segments (i.e. 'A', 'B' and 'C') which cover small vehicles, and in segment 'F', (large), but with no models in segment 'D' (medium) and 'E' (medium-large). Peugeot too, in common with Citroën and Opel showed a badly balanced product line, although in a less accentuated way. (See table 8.2.)

Apart from this, the low level of compactness in the product lines was reflected in the low standardization of mechanical groups and body-work. Fiat, Peugeot, Ford and Opel found themselves working with a number of body-pans and engines greater than the number of market segments in which they were operating.[14]

In the components field, only Germany and Great Britain could rely on firms of considerable size and high technological level. In France and Italy the structure of components supply was very fragmented, and there was heated competition to win orders from the car companies.[15]

All this brought about a considerable rise in costs in every phase of production (foundry, forging, stamping, machining, assembly), greater rigidity in production and surplus stocks.

Faced with the challenge of Japanese cars[16] the strategies of the European companies were orientated towards reconsidering the overall range of cars and the reorganization of the structure of component supply. Acceleration in model renewal, though necessary, became a kind of by-product of the rationalization and standardization of mechanical groups and bodies. The very need to reorganize product lines and components dictated an acceleration in model renewal based on a cloning process, i.e. the same engine for different models, the same pans for different bodies. All of this fitted together in the aim of probing the market for niches still not adequately served by other producers.

The Japanese car industry

The basic strategic direction of the Japanese car industry can be summarized by the single concept 'consolidation'. It has already been pointed out how, in the American industry, recovery of competitiveness is tied to the acquisition of new technologies together with greater productivity through a programme of massive investment in rationalization of products and car plants. In Europe, partly due to the institutional mechanisms which limit Japanese import penetration, the competitive front is concentrated on the reorganization of the product range in order to speed up model replacement and increase the number of versions, in response to a demand which spreads over many segments and which is becoming increasingly specialized. For the Japanese makers, the objective of the 1980s was a strategy of consolidation aimed at stabilizing their established competitive advantages. The rapidity with which these advantages had been acquired had brought with it an inevitable fragility.

The most innovative aspect of the Japanese approach to automobile production was the planning and building of a comprehensive technological system which attempted to perfect all the sequences of operations both in the *vertical* sense (components, supply, production and distribution) and in the *horizontal* one (planning connected to productive processes and product line).[17]

The achievement of this philosophy, much more complex and advanced in its criteria of optimalization than those of the American and European industries, has allowed it to reach a much higher level of productivity. This is based on:

a availability of modern, extensively automated and very flexible production plants
b a very favourable system of industrial relations involving a low level of conflict, negligible absenteeism, active collaboration and low wage rates, especially for the small component-producing companies
c a highly professional managerial system which has brought considerable results, from quality control to the 'just in time' organization of component supply and an efficient and assiduous after-sales service.[18]

These advantages are likely to be durable. Above all, the production area is the fulcrum of Japanese competitiveness. The commercial side of their business is however, less developed, particularly their undeveloped image for technology and style in the highest segments of the product line.

Currently, Japan depends on a very high number of exported cars. But their future prospects are linked to their policy of internationalization. This involves going beyond the export phase and building up production and assembly of cars with a large local value-added content.[19]

As for innovation strategies, however, the companies are perfecting what is seen as the 'third phase' of Japanese car-industry policy. The first phase was essentially based on highly competitive prices, the second on tenacious research into car reliability through accurate systems of quality control. The third is the development of sophisticated engine technologies and a stylistic image of excellence.

The Japanese market has never had the sort of elite production phase which America and Europe went through and which, among other things, led to the development of specialized firms dealing exclusively in luxury vehicles. The rise of the Japanese car industry in the fifties coincided with a mass demand based on large-scale production of the most standardized possible kind. This situation still prevails today when we consider that the only vehicles imported into the Japanese market are prestige cars.

Hence, the present-day effort towards consolidation, which takes place in much more favourable financial and economic conditions than in America and Europe is organized around investment in research for, and development of, modern and sophisticated technological solutions.[20]

The Japanese industry, therefore, allocates its investments quite differently. In the United States the priority in investments goes to process innovation. In Europe this appears less urgent and investments are mainly in rationalization of product lines and model renewal. In Japan stress is laid on innovation of product features. The early steps in this 'third phase' strategy were first to be seen in the development of electronic gadgets. More recently, however, the policy of putting stress on research and development is producing much more significant results. Every motor show in the international calendar exhibits new and outstanding products from the Japanese car-makers.

PERFORMANCE

The Japanese car companies

The economic results achieved by the Japanese car makers are excellent. Compared with the considerable losses sustained by the European and American companies as a result of the 1973 crisis, only Mazda showed a slight loss, in 1976. The Japanese companies have a particularly strong financial structure. Their profits turn out to be higher than declared in the official balance sheets if one measures them according to accounting criteria used in the United States and Europe. Japanese fiscal legislation allows the accumulation of non-taxed reserves to be put into research and development. Not only this, the policy followed in the distribution of dividends raises reinvestment levels. Considering that a very high level of shares belongs to other companies, principally banks, the remuneration of capital through dividends is low, and there is a bias towards the expansion of reserves and the raising of stock quotations.[21] This has decisively contributed towards reducing the level of debt and allows the firms to finance their own development. This is an extremely important fact for making possible investments in research and development which, because of their very nature, represent the highest level of risk.[22]

As far as the strategic objective of technological development is concerned, the Japanese firms have already had some significant results. According to estimates made by Dan Jones of the Science Policy Research Unit, the number of automobile patents registered in the United States has increased very rapidly. Between 1965 and 1966 there were 28 Japanese patents and 201 West German ones. In 1980–1 the former had gone up to 513 while the West German figure had increased to only 356.[23]

In terms of particular companies, Toyota, which is the biggest company, shows a somewhat more conservative attitude than the other Japanese companies. It particularly concentrates its attention on safety and environmental problems. However, it is also conducting high priority research into the optimal balance of high performance and fuel economy in engines. It is perfecting a new series of light and compact engines which will make wide use of electronic control devices.

Nissan's policy is more aggressive. Since 1982 it has built a new technical centre, a 203-million-dollar investment with a staff of 3,400. With this centre, Nissan intends to develop further electronic control systems for better engine functioning. Examples of this orientation are to be seen in the realization (for the first time by a Japanese firm) of a skid control device and a 16-valve double overhead camshaft engine.

Moving on to the smaller Japanese firms and to Mazda in particular, there is more evidence of the perfecting of a more sophisticated car. In Mazda's case the crises of the seventies were prevalently bound up with its unsuitable position in the market. With a production of less than 400,000 cars in these years, this firm attempted to break into the medium-large cars segment, in direct confrontation with Toyota and Nissan. Honda, Mitsubishi, Fuji, Daihatsu, Suzuki and Isuzu, on the other hand, decided to opt for the lowest segment of the product line. With the help of the Sumitomo Bank of Tokyo as its main shareholder, Mazda set about reorganizing the product line towards cars of a more economic class, which allowed for a rapid financial recovery.

On the technological front, Mazda's strong point lies in the process innovation at their new Hofu plant. It has been designed with the most modern flexible manufacturing and assembly systems. In product innovation Mazda has undertaken a sweeping reorganization of their research and development methods leading to a considerable reduction in the lead-in times for new models by the integrated use of CAD/CAM techniques. In 1983 Mazda brought out its '626', with an electronic shock-absorber regulator. In addition, Mazda is continuing a development programme for its rotary engine. This type of engine is still at a disadvantage on the mass-consumer level, but the stabilization of petrol costs could well renew its competitiveness in the field of luxury and sports cars.

Honda's growth has certain aspects which are more extraordinary than Toyota and Nissan. Founded in 1948 to produce motorcyles, and having a staff of hardly 20, Honda became the main national motorcyle company at the end of the fifties. In 1962 it began producing cars. Throughout the sixties it dedicated itself to a slow but sure expansion. At the beginning of the seventies Honda was producing cars with considerable avant-garde features. It is, however, important to underline that the outstanding success of this firm does not so much depend on a low-price policy as on the adoption of innovative technical solutions before their time. The 'Civic', for example, introduced before the oil crisis, is one of the few hatchback cars of non-utilitarian dimensions. It has enough room for five people, as well as front-wheel drive, a system developed by the firm since 1967. Before 1973 there were practically no companies apart from Honda with complete know-how about the equipment necessary for large-scale production of front-wheel drive cars.

Another typical feature of Honda cars is independent wheel suspension. This, in common with other Honda solutions has since been widely imitated. Honda also leads in a very dynamic international policy. It was the first Japanese company to build a car production plant in the USA and to contract large joint ventures.

Given Honda's history, its orientation towards systematic technological modernization constitutes an obvious factor of continuity. In the annual reports of this company, investment in research and development is expanding not only in the absolute sense but also in relation to sales. This is a very significant fact when one considers its outstanding explosion in sales. Its research and development expenses went from 96 million dollars in 1977 (2.4 per cent of sales) to 222 million in 1981 (2.8 per cent of sales). In the whole Japanese car industry the technological innovation strategies under way constitute a far-reaching challenge. It is beyond doubt that before long the Japanese firms will be able to present a complete range of avant-garde cars even in the higher levels of the range. This is of crucial importance. As long as Japanese competition is mainly based on prices (low costs), this means having to produce in Japan, to be able to utilize the particular national conditions, and to export fully built cars. But should competition move on to the technological level, even production and assembly plants abroad could build a highly competitive product. This aspect is extremely relevant for the United States, but above all for Europe. Production in the EEC could, for example, overcome the import restrictions now in force in countries such as France and Italy in particular.

The American car companies

Any analysis of results obtained by the American car industry in recent years must be complex and in certain respects contradictory. In the short term, the 1983 financial results and those for the first half of 1984 seem remarkably successful. In 1983 General Motors increased sales by 24 per cent compared with 1982, and recorded profits of 3.7 billion (3,700 million) dollars. Similarly, Ford and Chrysler brought their balance sheets into the black. In all, the Big Three had total profit of 6.298 billion (6,298 million) dollars, beating all previous records and recouping almost completely the losses accumulated since 1978. In 1984 the net profits of the Big Three reached a new record, touching 9.8 billion (9,800 million) dollars. This result can be attributed to two factors. On the one hand, car demand was encouraged by declining petrol prices swinging back towards standard-size cars, assuring higher margins for American car makers. On the other hand these firms had already boosted their productivity by cutting back in employment, closing down less efficient plants and reaching agreements with the trade unions to reduce labour costs.

From 1979 on, the American car industry has been following a process of reorganization which is predicted to involve total investment of 80 billion (80,000 million) dollars by 1985. One result has been the closure of some 40 factories (30 production and ten assembly) with a reduction in employment of 600,000 out of a total of 1.9 million. These initiatives have allowed a considerable lowering of the break-even point. According to industry estimates, the volume of sales necessary for profits has been considerably reduced. Compared to 1979 it has gone from 2.2 million (cars and trucks) to 1.1 million for Chrysler, from 2.9 million to 2.5 million for Ford, and from 5.5. million to 4.3 million for General Motors.[24]

Beneath the euphoria of this indubitable recovery, however, there still remain numerous unresolved problems. Firstly, the possibility of recovering the markets lost to imports is far from certain. The Japanese companies in particular have a firm hold on 25 per cent of the American market, and without the policy of export self-restraint imposed by the Japanese government, the level could be raised considerably. Secondly, in the compact and sub-compact market segments the American companies have thrown in the sponge.[25] All have by now admitted that they cannot produce that kind of car in competition with the Japanese companies, and have chosen to set up a series of agreements. The Big Three will sell small Japanese cars imported or produced in the USA using their own dealer networks, as General Motors is already doing. General Motors has signed a contract with Suzuki for 100,000 mini-cars with one-litre engines. It has also negotiated an agreement with Isuzu

a to buy 200,000 cars a year which Isuzu will produce in Japan for sale in the United States by General Motors' dealers starting in 1984–5
b for the production of Isuzu R-cars in an American plant at the rate of 300,000 a year.

Finally, it has established a joint venture with Toyota for the annual production of 240,000 compact cars of Japanese derivation, in the California plant at Fremont.

Ford has raised strong objections to the GM–Toyota agreement, and has tried to block it at the Department of Trade, but meanwhile in Mexico they have set up a plant for the assembly of 130,000 sub-compacts a year from 1989.[26] Destined for the United States, they will include parts from Mazda, which is 24.4 per cent Ford-owned. Ford has also made contacts with European firms to examine the possibilities of joint production of small cars to be assembled in the United States.

Chrysler is already selling cars produced by Mitzubishi (of which it holds 15 per cent) and is setting up other agreements for building a sub-compact designed to replace the L-body (Omni-Horizon).

Finally, American Motors has been assembling Renault compact cars for two years now.[27]

American car industry profits, then, are tied, in the short term, to a demand preference for standard American cars. In the long term, however, these market segments could also feel the pressure of foreign competition, not so much on the price front as on that of quality and technical sophistication.

There is no doubt that American car manufacturers have shown a great capacity for adaptation in carrying through down-sizing in a period of time which is really short for such a vast and complex sector. It has been a gigantic effort, with projected investments of some 80 billion (80,000 million) dollars over 5 years. The actual investment has been somewhat less for a series of reasons[28] but in any case, between 1979 and 1983, the total capital investment of the Big Three was in the order of 52 billion (52,000 million) dollars with an average ratio on sales of some 8 per cent (See table 8.1). These are very high figures compared to what the Japanese manufacturers registered for the same period, having an average ratio on sales of 5.5.per cent.[29]

Much of the American investment has been directed into reorganization of production facilities for the production of smaller and front-wheel drive cars. This rapid change of product characteristics has also produced difficulties for the automobile original equipment suppliers. In part, the American suppliers have turned out to lack the technologies and machinery needed for the new course,[30] in part they have not had sufficient capabilities to supply newly-designed components to be able to grow fast enough to meet the assemblers' demand. In 1982 it was forecast that non-US suppliers would provide 26 per cent of auto components for US automobiles in 1985 and that this figure would grow to 36 per cent by 1990.[31]

The prospects of the American market are not easy to analyse. On the one hand, demand is markedly cyclical, while, on the other, state regulations on safety, speed limits, pollution and fuel economy standards can have a far-reaching effect in changing the terms of confrontation between American, Japanese and European car makers. There are many who argue that in former years low rates of economic development, inflation and the corresponding increase in the price of cars ('sticker shock') limited the growth of demand considerably.[32] For this reason the current economic recovery should bring a strong improvement in sales. Moreover, with petrol below one dollar per gallon, demand should reorientate towards US-built cars. If the so-called pent-up demand theory works, then the American car industry will definitely emerge from its crisis. If however, the events of the seventies have structurally modified American drivers' car-buying preferences towards more economic cars then there is a chance that the American car makers will go on suffering from the pressure of Japanese competition on the economy-car front and European competition on that of the luxury car.[33]

Government regulation has a very important role to play here, not only in determining the overall volume of demand, for instance through safety regulations which increase car prices, but also in competitive relations because of emission regulations and fuel-economy standards. Estimates made by the Motor Vehicle Manufacturers' Association indicate that, up to now the average domestic-car-fleet m.p.g. performance has been consistently above federal standards, but the recent reversion of demand towards big cars could well make the stipulations of the Energy Policy and Conservation Act a hurdle for the American car makers.

Another issue is the potential introduction of local-content regulations. Various bills have been brought before Congress in the past, but even though some of them gained the approval of the House of Representatives none has yet managed to reach the Senate, and beyond that there is the risk of a presidential veto.[34] It is clear, however, that if there is a new demand recession, its introduction will become more likely.

In general terms, the American market still presents a troubled picture in that several lines of evolution are possible in different economic and institutional scenarios. Much, too, will depend on negotiations about labour costs. In 1982 the car companies and the United Automobile Workers set out an agreement which allowed for a considerable drop in labour costs and a more cooperative union–management relationship. In 1984 relationships with the unions improved as market conditions eased, and a contract was negotiated protecting some workers from redundancy through technological change. In addition, management agreed to the creation of a job bank – a one-billion (1,000 million) dollar fund from which wages will be paid to laid-off workers until other permanent jobs can be found for them.[35] Nevertheless, worries remain about employment levels, not only in car assembly but also in the components-producing industries which are coming under increasingly severe pressure in the international market.

European car companies

Any analysis of European car builders' performance must start from the consideration that, despite the EEC, the economic and financial trends of the companies depend largely on movements of demand in their own countries.[36] Any judgement of the validity of strategies is made more

Table 8.1 Auto Industry Figures

	1979	1980	1981	1982	1983
General Motors					
Sales (million $)	66,311	57,729	62,791	60,026	74,582
Profit or loss	2,893	− 763	333	963	3,730
Capital investment (% S)	8.1%	13.4%	15.5%	10.3%	6.4%
R & D (% S)	2.9%	3.9%	3.6%	3.6%	—
Ford					
Sales (million $)	43,514	37,085	38,247	37,067	44,455
Profit or loss	1,169	− 1,543	− 1,060	− 658	1,867
Capital investment (% S)	7.8%	7.5%	5.8%	8.0%	5.6%
R & D (% S)	3.9%	4.5%	4.5%	4.8%	—
Chrysler					
Sales (million $)	12,012	9,225	9,972	10,045	13,240
Profit or loss	− 1,097	− 1,710	− 476	170	701
Capital investment (% S)	6.2%	9.1%	4.6%	3.7%	13.6%
R & D (% S)	3.3%	3%	2.3%	3%	—
Toyota (financial year ends in June)					
Sales (million $)	14,012	13,241	16,697	16,040	20,386
Profit or loss	510	574	632	590	839
Capital investment (% S)	4%	5%	8%	5%	4%
R & D (% S)	—	—	—	—	—
Nissan (financial year ends in March)					
Sales (million $)	11,533	10,955	14,363	13,328	13,282
Profit or loss	327	350	409	359	298
Capital investment (% S)	5%	4%	5%	6%	6%
R & D (% S)	—	—	—	—	—

Honda (financial year ends in February)

Sales (million $)	5,179	5,231	7,980	7,846	9,292
Profit or loss	70	111	441	274	301
Capital investment (% S)	7%	5%	6%	6%	8%
R & D (% S)	2.7%	2.7%	2.8%	4.3%	1.8%
Rate of exchange $1.00 =	¥200	¥250	¥210	¥240	¥240

Renault

Sales (million $)	9,374	8,748	8,003	8,813	9,335
Profit or loss	117	67	−154	−446	−548
Capital investment (% S)	3.8%	7.4%	9%	8%	8.3%
R & D (% S)	—	—	3.1%	—	—
Rate of exchange $1.00 =	4.0 F	4.5 F	5.7 F	6.7 F	7.6 F

Volkswagen A/G

Sales (million $)	14,269	13,253	11,261	11,257	11,674
Profit or loss	141	102	54	16	−34
Capital investment (% S)	4.1%	6.2%	5.1%	6.4%	8.4%
R & D (% S)	—	—	—	—	1-1
Rate of exchange $1.00 =	1.7M	1.9M	2.3M	2.4M	2.5M

Fiat auto

Sales (million $)	6,716	7,841	8,251	7,751	7,449
Profit or loss	−117	−151	−225	−59	—
Capital investment (% S)	—	5%	4.3%	8.2%	8.8%
R & D (% S)	—	—	1.8%	1.4%	1.5%
Rate of exchange $1.00 =	L 830	L 856	L 1,124	L 1,346	L 1,518

Source: annual company reports.

difficult by the marked cyclical nature of demand in each country. It is therefore necessary to evaluate these companies' activities by trying to locate long-run strengths and weaknesses.

This aim can be achieved by evaluating,

a The degree of product standardization and scale economies
b the balance on product line
c the technological up-dating of production processes.

In evaluating these points, I have compared production in European car companies in segments 'A' to 'G', in the years 1974 and 1983. (See tables 8.2–8.4.) Segments 'H' and 'I' have been left out for reasons of simplification. In all cases the percentage of total production considered is high, on average above 95 per cent. It is in this way possible to show both the structure of the product line at the level of the individual company and the strength of each manufacturer within each segment. To make comparison easier, points are given in each segment. The company with the best-selling model in a particular segment is given 1, and correspondingly diminishing values to those companies whose production is lower. This can be seen in table 8.2. An average taken of these points in the product line gives a ranking among the companies. It may be used as a proxy indicator of scale economies. (See table 8.5.)

An analysis of the companies' position with regard to volume of production per segment is only one aspect of a complex competitive confrontation. The fact of having the best-selling model in a certain segment is an obvious advantage, but there are other elements to consider. For this reason we have reclassified production data into a pre-segment oligopolistic ranking. This compares the average value of the market quotas for the car companies in the various segments for 1983. In this case not only is the leadership in model production taken into consideration but also the 'crowding level' for each segment. In fact opportunities of profit come not only from the exploitation of scale economies but also from the possibility of making use of the high unit-sales margins which come from operating in segments of low competition. This is to be seen in segment 'G' where, almost exclusively there are cars such as Mercedes, BMW and Jaguar. This confrontation has been calculated at group level because car producers are proceeding to the standardization of components (engines, suspension, brakes) even for models with different name-plates. (See table 8.6, column 1.)

Finally, the definition of oligopolistic ranking of the companies has been related to the overall situation of each group, weighting market quotas taken from each segment with the share of that segment in the total production in the group itself. (See table 8.6, column 2.)

The results of these calculations show up with considerable clarity the rationalization achieved in car manufacturers' product lines. In 1974, in Italy, Fiat had not yet integrated Lancia's product line more than five years after their take-over. In Germany even the Volkswagen–Audi group showed imbalances. Volkswagen was widening their product line after many years of production of the one model. But they had not yet harmonized their own position with that of Audi which was dispersed over too many segments. Opel too had a weakly characterized model line, especially in the higher segments, and was in no position to compete with the prestigious Mercedes cars. BMW appeared to be out of its difficulties of the sixties and aiming decisively at placing itself on the higher echelons of the product line.

In France there was a varied picture: Renault and Peugeot were well balanced, Citroën and Simca Chrysler were full of anomalies.

Finally, Leyland's position had deteriorated. Its product line was dispersed over all segments without any precise strategy being apparent.

As table 8.7 shows, a clear tendency has emerged in recent years towards product-line renewal and a clearer division of roles between marques belonging to the same group. In Italy, Fiat was almost doubling its model range, in the sense that it assigned the lower parts of each segment to the Fiat marque and the higher one to Lancia–Autobianchi. Beyond this, these two lines of production, even if outwardly differentiated, have many components in common. This change, together with a reduction in the labour force and with greater automation, permitted a significant rise in productivity. In 1979 Fiat was manufacturing 14.8 cars per employee, in 1983, 23.8. As a result, Fiat's break-even point went from 1.3 million cars (1979) to 1.14 million. In 1985 management expect to make money with a million units.

Alfa Romeo have still got numerous problems to deal with. Their link with Nissan made it possible for them to replace the 'Alfa Sud' by the 'Arna' with a low volume of investment, using a method already tried out by Leyland and Honda with their 'Acclaim'. Improvements in industrial relations, too, have done much for a recovery in productivity and absenteeism has dropped. The break-even point required the production of 320,000 cars in 1979, compared to the 208,000 in fact produced. By 1984 the break-even point had been lowered to 250,000 cars, but even that was not enough to achieve economic and financial stability and the firm closed the year with a loss of 139 billion (139,000 million) lira. The gravest handicaps for Alfa Romeo remain their large workforce, their lack of investment funds and the current high national rates of inflation.

British Leyland too seems to have finally started on the road to recovery. The early phases (1978–81) were above all concerned with the reorganization of production, reductions in employment, and a start to cooperation with other car manufacturers (Honda, Volkswagen and others). The second phase (1981–3) brought the introduction of new models. Having passed these two phases, British Leyland has started on a third which aims at putting itself definitively on its feet. In this strategy a particularly important role is that of product-line renewal, begun with the launching of the 'Metro' and then the 'Acclaim' (produced under Honda license), the 'Maestro' and the 'Montego'. In collaboration with Honda the new prestige Rover 800 range of models (segment 'F') has been launched in 1986.

Table 8.2 'Per Segment' Production 1974 (Makes)

Segments

	A	B	C	D	E	F	G	Total
Fiat	260,855	368,157	305,945	128,509	74,402	1,854	—	1,139,722 (94.5%)
Lancia[a]	—	108,314	—	14,894	28,669	—	—	151,877 (99.1%)
Alfa Romeo	—	—	100,030	44,655	44,142	—	—	188,827 (90.6%)
Volkswagen	—	—	189,890	432,503	348,573	—	—	970,966 (92.9%)
Audi-NSU	—	—	22,146	171,399	93,735	1,286	—	288,566 (100%)
Ford[b]	—	—	217,560	466,499	52,443	28,978	—	765,480 (94.8%)
GM[c]	—	—	354,636	119,358	166,509	24,390	1,754	666,647 (93.2%)
Daimler–Benz	—	—	—	—	—	305,181	23,736	328,917 (96.7%)
BMW	—	—	—	—	57,353	109,121	12,773	179,247 (97.1%)
Renault	241,039	302,182	137,279	325,111	126,591	—	—	1,132,202 (96.4%)
Peugeot	—	137,982	193,625	48,823	213,680	—	—	594,110 (99.7%)
Citroën	270,817	56,894	150,490	—	—	40,039	—	518,240 (97.6%)
Leyland[d]	—	173,964	122,926	184,138	81,226	40,457	6,000	608,711 (82.4%)
Chrysler F.	—	77,460	216,794	66,071	22,546	—	—	382,871 (100%)
Total	772,711	1,224,953	2,011,321	2,001,960	1,309,869	551,306	44,263	7,916,383

Notes: [a]Lancia + Autobianchi. [b]Ford: D + B + UK. [c]GM: D + UK. [d]Austin + Jaguar + Rover + Triumph.
Sources: figures derived from Associazione Nazionale fra Industrie Automobilistiche (ANFIA); Chambre Syndicale des Constructeurs d'Automobiles (CSCA); Motor Vehicle Manufacturers' Association (MVMA); Verband der Automobilindustrie E.V. (VDA).

Table 8.3 'Per Segment' Production 1983 (Makes)

Segments

	A	B	C	D	E	F	F	Total
Fiat	184,466	408,475	262,767	90,182	24,999	—	—	970,889 (99.8%)
Lancia[a]	—	80,149	33,934	59,812	10,472	—	—	184,367 (99.6%)
Alfa Romeo[b]	—	—	44,659	112,035	34,507	2,027	—	193,228 (93.4%)
Volkswagen	—	166,246	591,259	218,649	—	6,160	—	976,154 (93.9%)
Audi	—	—	—	193,208	146,570	6,160	—	345,938 (95.4%)
Ford[c]	—	356,551	505,761	378,900	33,791	—	—	1,275,003 (95.2%)
GM[d]	—	246,300	459,834	377,694	146,876	20,032	—	1,250,736 (95.7%)
Daimler–Benz	—	—	—	—	109,837	189,403	150,902	450,142 (94.5%)
BMW	—	—	—	—	245,875	123,935	28,855	398,665 (98.0%)
Renault[e]	170,928	423,111	807,687	227,016	51,954	—	—	1,680,697 (96.3%)
Peugeot	44,928	154,995	—	189,434	212,739	3,470	—	605,566 (100%)
Citroën[f]	101,537	144,719	59,653	181,643	—	56,729	—	544,281 (100%)
Talbot[g]	87,052	85,300	112,702	46,392	1,302	—	—	332,766 (96.0%)
Leyland[h]	49,100	175,200	101,800	50,000	33,700	—	28,000	437,800 (92.5%)
Total	638,011	2,241,046	2,980,067	2,124,965	1,052,640	401,756	207,755	9,646,232

Notes: [a]Lancia + Autobianchi. [b]Alfa Romeo + Alfa Nissan. [c]Ford: D + B + UK + S. [d]GM: D + UK + S. [e]Renault: F + S. [f]Citroën: F + S.
[g]Talbot: F + UK + S. [h]Austin + Jaguar + Rover + Triumph.
Sources: figures derived from ANFIA, CSCA, MVMA, VDA.

Table 8.4 'Per Segment' Production 1983 (Groups)

	A	B	C	D	E	F	G	Total
				Segments				
Fiat[a]	184,466	488,624	296,701	149,994	35,471	—	—	1,155,256
Alfa Romeo[b]	—	—	44,659	112,035	34,507	2,027	—	184,367
VAG[c]	—	166,246	581,259	411,856	146,570	6,160	—	1,322,092
Ford[d]	—	356,551	505,761	378,900	33,791	—	—	1,275,003
GM[e]	—	246,300	459,834	377,694	146,876	20,032	—	1,250,736
Daimler–Benz	—	—	—	—	109,837	189,403	150,902	450,142
BMW	—	—	—	—	245,875	123,935	28,855	398,665
Renault[f]	170,928	423,111	807,687	227,016	51,954	—	—	1,680,697
PSA[g]	233,517	385,014	172,702	417,769	214,059	60,199	—	1,482,613
Leyland[h]	49,100	175,200	101,800	50,000	33,700	—	28,000	437,800
Total	638,011	2,241,046	2,980,067	2,124,965	1,052,640	401,756	207,755	9,646,232

Notes: [a]Fiat + Lancia + Autobianchi. [b]Alfa Romeo + Alfa Nissan. [c]Volkswagen + Audi. [d]D + B + UK + S. [e]D + UK + S. [f]Renault: F + S. [g]Peugeot + Citroën + Talbot. [h]Austin + Jaguar + Rover + Triumph.
Sources: figures derived from ANFIA, CSCA, SMMT, VDA.

Table 8.5   'Per Segment' Average Dimensional Ranking

Makes	1974	Makes	1983
Daimler–Benz	1	Daimler–Benz	0.816
Volkswagen	0.820	Renault	0.747
Renault	0.632	Ford	0.651
Fiat	0.553	BMW	0.615
Ford	0.464	GM	0.570
Citroën	0.427	Volkswagen	0.567
Peugeot	0.410	Fiat	0.526
GM	0.377	Peugeot	0.397
BMW	0.353	Audi	0.376
Leyland	0.305	Citroën	0.327
Chrysler France	0.257	Leyland	0.210
Audi NSU	0.175	Talbot	0.188
Alfa Romeo	0.168	Alfa Romeo	0.124
Lancia	0.136	Lancia	0.108

Sources: figures derived from *L'Argus de l'automobile*.

Table 8.6   'Per Segment' Average Oligopolistic Ranking and Overall Oligopolistic Ranking

	$\Sigma \dfrac{Q_s}{n_s}$ %		$\Sigma \, Q_s \cdot P_s$ %
Groups	1983	Groups	1983
Daimler–Benz	0.816	Daimler–Benz	0.466
PSA	0.698	BMW	0.246
Renault	0.670	Renault	0.220
BMW	0.615	PSA	0.201
Ford	0.600	VAG	0.176
VAG	0.537	Fiat	0.175
GM	0.536	Ford	0.165
Fiat	0.532	GM	0.151
Leyland	0.190	Leyland	0.063
Alfa Romeo	0.118	Alfa Romeo	0.041

Sources: figures derived from *L'Argus de l'automobile*.

The difficulties to be overcome by Alfa Romeo and British Leyland are, however, numerous. As our figures show, the scale economies of both companies are very low. Alfa Romeo and British Leyland are low on all the competitive lists, and as a result recovery capacity is bound up with a recovery in demand to lighten the pressure of competition. But even a major market recovery would not be enough. Without considerable investment in model renewal, it seems likely that the expansion of their stronger competitors will scotch their remaining chances of recuperation.

Table 8.7 Line Rotation

	1970-6			1977-83			1970-83
	New models introduced	Old models eliminated	Number of segments concerned	New models introduced	Old models eliminated	Number of segments concerned	Rotation index 1970-83
Fiat	5	8	6	10	2	5	3.00
Lancia	3	5	2	4	—	3	2.30
Alfa Romeo	5	1	3	4	2	4	2.25
Renault	6	2	4	8	4	5	2.80
Peugeot	5	2	4	5	1	5	2.00
Citroën	5	2	4	4	1	4	2.25
Ford	1	1	3	5	1	4	1.50
Opel	1	1	5	6	2	4	1.75
Volkswagen	5	2	3	4	1	4	2.25
Audi	3	1	3	6	1	2	4.50

Rotation Index = Ratio between: new models introduced (1970–83) and number of segments concerned (1983).

Source: Quattroruote.

In France the car-manufacturing picture shows contrasts. Renault and Peugeot both have numerous strong points. They have a vast internal market, second only to West Germany. In Europe, both have a wide range of models and are particularly competitive from segment 'A' to segment 'E'. Over the last three years, however, these two groups have been going through a difficult phase. Their domestic market share, which was at 80 per cent half-way through the seventies, has dropped to below 70 per cent. This is partly due to the difficulties encountered by Peugeot in restructuring Talbot production (formerly Simca–Chrysler). The greater aggressiveness shown by foreign manufacturers and production losses sustained through labour disputes led to considerable losses for both groups. By 1985 it was Renault who were facing the greatest difficulties: in 1984 they lost 1.4 billion (1,400 million) dollars. The core of their problem is slow growth in productivity and sluggishness in model replacement. Additional difficulties were presented by government price controls and a 13 per cent fall in French car registrations in 1984. George Besse, who succeeded Bernard Hanon in 1985, has started a drastic restructuring which aims at a return to profitability by 1987. In many ways this is a strategy similar to that of Fiat in 1980–3. It involves the elimination of non-car sectors of the business, automation and the renewal of models.

Table 8.8   Standardization Level (1983)

	Engines	Gear boxes	Body pans	Number of models	Segments
Fiat	6	8	8	12	A, B, C, D, E, H
Renault	7	8	5	8	A, B, C, D, E, F
PSA	12	14	11	20	A, B, C, D, E, F, H
VAG	2	8	4	10	B, C, D, E
Opel	4	6	6	7	B, C, D, E, F
Ford	6	6	5	5	B, C, D, E
BMW	3	3	3	4	E, F, G
Alfa Romeo	4	5	4	7	C, D, E, F, H
Volvo	4	3	3	3	D, E, F

Source: *Quattroruote.*

The current aim of Peugeot on the other hand, is to complete the commonization of components within their three makes. This group has the worst position on this question (see Table 8.8), but the launching of the Peugeot 205 and the Citroën BX has improved the position. In 1985–6 the management's aim is to cover all three makes with a product line over six segments, using four gear boxes, four engines and four body-pans.

The position of the German makes seems generally favourable, above all for Mercedes and BMW. For quite some time now, these two have been specializing in high-quality production, relying, at first, on their national market, the biggest and most receptive for large sedans, and then moving out into all the main markets. This entry into an elite consumer band has placed them beyond competition and has permitted a systematic, constant expansion in production, carried out deliberately and with an enviable financial solidity.

Mercedes' and BMW's performances can definitely be described as excellent. Mercedes' widening into segment 'E' with its '190' has been a complete success. BMW continues to reinforce its own technological image. After the debut of a particularly sophisticated turbo-diesel engine for their 5-series, this Munich company will introduce their new 7-series. This will bristle with electronics, underlining BMW's lead in this technology. It may also feature an all-alloy V12 power unit.[37]

The Volkswagen–Audi case is a little different. In the last few years VW has had to register unfavourable balance sheets, largely due to non-automobile production (in the computer and office-automation fields) and their car manufacturing operations in North and South America. Losses here have taken their toll on national car manufacturing. It has delayed the renewal of the 'Golf' and Audi 80. 1985, however, brought a definite recovery for the group. Audi has set itself the particular objective of entry into the prestige car market, changing its public image, previously a bit 'blue collar' in Germany. Their first step in this direction was with the '100', and the '90' should consolidate this line.

Overall, the German car industry is in very good health. In 1984 some difficulties arose because of a major strike by Industriegewerkschaft (IG) Metall for a reduction in working hours. In 1985, moreover, there was some stagnation in demand, largely caused by uncertainty about proposed emissions legislation. It is unlikely, however, that these indicate fundamental long-term problems for the German car industry.

Finally, we come to the European associates of Ford and General Motors. For some time now both of them have been pursuing a process of rationalization in their European production and assembly plants. This has been complex and hard and has meant closing down the least efficient plants and a reduction in staff. It has been all the more difficult because a part of the European financial resources was transferred to the United States to support the mother company. The operation can now be said to be complete in its general lines. Both companies are in the black, and Ford in particular has succeeded in widely renewing its product line as well as launching new models, while General Motors has concentrated on restyling. Ford and General Motors economic results seem definitely better than the positions they both have in the oligopolistic ranking (table 8.6), and in that of model renewal. Very probably this depends on the fact that Ford and General Motors have reorganized much faster than their direct competitors (Renault, Peugeot and Fiat), with a lower degree of vertical integration and a more marked standardization policy.

AUTOMATION AND EMPLOYMENT

The oil crisis also caused the technological trajectory of production systems to swerve. In the past, the car industry's pursuit of the highest levels of productivity had been based on the methods of Henry Ford, maximum specialization, maximum repetition and standardization of operations, large volume of production. This manufacturing system was rigid but proved adequate in the phase in which the car industry was in continuous expansion. But it was inadequate for new demands. In the face of demand subject to cyclical fluctuations inclined towards more personalized cars, there is a new problem: that of finding a new economic–financial balance at lower levels of production. Formerly, every competitive strategy was based on economies of scale at high levels of output. Now the problem has become one of modifying the cost structure and improving productivity and flexibility, so as to keep production costs down even where there has been a reduction in output.

Under the whiplash of the crisis, this resulted in an intensive automation of production, above all after 1979, with the adoption of flexible manufacturing systems (FMS) and robots.

The introduction of robots into the car industry began simultaneously in the USA, Japan and Europe in the early seventies. At that time robots were relatively simple machines with mechanically guided fixed movements. These features tended to employ the robot in fixed sequence operations and high output production according to schemes typical of rigid manufacturing, and it was introduced to substitute for manpower in the more risky and exhausting jobs.

Halfway through the seventies the designing of numerically controlled robots (NCR) opened up a whole new phase in the automation of car manufacturing in that these robots could now be utilized in much more sophisticated operations. The robots, however, were also installed to do single operations such as internal automation of one part of a production line (welding, stamping or assembly) which was still planned in conventional ways. One example is that of bodywork welding where it is usual to have a by-pass ready allowing bodywork to pass around the robot zone.

At the end of the seventies, coinciding with the launching of new models, the third robot phase came into being. Both the design of the product and the engineering of the process was thought out in terms of a robot line. In this more mature phase, the economic reasons leading to the introduction of robots are the following.

a *Productivity* With the use of robots there is a reduction in working time and the possibility of cutting out idle time on machines.

b *Flexibility* The robot is programmed to work in multiple production lines and to accept changes.

c *Quality* The quality of robot operations tends to be higher. Above all there is quality stabilization and a great reduction both in waste pieces and pieces to be rectified during the operations which follow.

d   *Safety*   The improvement in working conditions from the introduction of robots cuts out 'dirty jobs' and helps to prevent industrial injuries.

Industrial relations, particularly tense in the Italian car industry from the end of the sixties, have been a strong stimulus in the automation of processes at Fiat and Alfa Romeo. Fiat, in particular may be considered the car company with the highest world level of robot operations. (See table 8.9.) Their first application of robots on a large scale (a 16-robot group) was put into use in 1972 with the bodywork welding of the Argenta. A further step ahead was taken with the welding line of the '131' using a group of 23 robots, in 1977 a significant quality leap was taken with the introduction of 'Robogate'.[38] In the same year painting operations were carried out by robots in some plants, while in the area of mechanical assembly, in 1980, the new LAM (asynchronous engine assembly line) came into use.[39] (See table 8.9 and figure 8.1.)

The gains in productivity from these innovations are very significant. Fiat's experience shows that the installation of a robot (whose cost is between £45,000 and £65,000) replaces, on average 2.5 workers per shift with a production increase of 20 per cent per hour. Thus the investment is covered in two years. Added to this greater direct productivity, there are also indirect gains. Greater precision in operations allows new engineering systems and design. In the case of body welding, passing from the '127' to the Uno has marked progress from a body of 276 elements to one of 171, that is 36 per cent fewer. Welding spots have been reduced from 4,280 to 2,692. With the '127', 72 per cent of the welding spots were done with automatic machines. Now, the Uno has 99 per cent automatic welding, and 35 per cent of this is done by robots (see figure 8.2). Alfa Romeo has gone through a similar experience. Their welding line, in passing from the Alfa Sud to the '33', was reduced by 400 jobs. Of these, 220 depended on the higher productivity of the robot line, and another 180 resulted from fewer welding spots. By 1984 the total number of robots at Fiat was 765, and 189 more were planned for 1985. In Italian car companies, many of the gains in productivity can be attributed to automation. In 1979 Fiat made 1,230,579 cars, employing 83,000 production workers (i.e. 14.8 cars per

Table 8.9   Robots in Use, 1983

	GM	Ford	Chrysler	Fiat	Alfa Romeo	Renault	Volkswagen
Assembly	675	—	—	129	3	—	—
Welding	1,000	—	—	532	62	—	—
Painting	300	—	—	74	10	—	—
Others	325	—	—	30	6	—	—
Total	2,300	1,100	358	765	81	220	650[a]

Note: [a]This is a 1982 figure.
Sources: companies and *Automotive News*, September 6 1982.

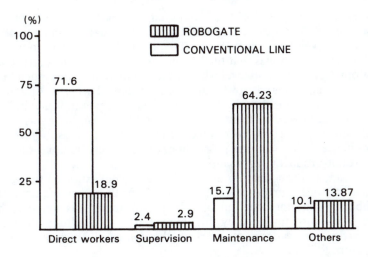

Number of workers: conventional line = 247
Robogate = 137

Figure 8.1   Fiat: Comparison between the Robogate and Conventional Body-Welding Technology
Source: Fiat.

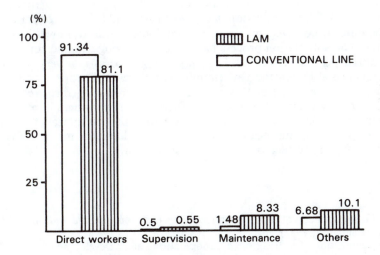

Number of workers: conventional line = 404
LAM = 360

Figure 8.2   Fiat: Comparison between the LAM (Engine Assembly Asynchronous Line) and Conventional Technology
Source: Fiat.

worker). In 1983, 1,157,880 cars required a work force of 48,700 (23.8 per worker).[40] Alfa Romeo's results are rather similar. Holding steady its production levels between 1979 and 1983, it cut its workforce from 40,000 to 25,000.[41] This implies that the labour-saving effect of the current wave of automation at a world level will permit productivity gains much higher than the average demand growth rate, which is about 2 per cent. Automation programmes are considerable. In Europe, apart from Fiat, Renault, Volvo and Volkswagen produce their own robots, and they have ambitious projects in the pipeline. By 1990, Volkswagen, for example, intends to have 2,000 robots in use, and is studying possibilities of developing joint ventures with other robot-producing companies.

In Japan, the robotization process is very advanced, even though any comparison with European levels is made difficult by varying definitions of robots.[42] The introduction of robots into Japan has not only been accepted but also favoured by the unions partly to eliminate 'dirty jobs' and partly from a desire to keep up the competitiveness of their own companies.[43]

In the United States the robot level seems to be lower than in Europe. At the end of 1983 the total of robots used by the Big Three was 3,758 (see table 8.9). They intend, however, to reach 25,000 robots by 1990. General Motors has begun to produce 'in-house' robots but also has an agreement with Fujitsu Fanuc, a Japanese high-volume robot producer, and will also use robots being developed jointly with the Unimation Company, the largest US robot maker. If the goal of 25,000 car-making robots is achieved by 1990, the reduction in the workforce will be about 20 per cent.

The impact, however, on changes in manpower utilization will be even greater. The automation process has brought a strong demand for highly specialized personnel with it. The up-grading process is a very positive consequence although the new training structures in Europe may prove inadequate for changes of this magnitude. Union–management relations have been very strained because of conflicts over employment levels. This is all the more important because the automation process appears to be the main opportunity European car manufacturers have for major gains in productivity in the face of Japanese competition.

NOTES

1 US Department of Transportation, *The U.S. Automobile Industry, 1981* (Washington, 1982).
2 Organization for Economic Cooperation and Development (OECD), *Perspectives à longe terme de l'industrie automobile mondiale* (Paris, 1983), p. 24: K. Bhaskar, *The Future of the World Motor Industry* (London, 1980).
3 G. Volpato, *L'industria automobilistica internazionale: Espansione, crisi e riorganizzazione* (Padua, 1983); *idem*, 'Crisis and new corporate strategic decisions: the case of the European car industry; *Economia Aziendale*, no. 3 (1983).

4   W. J. Abernathy, *The Productivity Dilemma: Roadblock to Innovation in the Automobile Industry* (Baltimore, 1978); W. J. Abernathy, K. B. Clark and A. M. Kantrow, *Industrial Renaissance: Producing a Competitive Future for America* (New York, 1983).

5   L. J. White, *The Automobile Industry since 1945* (Harvard, 1971).

6   W. C. Duncan, *U.S.–Japan Automobile Diplomacy: a Study in Economic Confrontation* (Cambridge, Mass., 1973).

7   A change in vehicle design demands a complex and diverse set of functions: (a) down-sizing, (b) conversion to front-wheel drive, (c) replacement of materials, (d) improving the efficiency of the vehicle through the development of new technologies. See US Department of Transportation, *The U.S. Automobile Industry, 1980* (Washington, 1981).

8   W. J. Abernathy, J. E. Harbour and J. M. Henn, *Productivity and Comparative Cost Advantages: Some Estimates for Major Automotive Producers* (US Department of Transportation, 1980).

9   US Department of Transportation, *Automobile Industry, 1980*, p. 29.

10 Half way through the 1920s, Fiat was producing seven different models with several versions (short and long chassis) with a total production of only 37,000 cars. See Volpato, *L'industria automobilistica*, p. 46.

11 Volpato, *L'industria automobilistica*.

12 Volpato, *L'industria automobilistica*, p. 205 and D. T. Jones, *Maturity and Crisis in the European Car Industry: Structural Change and Public Policy*, Sussex European Research Paper no. 8 (Brighton, 1981).

13 The structure of car demand can be subdivided into different 'segments'.

    A   super-utility car (e.g. Fiat Panda)
    B   utility car (e.g. Austin Metro)
    C   medium-small car (e.g. Ford Escort)
    D   medium car (e.g. Renault 9)
    E   medium-large car (e.g. Ford Sierra)
    F   large car (e.g. Audi 100)
    G   luxury car (e.g. Mercedes 380)
    H   sports car (e.g. Ferrari)
    I   speciality car (e.g. Land Rover)

14 For a detailed analysis of imbalance present in the product line of European manufacturers, see Volpato, *L'industria automobilistica*, ch. 15.

15 For a detailed analysis of the problems of the car component industry, see A. Enrietti, M. Follis, G. M. Gros-Pietro and G. Pescetto, *La ristrutturazione nell' industria metalmeccanica: il caso dell'auto e dei componenti* (Milan, 1980); G. Volpato, 'Crisi dell'auto e riorganizzazione dell'industria dei componenti', in G. Fornengo and E. Rullani (eds.), *L'industria dell'auto e dei componenti: integrazione e internazionalizzazione produttiva* (Milan, 1982); and Economist Intelligence Unit, *Comparative Economic Study of the Motor Vehicle Components Industry in the European Community and Japan* (Brussels, 1981).

16 The strength of Japanese competition varies considerably in Europe, depending on the presence or absence of 'national champions' and tariff policies, from 40 per cent of registrations in Finland to the limited quota of 2,200 vehicles for Italy. The success of Japanese sales initially depended on an underestimation of their competitiveness. 'In the case of the U.K., the first important Japanese penetration of the market coincided with the programme to rationalise the distribution network. Between 1968 and 1975, British Leyland, Chrysler, Ford

and Vauxhall "liberated" about 5,400 dealers who were then free to take up import representation. A sample survey of 300 such dealers estimated that 35% of the liberated dealers converted to import franchises.' See Top 70 Study Group, *Japanese–European Trade Relations: Restructuring or Co-operation? The Case of the Automobile Industry* (Geneva, 1978).

17 S. Shingo, *Study of Toyota Production System from Industrial Engineering Viewpoint* (Japan Management Association, Tokyo, 1981) and R. Prodi and P. Bianchi, 'Concorrenza e aggiustamenti strutturali nella industria dell'automobile', *L'industria*, no. 3 (1981).

18 See chapter 9 in this volume and also K. Shimokawa, 'Marketing and sales financing in the automobile industry: U.S. and Japan', in K. Nakagawa (ed.), *Marketing and Finance in the Course of Industrialisation* (International Conference on Business History no. 3, Tokyo, 1978) and A. Okochi and K. Shimokawa (eds.), *Development of Mass Marketing: the Automobile and Retailing Industries* (Tokyo, 1981).

19 L. Kraar, 'Japan's auto makers shift strategies', *Fortune, 11 August 1980;* G. Maxcy, *The Multinational Motor Industry* (London, 1981).

20 On the financial situation of the European car industry, see A. Mosconi and D. Velo, *Crisi e restrutturazione del settore automobilistico* (Bologna, 1982).

21 According to Harbridge House Europe, *The Japanese Motor Industry* (London, 1981), dividends paid by the Japanese firms vary from 1–2 per cent of the market value of the shares, compared to the 5–10 per cent or more distributed by the American and European firms.

22 For an evaluation of research and development levels across Japanese industries, see OECD, *Indicateurs de la science et de la technologie: ressources consacrées à la R & D* (Paris, 1984).

23 A. Altshuler, M. Anderson, D. Jones, D. Roos and J. Womack, *The Future of the Automobile.* (London, 1985), pp. 101–4; OECD, *Perspectives*, p. 93.

24 T. Dodsworth, 'Slim lines and fat profits', *Financial Times*, January 12 1984.

25 American hopes of managing to wring out a compact vehicle at costs that are competitive with Japanese ones have not entirely faded. All three big firms have launched programmes for new small vehicles. General Motors' Saturn project is the most ambitious, a clean-sheet programme involving an investment of three and a half billion (3,500 million) dollars which should produce its first car at the end of the 1980s. Ford and Chrysler are following suit with their similar, though less radical Alpha and Liberty projects.

26 *Automotive News*, 23 January 1984.

27 As early as halfway through the 1970s, The American Motor Corporation (AMC) found it impossible to make the necessary investments for renewal of its two product lines (passenger car and speciality vehicle – Jeep). Therefore it negotiated an agreement with Renault who, during 1980–2, have invested $350 million in AMC acquiring 46 per cent of its shares. In 1982 the production of Renault-designed compact cars began.

28 The most important factors were (1) the reduction of inflation and the strengthening of the dollar which made a 'buy' rather than 'make' policy more convenient; (2) the return of demand towards standard cars, with its consequent slowing down of the turn-over to smaller, front-wheel drive models.

29 *Automotive News*, 23 January 1984.

30 *Automotive News*, 23 January 1984.

31 *Business Week*, 21 June 1982.

32 The average age of US cars in use steadily increased from 5.7 years (1973) to 7.2 years (1981).

33 In 1982, GM entered a supply contract with the Italian luxury car body maker Pininfarina to import 8,000 bodies per year in an attempt to curb the rise of European luxury imports.

34 The bill which passed the House in November 1983 imposes local content ratios for components ranging from 3.3 to 30 per cent for 1985 and to 10 to 90 per cent for 1986, covering auto manufacturers selling over 100,000 units per year.

35 For these and other related changes, see the essay by Katz in this volume.

36 A detailed analysis of the difference between domestic and export price policies is to be found in Volpato, *L'industria automobilistica*, ch. 15.

37 *Automotive News* 27 February 1984.

38 This consists of a computerized control system to move bodywork mounted on 'Robocarriers' through a sequence of operations at successive work stations. Updated versions of Robogate were installed in seven General Motors Assembly plants in 1982–3: *Automotive News*, 6 February 1984.

39 This system is organized with a matrix scheme which can mount a vast range of engines. In this way the traditional working group no longer needs to move with the line but can do their work standing still.

40 In 1983 there were 62,900 production workers before 14,200 were permanently laid off in *cassa integrazione*.

41 10,000 were laid off and 5,000 took early retirement.

42 According to Japanese Industrial Robot Association data for 1980, there were 19,873 robots, 3,060 of them in the car industry.

43 This has been facilitated by the company-based structure of Japanese unions.

9

Product and Labour Strategies in Japan

Koichi Shimokawa

Since the second oil shock in 1979, the Japanese automobile industry, the last to develop among the three major auto producing areas in the world, saw its international competitiveness rapidly advance as radical structural change occurred in the US auto market, and Detroit auto manufacturers went into a drastic decline. Today, after four years of depression, Detroit is enjoying good profitability due to the renewed demand for big cars, but the Japanese auto industry maintains its comparative competitive advantage in small cars even while the voluntary export restraints on car shipments to the US continue. This international competitiveness of the Japanese auto industry is neither a temporary nor a casual phenomenon but flows from rationalization measures which are the product of mutual cooperation between management and labour and which have allowed the industry to realize high productivity and quality. Such rationalization measures, however, as typified by the 'just in time' (JIT) system, were not realized in a short time. Rather, they were established in a step by step manner as consensus and communication between labour and management were established at the latter's initiative. Another key element in rationalization has been the close cooperative relationship between assemblers and parts makers within corporate group organizations.

The Japanese auto companies' strategy of manufacturing small cars in low volumes using a flexible production system has played a crucial role in establishing rationalization. These strategies have promoted quick responses to changing market needs and improvements in quality levels linked to increased productivity. A decisive factor in carrying through these product strategies has been the cooperative relationship between management and labour.

In this paper, I will first take up the main reason why the competitiveness of the Japanese auto industry has risen so rapidly. Secondly, I will analyse how the Japanese auto manufacturers developed their product strategy, and the relationship between their product strategy and the rationalization of production. Following this, I will examine the history of Japanese auto makers' labour–management strategies and the response of the Japanese auto unions during the period of the establishment of JIT systems. Lastly,

I will consider how JIT systems contributed to the flexibility of production processes and to innovation in production-process technology, and what effect the introduction of robots into the production process in auto plants has had upon the upgrading of production process technology and the formation of new working skills.

THE RISE OF JAPANESE AUTO INDUSTRY COMPETITIVENESS

The rapid rise of Japanese automakers' competitiveness was directly linked to the rapid decline of the US industry. But was it simply brought about by US automakers' decline and the fast-growing demand for small cars? Moreover, is the relative ascendancy of the Japanese auto industry simply a temporary conjunctural phenomenon?

In fact, this relative superiority is not a passing phenomenon, but has been brought about by internal factors conducive to the continuous enhancement of competitiveness, in particular efforts towards high productivity and high quality and the combined strength of the materials suppliers and parts makers which support the auto industry.

Essentially, US automakers' competitiveness used to be built upon the high earning capacity of larger cars. During the heyday of large cars, they earned more than four times as much profit per car as the Japanese and West German makers of small cars.

Behind this facade, however, labour productivity and car quality continued to deteriorate, and US makers began to lag behind in technological innovation and capital spending. Moreover, the shift of demand towards small cars following the second oil crisis resulted in a total collapse of the earnings structure centred on large cars. The emphasis in competition moved from the pursuit of value added per car to the enhancement of labour productivity per employee.[1] US makers were forced to fight on the same ground as their Japanese counterparts, and as a result, the Japanese makers' strong competitiveness, which had been growing unnoticed, surfaced all of a sudden.

What were the internal factors that rapidly improved the Japanese automakers' international competitiveness? The fundamental ones were the success of Japanese-style 'micro-management' which made possible highly efficient operation of relatively small-scale equipment, and the close cooperative relations with suppliers and related industries.

These were reinforced by stable labour relations, the success of new forms of work organization and participatory systems, the spread of JIT systems, the improvement of technical standards, and the international competitiveness of related industries.[2] Another important factor was that since the Japanese auto industry made a late start, it could introduce the most advanced techniques to catch up with its Western counterparts quickly. Although capital investment was smaller than in the US and Western Europe, Japanese auto and parts makers introduced highly advanced equipment.

The fact that Japanese automakers had to face the problems of recalling defective cars for safety reasons and coping with environmental pollution in the early stage of their development also had a favourable impact on the improvement of their technologies and the expansion of the scope of their development efforts.

All of these factors combined together to have synergistic effects. Japanese automakers succeed in organizing the most efficient production with equipment which is relatively advanced but limited in scale and by so doing they achieved both high quality and high productivity.

In particular, Japanese-style rationalization measures, as seen in the QC (quality control) circles and the *kanban* (just in time) systems have enabled workers to take a positive role in the production process and bring their creativity and innovations into full play, thereby minimizing defects in their own work process and maximizing the effective operating hours of capital equipment.[3] Workers' standards of technical competence and knowledge have vastly improved and they are able to contribute to the development of new products, the improvement of equipment, in-house manufacture of robots, machine tools and metal moulds, and the maintenance and layout of equipment. These practices have also facilitated the introduction of new techniques such as electronics and new materials and, in particular, have increased the flexibility of the production process, easing remodelling and the adoption of new technologies such as front-wheel drive and turbo charging.[4] The most effective use of limited production equipment to achieve high productivity has led to strong international competitiveness even though the equipment and management scales of the Japanese auto industry are smaller than those of their American and European counterparts. That is, the minimum efficient scale of operations and the break-even points of the automakers have been reduced, enabling the maintenance of 11 mass-producing automakers in one country – the highest number in the world.

PRODUCT STRATEGIES OF JAPANESE AUTO MAKERS

The patterns of market structure and product strategies are clearly different in the US and Japanese auto industries. In the US case, there have been four stages: first, a period of an expanding mass market met by practical and popular cars such as the Ford Model T; second, a period of replacement demand met by a full-line policy; third, a period of increases in size and power met by larger cars; and fourth, a period of expanding second-car and third-car demand met by introducing compact cars. In Japan, because of its small land space, bad road conditions, and low income levels, personal transportation methods were first met by the bicycle, followed by the motorcycle and taxi, and only finally by the popular small car. Because of these historical conditions, Japanese automakers pursued a small-car product policy, and from around 1960, when the period of the mass-market popular passenger car began, introduced a full-line policy within the small car category.[5] Following this, however, when capital liberalization began, the Japanese auto industry was confronted by international competition, especially from Detroit's Big Three. As a result, an unexpected situation began to appear.

In the 1970s the product strategies of the Big Three shifted towards compact cars and their full-line strategies were downgraded. But this shift toward compact cars was only partially carried out and Japanese small car makers were given an opportunity to expand their overseas sales, especially in the USA. After the second oil crisis the small car boom accelerated and the Big Three were caught unprepared. In this sense, it was true that the Japanese auto industry was favoured by unforeseen shifts in the market. Yet, it was no accident that their international competitiveness in small cars rose rapidly. Rather, it rose because each Japanese automaker's product policy already had a clear orientation toward diminishing the technology gap and accumulating small-car production technology.

Individually, how has each Japanese automaker developed their product strategy? As mentioned previously, a full-line policy developed during the period of expansion of the popular car market. Toyota led the way in introducing this full-line policy while Nissan followed.

After Toyota separated its motor sales organization from Toyota Motor Company in 1950, a very aggressive market policy was pursued and a nationwide dealer network was set up using local capital. With this network, Toyota responded very sensitively to changes in the structure of the market.[6] In the first stage, for example, their full-line policy started with only two market segments, consisting of the high-priced small cars, Crown and Corona, and the low-priced small car, Publica, with a 700 cc engine. With the higher-priced cars they pursued high profits while with the lower priced Publica they aimed at increasing sales volume.

Their full-line policy was thus quite different from GM's full-line policy in the 1920s, which had been to introduce all types of cars simultaneously in all of the market segments. Yet, Toyota did watch the expanding market and from time to time introduced a new type of car to respond to the changing market structure. Examples were the introduction of the 1100 cc popular car, the Corolla in 1966, the Mark II in 1968, a new speciality car the Celica in 1970, and a new luxury speciality car the Soara in 1981. During the period of an expanding domestic auto market up until the first oil crisis, Toyota not only increased the number of their car lines but also expanded the amount of variation within each car line, within the limits of the same production capacities, and called this a 'wide-selection' system.[7] From the late 1970s, in an increasingly mature domestic market, they introduced twin cars such as the Cresta and Kamuri with a common chassis and basic components, and have upgraded established car lines, thereby stimulating replacement demand. Toyota's product strategy, thus, can be characterized as introducing new cars well matched to market needs and attaching importance to a car product mix combined with skilful model variation.

Behind this, however, has been their pursuit of high quality and low cost through complete rationalization of the production process.

In Japanese business journalism, Toyota's product development has been characterized as an '80 per cent principle', which always targets certainty and safety. Such a principle emphasizes the production of cars which will have maximum saleability. As a result, Toyota has not had many cases of bold product development or big risk taking. Today, Toyota's goal is to introduce more special features into their existing cars and they are gradually moving in this direction in terms of their product strategy.

Like Toyota, the other full-line maker, Nissan has been developing new products by using their strengths in engineering and the development of new technologies. Nissan, nevertheless, allowed Toyota to take the lead in the development of a full-line policy and in the competition for domestic market share. This was largely due to Nissan's disadvantage in terms of dispersed plant locations (a legacy of wartime expansion) and their slow development of a nationwide domestic sales network. Nissan introduced the first mass-produced passenger car in Japan, the mini-car Datsun, in the prewar period. Following the war, they established business ties with Austin in 1952 in order to acquire passenger-car production know-how.[8] Soon after this, in 1957 and 1958, they successfully introduced to the Japanese market their own self-designed small car, the Cedric (1500 cc) and the popular car, the Bluebird (1000–1200 cc). These two types of cars were used to compete with Toyota's Crown and Corona. Later, Nissan saw the necessity for expansion in the popular car market and introduced the Sunny (1000 cc) in 1966, ahead of Toyota's Corolla. Since then, these two cars have competed for sales volume as rivals.

In 1966, Nissan merged with the Prince Motor Co., an independent maker of medium-sized autos with excellent design and engine technology, and took over Prince's car lines, consisting of the Gloria and Skyline as the basic models.[9] With this, Nissan established itself as a full-line maker. Since then, Nissan has extended the variation of its basic models to meet the needs of the domestic auto market and has upgraded established models and added new models or twin cars. As a result, the structure of Nissan's product mix has become almost the same as Toyota's.

In comparison with Toyota, however, Nissan has more often attempted unique product developments and the introduction of new models. Examples have been using pick-up trucks as the spearhead of car exports to the USA; the introduction of a small sports car for the youth market, the Fairlady; the first introduction of a turbocharged passenger car; the introduction of a one-litre car, March; and the development of a new six-cylinder high performance engine, Pluzma. Nissan also has introduced a higher percentage of front-wheel-drive cars in its lineup than Toyota, after this became more important for fuel economy. Thus Nissan has been superior to Toyota in terms of unique product developments, but in an overall evaluation of the two makers, Nissan tends to be inferior because of an imbalance in its car lines. Moreover, while Nissan's product strategy emphasizes a 'product out'

Table 9.1   Total Production of Passenger Cars in Japan by Manufacturer 1961-83 (thousand units)

Year	Toyota	Nissan	Mazda	Honda	Mitsubishi	Fuji	Daihatsu	Suzuki	Isuzu	Total
1961	74	77	32	—	8	22	—	—	11	224
1962	75	89	42	—	8	12	—	3	15	244
1963	129	119	54	—	16	19	—	2	22	361
1964	182	169	60	5	29	26	6	2	34	513
1965	236	170	81	9	46	37	11	2	31	623
1966	316	232	92	3	76	59	22	3	33	836
1967	477	352	129	87	106	90	60	26	39	1,366
1968	659	572	178	187	130	104	89	96	39	2,054
1969	964	698	201	233	128	125	105	122	36	2,612
1970	1,068	899	225	277	246	158	142	145	19	3,179
1971	1,400	1,102	301	215	261	115	158	151	15	3,718
1972	1,488	1,352	380	235	223	130	110	90	13	4,021
1973	1,632	1,487	466	257	281	131	114	88	15	4,471
1974	1,485	1,257	379	316	233	102	78	55	28	3,933
1975	1,715	1,533	387	328	289	109	92	51	65	4,569
1976	1,731	1,610	447	474	403	158	71	43	91	5,028
1977	1,884	1,616	499	577	486	156	83	56	75	5,432
1978	2,039	1,733	493	653	629	140	123	62	103	5,975
1979	2,111	1,739	647	706	529	154	134	70	86	6,176
1980	2,303	1,941	737	846	660	202	156	88	107	7,040
1981	2,248	1,864	841	852	607	190	147	95	130	6,974
1982	2,258	1,816	824	854	573	201	128	114	113	6,881
1983	2,381	1,859	862	858	524	230	185	138	116	7,153

Source: Economist Intelligence Unit, *Japanese Motor Business* 1, no. 1 (September 1984).

orientation, developing and then promoting new products, Toyota's has been 'product in', a more consumer-oriented strategy to fit market needs. Hence, Nissan's introduction of unique products and new types of cars have not always been a 100 per cent success. In many cases, Toyota has caught up and overtaken Nissan's lead in such areas as the introduction of new types of cars and exports to foreign markets. Nissan's product and marketing strategy has emphasized from an early period the overseas market and business tie-ups with foreign automakers.

Compared with Toyota's and Nissan's yearly production of 3.1 million and 2.1 million vehicles respectively, the production of Mazda, Honda and Mitsubishi have been around one million each. These makers, however, are not full-line makers like Toyota and Nissan and their basic car lines, limited to about three categories, reflect an interest in the development of new specialized products.

Mazda, starting with a license for the rotary engine from NSU, aimed at the successful utilization of it in passenger cars. Because of the engine's fuel inefficiency in its early stage, however, the sales of rotary-engine cars dropped off suddenly after the first oil crisis and the company came to the verge of bankruptcy. More recently, Mazda has made a recovery as the fuel efficiency of the rotary engine has been improved and the sports car RX-7 and popular car, Familia, have become big successes.[10] The special features of Mazda's product strategy are the three types of engines used (rotary, diesel and recipro), the emphasis placed upon high performance and driveability, and target-oriented development of models.

Mazda was also the pioneer of mixed-model production systems in which several models are assembled on one final assembly line using computer-aided production schedules. It has used the strength of its production system to support product development.

The latest newcomer to passenger-car production, Honda, entered the area from the production of motorcycles and mini-cars and used its excellent internal combustion engine technology successfully to develop the new antipollution CVCC engine.[11] Honda's product strategy is characterized by the development of unique products based upon detailed market research. In all of their car lines, they have been installing front-wheel-drive mechanisms from an early date. They also introduced early on the so-called 'two-box' popular car, Civic, which emphasized the minimum practical necessities in a car. Later, they introduced the Accord, which gained a good reputation in the US market. Most recently, they introduced to the domestic market a new concept one-litre car, City, developed by a group of young Honda engineers all under 30 years old. These examples of unique product development and overseas market orientation as well as cooperation with a foreign automaker such as BL in new car development, are the characteristic features of Honda's product strategy.

Mitsubishi, which inherited a talented group of engineers from the aircraft field, has enjoyed an advantage in being able to gain the cooperation of other excellent companies in the Mitsubishi group, such as Mitsubishi Heavy

Industry and Mitsubishi Electric Co. Mitsubishi's product line is a peculiar combination of heavy trucks, buses, small passenger cars, and mini-cars. As a result, their research and development people have difficulty covering all of these fields, and in addition, because of Mitsubishi's shortage of sales and marketing ability, their product development has often been badly timed.

Mitsubishi's product line consists of three basic models and they have enjoyed success with the new Galant series and the two-box Mirage series since 1977. Since then, however, their model changes have tended to be delayed. They are now planning to emphasize mecatronization (mechanical electronics) – from engine and steering to transmission and body structure, and are hoping to make it the core of a synthesized technology. Their future themes will have to be increasing their research and development ability and producing a distinctive company character for their products while focusing on particular market segments.

Although their production capacities are lower than the makers mentioned above, other auto manufacturers have been developing products with special features. Isuzu, for example, a producer of heavy-duty trucks and passenger cars, has been developing common components for its vehicles through a collaborative relationship with GM and is now emphasizing diesel engine development and using new techniques for car bodies. Fuji Heavy Industries, on the other hand, is emphasizing four-wheel-drive vehicles, while Daihatsu is famous for their one-litre car installed with a three-cylinder engine. Suzuki, which specializes in mini cars, is going to enter the one-litre car market following their business collaboration with GM. The main weaknesses of the smaller companies are their weaker marketing networks and limited dealerships. They also have problems of limited access to parts suppliers. In research and development it is harder for them to sustain high levels of investment, but most of them offset this by focusing their research on particular products or by drawing on the research resources of related companies. For instance, Mazda is linked to Ford, Daihatsu to Toyota and Subaru to Nissan.

As we have seen the product strategies of Japanese auto-makers vary from company to company. In general, however, they can be divided into three groups:

1 two companies following a full-line policy within the small-car category
2 three companies which pursue target-oriented special characteristics within three basic categories of cars
3 four companies which pursue certain engineering characteristics among a few types of cars.

The product strategies of Japanese automakers, however, cannot be divided up vertically according to car category in the same way as the German auto manufacturers who specialize in luxury, middle-class, and popular car categories. Instead, Japanese makers continue to compete with each other in the same market segments and as a result, within the total

		1978	1979	1980	1981	1982	1983
Corolla	(Toyota)		Ⓕ		Ⓜ		Ⓕ
Sprinter	(Toyota)		Ⓕ		Ⓜ		Ⓕ
Corsa	(Toyota)	Ⓝ		Ⓜ		Ⓕ	
Tercel	(Toyota)	Ⓝ		Ⓜ		Ⓕ	
Starlet	(Toyota)	Ⓕ		Ⓜ	Ⓜ	Ⓜ	
Corolla II	(Toyota)					Ⓝ	
Carib	(Toyota)					Ⓝ	
Sunny	(Nissan)		Ⓜ		Ⓕ		Ⓜ
Pulsar	(Nissan)	Ⓝ		Ⓜ		Ⓕ	
Langley	(Nissan)			Ⓝ		Ⓕ	
Laurel Spirit	(Nissan)					Ⓝ	Ⓜ
Liberta Villa	(Nissan)					Ⓝ	
March	(Nissan)					Ⓝ	
Familia	(Mazda)	Ⓜ	Ⓕ				Ⓜ
Lancer	(Mitsubishi)	Ⓜ	Ⓕ		Ⓜ		
Mirage	(Mitsubishi)	Ⓝ				Ⓜ	Ⓕ
Charmant	(Daihatsu)	Ⓜ			Ⓕ		
Charade	(Daihatsu)			Ⓜ	Ⓜ Ⓜ		Ⓕ
Leone	(Fujijuko)		Ⓕ		Ⓜ		
Civic	(Honda)		Ⓕ	Ⓜ	Ⓜ		Ⓕ
Quint	(Honda)			Ⓕ	Ⓜ		
Ballard	(Honda)			Ⓝ		Ⓜ	Ⓕ
City	(Honda)			Ⓝ	Ⓝ		
Fiore	(Mitsubishi)					Ⓝ	Ⓕ
Cultus	(Suzuki)						Ⓝ

Figure 9.1   Sub-Compact Car Market in Japan: Ⓝ New Model, Ⓕ Full Model Change, Ⓜ Minor Change/Face-Lift

market there is a wide variation of car lines even though it is only within the small car category. In contrast to the old VW Beetle concept, which emphasized practical use and a completely standarized design, the interior and styling of Japanese cars have varied greatly. In this sense, it can be said that Japanese makers have put the image of big or mid-size cars into the small-car category. Recently, they have also been aggressively competing against each other in terms of the use of new materials and the installation of electronic devices. As a result, their frequency cycle of introducing new models and undertaking model changes is becoming shorter (see figure 9.1).

   This type of product development by Japanese automakers owes much to the uniqueness of the Japanese makers' production systems and their superiority in production-process technology. One example is the assembly of many types of cars and their variations on one assembly line, symbolized in the mixed-model production system. Japanese makers are also able to easily undertake model and product-design changes since they have flexible production systems in which tooling and changes in die and equipment layout in the plant can be done very quickly. Furthermore, each Japanese producer searches for its own way to find a competitive edge in its manufacturing process and has its own distinctive preferences about how things should be done.[12] One of the main reasons that Japanese makers are able to undertake this type of product development is their stable labour–management relationship and use of 'just in time' systems.[13]

RATIONALIZATION AND LABOUR RELATIONS IN THE JAPANESE
AUTOMOBILE INDUSTRY – THE CASE OF TOYOTA

The late Professor W. J. Abernathy observed in his *Industrial Renaissance* that the differences between the United States and Japan in terms of the manufacturing cost and quality of economy passenger cars cannot be explained satisfactorily by differences in wage scales, a reasoning frequently employed in the past:

The Japanese advantage rests not on a substitution of capital for labour or labour for capital; it rests, instead, on diligent control of the whole system of production. . . . There is, instead, only an insistent effort to manage the whole manufacturing process as a coherent, integrated system. . . . [Therefore] Japanese manufacturing systems keep their lines operational a high percentage of the time, make greater use of materials handling equipment, process fewer defective parts, enjoy lower rates of worker absenteeism, and match workers better with their tasks than do most comparable systems in the United States. . . . They are all the direct result of a production philosophy that stresses not volume, as does the American philosophy, but quality – of process as well as product. . . . American companies . . . often beset with fluctuations in demand, chose to build a system dominated by scale economies and long production runs and thus, by extension, the loss of flexibility inherent in standardisation.[14]

Unlike the United States, a production system that assures high quality and eliminates waste has been nurtured in Japan. Under this system, uptime or the operation ratio of facilities is very high. In addition, the production system integrates flexibility of production, for instance in the ability to do quick die or plant layout changes and having a number of models assembled on one line.

The above observation by Abernathy is extremely significant to industrial relations and labour management in the Japanese automaking industry. The establishment of a cooperative relationship between management and labour is what made the Japanese type of production system possible. It was only after the establishment of this cooperation that the *kanban* or 'just in time' (JIT) system materialized.

In general explanations of the JIT system, there is a tendency to put excessive emphasis on the aspect of stock-control and the minimization of inventory. In fact, the reduction of the amount of inventory to an extreme if not absolute minimum also plays an important role in uncovering waste of time and material, usage of defective parts and components, and inappropriate machinery movements. In order to reduce inventory to a

Table 9.2 Changes of Employment in the Major Automobile Companies in Japan

Fiscal year[a]	Major 26 automobile and automobile parts manufacturers[b]		Toyota		Nissan		Honda	
	No. of employees	Index	No. of employees	Index	No. of employees	Index	No. of employees	Index
1963	—	—	18,809	77.5	22,263	86.5	7,696	90.4
64	—	—	22,647	93.3	25,744	100	8,481	100
65	151,493	100	24,278	100	26,926	104.6	9,129	107.6
66	162,199	107.1	28,274	116.5	33,519	130.2	11,555	136.2
67	188,305	124.3	32,134	132.4	38,987	151.4	13,539	159.6
68	214,931	141.9	36,032	148.4	40,034	155.5	16,916	199.5
69	227,605	150.2	37,946	156.5	41,694	161	18,564	218.9
70	236,785	156.3	40,415	166.5	45,410	176.4	18,332	216.2
71	247,337	163.3	41,403	170.5	51,395	199.6	18,554	218.8
72	261,071	172.3	42,561	175.3	52,819	205.2	18,597	219.3
73	271,225	179	44,228	182.2	50,636	196.7	18,781	221.4
74	271,778	179.4	44,584	183.6	50,956	197.9	18,804	221.7
75	270,383	178.5	44,474	183.2	52,669	204.6	19,084	225
76	265,244	175.1	44,798	184.5	54,709	212.5	20,348	239.9
77	270,564	178.6	45,203	186.2	56,068	217.8	21,334	251.5
78	273,699	180.7	45,233	186.3	55,367	215.1	21,220	250.2
79	275,068	181.6	47,064	193.9	56,030	217.6	23,362	275.5
80	286,121	188.9	48,757	200.8	57,560	223.6	25,488	300.5
81	296,222	195.5	51,034	210.2				

Notes: [a]The fiscal year differs for each company. Toyota's term was from June to May until 1974 and was changed from July to June from 1975; Nissan's has been from April to March; Honda's has been from March to February. [b]Major 26 companies whose stocks are listed in the Tokyo 1st Class Stock Exchange.
Source: financial reports of companies, compiled by the Data Bank of Nihon Keizai Shinbunsha; cited from Kazutoshi Koshiro 'Personnel Planning, Technological Changes, and Outsourcing in The Japanese Automobile Industry', in W. Streeck and A. Hoff (eds) Workforce Restructuring, Manpower Management and Industrial Relations in the World Automobile Industry, vol. 2, Case Studies, (Berlin, 1983), p. 46.

minimum it is necessary to eliminate any wasteful use of raw materials as well as defective operations and unnecessary work time, and to have every one of the workers directly involved in trying to discover problems and come up with creative ideas and means to correct them. Under this system, when an aberration in either quality or equipment occurs, an automatic device installed in every work station stops the line. As a result, there is no chance of accumulating defective parts or rectification operations. The system thereby generates unavoidable pressures to maximize uptime, or effective operation time, and to minimize defective parts or products. Such pressure not only requires excellent maintenance of machinery but has to be reflected in the relationship with parts and components suppliers and in the standard operational practices on the production lines. Suppliers, in this system, have no choice but to try to maintain and meet high quality standards. The workers directly involved at a work station that is installed with an automatic line-stop device, on the other hand, are also compelled to try to thoroughly eliminate waste and find problems. The effective operation of this system also necessitates a form of job structure that induces workers to participate in planning and management as well as to maintain a strong loyalty to the company and very low rates of absenteeism.

The enormous significance of the JIT system lies in the fact that actual management operations, which are a consolidation of production planning and production control, are carried out with the participation of all direct-line workers rather than relying solely upon a group of specialists. The system is characterized by its generation of chain reactions in that once an automobile manufacturer begins to implement it, the effect is extended to suppliers, and prompts awareness of the need for improvements on their part as well. In this way, both the automaker and its suppliers accomplish an integrated and unified rationalization. The high productivity made possible through this system also debunks the American myth that productivity is a trade-off of cost and quality, which is almost a type of common sense among automakers in the United States. In Japan, a sizeable improvement of quality and productivity is achieved at the same time through building high quality into the product in the process of manufacturing.[15]

It was Toyota that took the lead in implementing this JIT system among other Japanese automobile manufacturers. Yet, the system was not 'built in a day' even at Toyota. Although Toyota experienced a labour dispute in 1950, since then there has been no occurrence of any dispute. In 1951, the labour agreement that had been operating until then was abolished and there was no comprehensive labour agreement until 1974. During this time, however, Toyota had a principle of paying respect to customary practices that were agreed upon at management and labour council meetings and when problems relating to production arose, Toyota held detailed discussions with labour. By so doing, Toyota standardized the customary practices while the problems regarding the relationship between management and labour have been solved at council meetings under the principle of discussion rather than through a notion of collective bargaining. Although a management–labour conference exists and a production sub-committee within it, discussions relating to production problems are basically carried out at informal gatherings called management and labour meetings and under them, plant meetings and shop meetings, that are organized according to job units. In discussing methods of production or methods of developing rationalization, the shop meetings in particular serve as a convenient channel to ensure communication by inviting the participation of all concerned personnel. These shop meetings work in conjunction with the activities of quality control circles (QC circles), and as such, opinions and observations of rank and file workers are drawn upon in the meetings. The meetings also help to establish team work among members. According to the type of problems that are to be discussed, the participants in these meetings range from rank and file workers to assistant foremen, foremen, supervisors and section managers who are working members at the production site, and at time, include department managers and other managerial and executive personnel. It should be pointed out that assistant foremen, foremen and supervisors, who are managerial personnel at the production site, are all organized members of the labour union. Among the production site personnel, the one who holds the key to actual operations is the foreman who, as the leader of operations, has responsibility for cost and production volumes in his unit of operation. At the time of election of union committeemen, there is a strong tendency for assistant foremen and foremen who are capable of getting things done well to be elected. The fundamental principle that Toyota follow in solving production problems is to pay maximum attention to solving them by worker-initiated ways and means. Through these meetings, both official and unofficial, the actual conditions and circumstances of the company are conveyed to workers just as they are to top management and in turn, management has ample opportunity to explain in advance its plans and policies of rationalization to the labour union and rank and file workers at the production site. Management officially announces all information about fundamental problems that relate to the rationalization of production to all workers through the labour union and spares no effort in trying to have its rationalization requirements well understood. At the same time, the responsibility of problem-solving is dispersed and diffused and therefore quicker feedback is ensured even before a problem is likely to occur. Discussions on the rationalization of production aim to clarify what the *potential* problem is and where it will occur rather than to take action after the problem has already occurred.

As a result of having such detailed discussions which are directly linked with the actual circumstances of the production line, an established grievance committee between management and labour has never had an opportunity to function since various improvements based on the discussions are put into effect well before problems take shape.

Table 9.3 Recruitment of Workers and Labour Turnover at Nissan

| Fiscal year | Sources of Recruitment | | | | | Total employment at the end of previous fiscal year (B) | Entrance rate (A/B) % | Estimated number of separation (C) | Separation rate (C/B) % | National average annual separation rate in the manufacturing industries (%) |
	Ordinary workers	Probational workers	Seasonal workers	Temporary workers	Total (A)					
1968	4,206	5,730	8,776	2,172	20,884	33,519	62.3	15,416	46	30
1969	3,105	3,671	9,657	2,293	18,726	38,987	48	17,679	45.3	28.8
1970	2,637	4,213	9,361	1,365	17,576	40,034	43.9	15,916	39.8	30
1971	2,433	3,709	9,727	2,516	18,385	41,694	44.1	14,669	35.2	24
1972	3,430	2,643	7,944	5,283	19,300	45,410	42.5	13,315	29.3	21.6
1973	3,108	2,804	5,789	6,542	18,243	51,395	35.5	16,819	32.7	24
1974	1,804	73	2,536	0	4,413	52,819	8.4	6,596	12.5	22.8
1975	1,140	203	2,351	1	3,695	50,636	7.3	3,375	6.7	20.4
1976	2,040	176	6,291	1	8,508	50,956	16.7	6,795	13.3	18
1977	3,672	66	2,976	18	6,732	52,669	12.8	4,692	8.9	18
1978	2,697	1	0	1	2,699	54,709	4.9	1,340	2.4	16.8
1979	291	26	3,322	1,185	4,824	56,068	8.6	5,525	9.9	16.8
1980	901	1,013	4,696	1,467	8,077	55,367	14.6	7,414	13.4	16.8
1981	2,337	0	3,532	1,865	7,734	56,030	13.8	6,204	11.1	16.8
1982	—	—	—	—	—	57,560	—	—	—	—

Source: Nissan Motor Company; Ministry of Labour, Maigetsu Kinro Tokei Chosa (Monthly Survey of Labor Statistics); cited from Koshiro, 'Personnel Planning', p. 48.

The full-fledged launching of the so called *kanban* system at Toyota occurred in the 1960s. Later on, as motorization in Japan expanded and the requirements of automobile users diversified, it became increasingly necessary to produce smaller volumes of a large number of body types – often referred to as a full-line policy or full-choice system. In the process of this diversification of models, the *kanban* system exercised its formidable potential. In particular, at the time when Japan was about to undergo capital liberalization, both management and labour became increasingly anxious over the prospect of foreign investment in Japan. The notion that corporate health had to be reinforced by promoting internal rationalization came to the fore. This in turn acted as a trigger to further development of the *kanban* system in particular as a way to produce smaller volumes of a larger number of body types.

At the same time Toyota developed its rationalization in two interrelated directions. One was to exercise quantitative inventory control for every station in the production line, while a second was to have a worker handle several machines or a few stations in order to increase the efficiency of operations with a smaller number of workers. Inventory control of batch production operations such as stamping was reorganized. Only after a *kanban* or signboard was delivered to the stamping shop indicating that the inventory of stamping parts at subsequent operations was reduced to a predetermined volume, was the stamping operation of the parts in question performed. If an individual operation at a work station was solely done by one person, he could accumulate inventory at his discretion, and this made it easier to deal with the occurrence of problems. At the same time, however, a high level of inventory played a role in camouflaging the occurrence of problems. Therefore, another method of reducing inventory was to shift from batch production that could result in the accumulation of inventory, to flow production. In this case, the efforts of reducing inventory at each station and having a worker handle a few stations were closely interrelated: by making workers versatile enough to handle a few stations in line and a sequence of operations, the flow production was greatly facilitated and at the same time the accumulation of inventory at each station became difficult.

The introduction of the *kanban* system in the 1960s as illustrated above, did not take place at all work stations at the same time, let alone at all of Toyota's plants. Upon agreement between management and labour, the system of rationalization was gradually introduced, starting from those stations that could cope with it most easily. For example, multiple station handling was started in the machining shops. The JIT system required that suppliers deliver parts and components at a predetermined time and place in pace with the production of automobiles at the assembly plant. The automobile assembler, however, did not oppress parts suppliers with unilateral pressures for inventory reduction. Rather the first step was for the assembler himself to make efforts to reduce his inventory in the process of production and find out the problems involved. Such efforts only bore fruit after long and time-consuming discussions between management and labour at a great number of meetings and QC circle activities. Before long, however, these would give birth to Toyota's corporate-wide total quality control campaign.

When the first oil crisis occurred at the end of 1973, domestic market demand began to shrink and Toyota grappled with further rationalization in order to create an organizational structure that could withstand even a 70 per cent operation rate. In this effort, the *kanban* system and total quality control (TQC), which Toyota had already begun to develop played a vital part. Both were introduced not only into Toyota's factories but also into its related parts and components suppliers on a large scale.

What Toyota actively tried to realize at this stage was the mobility of labour in its factories or in its shops within factories, the so-called practice of 'lending a hand' in order to minimize imbalances of production generated by changes in demand and product diversification. As the union agreement on this subject stipulates:

'Lending a hand' refers to the situation where a certain section – an assembly line, for example – discovers that a sudden increase in production will leave it short of manpower and requires temporary – repeat, temporary – assistance from other manufacturing or no manufacturing sections. It has no connection with job rotation. Such temporary loans of personnel from the non-manufacturing sector into the manufacturing one are subject to three stringent restrictions:
a   the basic term is three months – with no possibility of extension
b   a person may only be transferred in such a fashion once a year
c   the full details of the transfer shall be submitted for union review at least seven working days before it is due to take effect.

Toyota also developed a working system to enable certain workers not only to handle several machines or stations but to perform many different jobs rather than just expanding their ability through job rotations inside the factory. Although Toyota rarely relocates workers except when a new factory is established, it has coped with demand change and model changes by increasing the mobility of labour. No rule has been made by labour and management regarding relocation of workers. Although it is stipulated simply that the union must receive notification on the period and frequency of relocation of workers at least one week before it takes place, these

Table 9.4   Agreement at Toyota on Overtime

	Work outside and in addition to regular working hours		Work on scheduled holidays
	Per day	Per month	
Manufacturing sector	4 hrs per day	55 hrs per month	2 times per month

Source: All-Toyota Workers' Union, *Toyota no Kumiai Katsudo* (*Union Activities at Toyota*) (Toyota City, 1984), p. 26.

procedures are normally handled in practice by detailed consultation between union and management.[16] The development of workers' ability to handle different types of jobs is connected with promotion and forms part of their on-the-job training. Efforts to eliminate work that requires some intuition based on experience and know-how, by improving tools and jigs, is also being pushed forward.

What is noteworthy in the development of the JIT system since the first oil crisis is its success in unifying workers' ways of thinking and deepening their understanding of the system, and as a result raising the level of skilled labour. Taking a typical example, a die change which formerly required 90 minutes at Toyota was reduced to two minutes and a half, and in line with the diversification of stamping operations, the method of production was changed from a batch system, producing batches to last half a month to a flow system that produced stamped parts for a one-and-a-half-day supply.

These achievements were made possible by the work of QC circles. Basically, QC activities were voluntary in nature, but the type of QC activities that were designed for the improvement of operations or work environment were clearly defined as part of normal working operations. Also as an established rule, the methodology of improvement was clarified and well understood so that both management and labour were able to ensure that no over-strain would occur in the process of improvement and no irrational method would be applied. A 'visible control', through which a defective operation or break-down of machines could be monitored by means of a gauging instrument or panel, was directly linked with a device to stop the production line. By the introduction of this automatic line-stop device, often referred to as 'foolproof', the line automatically stopped when a defect occurred. Before its introduction, stops were manually operated. When a line stopped, a foreman or an assistant foreman acted as the leader to solve the problem in conjunction with all the other team members. Such teamwork in solving problems was often the key to success.[17]

A final aspect that requires mention is robotization. Robotization was used to transform single-purpose machines to multiple-purpose ones, or to even more refined multiplication. By adopting robots, the investment needed for model changes could be reduced, and the incessant quest for rationalizing operations became easier and smoother. The major subject in the future in this area will be to robotize the whole assembly line by making use of robots with intelligence, not just limiting the area of robotization to paint and welding shops. At present, the utilization of robots does not necessarily mean a threat to employment, and workers themselves have shown understanding toward their introduction, since robots have made workers' jobs easier. Robotization has also had the effect of making workers study the areas of overhauling and maintenance of robots and the techniques of handling computers. Manufacturing and renovation of robots for specific operations is done by partially relying upon the creative thinking of the workers in each company or plant. Both labour and management, however, recognize that robotization, especially robotization as a total system making use of intelligent robots, will probably have an impact upon employment. This will be a theme for discussion in the future. The recent agreement between Nissan and its labour union regarding the introduction of robots, reflects the importance of this issue.[18]

CONCLUSION

Although we examined how the 'just in time' system has blended with cooperation between management and labour by focusing on Toyota, it should be said that Nissan, Mazda, Honda, Mitsubishi and others have also made similar efforts. Upon detailed inspection, however, it is clear that each company has its own JIT method. These various JIT methods have evolved from differences in manufacturing processes and designs of production and component supply systems, based upon where the plants are located, and upon each company coming up with something original depending on its needs.

For instance, Nissan's action-plate method allows for flexibility in production by keeping certain components in stock and thus enabling an autonomous control of production through stock. Depending on the types of components, some are supplied by the suppliers at a specified spot and time; but in the case of Nissan, because its factories and parts suppliers are spread out more, it keeps a larger stock. Also at Nissan, the development of information technology in recent years has made it easier to decrease the number of plates.[19]

Both in JIT methods, and in the introduction of robots, limited mainly at the moment to painting and welding areas, each company has come up with its own ideas. Some companies have experimented with the introduction of robots even though the necessary reorganizations of manufacturing processes from time to time result in frequent changes of the layout of facilities. These trends suggest that JIT methods make it easier to decide on introducing robots and choosing the pattern of introduction.

As we have outlined, Japanese-style rationalization has been able to promote flexible production allowing adjustment to various product marketing strategies, and shortening the time required for design developments. It has also been able to blend quality and productivity together and has proved flexible enough to allow the rapid development of new industrial materials, electronic equipment and other technological innovations. But it is only through mutual trust between labour and management that it has been possible to sustain such rationalization until the present. This has been built by the initiatives of factory management matched by group cooperation and QC circles among factory workers. It is supported by recognizing problems in each factory and solving them through formal and informal consultations as well as total communication between labour and management. Of course, in Japanese auto factories, various controversies and conflicts do exist, and in some cases agreement cannot be reached. But by exchanging views patiently, it is possible to come to an understanding of each other's position even though an agreement may not be reached.

The Japanese auto industry experienced industrial disputes in 1950 and 1953 because of personnel reduction, and as a result of these strikes labour unions realized that without company growth, a real rise in living standards or improvements in labour conditions could not be gained. This led to their coming to share a common outlook with management and as a consequence there have been hardly any strikes in the past 30 years, although this is not due to weaknesses on the part of the labour unions.

The labour unions are fully aware that no hostility or mutual distrust between labour and management should exist and management pays serious attention to this. A stable relationship between labour and management in the Japanese auto industry has been achieved in this way and workers have come to perceive the company as being a certain type of community and identify with it strongly.

The key to the Japanese auto industry's competitiveness in the international market is Japanese-style rationalization and the cooperative relationship between labour and management. But it is still unknown whether this effectiveness and comparative superiority will continue in the future.

First of all, it will be imperative that Japan's socio-economic system continues to function without disturbance. As the working population rapidly ages, a lot will depend upon whether the younger generation will accept Japanese-style rationalization and labour–management cooperation. Another problem from a product-strategy point of view is whether the Japanese auto industry can keep up with the varied and changing demands of new auto products considering the overdependence of its product development on a high level of manufacturing technology alone. Emphasis will continue to be placed upon manufacturing-process technology and versatile skilled workers but other countries becoming aware of these aspects will take steps to rectify their situation, in which case Japan will no longer be able to maintain the superiority it now has. What needs to be done in the Japanese auto industry is to meet the demands of new technology and market changes without lowering the level of manufacturing-process technology and at the same time raising the level of design skills and basic component techniques that lag behind.

NOTES

1 Koichi Shimokawa, 'Nichibei Jidoshasangyo no Seisansei Kokusaihikaku' ('International Comparison of Productivity in the Automobile Industry: USA and Japan'), *Keiei Shirin*, (*Hosei Business Journal*) 18, No. 4, p. 22.
2 Koichi Shimokawa, 'Gensantaiseika no Jidoshasangyo' ('Japanese Automobile Industry under Self-Restraint') *Keizai Hyoron*, July T1982, p. 21.

3 Shimokawa, 'Productivity in the Automobile Industry', p. 20.
4 Shimokawa, 'Japanese Automobile Industry', p. 23.
5 Koichi Shimokawa, 'Jidoshasangyo Jugonen no Kaiko to Tenbo' ('Fifteen Years Reminiscence and Future Perspective on the Japanese Automobile Industry', *Jidosha Journal*, June 1975, p. 14.
6 Shotaro Kamiya, *My Life with Toyota*, (Toyota City, 1970) pp. 57-67.
7 Toyota Motor Sales Company, *Motorization to tomoni* (*Our way with Motorization*) (Toyota City, 1970), pp. 361-9.
8 J. B. Rae, *Nissan-Datsun: A History of Nissan Motor Corporation in the U.S.A., 1960-1980*, (New York, 1982), p. 10.
9 Nissan Motor Corporation, *Nijyusseiki eno mich* (*Our way toward the 21st Century*), 50th Anniversary Company History, (Yokohama, 1983), pp. 140-1.
10 Osamu Yamamoto, *Mazda no Fukkatsu* (*Come-Back for Mazda*) (Hiroshima, 1983), pp. 109-14, 214-15.
11 Koichi Shimokawa, 'Honda's entry into the worldwide Automobile Industry', in D. H. Ginsburg and W. J. Abernathy (eds.), *Government, Technology and the Future of the Automobile* (New York, 1979), pp. 310-1.
12 W. J. Abernathy, A. M. Kantrow and K. B. Clark, *Industrial Renaissance* (New York, 1983), p. 75.
13 W. J. Abernathy, A. M. Kantrow and K. B. Clark, 'The New Industrial Competition', *Harvard Business Review*, September-October 1981, p. 71.
14 Abernathy et al., *Industrial Renaissance*, pp. 62, 77, 78.
15 Shimokawa, 'Japanese Automobile Industry', p. 22.
16 All-Toyota Workers' Union, *Toyota no Kumiai Katsudo* (*Union Activities at Toyota*) (Toyota City, 1984), p. 27.
17 These descriptions are based on interviews in the Toyota Motor Corporation and the All-Toyota Workers' Union.
18 *Nippon Keizai Shinbun*, 1 March 1983.
19 These descriptions are based on interviews in the Nissan Motor Corporation.

10

The New International Division of Labour, Labour Markets and Automobile Production: the Case of Mexico

Rainer Dombois[1]

In the recent past the tendency to internationalize automobile production has attracted considerable attention. Joint ventures have been formed, new plants have been established outside traditional industrial centres and networks of worldwide sourcing have been developed. This indicates not only a widening of international competition in established markets marked by a new stage of capital concentration, but also a new distribution of locations in the automobile industry.

The aim of this paper is to examine some traits of the international division of labour within one company, Volkswagen (VW). The case study of car production and the labour market in Mexico investigates why companies such as Volkswagen have established plants in Third World countries and what development prospects exist in new production subcentres outside the traditional centres.

The focus of our attention will be on the connection between the labour market and automobile production. What is the role of the labour market situation in a developing country in the decision of automobile companies to establish production there? How does the intense competition in the external labour market affect the labour market in the plant? Mexico appears to be a very good testing ground for current hypotheses. For as well as having the general advantages of semi-industrialized countries, that is, an almost inexhaustible, cheap, highly motivated and expanding labour force, Mexico particularly benefits from its geographical proximity to the USA.

The following is a rough outline of the internationalization of VW production, examining in particular the reasons for setting up plants in Mexico. A further section deals with the plant labour market structure. Finally some general conclusions are drawn.

244

INTERNATIONALIZATION OF PRODUCTION AT VW

In the early 1960s when US companies had already established production plants in many countries, VW production was still limited almost without exception to plants in West Germany.

For a long time the VW Beetle was the only model of passenger car produced in Germany aimed to a considerable extent for export. Thus, in 1962 almost 95 per cent of VW production came from West German plants, and nearly 60 per cent was exported.

During the last 20 years however, the company has been establishing production and assembly plants in many countries. Approximately one third of current production comes from foreign plants (see table 10.1) and one out of every three company employees nowadays works at a foreign plant. Roughly one fourth of total production comes from semi-industrialized countries, mainly Brazil, Mexico, South Africa and Nigeria.

Such internationalization has brought about structural changes within the company. Domestic production in the German plants has only increased slightly, when compared with overseas production, and production and employment abroad have been growing at the expense of the German plants. In addition to pure assembly plants such as those in Belgium, the USA, South Africa and Nigeria, production plants have come into being with a high level of vertical integration, which depend to only a small extent on sourcing from West Germany. The plants in Mexico and Brazil operate at all stages of production, Brazil even develops its own models.

A look at the export structure affords a striking picture of the regional shift (see table 10.2): with the same export quota as 20 years ago Volkswagen AG (the main subsidiary in Germany) now exports mainly to European countries, whereas other market regions, particularly South America and the USA, have undergone a loss of importance. This is not only the result of changed market positions. Far more important is the tendency to draw off production from domestic to foreign plants. VW AG produces mainly for West Germany and other European countries; VW of America for the USA; VW do Brasil for South America, and VW de Mexico for Central America. The foreign subsidiary companies sell their products exclusively, or at least to a large extent, on the domestic markets, and some plants such as those in Brazil and Mexico, also export to some degree. Distribution is arranged so that the VW subsidiaries do not compete in the same markets with the same products. Parallel production such as that of the Golf and Jetta takes place in different countries and there is a certain specialization in specific types.

The regionalization of production and markets is supplemented by an international system of integrated cooperative production through which certain plants assume sourcing functions for others. The Mexican plant, for example, supplies the US subsidiary with engines and pressed parts, and receives gear transmissions from Brazil. Even the domestic plants have been assembling parts produced in Brazil and Mexico.

Table 10.1 Production and Employment of the Most Important Subsidiaries of Volkswagen

	Production (in thousands)	Percentage of total production	Employment	Percentage of total employment
Germany:				
Volkswagen AG[a]	1,024	} 66	} 155	} 67
Audi-NSU	389			
Abroad:				
Brazil	328	15	34	15
Mexico	87	4	13	6
USA	92	4	7	3
Argentine	18	1	3	1
South Africa	42	2	7	3
Belgium	121	6	5	2
Others (Nigeria/				
Jugoslavia)	15	1	7	3
Total	2,116	99	232	100

Note: [a]Without CKD (Completely knocked down kits).
Source: Annual Company Report, 1983.

Table 10.2 Volkswagen[a] Exports 1960 and 1982 (per cent of total production)

Importing country	1960	1982
Europe	22	38
America	25	14
Africa	3	2
Asia	2	2
Australia	4	0
Total exports	56.6	55.8

Note: [a]Without Audi.
Source: Annual Company Reports.

It is obvious that VW has established new subcentres of production, which have changed the role played by its plants at home. It is indeed true that research and development are still concentrated in Wolfsburg just as before, and that decisions regarding investment and production programmes are also made there. Yet considerable segments of production including capital-intensive high technology operations have been moved into foreign countries, mainly in the Third World.

CAUSES OF THE ESTABLISHMENT OF SUBSIDIARIES IN THIRD WORLD COUNTRIES – A CASE STUDY

What are the causes of these structural changes within Volkswagen? Why has Volkswagen, like other automobile companies, selected and developed production sites in the Third World? What is the dynamic of this development?

In the social sciences there has been a heated debate as to the causes of the internationalization of production in recent years. The most general interpretation was suggested by Fröbel, Heinrichs and Kreye as follows. Processes of mass production are standardized to a high degree and have, by using Taylorist methods, been separated into simple, timetabled, closely standardized operations. Given modern technologies of transportation and communication, operations of this nature can be best carried out in Third World countries. The aim is to utilize the 'international industrial reserve army', that is, a labour force which is adequately skilled, almost inexhaustible in number, highly motivated, and satisfied with low wages.[2] Cohen has described similar trends towards an international division of labour in the automobile industry. Ancillary relationships in production between plants allow companies to benefit both from the advantages of location and from economies of scale. Hence a division of labour within a company develops. In industrialized countries, with their high payroll costs, the emphasis is on 'high value-added work', while in developing countries labour-intensive stages of production or component-part production prevail.[3]

Whereas these authors stress the importance of the labour market (i.e. costs and qualifications of the labour force), Jenkins and other investigators of 'dependent industrialization' hold a different view. They attribute the presence of the automobile industry in the Third World to tight political restrictions by host governments which force the hand of the companies. Here the establishment of new plants is seen as the result of protectionist policies of the national governments which subject access into attractive markets to certain constraints.[4]

The two interpretations naturally lead to different conclusions. If the companies are making their decisions 'freely' and particularly if they can make use of differences in labour markets, then increased movement of car production away from the traditional industrial centres can be expected. However, if developments are based on political conditions and concessions, then the extent to which the pattern can be expected to continue seems more limited.

What follows here is an investigation of the reasons for this colonization, undertaken by other companies as well as VW, and an assessment of how far it will continue, based on the example of Mexico.[5]

In the 1950s CKD (completely knocked down) parts were assembled in Mexico in nominal numbers for the VW company. The subsidiary VW de Mexico was founded in 1964 and first began assembly in its own plant. In 1967 the plant in Puebla began production, encompassing almost all stages of automobile manufacture – foundry, engine plant, stamping shop, body shop, paint shop and assembly. The Beetle and the light truck have been produced in Puebla since then; recently the Golf and the Jetta were added; all were produced almost exclusively for the domestic market until the 1970s. Exporting began with the Safari to the USA and this remained at modest

Table 10.3   Car Production in Mexico and Production and Export by Volkswagen de Mexico (in thousands)

	1970	1972	1974	1976	1977	1978	1979	1980	1981
Total production	190	230	351	325	281	384	444	490	597
Total exports				4	12	26	25	18	14
VW production	36	58	115	83	52	94	109	127	138
VW exports				0.7	5.2	18.3	19.1	13.1	9.3

Source: Secretaria de Programacion y Presupuesto (SPP), *La Industria Automotriz en Mexico*; Asociación Mexicana de la Industria Automotriz (AMIA).

levels even after the Mexican plant had begun to supply the European market with the Beetle (see table 10.3). The production of engines was started in 1981, but almost exclusively for export, mainly to the US plant at Westmoreland. This new engine plant is equipped with up-to-date technology.

VW, like the other transnational companies (Ford, GM, Chrysler and Nissan), shows a typical segmentation of production structure. Production aimed chiefly at the domestic market employs methods used mainly in the 1960s. The standard of mechanization is nowhere near that of the parent company, as there are for instance neither robots, computerized production control, nor flexible manufacturing systems. Plants which were set up for the export market, however, have the highest standards of mechanization. The new engine plants of VW and Ford, for example, are equipped with complicated transfer lines and partly with automatic transport and storage facilities, while the old ones, producing as before for the domestic market, operate predominantly with individual machines. The assembly of engines also shows a higher degree of mechanization.

It appears paradoxical at first that the production of cars or parts to be exported, is characterized by forms of production in which the level of mechanization is high, the costs of labour play a subordinate role, and where more highly skilled workers are needed. This appears to waste the advantage of being located in Mexico, where the labour force is inexpensive yet lacks the special skills necessary in the production of highly specialized products. The particularly labour-intensive segments of production and processes with comparatively low levels of mechanization are concentrated much more on production for the domestic market.

The most important reasons for this production structure lie in

1 government economic policy
2 production cost structure
3 price levels.

Government economic policy

Like other transnational companies, VW was forced to set up a production plant in Mexico following the Decree of 1962, if it was not to lose its market share to its competitors. In 1962 the Mexican government issued a Decree calling for the total replacement of imported automobile CKD parts by domestic production.[6] In addition, local content had to correspond to 60 per cent of total production, and certain parts (including engines, tyres and batteries) had to be produced in Mexico. Mexican contractors were forced to produce engines themselves and obtain ancillary parts from Mexican firms. The government admitted ten companies which specialized in certain types, VW being assigned the production of the small car. The firms were issued production quotas and prices came under the direct control of the state.

After 1962, the firms expanded assembly plants, foundries and engine plants. Simultaneously a national ancillary industry came into being under the protection of government economic policies.

The balance of payments remained negative in the automobile sector owing to the still-high share of imported component parts. This has, since the end of the 1960s induced the government to issue additional decrees calling for more exports, in order to even out the balance of payments and to make the Mexican automobile industry more competitive internationally. These measures had little initial success, but the Decree of 1977 produced some results. The firms, having had more and more to deal with their own problems of foreign trade, set up modern engine plants aimed at export markets: VW in Puebla, Ford in Chihuahua, GM and Chrysler in Ramos Arizpe and Nissan in Aquascalientes. The recession and consequently exchange controls worsened in 1982, resulting in yet another decree which made the number of a given firm's models produced for the domestic market dependent on its export performance.

Government policies caused VW (and others) to set up plants in Mexico. To avoid losing the Mexican market, transnational companies had to set up plants with a high level of vertical integration, including capital-intensive plant such as foundry and engine production. Finally firms turned to production for foreign markets when compelled to do so by the government system of restrictions and incentives.

Structure of costs in production

The establishment of VW in Mexico may be seen as merely a reaction to the protectionist policies of the Mexican government. But were there other economic advantages which also encouraged these developments? Research indicates that production costs in Mexico (as in other developing countries) are far higher than in West Germany[7] even though, in 1983, the Mexican workers at a VW plant earned only about one fifth of their German colleagues. The plants produce in volumes which have never reached optimal range, although estimates of the threshold of economies of scale vary considerably. For production in developing countries it is estimated that at least 100,000 vehicles of one basic model would have to be sold if the product were to be competitive internationally.[8]

For those areas of production requiring large capital assets such as engine production or even moulding, the estimates of these thresholds are naturally much higher.[9] The Mexican firms have never even approached these levels hence the higher unit costs when compared with those mass produced in the industrialized countries.[10]

In addition to the higher costs incurred through transportation and packing of the parts imported from the mother plant, the national ancillary suppliers' high prices also raise the costs of Mexican producers. Ancillary industry operates on a narrow production base, rendering it incapable of using economies of scale to the same extent as in the industrialized countries. It is also monopolized to a large extent. Often two or more enterprises divide the national market for parts. The ancillary industries' prices lie far above the average in world-market levels.

It is due to these conditions that production costs for the domestic market are higher than those of corresponding production in industrialized countries.[11]

In view of the narrow domestic market, one option for the companies is to expand production to supply the world market and thereby take advantage of the economies of scale.

They first attempted this with engine plants, which have entered production in recent years with capacities of production comparable with those in the industrialized nations, much too large for the domestic market. But even though they produce predominantly for the export market, it is still hard to attain the cost levels of the industrial centres. According to the company's own calculations, the engines produced in Puebla for the VW Golf are still more expensive than those produced in Salzgitter. This is due mainly to the lack of an industrial infrastructure, especially problems of quality and cost arising from the ancillary industries. Calculations made by Ford, as published by Cohen in 1982, show that it is only tax and excise benefits which make it worthwhile to produce engines in Mexico.[12] Interestingly enough these were benefits which were aimed at stimulating traditional production for the domestic market and which became effective only through a mixed calculation.

Prices

The higher costs of production are more than outweighed by higher market prices. The bigger US models cost up to 75 per cent more in Mexico than in the USA. In 1981 the Beetle as produced in Mexican plants cost about 40 per cent more than in West Germany, and in the case of the Golf the figure was 50 per cent. These prices, only available on the domestic market, enabled firms to absorb the higher production costs and to yield big profits.[13] This is what attracted companies to operate in Mexico in the first place. The domestic market is shielded from the competition of the world market, so production takes place at higher profit rates, even though production costs are higher than in industrialized nations. The government has control over who is allowed to compete in the domestic market, a powerful trump in its hand, by means of which it can force companies into structural changes which serve the needs of the national economy. Access to a protected and progressive market was the most important motive of the firms in meeting the stipulations of the 1962 decree and in establishing production with a high level of domestically produced components, despite the fact that the size and fragmentation of the market in no way allowed a cost structure that could compete with the industrialized countries.

Again, the risk of losing this profitable domestic market to competitors induced companies to undertake production for the foreign market and to establish capital intensive plants in Mexico. The high profit margins in the domestic market are the incentive for exports. VW improved its foreign exchange by exporting the Beetle, and compensates for the comparatively low prices in West Germany by its high prices in Mexico. The advantage of producing engines for export is that the state is therefore willing to facilitate the import of cheaper ancillary parts. Exports thereby result in lower costs of production for the domestic market.

PLANT LABOUR MARKETS IN THE MEXICAN AUTOMOBILE INDUSTRY

Employment policy and internal labour markets

The structural features of the Mexican labour market, namely an inexhaustible supply of efficient, hard-working and cheap labour, a shortage of jobs in industry and in the traditional sectors of industry in general, seem to be of very little significance in the establishment of an automobile industry in Mexico. But how do these conditions affect the internal situation in the automobile industry, and the employment and working conditions of the automobile workers?

Fröbel, Heinrichs and Kreye emphasize the 'competition' of the industrial labour reserve, cheap labour and a hire-and-fire system.[14] Conversely, some writers insist on the dualism of the labour market in developing countries. Munoz argues that there is a high wage level and a regular workforce in the modern oligopolistic sector, to which the automobile industry belongs. Recruitment and allocation of the workforce follow patterns which are characteristic of internal labour markets. Jobs are arranged into 'mobility chains' or 'job ladders'. Workers gain promotion with increased seniority, and change their position on joining the company by moving into more specialized and better-paid jobs.[15] All in all, the plant labour market is screened from the external labour market.

In companies belonging to the traditional sector (with low capital intensity, concentration and market control), however, pay levels are low. An unstable workforce level and high fluctuation have provided for an intensive exchange with the external labour market.

Although Mexican automobile workers earn only a fraction of the wages of their American and European counterparts,[16] despite the longer working hours in most plants, and although the social benefits are much lower than in industrialized countries, employment in the automobile industry is a very attractive prospect. Workers earn much more than the legally prescribed minimum wage, and can lay claim to social benefits from which the overwhelming majority of the population is excluded.[17]

The conditions of work and employment within the automobile industry vary from company to company. The highest wages and the shortest working hours are to be found in the older plants in the Mexico City area, and the lowest level is to be found in the new engine plants in the north of the country.

The employment structure of the Mexican automobile industry is characterized by the division of the workforce into permanent employees and workers with temporary contracts. Workers employed by VW on a temporary basis comprised 45 per cent of the total workforce in 1979, while in 1981 38 per cent of Ford workers had a limited contract. The length of contracts varies from a few weeks to 11 months. At times of falling sales and production the contracts are not renewed as has been the case since 1982. The allocation of limited-term contracts cannot be explained solely on the grounds of production fluctuation. After all, even in the extended periods of uninterrupted growth, the level of temporarily employed persons did not fall. The temporary workforce has the function of extended selection and probation. Workers proving themselves efficient and disciplined receive permanent contracts and have the opportunity to be absorbed into the company's permanent work force. The latter is recruited exclusively from the circle of temporary workers. Workers with temporary contracts receive the contractually agreed pay levels and social benefits but have no defined rights and claims to jobs, training and promotion to higher-paid job categories and can be assigned as the company wishes, mainly of course at the foot of the job ladder. Conversely, permanent workers gain seniority and can lay claim, on this basis, to better jobs. In some cases the company and trade unions negotiate the selection for promotion.

Finally the permanent workforce is protected better by means of high contractually prescribed minimum wages and by strong codetermination rights for the trade unions in cases where the regular workforce is reduced by redundancies. The chances for better earnings, defined work rights and relatively stable employment of the permanent workers are, however, the counterpart of the uncertain buffer situation of those workers employed on a temporary basis.

This description applies only to the older main plants of the companies. In the new Ford plant in Chihuahua so far *only* temporary workers have been recruited. The principle of seniority does not apply here, and the use of labour is far more flexible than in the main plants. Promotion to higher pay levels is dependent on the qualifications of the workers. The workers however do not even earn half as much as their colleagues in the main plants, and have to work longer hours.

Trade unions and the internal labour market

The extent of trade-union control over the internal labour market is remarkable. The trade unions organize in the automobile industry on a plant basis, or – as in the case of Ford – on an enterprise basis, and negotiate plant or company contracts.[18]

The contracts extend the minimal norms of labour legislation and grant the union and especially the executive committee far-reaching rights of codetermination:

1   The companies are closed shops. The unions have the exclusive right to propose workers to be employed to the company. The union can compel the company to suspend a worker or, upon exclusion from the union, to dismiss him.
2   Union and company arrange jobs in hierarchical ladders, and the permanent workers are placed in job categories according to their seniority.
3   Promotions take place either (as with VW) in strict accordance with seniority, or after negotiations. Negotiations are also required when permanent workers are to be transferred to other departments or promoted.
4   The number and structure of permanent jobs and permanent workers is stipulated and can only be reduced after negotiations with the trade union. Such negotiations include work standards and the selection of workers for redundancy and wage increases.

The trade unions have thus gained strong control over the plant labour market, but only for permanent workers. The employment and use of temporary workers is beyond the control of the trade unions, even though in some collective agreements the passage into the permanent workforce is also controlled. Companies endeavour therefore to maintain the number of temporary workers employed so as to preserve a greater flexibility and maintain the pressure of competition on the permanent workforce.

Internal labour market and development

In contrast to common assumptions, we have found in Mexico a strongly protected, controlled and screened internal labour market which directs and limits the competition between various groups of employees and between employees and the workers of the external labour market. However this structure does not correspond fully to the model of a dual labour market. A large part of the workforce, those workers with limited contracts, are exempted from the rights and guarantees which are supposed to characterize the labour market of the modern oligopolistic sector. Workers employed on a temporary basis have only uncertain employment prospects, and training and promotion chances. The two sides of the internal labour market, the stable and the unstable, complement each other.

What is the basis of the strong control which the unions have won over at least one side of the internal labour market? State industrial legislation promotes such a control. It sets out fixed minimum norms for pay, working hours, redundancy payments and selection criteria in promotions, and facilitates, in principle at least, the development of strong and competent trade unions in the company. Nonetheless the differences between the companies suggest that labour legislation only takes effect when it is used by strong trade unions. Trade unions in the older plants of Ford, General Motors and VW, which have a long tradition of collective bargaining, have most strongly gained control of the plant labour market, especially in the cases of Ford and General Motors. The limitation of trade unions and collective agreements to plants or companies, together with the competition between the union confederations, ensure that the advanced norms and procedures are not generalized and extended to other firms. Ford and General Motors have used the construction of modern plants in the north as an occasion for negotiating collective agreements which lie way below the level of the main plants in the area of Mexico City, thus giving back to the companies the control of the plant labour market which they were forced to share with the trade unions in the older plants. Thus the extent to which the plant labour market is controlled, and the claims and rights of the workers are defined, is strongly dependent on the experience, strength and authority of the trade union.

Why do the trade unions attribute such importance to labour market control, recruitment, selection and to definition of employment terms? Where the labour market enables companies to make use of a broad industrial reserve army, the control and limitation of competition among workers becomes more important than in industrialized countries. The authoritarian internal structure of many trade unions in the automobile sector is not simply the result of strong trade-union influence on recruitment and allocation, nor a product of schemes of oligarchic control over the membership. They are also structural means for maintaining solidarity, forced or otherwise.

CONCLUSIONS

The establishment of VW and others in Mexico may initially seem to be a special case. Internationalization of production follows no unified logic. The VW company had, for example very different reasons for setting up plants in the USA.[19] But observations based on the Mexican case study are valid for a number of other countries. Many Latin American countries have by their limitations on imports and production compelled the establishment of an automobile industry controlled by transnational companies, using the weapon of being able to refuse entry to developing and protected markets. In Brazil and Mexico, high local content was compelled, in line with the import substitution policies of the two countries. When the deficit in the balance of payments grew enormously, the government attempted to move the companies to produce for export by means of tax and excise benefits, and currency exchange allocations. In other nations too such as Yugoslavia, South Africa and Spain, the establishment of new plants was caused by protectionist governmental policies. For VW, as for other companies, it is the opportunity for outlets into the big, protected markets which are likely to develop, which makes production there so attractive. Companies do not want to surrender such markets to competitors and are therefore ready to submit to governmental constraints. The price situation in protected markets also permits the establishment of production structures which would not be profitable in the industrial centres.

Payroll costs, and in fact the entire labour market, play a subordinate role in these calculations, since lower wages are outweighed by other factors such as lower productivity, small volumes of production, expensive national ancillary suppliers and an inadequate infrastructure.

The tight governmental control of production also reduces the strategic flexibility of the big companies. They are forced to choose less-than-ideal sites in return for access to protected markets. In fact, it may be more profitable to transfer high-technology manufacturing segments of production in order to overcome deficits in the balance of payments rather than to locate assembly operations (which require a complex infrastructure) in Third World Countries.

The international distribution of work within the companies is undertaken to achieve and maintain a position in attractive but regulated markets. The choice of location for export production is the result of complex calculations which take into consideration its impact on the domestic market. For instance, the establishment of production capacities for export can be profitable if it induces the state to facilitate production and sales in the domestic market.

We can conclude that the tendencies towards a 'new international division of labour' are limited within the automobile industry. As table 10.4 shows, the percentage of automobiles produced in Third World countries has

Table 10.4   Percentage of World Car Production by Region

	1970	1980
North America	32.1	24.2
Latin America	3.2	5.6
West Europe	39.9	31.1
East Europe	5.4	9
Japan and Asia	18.4	29.1
S. Africa	1	1
	100.0	100.0

Source: Asociación Mexicana de la Industria Automotriz (AMIA).

remained relatively small in the last decade.[20] The growth that has been experienced there appears to be due more to the general expansion of markets than to a long-term tendency towards a new international distribution of locations and production areas to the detriment of the industrialized countries. The changes observed here are closely connected with the protectionist political practices with which developing countries force industrialization and which push their domestic prices far above the world market levels. The state then needs to offer major incentives if they wish to push the companies to produce for export so as to ease national balance of payments constraints.

NOTES

1 Translated by Ian Armstrong.
2 F. Frobel, J. Heinrichs and O. Kreye, *The New International Division of Labour: Structural Unemployment in Industrialised Countries and Industrialisation in Developing Countries* (Cambridge, 1980).
3 R. Cohen, 'The international reorganisation of production in the auto industry', unpublished paper, 1979, p. 5.
4 R. Jenkins, 'Internationalisation of capital and the semi-industrialised countries: the case of the motor industry', unpublished paper, 1983.
5 This paper is based on a comprehensive study of automobile production and the labour market in Mexico which I am undertaking at the Wissenschaftszentrum, Berlin. See also, R. Doleschal and R. Dombois (eds.), *Wohin lauft VW? Automobilproduktion in der Wirtshaftskrise*, (Reinbek, 1982).
6 D. Bennett and K. Sharp, 'Transnational corporations, export promotion policies and U.S.-Mexican trade', the Wilson Centre, Working paper no. 104, (Washington DC, 1981); R. Jenkins, *Dependent Industrialisation: the Automotive Industry in Argentina, Chile and Mexico* (New York, 1977); Secretaria de Programacion y Presupuesto/Secretaria de Patrimonio y Fomento Industrial (SPP/Sepafin), *Analisis y Expectativas de la industrial Automotriz en Mexico, 1982-6*, (Mexico City, 1982).
7 J. Baranson, *Automotive Industries in Developing Countries* (Baltimore 1969); Jenkins, *Dependent Industrialisation.*; SPP/Sepafin, *Analisis.*
8 G. Maxcy, *The Multinational Motor Industry* (London, 1981) p. 214; K. Bhaskar, *The Future of the World Motor Industry* (London, 1980), p. 46ff.
9 In the boom year of 1981, VW produced an average 40,000 units per basic model and shared the lead for production in Mexico with Nissan.
10 One estimate is that unit costs fall by between 15–20 per cent when production is increased from 50,000 to 100,000 units. United Nations Centre on Transnational Corporations, *Transnational Corporations in the International Automobile Industry* (New York, 1983).
11 In the late 1960s, Baranson presented a detailed cost-production analysis of Mexico, Brazil and Argentina showing average costs far above those in the USA. He calculated that costs in Mexico were 164 per cent above those in the USA. Baranson, *Automotive Industries.*
12 R. Cohen, 'International market positions, international investment strategies and domestic reorganisation plans of the U.S. automakers', unpublished paper, 1982.

13 Jenkins, *Dependent Industrialisation*, p. 110.

14 Frobel et al., *New International Division of Labour*, pp. 50–60.

15 O. Munoz, *Dualismo, organizacion industrial y empleo*, Estudios cieplan, no. 19 (1977), p. 29; P. B. Doeringer and M. Piore, *Internal Labor Markets and Manpower Analysis* (Lexington, MA, 1971).

16 In 1983 workers at Ford Mexico and GM Mexico earned about one sixth of their US counterparts: VW Mexico and GM Mexico earned about one sixth of their US counterparts: VW Mexico workers earned about one fifth of the earnings of their German counterparts.

17 VW workers earn about three times the minimum wage and Ford and GM workers about 3.5 times the minimum wage. In the more modern engine plants, however, Ford and GM workers average only 1.5 times the minimum wage and working hours are longer and social benefits less favourable.

18 I. Roxborough, *Unions and Politics in Mexico: the Case of the Automobile Industry* (Cambridge, 1984).

19 W. Streeck, *Industrial Relations in West Germany: A Case Study of the Car Industry* (London, 1984).

20 Automobile imports from countries outside the OECD increased from 0.2 to 1.29 per cent between 1970 and 1980, and imports of automobile components from 0.73 to 2.70 per cent according to OECD Statistics on Foreign Trade.

11

New Production Concepts in West German Car Plants

Ulrich Jürgens, Knuth Dohse,
Thomas Malsch

The West German automobile industry is currently undergoing unprecedented changes in its technical structures and social relations of production. This situation has provided an opportunity for new production concepts to emerge. Even in the recession years 1981–2, modernization activity in the automobile industry was far greater than in the other sectors of durable goods manufacturing.[1] Since the beginning of the 1980s, the level of investment in tools and equipment has been at least three times as high as during the 1970s.[2]

There are differences in the level of investment activity among the six automobile firms in the Federal Republic (disregarding Porsche which only produces sports cars). These differences, however, are largely in the timing of investments rather than investment levels. While the four German-owned firms (Daimler–Benz, BMW, Audi and Volkswagen AG)[3] began their investment leap around 1978, the two subsidiaries of US firms, Ford and Open (GM), did so only around 1983.

The explanation for this investment leap at the beginning of the 1980s lies, as is well known, in the changing world market, particularly the success of Japanese exports in Europe and the United States. However, the modernization efforts of the West German producers were not undertaken 'with their backs to the wall', out of sheer economic necessity, as was the case, for example, at British Leyland or at Chrysler and Ford in the United States. None of the six West German firms has encountered serious economic problems since the middle of the 1970s. On the contrary, the three producers covering mainly the upper segments of the market, (Daimler–Benz, BMW and Audi), showed consistent growth in production and sales during the last ten years (with the exception of Audi in 1980/81). The three producers for the mass market segments, (VW, Ford and Opel) experienced, in contrast, temporarily stagnating and declining production and sales figures in 1981–2.

It is thus necessary to distinguish between:

1   The group of mass producers whose product spectrum was directly affected by the penetration of competitive Japanese products. They had

258

to reduce production costs markedly in order to counter the price advantages of Japanese competition and to be able to produce more flexibly in response to market demand by means of increased product differentiation and more frequent model changes.

2 For the group of up-market producers, the necessary adjustments related to the need to respond to changing market opportunities through more flexible production, rather than the need to reduce production costs. Naturally, this group of producers also exploited the potential for more cost-efficient production, even for smaller production runs, through flexible automation.

Although their situations were somewhat different, both groups of producers pursued the same strategy: their restructuring focused on the technical aspects of production. The goal was the comprehensive introduction of flexible, computer-based techniques (industrial robots, computer numerically-controlled (CNC) machine tools, etc.) in place of predominantly manual forms of production and earlier less flexible single-purpose machines.

Internationally, the auto industry is pursuing four major strategic options to increase productivity. These can be characterized as follows:

a Human-resources strategy: The expanded utilization of human resources primarily through measures for enhancing motivation, tapping shop-floor knowledge of production and corresponding measures for training and work organization. (Because the transfer of Japanese concepts is particularly important here this can also be called the 'Japanese strategy').

b Organizational strategy: The reduction of labour costs through work reorganization, either through changes in the division of labour or through the elimination of idle time through work intensification.

c Concession strategy: The recovery of bargaining terrain through 'give-back' wage agreements, increases in working time or the elimination of previously accepted working practices.

d Technology strategy: The introduction of technology, particularly more flexible mechanization.

The West German automobile producers have emphasized the technology strategy in combination with an organizational strategy. Up to now, the human-resources strategy and the concession strategy have played no role in West Germany comparable with their importance in the US automobile industry. There is – in comparison with the situation in other countries – relatively little need for the human resources strategy in the Federal Republic. Communication barriers between the workforce, employee representatives and management that constrict productivity are much less of a problem in the Federal Republic than in Britain and the USA. A concession strategy is less necessary because in the Federal Republic, in contrast to Britain and the USA, work practices that constrain production (for example, demarcation rules) are much less of a problem. A concession strategy would have to be primarily directed at wage and working-time issues and would destabilize the system of industrial relations in the Federal Republic as a whole. While the labour unions have relatively little control over the labour process they enjoy a relatively high level of wages, relief time and shorter working hours. Any attack on this situation would strike at the core of the Germany productivity coalition.

In the technology strategy, new forms of work organization, such as a changed division of tasks between groups of employees, new skill and performance requirements and flexible labour deployment are of central importance. These are also the focus of internal union policy discussions. Because the level of employment in the German automobile industry increased by about 2 per cent in the five-year period 1978 to 1983 (while it declined in the USA by 28 per cent, in France by 14 per cent, in Italy by 18 per cent and in Great Britain by 30 per cent), union policy discussions in the Federal Republic have not been dominated by the problem of redundancies and job security. Rather, the changing job situation of those in employment was the principal concern. This is reflected in the strategy of Industriegewerkschaft (IG)-Metall:

'The benefits of increased productivity should . . . not primarily be used to reduce the number of workers. Rather they should be utilized in the following areas in the form of decreased working time: humanization of work as well as the improvement of production structures; a training offensive to improve skills.'[4]

At the same time, the basic approach of the West German labour unions – the principle of accepting and cooperating with the introduction of new technology[5] – remains unchanged in the automobile industry.

In the following essay we wish to examine more closely the relationship between the technology strategy and concepts of work organization. Our focus is the extent to which the functional requirements of automated production are compatible with labour-union and works-council demands with regard to job structures and work organization.

In the following section some basic aspects of the mechanization and automation strategy of firms and the related changes in work organization are presented in order to sketch the principal trends in the industry. In the section after that the development of automation-oriented job structures in the Federal Republic in the context of the conflict between management goals and labour union demands is examined. In a final section the issue of new production concepts without automation (the human-resources strategy), is briefly considered.

OPENING NEW AVENUES FOR AUTOMATION

Modular product design and automation

There had been considerable investment in new technologies in the 1960s and 1970s, and in many areas of manufacturing the level of mechanization was already very high at the beginning of the 1980s. What distinguishes the new rationalization strategy is that the emphasis is no longer on the mechanization of individual work functions or areas but on the total system of automobile production, particularly at the interfaces between suppliers and producers, production planning and actual production manufacturing and maintenance. Thus a more comprehensive planning approach is now typical. In implementing their technology strategy, the auto producers can draw on a comprehensive 'new technological repertoire'.[6] Microprocessor technology which matured in the course of the 1970s is now ripe for mass application.[7]

In this context two developments should be particularly emphasized. Firstly, greater attention is given to production problems in the phase of development and design of new models.[8] The techniques of computer-aided design and computer-aided manufacturing offer new possibilities that have only just begun to be utilized in the Federal Republic. Secondly, intensified computer-based control of material flows and manufacturing has led to a re-examination of traditional principles of production and work organization, particularly in the area of assembly operations.

One result of this development is the concept of modular construction. By dividing assembly-line work into work segments, such as separate modules for door assembly, instrument panel assembly, or assembly of the power train, more work content can be shifted to subassembly areas. This is often regarded as the first step to new forms of work organization such as autonomous groups, combining aspects of the human-resources strategy and the organizational strategy. But such shifts towards subassembly operations are also frequently preliminary steps towards mechanization (technology strategy). Thus, for instance, the new concept of separate door subassembly (removing the doors from the body after the paint shop and assembling them independently on a separate line), paves the way for the assembly of doors with flexible technology.[9]

The new conception of assembly work is as yet in its infancy, and its implementation is thus far experimental and piecemeal. For this reason it is hard to predict the future course of the development of work organization in assembly operations. Because of the large capital investments that such measures entail and the many unresolved problems of technology and work organization, it is not surprising that such concepts have only been slowly implemented and limited to particular areas of production. A notable example of advanced assembly technology is VW's Hall 54, the new trim and final assembly facility for the VW Golf in Wolfsburg. In Hall 54, Volkswagen has increased the level of automation from 5 per cent to more than 25 per cent.[10] Here, for instance, the fully automated power-train assembly eliminates a labour-intensive manufacturing stage that is still a test area for semi-autonomous group work in many other plants. This automation of assembly operations in Wolfsburg is only one part of a mosaic of mechanization efforts in different parts of Volkswagen assembly operations. At Wolfsburg, automation affects primarily the front part of the car. In the Emden assembly plant, which was modernized about the same time, the assembly of the rear is automated and in the Ingolstadt plant (Audi) it is the roof.[11] Only when these three pieces of the automation mosaic are put together in one plant for the production of the next generation models will the real potential rationalization become evident.

The development of new production concepts based on flexible technology in trim and final assembly is not limited to VW, although it was the first to implement them on a large scale. In 1979 BMW in Munich introduced a pilot plant 'to develop new production methods for assembly in normal large volume production';[12] Daimler–Benz has raised the degree of automation in its new assembly plants in Sindelfingen and Bremen to 18–20 per cent; Opel has also introduced new concepts for trim assembly in its modernization program at its two large domestic plants in Bochum and Russelsheim.

The example of Hall 54, however, has shown that modular construction methods are not necessarily identical with group work or the use of off-line 'assembly islands'. In Hall 54, most parts of the trim area of the assembly line remain conventionally organized. In this area the percentage of subassemblies that are disconnected from the cycle of the main line has not been markedly increased. But alongside this there is a large complex of highly automated machinery and equipment in the final assembly area in which few traditional assembly operations still remain.

General Motors, by contrast, has combined the modular approach with the concept of assembly islands in trim and final assembly operations in its most recent model changeover for the production of the new Opel Kadett (Astra). Certain items such as doors and fascia panels are assembled off-line. The new methods have been introduced in the UK at the Ellesmere Port plant where the Vauxhall Astra is being built, at Antwerp in Belgium, and Bochum in Germany where the Opel Kadett is manufactured. In these plants the percentage of subassembly operations is considerably larger than in previous line assemblies.[13]

Automation and changes in job functions

The current efforts to automate production are concentrated above all in parts production, stamping plants and body shops. Figure 11.1 shows the degree of automation[14] of the most important production departments of West German automobile producers in 1983. These trends affect both the level and structure of employment.

The actual number of redundancies that are associated with the current modernization wave is controversial. It depends upon many assumptions about market and sales trends, investment, vertical integration or changes in the gross value of the product.[15]

IG-Metall has published estimates of the redundancies expected to result from rationalization in the period 1984–90 (table 11.1), *excluding* possible off-setting effects resulting from the factors mentioned.[16] This projection

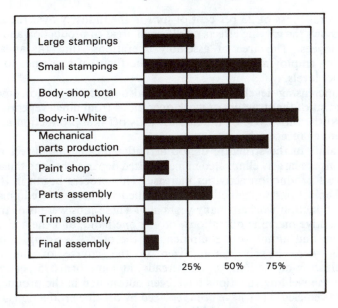

Figure 11.1   Degree of Automation in Car Production
Source: Wolfgang Reitzle, 'Der Trend beim Einsatz von Industrierobotern: Abkehr von der starren Automatisierung und Einsatz flexibler Industrieroboter', *Management-Zeitschrift* 52 (1983), no. 6, pp. 267–70.

Table 11.1   Projected Manpower Reductions 1984–90

Production department[a]	Distribution of employment[b]	Number of employees[c]	Reduction in personnel as a result of new technologies[d]
Development/design	8%	52,800	up to 10% = 5,280
Production planning administration	20%	132,000	up to 10% = 13,200
Stamping	8%	52,800	up to 40% = 21,200
Body shop	20%	132,000	up to 30% = 39,600
Paint shop	4%	26,400	up to 20% = 5,280
Assembly	32%	211,200	up to 30% = 63,360
Maintenance	2%	13,200	up to 0% = 0
Inventory	2%	13,200	up to 10% = 1,320
Parts production	4%	26,400	up to 10% = 2,640
Total	100%	660,000	151,780

Notes: [a]In producers of automobiles, trucks, trailers, special loading constructions and components. [b]Data issued by the German Automobile Industry Association (VDA) on the distribution of employment in typical automobile plants. [c]Calculated from VDA data on the distribution of employment. [d]Assumes constant volume of production.
Source: *Der Gewerkschafter*, April 1984, p. 3.

of an average loss of 23 per cent of jobs in the industry over the six-year period shows the varying effects on different areas of production and groups of employees. The area of assembly operations – thus far an area of expanding employment – is increasingly the focus of strategies to reduce personnel levels.

The increasing level of automation also leads to a corresponding realignment of the structure of work operations from direct repetitive work linked to the time-cycle of the line towards off-line production activities and maintenance work.

This shift in the structure of job activities means that direct manual operations are largely eliminated in mechanized departments and the amount of indirect production activities increase. This process began in the area of mechanical parts production where skilled workers were eliminated as direct production workers many years ago. These jobs were broken down into repetitive machine operations, on the one hand, and the activities of setting up and monitoring equipment on the other. Welding, soldering, finishing were largely marginalized in the course of the current mechanization of the body shop. Already, at some firms 95 per cent and more of the welding functions have been automated in the production of standard vehicles. They have been replaced by off-line production activities which require maintenance skills, the monitoring of complex equipment and machine-setting. Assembly work too is now about to be restructured. The function of placing pieces into and removing them from equipment has become even more repetitive but new off-line work activities such as equipment monitoring and setting have been introduced.

The changing pattern of automation has also made the prevention of production stoppages (or at least reducing their frequency and duration) more important in the economic calculations of management. Management has, therefore, shifted its emphasis toward avoiding or reducing idle time in the utilization of equipment. Reitzle has presented an example of the stages of automation on a production line in the body shop, which appears in table 11.2.[17] The table shows clearly that capital costs have greatly increased in comparison with labour costs in highly mechanized body-shop operations. Consequently, the determination of job structures is primarily guided by the need to ensure that equipment down-time is minimized.[18]

AUTOMATION-ORIENTED JOB STRUCTURES – BUT HOW?

The issue of job structures in automated areas of production is still undecided in the West German automobile industry. The discussion and the related innovations have occurred in the context of the conflict between the organizational goals of management and those of the trade unions and works councils. The most important issues have related to the maintenance of wages and acquired status; above all, the issue of the status of skilled workers. It would, however, be incorrect to see this conflict as growing in

Table 11.2   Levels of Automation on a Line in the Body Shop at BMW

Situation for different models	Number of welding points	Direct production and maintenance workers	Degree of automation	Investment (million DM)
Model E 21:	850	62	0%	6
Model E 28: (high automation through use of robots and contentional tack welding station)	1,000	6	90%	15.5
Model E 30: (high automation through use of robots and simplified conventional tack welding station)	800	4	100%	14.5

Note: data assumes production of 500 units per day.
Source: Reitzle, 'Industrieroboter', *Computer-gestütztes Produktions-management*, 3, ed. Horst Wildemann (Munich, 1980), p. 27.

intensity: there are new areas of compromise as well as new lines of conflict. Some of the main developments with respect to new job structures are examined in detail in the following discussion.

Job enrichment on automated equipment – the example of the Anlagenführer

The job designation *Anlagenführer* (AF) ('monitor of complex equipment')[19] has existed since the 1960s in the body shop at Volkswagen. A number of new AF positions were created in the course of the most recent restructuring at the beginning of the 1980s. According to company estimates the number of AFs in the body shop at Wolfsburg is at present around 290. Previously there were about 150. In the trim and final assembly area of Hall 54 where this job description did not previously exist there are now a total of about 80 AFs (in two shifts).

In addition to the increase in the number of AF positions, it was decided to expand the scope of their work, and maintenance tasks are now part of the new job descriptions. In the past, this work was the responsibility of the maintenance department, although it was frequently done by AFs. Among the new tasks that they now routinely perform are: changing or dressing of welding tips, moving robots into zero position, correcting welding spots in robot programs, changing welding cylinders and setting up equipment for different design options.

This job description was negotiated at the same time as the new VW wage system in a joint commission of management and the works council without serious resistance from the skilled trades departments. According to the job description, both production workers and skilled workers can become AFs. (The VW wage system is based on the principle of compensation according to job requirements and not according to training and skill level; therefore, it does not differentiate between unskilled and skilled workers).

At VW, the 'enrichment' of the AF job was the result of demands from those AFs already occupying this position. During the survey and classification of job activities for the new VW wage system, they pointed out that they regularly performed some skilled-worker tasks, although these were not part of their job description. In designing the new AF position, management designated the new position as a production job, but in practice tried to recruit people with a skilled worker's certificate. This is possible because at VW and other German automobile producers, skilled workers are, to an increasing extent, employed as production workers. As production workers and under control of the production supervisors they are under more pressure to 'make volume' and to keep the equipment running. Thus, for instance it would be a good sign when an AF is not working because this would mean that his equipment is functioning. In such a situation a worker belonging to the production department could be told to do other extra tasks. Production management can issue instructions to its own production employees, but not to skilled maintenance workers – who are supervised by their own departments.

The AF positions at VW are much sought after. There is a great deal of competition about whether primarily unskilled or skilled workers are to be chosen and about the selection of individual candidates. The goal of the works council is to open up the AF positions for production workers or at least – if that could not be achieved – to man them with skilled workers who are currently employed as production workers in the same department. Thus, for example, in the body shop of the Wolfsburg plant the AFs are predominantly former production workers. In the assembly area in Hall 54, by contrast, they are exclusively skilled workers who were selected jointly by the department managers and works-council representatives from among production workers with skilled trades certificates.

The AF position is the result of a definite negotiating process in the plant and not primarily the result of a technology-induced transformation in the utilization of manpower.[20] Thus, for example, in Ford-Germany the AF position is reserved for skilled tradesmen with certificates in electronics who will now be under the supervision of the production department. General Motors allocates this function to skilled tradesmen also, but they will remain under the supervision of the maintenance department. At their Opel plant in Bochum, this work structure is the result of a bargaining process. The works council had advocated job rotation. Due to wage-cost considerations, which highly qualified activities are included in the job rotation is of critical significance. In the area of robot lines, the demand of the works council was to include the setters. The following description is from works council members involved:

We proceeded erroneously from the assumption that we could succeed in fixing the group work on robot lines at the level of the setter. However, months later we observed at the negotiations on this demand that the employers' side had outmanoeuvred us. They had structured work organization in such a way that the setter and AF-operations were allocated to the skilled trades area, thus to the straight hourly wage category and the residual jobs, that is pick-and-place and repair work, to the incentive pay category. Now we were in a bind, because we could hardly ask that the work be taken away from the skilled workers. We managed to get out of this situation in a more or less satisfactory way because we were successful in fixing group work at the level of repair work in most segments. So we were at least partially successful achieving about 50% of our demands.[21]

Job protection on automated equipment – union demands for group work

The example described above illustrates that group work is not a management demand that arises naturally from technology. Group work has become an arena in which management and the workforce or works councils increasingly collide and compromises emerge. Labour-union representatives regard group work with job rotation and correspondingly higher qualifications for each group member as protection against downgrading and job loss as a result of subsequent rationalization measures: 'The goal is to take some realistic steps away from the exaggerated division of labour that prevailed in the past and towards production structures that entail the greatest possible amount of autonomy, skill and creativity. Residual functions have to be merged with skilled functions.'[22] The trade-union demand for group work is based on a risk analysis of so-called residual activities in automation. Simple activities such as machine-tending or parts handling constitute a large share of the jobs remaining after automation. This is evident, for example, in developments after the restructuring of VW's Hall 54. Approximately 40 AF jobs were created as well as 85 skilled-worker jobs for maintenance workers on each shift in the automated areas of production. In contrast to these newly created and upgraded jobs, there were 400 pick-and-place jobs for workers who place parts in loading devices, do stacking and so forth. Table 11.3 presents data on the restructuring process at Daimler–Benz which illustrates the importance of residual jobs. The data pertains to a changeover in an area of the body shop that is to be automated at Daimler–Benz, giving the past and future structure of work operations. The restructuring entails a 31 per cent reduction in personnel. By contrast, personnel in indirect production functions increase by 80 per cent.

An important point for job design is whether 'residual functions' within work subsystems are distributed among existing jobs or are bundled together

Table 11.3   Occupational Structure at Daimler–Benz Bremen Plant before and after
Restructuring

Type of work	Old product	New product
Manual production work (welding, soldering, cleaning, repair)	96%	37.8%
Control tasks	4%	14.5%
Simple machine tending and pick-and-place work	1%	47.6%

Source: Richard Helken and Udo Richter, 'Menschengerechtere Arbeitsgestaltung für DM 5,72 (Fünfmarkzweiundsiebzig)', in Heinrich Buhmann, Herbert Lucy, Rolf Weber and others, *Geisterfahrt ins Leere: Roboter und Rationalisierung in der Automobilindustrie* (Hamburg, 1984).

as residual jobs and thereby create residual workers. If the latter is the case, these activities are doomed to disappear as a result of automation.[23] For instance, 'just in time' delivery and the introduction of *kanban* would lead to the future elimination of a large number of these jobs.[24]

Job rotation that incorporates residual jobs thus constitutes a means of protecting employment. This was already an essential motive of the works council in negotiating the new wage system at VW with its 'work subsystems'.[25] However, the variation in job content and qualification level in the jobs incorporated in these work subsystems was slight. Although rotation between different activities was 'officially' desired, it was and is not very popular on the shop floor and has not been forced through by supervisors and works-council representatives.

In addition to securing employment, there are also other reasons for the union's support for group work such as monotony, underutilization of intellectual capacities, social isolation, one-sided strain and stress, and health problems. There are signs that union demands for group work in order to counter these effects *and* really to implement rotation have become more important recently. An example is the new body shop at the Daimler–Benz plant in Bremen. The changes in work design that management planned for this plant were sharply criticized by the works council:

In principle the layout of the line foresees that the construction stations for the body will consist of one main spot welding line of robots. Thereafter comes a finishing line where workers manually carry out arc-welding, soldering, finishing and repair tasks. One or two men working at the robot lines merely perform pick-and-place tasks – i.e. lay metal parts in the machine. By contrast at least five workers are employed in the finishing lines who do skilled work. In spite of good ergonomic design of the jobs, the work is physically very strenuous.[26]

In response to the demand of the works council the main line *and* the finishing line were combined in every case into a single work subsystem.

All work in this subsystem is supposed to be carried out by the workers in group work with job rotation. Similar examples can be found in the automated cylinder head assembly in the VW Salzgitter plant and the body-in-white department at the Opel plant in Bochum.

Teamwork and the reduction of indirect labour

The formation of production teams represents an alternative to the development of a broader spectrum of work requirements for selected employees, e.g. the *Anlagenführer*. The production team is quite different from the production group concept favoured by the unions. The unions' group concept involves the integration of unskilled production jobs, such as pick-and-place jobs, into work groups of direct production workers so that the overall skill of the workers involved should be raised. But the management team-concept is to integrate specialist indirect workers, such as maintenance and quality control workers, with direct production workers in teams.

Except as a 'task force' for resetting and changeover on the presses in stamping plants (see below), team-concepts have hardly been utilized by management until recently. Exceptions are the production teams at Audi, which thus far have been limited to the body shop in the Ingolstadt plant, and the new engine plant of General Motors in Aspern near Vienna. V. Haas, a management representative from the GM Aspern plant explained the purpose of this pilot project as follows:

Generally stated, each of the individual departments named has its own personnel that can be divided with respect to labour deployment into active time and idle or waiting time. This is mainly caused by more or less rigid departmental boundaries in the sense of division of labour and areas of responsibility. The team-concept took this as a starting point. The concept leads to production teams, that means that all those directly participating are in 'one boat', and all can do all of the work tasks within the area of responsibility of the team – quality, production, volume and capacity utilization. The joining together of previously separated individual areas of responsibility in a team opens up possibilities for reducing the sum of time lost. Or, expressed differently, to achieve the highest possible ratio of time worked within the working time of the individual employee. This ideal leads automatically to the formation of a team based on different areas of responsibility.[27]

The idea can be represented diagrammatically as in figure 11.2. The scheme concentrates on eliminating the unproductive time in the utilization of plant labour force which results from divisions between direct production and indirect production operations, in contrast to other schemes which focus on reducing idle time in the utilization of equipment, resulting from repair and changeover downtimes. Since 1982 these team-concepts have been tested in the GM Aspern plant in Austria. The team-concept is supposed to be fully realized in the Aspern plant by 1986; by then the workforce will have been divided into 98 individual teams. They appear to be a pilot project

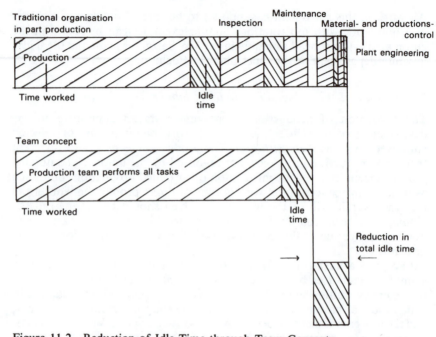

Figure 11.2   Reduction of Idle Time through Team-Concepts

Source: V Haas, 'Team-Konzept: Mitarbeiter planen und betreiben ihr Arbeitssystem'. Paper presented to the IAO – Arbeitstagung 'Wettbewerbsfähige Arbeitssysteme' 22–23 November, 1983. Böblingen.

for future changes in the major Opel plants in Germany. In contrast to the rather isolated quick-die-change-teams and production teams at VW and Audi, Opel's team-concept is not exclusively oriented toward increasing flexibility in labour deployment and reducing unproductive work time but also toward changes in the structure and responsibilities of management in the production process. Finally, the Aspern concept is not limited to the automated area of production but has also been applied to the area of labour-intensive assembly work.

The ideas behind this strategy, which seems to be conceptually similar to that in a number of General Motor's pilot project plants in the USA (for example, the engine plant at Livonia, Michigan), go considerably beyond the strategies of other companies in the auto industry of the Federal Republic. Central elements of this comprehensive program are:

1   the integration of the previously separate areas of responsibility for quality control, maintenance and production in one team and, hence, the elimination of foreman as a separate job status
2   free election of the team spokesman; active participation of the team in the selection of new co-workers; independent allocation of the

work within its area of responsibility; and independent loaning and borrowing of co-workers to and from other teams to compensate for fluctuations and absenteeism

3   shared responsibility in monitoring the budget, in particular monitoring the flow of material in order to minimize inventory (*kanban* system); participation in problem analysis, promotion of cost and quality consciousness

4   tendency towards forms of premium pay and pay-for-knowledge principles as in the USA.

General Motors expects 'significantly higher motivation and identification of our employees, higher machine utilization rates, improved quality and reduction of material flows. Hence, on the whole, higher process yield in association with higher productivity'.[28] It is also clear from Haas's contribution that, despite this far-reaching transfer of responsibility to production teams, management has no intention of giving up its prerogatives. Thus 'the installation of a highly capable electronic data processing system is planned as a means of coordination and control of success: the heart of the system will be its machine monitoring system.'[29] Moreover, the 'partial autonomy' of the groups is strongly controlled by the tight time standards, monitored on a world-wide basis.

Most of the goals cited have not yet been achieved. In particular, there were problems with a high rate of absenteeism among employees. GM has thus far not succeeded either in essentially altering the organizational boundary between production and maintenance, and they have only been able to include a limited number of tasks of the skilled-trades department in the spectrum of team work, thereby incorporating skilled workers in the teams.

The boundary between production and maintenance is, by contrast, much less pronounced in the production team concept at Audi. In the Audi Ingolstadt plant, production teams have been established – limited to individual areas of the body shop – which consist of an 'equipment monitor' with functions of group leadership, one or more 'robot monitors', one or more quality inspectors, several equipment operators (predominantly pick-and-place workers with an expanded spectrum of tasks) as well as additional workers in some cases, according to work requirements. Skilled workers have been recruited for the jobs of equipment monitor and robot monitors. Above all they have assumed certain servicing and maintenance work such as changing robot welding guns and checking their positioning, examining welding electrodes for signs of wear and renewing them, setting of equipment and so forth.

Training programs have been established in order to ease the transformation to team-work but there have been difficulties in transferring expanded functions to pick-and-place workers. At the present time there are no more than seven production teams in the body shop at Audi, though an expansion of the number of teams is planned for highly automated areas such as the stamping plant, parts production and other areas of the body shop.

*Team-work as the elimination of independent skilled work
or as a transitional form: quick-die-change-teams*

Where production runs have been shortened, the setting and changeover
functions for machinery such as stamping equipment have created
bottlenecks. According to (in part misleading) comparisons of the speed
of changeover in Japanese and Western stamping plants, in Japan the change
takes about ten minutes, whereas in the English, American or German plants
it used to last sometimes more than four hours. Quick-die-change teams
have been set up in VW stamping plants to tackle this problem. This began
with large investments in stamping technology at the end of 1976.[30] The
change in stamping technology to quick-die-change presses and the necessity
of reducing the time required for changeovers due to shorter production
runs and more frequent changeovers were the occasion for reconsidering
the organization of the division of labour.

Changeover teams such as those that were formed in the VW plant at
Kassel consist of a team for every stamping line with two line leaders, a
setter, a fitter, a tool-maker and an electrician. Other specialists are called
upon as needed. The stationary pressline monitors (*Strassenführer*), are,
according to their job description, obligated to 'assist in changeovers'. There
are in addition three to five pick-and-place workers for each line that are
not part of the team. This is an example of the problem of residual work
mentioned above.

In the VW stamping plant at Wolfsburg these changeover teams are not
assigned to specific lines, but to departments with several stamping lines.
The establishment of these changeover teams was complemented by a
restructuring of the job requirements and status to create jobs which are
very similar to the AF positions. The job responsibilities of the maintenance
mechanic (skilled worker) and the die-setter (unskilled worker) were fused.
The resulting job description is that of the 'setter-mechanic' who is classified
as a production worker (since 1980) and receives incentive pay.

This fusion of maintenance mechanics and die-setters in the changeover
teams required considerable retraining; the die-setters were trained by the
production mechanics and vice versa. The new teams are assigned to minor
tasks of maintenance and repair of defective equipment. Larger repair jobs
(repairs that last over one hour) are, as in the past, the responsibility of
the central maintenance department.

The formation of changeover teams led to a bottleneck in advancement
by cutting the traditional line of promotion from pick-and-place jobs to
the die-setter position for unskilled and semi-skilled workers. The
Strassenführer is now the end of the job ladder for pick-and-place workers.
Previously the *Strassenführer* was the entry qualification for die-setters.
For this reason the reorganization was criticized by the *Strassenführer* who
were close to being promoted to die-setters. There is also considerable
dissatisfaction among the production mechanics who previously belonged

to skilled-trades departments and now fear deskilling. On the other hand, the group of die-setters benefited from the change – they advanced in status and pay as well as in skill.[31]

Nevertheless, it is by no means clear that the changeover teams and the setter-mechanic represent the last word in the adjustment of job structures. Management sees further need for 'workers of the stamping shop to provide one another with more information, to have their work areas overlap more, to extend their activity beyond its present scope, to learn more, understand more and to work in overlapping shifts'. This indicates that 'there are obstacles to the type of co-operation that supervisors would like to have and which is required by the production process.'[32]

The problem of knowledge of production being withheld by individuals or within a work group is not resolved merely by the formation of teams. Thus, for example, it is not really a question of ability that many die-setters have not mastered the skills that are expected of them now.

The former maintenance workers who are supposed to transfer their knowledge in on-the-job training, have proved reluctant to do so. These difficulties make it likely that VW will go beyond team formation with a mixture of production and skilled-worker operations. This may be only a transitional solution and the first step in the development of a 'stamping-plant skilled worker' with an all-round skill.

The job of the 'equipment mechanic' (*Anlagenmechaniker*) is presently being considered at VW with such a goal in mind. In contrast to the setter-mechanic, who is only responsible for the changeover process and not for any production operations, the 'equipment mechanic' would be responsible for both changeover and production work (equipment monitoring). The team in a stamping area would then consist of a number of equipment mechanics recruited predominantly from among young skilled workers, who would carry out the previously divided maintenance, setting and monitoring activities. In addition, there would also be, for a transitional period, residual pick-and-place jobs that in time would be carried out by 'iron hands'.

NEW PRODUCTION CONCEPTS WITHOUT AUTOMATION?

Our claim in this paper is that the development of new production concepts in the automobile industry of the Federal Republic is dominated by automation or preparations for automation. This is in contrast to the fact that the attraction of the 'Japanese model' seems to lie in the promise of increasing efficiency and reducing costs without requiring investments in technical hardware. It seems quite simple: if one gives production workers responsibility for quality, one can save the costs of quality inspectors; if one forms problem solving groups among shop-floor workers, one can use their knowledge of production to increase efficiency – without any additional costs.

Our contention is that German producers are cautious and conservative in responding to the prospective gains to be derived from adopting these Japanese organizational forms. Nevertheless, similar measures have been attempted in Germany. They are (excluding the problem area of inventory/material flow), the formation of work subsystems/work groups to make labour deployment more flexible; the 'enrichment' of production work and the formation of quality circles and similar groups.

Work flexibility and job rotation

We are dealing here with much the same set of problems discussed in connection with group-concepts. Elements of group-concepts in a much reduced form have been systematically introduced since 1978 by Volkswagen over large production areas. Its basis is the *Lohndifferenzierungs-Tarifvertrag* (LODI).[33] The main function of this system is to simplify wage determination in cases of temporary transfer and thus ease the conflict potential when temporary transfers occur, which entail work with a different content or at a different work place. LODI replaces the system of analytical job evaluation. The basis for the evaluation is no longer individual jobs but certain defined work subsystems (*Arbeitssysteme*), which as a rule include 15 to 30 employees. Which jobs are included in a work subsystem is negotiated between management and the works council. The employees within a given work subsystem receive the same wage even in the case of slight differences in work activity and independent of which job they are performing at a given time. As a rule, however, similar jobs within a large work area, i.e. those at the same skill level, are joined together in a given work subsystem (i.e. not the jobs representing the actual division of labour within small production units).[34] The company's expectations of the new procedure of wage determination are to achieve greater mobility and flexibility through a quick and smooth adjustment of personnel assignments to changing production requirements. The works council in contrast regards the new wage determination procedure, among other things, as an instrument for shaping work organization and influencing job content, job stress and strain factors. With the aid of the formation of work subsystems, the works council foresees the possibility of combining the semi-skilled job operations with 'residual' operations in order to partially elevate skill levels or to maintain a certain minimum skill level. Also, the works council hopes to reduce job stress by coupling more difficult jobs with easier job tasks within a single work subsystem and through job rotation within the subsystem.

In practice, the VW system is limited to increasing the spatial flexibility of labour deployment. Voluntary job rotation between jobs with different job requirements to prevent one-sided stress or deskilling hardly exists. It is not popular with the workforce and not enforced by supervisors and works council representatives.

The establishment of groups with the goal of job rotation to compensate for work-related stress and strain is currently a prominent theme in labour-union discussions in German automobile plants. At the Opel plant in Bochum, for example, the criteria for the creation of systems of job rotation have been specified as follows:

1 Work content in a segment must be so different in terms of the motions involved that some change actually takes place between different physical postures and sequences of movement. It makes no sense to alternate a deep bend on the right side of a car merely with a deep bend on the left side.
2 The system of job rotation has to be really understandable in order that the rotation can take place several times a week and not disrupt work routines. . . . Secondly, we want to achieve a job rotation system with only five to six workers that does not undermine personal interaction between colleagues on the job.[35]

The introduction of job rotation is also perceived as a problem of solidarity, and of mobilization of a broader consciousness within the plant. Thus, for example, the leadership of the shop stewards in the Bremen plant criticized developments in the Daimler–Benz sister plant in Sindelfingen as follows:

In Sindelfingen management wanted to introduce group work in metal finishing of the roof. The 'final finishing workers' rejected that, because they were not willing to also do 'rough finishing'. Not only would stress and strain have been lessened for the rough finishing workers, but they would also have received a higher wage classification.[36]

Enlargement of work for production workers in labour intensive areas

One focus in the expansion of the responsibilities of production workers is the transfer of responsibility for quality control back to direct-production workers. Such measures have been undertaken by a number of German manufacturers. They were, however, always accompanied by the introduction of computer-based automated measurement procedures, reporting and alarm systems. The return of inspection functions to the production department has been associated with the formation of new job profiles only at Ford where the integration of repair and quality control led to a newly created classification called 'repair inspector', who gets a corresponding wage supplement.

At VW, by contrast, the transfer of quality-control functions was absorbed by the production department and integrated into the standard job descriptions for individual jobs without creating new job designations. The tendency at VW is to decentralize quality-control functions by creating quality-control subsystems (*Qualitätsregelkreise*) and to form 'pairs' of one quality-control inspector and one repair worker. This constitutes a move towards bringing the two areas of responsibility closer together and raises the prospect of a merger, but currently it does not constitute a basic change.

The formation of quality circles

The picture of a relatively cautious and experimental application of production or – better – productivity concepts that are not associated with a technical transformation of work is reinforced by experience with quality circles. Quality circles and their functions of mobilizing employees' knowledge of production for optimizing production flow, increasing efficiency, and securing loyalty through peer-group control are well known[37] and are, naturally, also attractive for German car producers. All have made efforts to introduce them under one name or another.

Opel has a low level of quality control activities, but it should be noted that its production-team concept would incorporate the goals and functions of quality circles in a more comprehensive way. BMW and Ford are the most advanced on these issues. The Ford management made considerable efforts to propagate the idea of quality circles and to push them through. In 1981 there were about 230 quality circles in the continental Ford plants and about the same in the English plants.[38] There are also quality circles at VW, although only to a limited extent, and there is no sign of any large-scale campaign to introduce more of them. Except for the VW Hannover plant with currently 120 quality circles, there is at VW only a relatively small number of 'action circles'. These address a particular goal and are disbanded after solving their specific task. After long expressing a positive attitude towards quality circles, the VW works council recently seems to be developing a rather sceptical attitude towards them.[39] Quality circles are increasingly mistrusted by union representatives, particularly when they elect their own spokesman and are responsible for the independent solution of problems. They see a danger that the union representation of workers' concerns with how jobs are performed – an aspect long neglected by unions in the Federal Republic – could be usurped by management through the institution of quality circles. This negative attitude has also prevailed at the Daimler–Benz and Opel works councils which have not allowed quality control activities to develop very far.

FUTURE TRENDS: ABOLITION OR RENEWAL OF THE DIVISION OF LABOUR?

The importance of new production concepts in the automobile plants of the Federal Republic is particularly associated with preparations for or the implementation of, automation measures, though each company has a slightly different approach.

Ford up to the present has confined itself largely to measures affecting work organization, integration of responsibility and quality circles. Opel has given its attention primarily to their partly supervised plants in Saragossa and Aspern, where the interplay of new production and organizational techniques is being systematically tested.

In the world empire of General Motors the 'green-field site' approach seems to be preferred, with the advantage of applying the newest technology with one push, building up a new organizational structure, and taking into consideration the positive and negative experiences of other plants.[40] It remains to be seen what will be tried in the new plants at Bochum and Russelsheim. At VW, where the automation of the assembly operation represents the most significant effort to implement the technology strategy, controversies about labour policy focus on questions of job structures. The principal issue now is the development of a new job category, complex equipment monitor (*Anlagenführer*), and the delimitation of this new job category both with respect to skilled work as well as in regard to residual work on equipment. At Audi, by contrast, the emphasis is on the further development of the production-team concept. Daimler–Benz and BMW are not thus far known to have undertaken any spectacular automation projects or experiments with new job structures. In both firms the expansion of capacity still plays a dominant role – as is shown by establishment of new plants (Daimler–Benz in Bremen, BMW in Regensburg). Nevertheless, here, too, there is experimentation with new job structures.

The examples and trends described here, provide no clear picture of future developments. As we have seen, there is some definite area for compromise between management and union representatives at the plant level. There is no conflict in principles between the union goal of protecting residual work and management's goal to increase process yield.

Therefore, management may not have any objections towards work structures like production teams, practising job rotation, and raising the average skill level, if this can be isolated to single pieces of automated equipment. The increase in the wage level which would be unavoidable in such cases, would not count very much as compared to the amount of capital invested in the equipment. Also, the wage systems of the West German companies do not pose problems of classifying semi-skilled workers and skilled tradesmen into the same wage group. The system of analytic wage differentiation (as practised at Daimler–Benz, Opel etc.) as well as measured day-work systems are both based on the principle of wage determination according to the actual work performed and not by training or status. Nevertheless, from the point of view of management these wage systems do not provide sufficient incentive for the employees to maintain high utilization of equipment by performing all necessary work tasks flexibly and without regard to formalized job descriptions. For this reason, consideration is being given to altering the incentive wage system: in practice there exist thus far only small experimental projects.

A further problem from the point of view of management results from the fact that 'generous' regulations that are justified for particular pieces of equipment encourage workers in neighbouring work areas and departments to demand equal treatment. Thus, for example, there is at present a controversy at VW as to whether *all* employees in highly mechanized areas of production should be classified as equipment monitors and paid correspondingly in order to overcome polarization between enriched quasi-skilled work on the one hand and deskilled residual work on the other. This also reflects the strategy of IG-Metall with regard to job structures and automated production.

This intensifies the already strong tendency of management to even further reduce the manning of equipment in so far as they are able to cope with the problem of maintaining a high level of equipment utilization through preventive maintenance and automated control systems.

Even if there is a tendency towards equalization of wages and skills at a higher level on automated equipment, it is nevertheless doubtful whether this will benefit current production workers much, the majority of whom are semi-skilled. The question of the future of skilled work can be expected to become an important area of tension in the automobile industry in the Federal Republic in the 1980s. There is currently an increasing tendency for production tasks to be carried out by certified skilled workers who thereby lose their skilled status. It has been traditional in the Germany automobile industry to recruit skilled workers for production jobs. According to our interviews the percentage of production workers who have completed an apprenticeship in metal-working skills is, on the average 20 per cent; in plants in less industrialized regions it can be 60 to 80 per cent in some production departments.

The competition for the new jobs in production is for jobs which have been only slightly supplemented by traditional skilled tasks in maintenance and servicing. The boundary line of the corresponding skilled-trade departments has remained largely stable in German plants. The plan to have the highly mechanized equipment operated as far as possible by universally qualified skilled workers has in the meantime been abandoned because these qualifications were too seldom needed in routine maintenance work and production.[41] There remains a need for independent maintenance specialists who are not bound to routine production tasks, and there is an upper limit to the potential of integrating the more highly skilled tasks in team work.

The future will show how effective the union strategy of a 'training offensive' can be in countering tendencies towards a renewed polarization of skilled and unskilled work and related competition within the workforce. At present IG-Metall is calling for an 'offensive training policy for all employees in the automobile industry' and is attempting to counter possible conflicts of interest among the workforce by disseminating a more comprehensive social perspective through the use of work groups:

The new form of work organisation requires above all a learning process in groups. Only in this way can co-operative and communicative abilities be further developed that suffered under the use of Tayloristic fragmentation of work. Expertise and social skills are, however, not only important for the plant level work process. They also make possible broader engagement in social affairs and are therefore a basic element of a humane social structure.[42]

NOTES

1 Wolfgang Gerstenberger, *Strukturwandel unter verschlechterten Rahmen-bedingungen: Strukturberichterstattung 1983* (Berlin, 1983).
2 Aggregate investments of the six German firms BMW, Daimler–Benz, Ford, Opel, VW and Audi in billions (thousand millions) of DM are as follows:

1975	1976	1977	1978	1979	1980	1981	1982	1983
1.90	1.90	2.50	3.70	4.80	5.90	6.50	7.60	7.00

Source: IG Metall, *Beschäftigungsrisiken in der Autoindustrie: Vorschläge der IG Metall zur Beschäftigungssicherung und zur Strukturpolitik in diesem Industriebereich* (Frankfurt, 1984) p. 21.
3 Audi is 100 per cent owned by VW and is thereby part of the VW Corporation.
4 K. Pitz, 'Bildungsoffensive gegen Beschäftigungsverluste', in *Der Gewerkschafter, Monatsschrift fur die Funktionare der IG Metall*, December 1984, p. 42 f. See also the position paper of the IGM: *IG Metall Vorschläge 1984*, p. 50 ff.
5 Wolfgang Streeck, *Industrial Relations in West Germany: A Case Study of the Car Industry* (London, 1984).
6 Horst Kern and Michael Schumann, *Das Ende der Arbeitsteilung? Rationalisierung in der industriellen Produktion* (Munich, 1984), p. 44 ff.
7 Horst Kern and Michael Schumann, 'Arbeit und Sozialcharakter: Alte und neue Konturen', in: Joachim Matthes (ed.), *Krise der Arbeitsgessellschaft? Verhandlungen des 21. Deutschen Soziologentages in Bamberg 1982* (Frankfurt/New York, 1983), pp. 353–65.
8 See the proud observation in the 1983 VW annual report: 'The new Golf represents, for the first time in the hundred-year history of automobile production, a car that is designed to be largely produced with automated equipment. This model represents a drastic change in industrial practice.' The greater attention given to manufacturing problems in the phase of development and design results from an awareness that a high proportion of final cost is determined by this phase. According to some estimates, 70 per cent of the final cost of the automobile is already determined in the phase of development and design while only about 10 per cent of the final cost is determined in the phase of actual production. See Wolfgang Reitzle, 'Industrieroboter', *Computergestütztes Produktionsmanagement* 3, ed. Horst Wildemann (Munich, 1984).
9 Joachim, Milberg, 'Montagegerecht-designfeindlich', *Produktion*, 2, no. 5 (February, 1984).
10 'Degree of automation' is the percentage of mechanized or automated functions in the total number of functions in a system: for these calculations there is a standard of DIN (German Industrial Norm) 19233.
11 *Zeitung der Industriegewerkschaft Metall für die Bundesrepublik Deutschland* 39 (1984), no. 4, p. 14.
12 *BMW Annual Report (Bericht uber das Geschaftsjahr 1979)* (Munich, 1980).
13 See *Assembly Automation* 4, no. 4 (November 1984), pp. 194–6. This involves the manufacture and testing of the cockpit module. The cockpit consists of the whole of the fascia with its instrumentation, heater and controls, steering wheel, ignition key lock, plus clutch, brake and accelerator pedals and linkages.

14 Reitzle, 'Industrieroboter', p. 26; Kern and Schumann, *Das Ende der Arbeitsteilung?* p. 66 ff. For the increasing use of robotics see: Thomas Malsch, Knuth Dohse and Ulrich Jürgens, 'Industrial Robots in the Automobile Industry. A Leap Towards "Automated Fordism"?', Publication Series of the International Institute for Comparative Social Research/Labor Policy (Berlin, 1984).

15 On the current controversy about employment effects see IG-Metall, 'Vorschläge'; Federation of the Automobile Industry (Verband der Automobilindustrie), *Stellungnahme des VDA zur Unterschung der IG Metall über 'Beschäftigungsrisiken in der Autoindustrie . . .'*, VDA press release no. 20a, 20 December 1984; Alan Altshuler et al., *The Future of the Automobile: The Report of MIT's International Automobile Program* (London, 1985), p. 199 ff; Kern and Schumann, 'Das Ende der Arbeitsteilung?', p. 67 ff.

16 The prognosis was published in *Der Gewerkschafter* 4 (1984), p. 3; according to the source it is attributed to internal plans of the auto companies.

17 Reitzle, 'Industrieroboter', p. 27.

18 According to William J. Abernathy, Kim B. Clark and Alan M. Kantrow, *Industrial Renaissance: Producing a Competitive Future for America* (New York, 1983), p. 84 ff. The most important reason for the lower Japanese production costs is their ability to maintain high levels of process yield. The management sample attributed 40 per cent of the Japanese cost advantage to this factor alone. The principle determining factors of process yield are machine cycle, running time and reliability conditioned by methods of controlling material flow, maintenance and work organization. Technological structures, by contrast, are estimated by Western managers to be much less important (about 17 per cent of the cost advantage was attributed to technological factors).

19 The job of monitoring complex equipment has been recently discussed in the literature on industrial sociology in the Federal Republic as an example of a current transformation in the utilization of manpower with long-term effects on qualification requirements and, thereby, also on the possibilities for self-fulfilment in the work process. For Kern and Schumann, who are very influential in German industrial sociology, this transformation represents a step toward the final overcoming of Taylorism (see Kern and Schumann, 'Das Ende der Arbeitsteilung?').

20 Knuth Dohse, Ulrich Jürgens and Thomas Malsch, 'Die Entwicklung von Arbeitsstrukturen in hochmechanisierten Bereichen der Automobilindustrie', in: *Automobil Industrie* 30, no. 1, (March, 1985).

21 Willy Gröber, and Günther Zimmermann, 'Notfalls machen wir mit dem Nein ernst', in Heinrich Buhmann, Herbert Lucy, Rolf Weber and others, *Geisterfahrt ins Leere: Roboter und Rationalisierung in der Automobilindustrie* (Hamburg, 1984), p. 100.

22 Pitz, 'Bildungsoffensive', p. 42 f.

23 Projektgruppe Automation und Qualifikation, 'Zerreißproben – Automation im Arbeiterleben: Empirische Untersuchungen', part 4, *Das Argument* Sonderband 79 (Berlin, 1983), p. 168.

24 Manfred Muster, 'Rationalisierung in der Automobilindustrie', in Buhmann et al., *Geisterfahrt ins Leere*, p. 16.

25 Eva Brumlop and Ulrich Jürgens, 'Rationalisation and Industrial Relations in the West German Automobile Industry: A Case Study of Volkswagen', in O. Jacobi et al. (eds), *Technological Change, Rationalisation and Industrial Relations* (London, 1985).

26 Richard Helken and Udo Richter, 'Menschengerechtere Arbeitsgestaltung fur DM 5, 72 (Fünfmarkzweiundsiebzig), in Buhmann et al., *'Geistfahrt ins Leere'*, p. 34.
27 V. Haas, 'Team-Konzept: Mitarbeiter planen und betreiben ihr Arbeitssystem'. Paper presented to the IAO-Arbeitstagung 'Wettbewerbsfähige Arbeitssysteme' 22–3 November, 1983. Böblingen, p. 137 f.
28 Ibid, p. 135.
29 Ibid.
30 *VW AG Annual Report*, 1980, 1982.
31 Klaus Wagenhals, 'Möglichkeiten von Kompetenzentwicklung in Zusammen-arbeitformen, wie sie sich in Zuge der Automatisierung eines Produktion-prozesses entwickelten – dargestellt am Beispiel der Einführung von Teams im Presswerk eines grossen Automobilkonzerns', Psychology Diploma, Marburg, 1983, pp. 78–83.
32 Ibid., p. 81.
33 Brumlop and Jürgens, 'Rationalisation and Industrial Relations', p. 41 ff.
34 Eva Brumlop, *Veränderungen der Arbeitsbewertung bei flexiblem Personal-einsatz: Ergebnisse einer Untersuchung zum Lohndifferenzierungsprojekt bei VW 1984* (Frankfurt, 1985).
35 Helken and Richter, 'Menschengerechtere', p. 35.
36 Ibid.
37 Knuth Dohse, Ulrich Jurgens and Thomas Malsch: 'From "Fordism" to "Toyotism"? The Social Organization of the Labor process in the Japanese Automobile Industry', Publication Series of the International Institute for Comparative Social Research/Labor Policy (Berlin, 1984).
38 *Financial Times*, 1 May 1981.
39 *Gewerkschaftliche Monatshefte* 34 (Koln, 1983), pp. 740–5.
40 Haas, 'Team-Konzept' p. 135.
41 Kern and Schumann, 'Das Ende der Arbeitsteilung?', p. 59.
42 Pitz, 'Bildungoffensive', p. 43.

12

Recent Developments in US Auto Labour Relations

Harry Katz

Under the pressure of enormous declines in sales and employment, a number of unprecedented events occurred in relations between labour and management in the US automobile industry between 1979 and mid-1983. These events included the negotiation of pay freezes as part of efforts to stave off the bankruptcy of the Chrysler Corporation in 1980. Early renegotiation at General Motors and Ford of their national agreements with the United Autoworkers (UAW) in 1982 also produced unprecedented wage and fringe benefit concessions. Meanwhile, in a number of plants major work-rule changes were being negotiated and in some plants worker participation programmes expanded dramatically. Inside GM, a particularly noteworthy development was the expansion of the use of team forms of work organization which replaced the traditional highly detailed job classification system and challenged the industry's traditional form of job-control unionism. Some observers went so far as to suggest that these developments amounted to the emergence of a new industrial relations system in the United States. Yet, prompted by high corporate earnings and some signs of a return to traditional bargaining, by 1984 questions began to be raised as to whether conclusions regarding the emergence of a new industrial relations system had been premature.

This paper argues that to understand the implications of recent labour-relations conduct in the auto industry, it is necessary to adopt a systems view and assess the extent to which concession bargaining or worker-participation programmes challenge the industry's traditional labour-relations system.[1] The traditional auto labour-relations system was structured by the following three key features: the determination of wages through formula-like wage rules in multi-year national contracts; a connective bargaining structure defining the relationship between national and plant-level bargaining; and a job-control focus premised on the contractual resolution of disagreements and the linking of worker rights to strict job definitions.

The next section of the paper describes how each of the three features of the auto labour-relations system operated over the period following the Second World War and clarifies the interactions that occurred across the three key features. The following section discusses how modifications made to the three key features after 1979 led to an erosion of the traditional labour-relations system. Then, recognition of the system nature of auto bargaining is used to outline the alternative paths that stand before labour and management as future options. The paper then discusses the 1984 contract renegotiations at GM and Ford and the implications for the future course of auto labour relations.

THE THREE KEY FEATURES OF THE TRADITIONAL AUTO LABOUR-RELATIONS SYSTEM

Wage rules

Formula-like mechanisms have been utilized to set wage levels in collective bargaining agreements in the auto industry since the historic General Motors–United Auto Workers agreement in 1948.[2] These collective bargaining agreements have been national, company-specific, and multi-year (since 1955 they have been three-year agreements). The formula wage-setting mechanisms traditionally included in the contracts are an annual improvement factor (AIF) that since the mid-1960s has amounted to 3 per cent per year, and a cost-of-living adjustment (COLA) escalator that originally provided full cost-of-living protection and provided in the 1970s roughly an 0.8 per cent wage increase for every 1 per cent increase in the national consumer price index.[3]

The importance of these formula-like mechanisms is that they provided continuity in wage determination across time, and across the auto industry at any given point in time. The continuity across time was provided by the fact that, except for minor adjustments, the formula mechanisms rigidly set wages from 1948 until 1979 among the Big Three companies (GM, Ford and Chrysler).[4] Continuity across the industry was provided by the inter-company pattern-following well documented by Levinson,[5] and by the fact that in the plants covered by the company agreements, the national contract wage was not modified at all in local bargaining.

The COLA and AIF formula mechanisms can be viewed as a form of 'wage rule' which guided the behaviour of labour and management bargainers in a manner analogous to the function served by shop-floor work rules.[6]

For national union leadership, the steady adherence to wage rules served an important function by providing a standard of good performance in bargaining: the rank and file could not fault the union leadership for securing wage increases satisfying the rule during contract renegotiation. Furthermore, over time these wage rules became a secure standard continually legitimated by the efforts of the union's national leadership. Support from union members for these wage rules also derived from the fact that continual adherence to the wage rules provided steadily improving real wages.[7] Meanwhile, pattern-following within the industry satisfied workers' equity concerns.

On the other side of the bargaining table the use of wage rules was appealing to management both as a means of reducing the likelihood of overt conflict with labour, and as a way to facilitate long-term planning. The continuity in labour costs provided by the wage rules was especially attractive to auto-industry management in light of the long lead time associated with new-product development and investment planning.

The use of wage rules had a number of other important implications for bargaining in the auto industry. The ban on local modification of nationally set contract wages was a critical part of the connective bargaining structure which defined the relationship between national and local bargaining in the industry. Secondly, the use of formula-like wage rules to set compensation narrowed the range of national union participation in corporate decision-making, and thereby was a key part in the contractually-based job control focus of labour-management relations. In this way the use of wage rules was closely linked to the two other features of the auto labour-relations system. These links and the two other key features that structured auto collective bargaining are outlined in detail below.

Connective bargaining

According to Ulman,[8] connective bargaining

involves the negotiation of wages, fringes, and some work conditions between company and one or more national unions, the latter connecting the company-wide wage settlements in an industry via pattern bargaining. Working conditions and, to a lesser degree, some pay questions are also negotiated at the plant level with local unions; and local and national unionists are sequentially involved in grievance handling.

Within the auto industry's connective bargaining structure, compensation is set by national company-specific agreements. Some work rules such as overtime administration, employee transfer rights, and seniority guidelines are also set in the national contracts. Local unions, in turn, negotiate plant-level agreements which supplement the national agreements. These local agreements define work rules such as the form of the seniority ladder, job characteristics, job bidding and transfer rights, health and safety standards, production standards, and an array of other rules which guide shop-floor production. The local agreement does not regulate either wages or fringe benefits which are set in the national contract. Some indirect influences on wage determination do occur at the plant level in the definition of job classifications provided through the local agreements. The operation of piece-rate systems also modify wage levels, but by the late 1950s piece rates, with very few exceptions, had been eliminated from the industry.[9]

Local bargaining over work rules allowed for the expression of local preferences and some adjustment to local conditions. This facilitated the sort of shop-floor 'fractional bargaining' described by Kuhn.[10] In this system the grievance system, with binding third party arbitration, served as the end point of contract administration, although disputes concerning production standards, new job rates, and health and safety issues were not resolved through recourse to arbitration. Occasionally, as revealed in Bureau of Labor Statistics figures, strikes did occur in the postwar years as part of both local contract negotiation and shop-floor bargaining.[11] In the main, however, this connective structure succeeded in diffusing plant level labour–management disputes.

Although local UAW unions are provided with the right to negotiate the local agreement with plant management, a critical element in this connective bargaining structure is the active role the national union plays in monitoring plant-level bargaining and agreements. The formal power to do so comes from the fact that many features of local agreements such as the seniority ladder and local strikes require the approval of the national union.

The separation between compensation determination and plant-level work-rule bargaining, and the limits on local bargaining placed by the national union ensured that local work-rule bargaining was not significantly influenced by the employment consequences of shop-floor work rules. Over the postwar years the recourse to either foreign or domestic non-union supply of parts previously produced in union plants occasionally had significant employment consequences within selected plants. This could have led to wider local work-rule modifications and inter-plant divergence as part of the effort to lower in-house union costs so as to more effectively compete with alternative suppliers. Yet, two factors worked to severely lessen this pressure. For one thing, the industry's output and employment were on an upward long-run path in the post war years. Business lost to an outside supplier was made up for by an expanding volume of business activities left in-house. Secondly, liberal transfer rights and allowances were provided within the union's national agreements, which allowed workers displaced in one plant to bid on new jobs in other plants of a company. As a result, and in contrast to the recent period discussed later in the paper, local unions were not under pressure to relax work rules in order to save jobs.

With pay set strictly at the national level, the bargaining structure did not promote any linkage between pay and local work rules, and in that sense the system was not 'connective'. The system was connective, however, due to the fact that the national union was heavily involved in monitoring local union affairs and functioned as a channel of communication up and down the union hierarchy.

This process shifted political power inside the union to the national union officers. In this way, the imposition of the connective structure in the immediate postwar years was associated with the rise and solidification of the Reuther faction within the UAW.[12] The elaboration of the connective structure in the auto industry in the 1950s also paralleled the similar centralization underway within national unions throughout US industry.[13]

By producing a separation between work-rule bargaining and compensation determination, this connective structure also discouraged local unions and workers from concerning themselves with business decision-making at either the corporate or shop-floor levels. Consequently, the connective structure is closely linked to job-control unionism, another key feature of the postwar US auto collective bargaining system.

Job control

At both national and shop-floor levels, the labour relations system in the US auto industry relies on contractually defined procedures to regulate disagreements between labour and management. The contractual regulation of these procedures are heavily focused on 'job control'.[14] For one thing, wages are explicitly tied to jobs and not to worker characteristics. In addition, much of the detail within the contract concerns the specification of an elaborate job classification system with much attention paid to the exact requirements of each job, and to seniority rights that are tied to a job ladder which guides promotions, transfers and layoffs.[15]

At the corporate level in this system, labour and management negotiate over compensation levels and a limited number of work rules. During negotiations over compensation, the use of wage rules keeps the parties away from discussion of either company pricing or profits. Note, this was an explicit motivation for the adoption of the AIF and COLA formulas in 1948, when Charles Wilson, then president of General Motors, was searching for a way to answer and avoid Walter Reuther's request explicitly to discuss company profit and pricing policies.[16] The use of wage rules and the enforced narrow range of local work-rule bargaining also discourages discussion of other broad corporate concerns such as investment planning, outsourcing and the problems associated with the introduction of new technologies. Meanwhile, at the local level similar pressures discourage shop-floor discussion of business and production decisions. The resolution of disagreements through the grievance procedure and the extreme job-control focus leaves little room for alternative forms of worker participation in decision making.

For management, this labour-relations system served the important function of containing the union's and workers' penetration of issues that were deemed to be managerial prerogatives. As Harbison and Dubin note, containment of the union was a central objective for auto management in the union's early years.[17] The labour-relations system which emerged largely resolved this concern by limiting the bargaining agenda.

Though the limited bargaining agenda did not satisfy all of Reuther's initial goals, this system satisfied important political needs within the UAW. In particular, the national union was placed in firm control of what periodically had been restive local unions and workers.[18] The multi-year agreements signed after the war also satisfied an important union goal by contractually insuring union security.[19]

Furthermore, given the limited import penetration of domestic sales, the national coverage of the company agreements matched the geographic extent of the relevant product and labour market throughout the 1950s and 1960s. Along with the steady rise in auto sales this provided workers with large real increases in pay and the Big Three firms with high profits.

The three features of auto bargaining – wage rules, connective bargaining, and job control – thereby historically have been linked together into a reinforcing labour-relations system. In broad terms this is a highly centralized system. Wages are set at the national level and local work-rule bargaining is bounded within limits imposed by the national union. In addition, union and worker participation in business decision-making is limited and contractually based. Until the late 1970s, this was a well-functioning labour-relations system consistent with the economic environment in which it was embedded.

THE EFFECTS OF THE STRUCTURAL DOWNTURN

In the late 1970s the economic environment of the US auto industry changed dramatically. A prolonged recession, a rise in imports, and structural shifts in the demand for automobiles led to enormous declines in auto sales and employment. The employment of production workers in the auto industry dropped from a peak of 800,800 in December 1978 to a low of 487,700 in January 1983.[20] Imports, as a fraction of total car and truck sales in the United States, rose from 14.6 per cent in 1970 to 25.2 per cent in 1981. The enormous decline in sales and employment after 1979 precipitated major modifications in all three of the key features of the labour-relations system in the US auto industry.

Wage rules

The wage rules traditionally used to set wage levels have been modified significantly, first as part of the effort to avoid bankruptcy at Chrysler in 1979, and then as part of the early agreements reached at GM and Ford in March of 1982.

Under the threat of bankruptcy and pressure from the Federal government which was providing loan guarantees to Chrysler, the formula mechanisms were modified in the UAW–Chrysler agreement. A new three-year agreement negotiated at Chrysler in 1979 maintained the formula mechanisms, but deferred payment of the annual improvement factor and the scheduled cost-of-living payments. Under further direct pressure from the Federal government in 1980, the deferrals were extended and accompanied by a substantial reduction in the number of paid personal holidays. When Chrysler's financial difficulties continued, labour and management returned to the bargaining table for a third time in January 1981 and agreed to cancel the remaining AIF and COLA increases. The total effect of all these pay concessions was to lower the hourly pay of Chrysler's workers $2.50 below the pay received at Ford and GM.

Although these agreements entailed major modifications in the old wage formulas, later events at Chrysler reveal the continued strength of the union's and workers' attachment to the historic wage rule. In December 1982, after rank and file rejection of an earlier agreement, the UAW and Chrysler signed a contract providing an up-front wage increase equal to the traditional 3 per cent annual improvement factor increase, restored the old cost-of-living escalator, and removed the profit-sharing plan introduced in 1980.

In the face of the continuation of Chrysler's financial upturn a new two-year agreement was reached between Chrysler and the UAW in September 1983. The agreement includes a 3 per cent AIF increase and continues the full COLA escalator. These wage increases amount to full restoration of the traditional wage rules.

At Ford and GM, in three-year agreements negotiated in March of 1982 (before the scheduled expiration of the existing contracts in September) the parties eliminated any AIF increase and deferred some of the scheduled COLA increases.[21] In addition, annual work hours were increased 4 per cent through the removal of nine paid personal holidays and one scheduled holiday.

One thing that stands out in these changes is the parties' effort to maintain the structure of the wage rules even in the face of building economic pressure. The pattern is that first, implementation of the wage-rule-generated increases is deferred and only later are those wage increases cancelled. Then, if economic conditions improve (as at Chrysler) workers first press for restoration of the form, though not necessarily the complete structure, of the old wage rules. Throughout this adaptation process, labour and management reluctance to abandon the use of wage rules reveals the strength of those rules.

At Chrysler, Ford and GM, the modification of the wage rules was accompanied by the introduction of company based 'contingent' compensation schemes. These profit-sharing plans tie future wage increases to the economic performance of each company. The continuation of these plans at GM and Ford leads to a further weakening of pattern-following across the companies. The pressure for a lessening of inter-company pattern-following comes from the fact that in the face of low sales volume, strict pattern-following might produce larger employment losses, particularly in the poorest-performing companies. In the past, although the economic performance of the Big Three varied significantly, the industry's sustained long-term economic growth had insured that adherence to pattern-following, though perhaps reducing employment growth in the relatively poor-performing companies, did not lead to explicit employment losses.[22]

Connective bargaining

The pay concessions and the move to contingent compensation schemes which tie wages to company performance have increased the variation in employment conditions across the companies. At the same time, across plants the contemporaneous erosion of the old connective bargaining structure has produced increased variation in work rules.

The threat of increased employment loss due to either the further outsourcing of parts production or further production-volume reductions has led labour and management to modify local work practices. At the core, these modifications entail efforts to modify work practices so as to lower costs. The pressure for increased inter-plant work rule divergence comes from the same source as the pressure for inter-company pay variation, the even greater explicit losses in employment that would result if previous policies were maintained.

Some of these work-rule changes involve increases in the 'effort bargain' through a tightening of production standards. Other work-rule changes include efforts to lower production costs by increasing the flexibility by which labour is deployed. Common examples of the latter include classification consolidation and limits imposed on job-bidding rights.[23]

Work-rule revisions first were carried out by local unions that had experienced severe layoffs with informal sanctions provided by the national union. Then, in the 1982 Ford and GM contracts, the national union formally empowered local unions to modify local work rules when faced with a major outsourcing decision with the following contract language.

In the event that changes in labor costs can make a difference in the reasons for a major outsourcing action, the Union shall have 30 days from the notice to propose any changes in work practices or any local deviation from the Collective Bargaining Agreement that might make it feasible for the company to continue to produce without being economically disadvantaged.[24]

This new clause legitimizes a wider range of inter-plant work rule divergence than was allowed in the past but does so in a manner that illustrates the national union's desire to preserve as much as possible of the old bargaining structure. For instance, note that the new clause appears in a letter concerning outsourcing which supplements the national agreement and not in the main part of the contract where national versus local responsibilities are delineated. In practice, the narrow application of this clause does not hold. Field interviews reveal that employment declines became so severe over the last few years as to induce many local unions to make significant work-rule changes even where there was no impending outsourcing decision.

As mentioned above, in many plants the modification of work rules interacts closely with ongoing worker-involvement programmes. In this way, the erosion of the connective bargaining structure is linked to a shift away from the job-control focus that characterized postwar auto bargaining.

*A shift from job control to increased worker involvement in
business decision-making*

Broader worker involvement in business decision-making was first initiated
through programmes that were viewed as supplements to collective
bargaining. However, recently the expansion of these programmes and the
introduction of team forms of work organization in some plants has led
to significant movements away from the traditional job-control orientation
of shop-floor labour relations.

The earliest worker participation programmes were the quality of working
life (QWL) programmes at GM. At one point Irving Bluestone, a former
vice-president of the UAW and one of the chief designers and proponents
of these programmes, wrote that a guiding principle of QWL is that, 'The
provisions of the national agreement and of the local agreements and
practices remain inviolable.' Furthermore, Bluestone stated that where QWL
is introduced, 'The local understands that normal collective bargaining
continues.'[25]

At the local level, in the early QWL efforts these guidelines were carried
out through the maintenance of a clear and sharp separation between QWL
programme activities and normal collective-bargaining issues and
procedures. This separation symbolized the fact that labour and
management viewed QWL programmes as a supplement to and not a
fundamental alteration of the existing collective bargaining system. QWL
programmes were initially conceived of as experimental efforts designed
to address worker concerns with the work environment and the climate of
the relationship between workers and supervisors.[26] In such a system in
which QWL activities functioned only as a supplement to normal bargaining,
it would be possible for labour and management to continue their basic
contractual job-control focus.

Yet, in response to the industry's decline, at corporate and local levels
there is no longer a clear separation between QWL activities and 'normal
collective bargaining'. Rather, worker involvement is now inextricably linked
with other aspects of labour relations. In the process, labour and
management have taken significant steps away from the traditional job-
control bargaining orientation, and thereby contributed further to the
erosion of the old labour-relations system.

Corporate-level steps include the placement of Douglas Fraser, then
President of the UAW, on the Chrysler Board of Directors; 'mutual growth
forums' initiated at Ford and GM where broad business decisions such as
investment and outsourcing are discussed; and an informal exchange of
information between national company and union officials that is part of
the implementation of the new contracts' outsourcing, plant closing and
other novel clauses. The Saturn project at GM, where labour is participating
in planning discussions concerning production of a small car in the United

States, is another illustration of how labour is now participating in a wider array of decisions.

New activities underway at the local level include worker involvement in shop-floor quality circles; local mutual growth forums analogous to national forums; and wide ranging discussions between plant management and union officials concerning outsourcing, new technologies and production problems.

The range of worker participation now varies widely across plants. In some plants labour–management relations are much as they were years ago. In some other plants up to one third of the workforce participate in quality circles. A more extensive form of worker involvement occurs in the ten GM plants (including three new assembly plants) utilizing an 'operating-team' concept. In these plants there is a single classification for all production workers and a 'pay-for-knowledge' system which rewards workers for learning a wider variety of jobs. The team-work groups typically receive advance warning regarding new technology and production plans, can voluntarily create job rotation schemes, and have input into the work area layout and production decisions. In some Ford plants a similar team system has been adopted in a few departments, though management in these plants hopes to gradually increase the use of teams to the whole plant.

The increased involvement of workers and the union in business decision-making appears to have been encouraged by a number of factors. On the one hand, the movement toward company-based compensation at the national level and work-rule concessions at the local level have required wider access by the union to corporate decisions. The negotiation of company-based compensation leads the union to request corporate information as part of their consideration of the terms of the contingent compensation scheme, and also leads the union to desire to monitor corporate earnings and decisions when the scheme is in place. Similarly, at the plant level, the local union and workers request to see and debate plant business plans before they will accept work-rule concessions. Once local concessions are in place, the local union then demands to continue to receive business information as part of a monitoring function.

In addition, the union and workers have asked for increased participation as a trade-off for their willingness to accept either compensation or work-rule concessions. Here, the increased involvement is perceived by the union and workers as a gain to be traded for the relaxation of other contract terms rather than only as a means by which information is gathered so as to determine the union's willingness to agree to concessionary terms in the first place. Increased worker involvement also contributes to the companies' efforts to reduce costs and increase the flexibility of human-resource utilization. The team system, through its broadening of job definitions, is particularly well suited to provide greater flexibility in production processes.[27]

*Overview of modifications made to the traditional
labour-relations system*

The last three years of bargaining in the US auto industry have seen: the
use of wage rules modified and lessened; a wider divergence in local
practices; and increased involvement by the UAW and workers in corporate
and shop-floor decision-making. These changes have eroded the labour
relations system that historically has operated in the US auto industry. An
important point to note is that it is no accident that all three key features
of the auto labour relations system are changing simultaneously. For, the
same factors that linked the key features and created a labour-relations
system in the first place make system-wide rather than piecemeal change
inevitable.

The modifications made to wage rules, connective bargaining and job
control all initially occurred through amendments that preserved the
structure of the old labour-relations system. The wage rules were first
deferred and revised; work-rule changes emerged through informally
sanctioned local actions; and worker involvement began as part of
experimental programmes kept separate from normal bargaining. The
reluctance of labour and management to revise the three features in a more
flexible or comprehensive manner supports the contention that these features
reinforced one another to form a labour-relations system.

THE FUTURE COURSE OF US AUTO LABOUR RELATIONS

What is likely to happen to the US auto labour-relations system in the years
ahead? Will the dominance of the three features of the traditional system
re-emerge? Or, will worker participation and work organization reforms
expand to the point that a fundamentally new labour-relations system
emerges?

The history of auto bargaining shows that environmental factors shaped
the labour-relations system. The steady adherence to wage rules from 1948
until 1979 was supported by the industry's long-run growth in sales and
employment. The connective bargaining structure, in turn, was feasible given
the low level of import sales and the complete unionization of the Big Three
which produced an overlap between labour and product markets. The steady
growth in autoworkers' earnings and Big Three profits also contributed to
the acceptability on both sides of the bargaining table of the continuation
of a job-control focus. It was only the sharp economic slump after 1979
that led to major modifications in the traditional auto labour-relations
system.

The central role of the economic environment in shaping the choices
before labour and management implies that future economic developments
must be assessed in order to arrive at predictions regarding the future course

of auto labour relations. Yet, the history of auto bargaining also shows that labour and management retained a degree of *strategic choice* in the design of the labour relations system. The bargaining system that emerged out of the instability of the environment immediately following the Second World War had to be consistent with the economic environment, but was not strictly determined by environmental factors. Thus, in terms of future developments, even in the face of any given set of environmental pressures, labour and management will exercise some independent control over the course taken. This suggests the need to consider both likely future economic pressures and the likely strategic choices of labour and management.

Pressures for greater flexibility

Recent changes in the world auto industry have generated the need for cost reduction and greater flexibility in the production process. For a number of reasons these pressures are likely to persist in the years ahead.

Factors contributing to the need for greater flexibility in the production process include: developments in the product market, new technologies, and macroeconomic events. On the product market side, US auto producers have moved away from a strategy of producing a wide range of vehicle types and increasingly are focusing their product lines along a specialty or 'niche' strategy. Associated with this switch is the abandonment of the small end of the car market by American producers and the world-wide erosion of distinct national auto markets.[28]

This shift in product-market strategy has important implications for the production process, because production schedules for specialty vehicles are more subject to changes in consumer preferences or competitive offerings. Consequently, on the shop floor there is greater need for the capacity to rapidly adjust production volumes and type. One way to acquire this sort of flexibility is to replace the traditional job-control form of workplace regulation with team forms of work organization and a more informal system of work-rule regulation.

The increased use of robotic and microelectronic technology provides additional pressure for more flexible work rules since the ability to rapidly switch product types appears to be the critical advantage robots have over earlier forms of automation. A machine that is frequently reprogrammed, or an assembly line that is frequently rearranged, requires workers and work rules that flexibly adjust.

A third factor that has contributed to the industry's search for greater flexibility in labour relations and work rules is the volatility in product demand generated by macroeconomic flux and structural economic developments. The likely continuation of the structural problems creating heightened macroeconomic flux – oil-price shocks, government policy responses to the inflation–unemployment trade-off and the increased exposure of the US economy to world economic events – suggests a continuation in this trend of greater macroeconomic instability. On balance then, there are a number of factors likely to contribute to the pressure for increased flexibility in the auto labour-relations system.

Cost pressure

In the face of a slump in auto sales that continued from 1979 until mid-1983 and heightened competition from the Japanese, the American auto industry also came under intense pressure to lower costs. The sharp rebound in auto sales and corporate profits which started in late 1983 and continued through 1984 led some to predict that the industry has returned to a long-run growth path similar to that of the 1950s and 1960s. Are these predictions accurate?

To derive a good forecast of future trends, a number of critical factors which influence future domestic auto sales must be considered, including: the growth rate of the USA and other economies; the competitive pressures generated by foreign producers; and the course of government protectionist policies which potentially might insulate American producers from foreign competition. And even with a projection of domestic sales in hand, it is necessary to consider the role that technological change and outsourcing will play as factors that might reduce auto employment and add to the pressure on the UAW to change labour-relations practices so as to expand auto sales and employment.

Assessment of these factors leads me to conclude that the economic environment is likely to provide continued pressure on labour and management in the US auto industry to moderate costs.[29] Although cyclical slumps and competitive problems may lead to extreme pressure for some firms, most American firms probably will face moderate to strong pressure for cost reduction, but pressure that is not as extreme as during the 1979–83 sales slump.

ALTERNATIVE FUTURE PATHS OF LABOUR RELATIONS

How will environmental economic pressures influence the future course of US auto labour relations? The fact that labour relations practices tend to evolve into a well-connected system implies that labour and management do not face a large number of alternative labour relations options each of which is only slightly different from some other alternative option. As the history of auto collective bargaining shows, the basic operation of a labour-relations system resists fundamental change and encourages incremental change only so long as such change does not call into question any of the key terms of the system. In addition, the logic of the operation of a labour-relations system requires that the various features of any new system fit together well with each other. For example, pay procedures will not persist if they are not well tailored to the structure of bargaining or do not mesh with the defined terms of worker participation in decision-making. Therefore, labour and management will be choosing from a limited number of alternative *paths* each of which entails a *set* of pay, bargaining structure and worker involvement procedures. The three paths outlined below appear to be the alternatives available to labour and management in the US auto industry.

The status quo path

One potential path is continuation of the traditional labour-relations system. The more favourable are environmental economic conditions, the more likely this path and the retention of the traditional labour-relations system. History suggests that unless there is strong pressure to do otherwise, the parties and the inherent features of the traditional labour-relations system exert strong pressure for the systems continuation. Both labour and management are attracted to the stability and continuity provided in the traditional system. Furthermore, the interconnections that exist across the key features of bargaining strongly reinforce continuation of the current system.

The continuation of the traditional labour-relations system might include QWL-type programmes possessing a limited focus as a supplement to the traditional key features. These QWL programmes could be used as a vehicle to address housekeeping issues, provide a forum for increased worker-supervisor communication and include quality programmes or some other mechanism for workers to make suggestions concerning production problems. These programmes would then look very much like the QWL programmes underway in GM in the early and mid-1970s and would not confront the more serious issues raised by more extensive forms of work reorganization and work-rule change.

A conflict path

In the face of severe pressure to reduce costs in order to improve sales and competitive world standing, it is possible that a conflict path would emerge. A conflictual path is most likely to emerge if pressures to reduce costs lead management to bargain hard for further pay and work-rule concessions, and make substantially greater use of outsourcing. Conflict ensues on this path if eventually the UAW responds to increased outsourcing by initiating strikes or other actions to try to limit its scope. Or, if repeatedly frustrated by earlier pay concessions, at some point workers and the UAW leadership refuse further pay and work concessions and initiate militant strike and shop-floor actions as part of their resistance towards management's demands.

The conflict scenario would entail a breakdown of the traditional system and the re-emergence of the kind of prolonged conflict and instability characterizing the union's organizing drives in the 1930s and immediate postwar auto bargaining. It is possible that, unlike in the late 1940s, this conflict would not rapidly lead to stabilized labour relations, but rather lead to prolonged strikes or the transformation of the UAW into a radical union. A critical factor would be the form of any governmental intervention applied to resolve the conflict. Needless to say, it is difficult to predict the form and timing of the return to any more stable pattern of labour relations that might follow this conflict phase. However, the enormous costs this conflict would impose on both management and labour makes the emergence of this path only likely if the industry were to face a sustained sales decline and extreme pressure to lower costs.

A cooperative path

A third potential path is the introduction of greater flexibility into pay and work rules and increased worker involvement in decision-making. This path is more likely if the industry were under some pressure to reduce costs and introduce greater flexibility, but the pressure was not extreme. Moderate economic pressure might induce labour and management to extend recent movements toward an alternative to the existing system. However, a cooperative path is less likely in the face of *extreme* economic pressure because the parties would probably pursue more radical alternatives in this case.

One part of this cooperative path might entail making autoworker wages more responsive to macroeconomic conditions and simultaneously allowed to vary more significantly across companies through an expansion in the use of profit sharing or some other form of contingent compensation. This could be accomplished by way of an increase in the profit-sharing plans in place in the GM and Ford 1982–4 national contracts with the UAW.

Greater flexibility in the production process also could be developed through a movement away from the traditional job-control orientation of labour-management relations. One way to increase flexibility is to broaden job responsibilities and training which would simplify adjustments in production volume and type. GM's operating team system may well provide a model of how job-broadening could be expanded in the US auto industry. The operating team system is particularly interesting because it includes some of the procedures which provide the Japanese auto industry with its high degree of flexibility and adaptability and is so similar to the *Lohn-differenzierungs-Tarivrertrag* (LODI) pay system adopted at Volkswagen in 1980.[30]

If a cooperative path were to emerge in the US auto labour-relations system, changes in corporate labour–management relations also would be required. In a cooperative path, at the national level labour and management would have to develop a more informal relationship in which greater communication regarding business and production decisions was regularly provided to the union leadership. In part, the union's involvement in a broader array of business decisions would likely grow out of the union's desire (or insistence) that it be informed of such decisions before it would be willing to agree to any form of contingent compensation scheme.

This provides another illustration of the interconnected nature of the labour-relations system. Changes in pay-setting procedures such as profit sharing would lead labour and management towards a more informal and broader range of contacts and away from a job-control orientation. In an analogous manner, the introduction of work teams and the expansion of worker participation on the shop floor would lead to modification of another basic feature of the auto labour-relations system, the connective bargaining structure.

Work-team systems and worker involvement would inevitably lead to diversity in pay and employment conditions across work groups and firms. The standardization that is part of the traditional connective bargaining structure would be lessened; although the UAW might still want to maintain standardization in some employment conditions or limit the range of variation allowed in particular items. The difficult task for the union would be to maintain the desired degree of standardization while at the same time allowing the experimentation and other by-products of increased worker involvement in production decisions.

If team systems were to expand, the union also would face the difficult task of developing an institutionalized procedure that could mediate any tensions arising between participatory and bargaining processes. In some of the existing team plants, a joint steering committee appears to play this role.

THE 1984 NATIONAL CONTRACT NEGOTIATIONS

The negotiation of new national contracts covering UAW workers at GM and Ford in the autumn of 1984 provides an indication of emerging corporate and union strategies. These negotiations occurred in an economic environment that shifted bargaining power to labour's advantage. From early 1983 on, auto sales and profits were buoyed by a strong macro-economic recovery and the advantages provided by the continuation of voluntary import restrictions on Japanese cars. In 1983, GM and Ford respectively posted profits of 3.7 billion (3,700 million) and 1.9 billion (1,900 million) dollars and earnings in the first half of 1984 of 3.2 billion (3,200 million) and 1.8 billion (1,800 million) dollars. These profits were in part generated by the shift in consumer demand to larger cars and full-option models. By mid-1984, constrained by previous plant closings, Ford and GM assembly plants were running at or near full capacity, particularly for the production of large cars.

The union's bargaining stance also was strengthened by workers' angry response to the substantial bonuses awarded executives at Ford and GM as part of their 1983 compensation packages. For example, Philip Caldwell, Chairman of Ford, received a combined salary and bonus in 1983 of 1.4 million dollars and earned 5.9 million dollars through the appreciation of stock purchased in his long-term compensation package.[31] Roger Smith, Chairman of GM, was awarded 1.5 million dollars in salary and bonuses. Many interpreted these bonuses as a signal that auto management believed the industry had fully recovered from its problems. One group of autoworkers (the coalition in favour of 'restore and more') called for a 1984 contract settlement providing substantially more than a restoration of 1982 contract concessions.

GM was eventually designated as the UAW's target company and when negotiators were unable to reach a settlement by the September 14 deadline, a strike was called. In contrast to traditional company-wide strikes, however, the UAW struck only 17 plants, although the targeted plants were those assembling relatively high-priced cars. Six days later the strike was ended with the announcement of a tentative contract of three years' duration. This contract was later approved by GM workers and a nearly identical agreement was negotiated at Ford.

The new settlement provides first-year wage increases of 1 per cent to assembly workers and up to 3.5 per cent increases to certain skilled trades, and average increases of 2.25 per cent. In the second and third year of the agreement workers receive lump-sum payments amounting to 2.25 per cent of their annual wages. In contrast to the first-year increases, these lump-sum payments will not be included in the base wages used to determine pensions, overtime and other benefits. Each worker also will receive $180 upon ratification of the settlement and the profit-sharing programme initiated in the 1982 national contract is continued. It is estimated that in 1984, GM workers will receive approximately $1,000 from the profit-sharing programme. The wage settlement also continued the COLA formula although 24 cents of COLA-generated increases were diverted to cover the cost of rising fringe benefits.

This wage package represents a compromise between the union's desire for full restoration of the traditional wage formulas and the company's desire to provide lower increases and a more direct link between future wage increases and company performance. On the one hand, the settlement restores the COLA formula intact. The traditional annual improvement factor, however, was eliminated. The scheduled 2.25 per cent average annual increases are somewhat lower than the traditional 3 per cent AIF, vary in size by job classification, and also modify the traditional pattern by not building all of these increases into base rates. In effect, the parties substituted profit sharing and lump-sum increases for the traditional AIF-formula wage increase. The retention of profit sharing also ensures that autoworkers' annual incomes will vary across the Big Three somewhat as a function of company performance, although the magnitude of this variation will be small.[32]

The most innovative part of the 1984 settlement is a new job-security programme covering current workers who in the future are displaced from their jobs due to either technological advances, corporate reorganizations, outsourcing or other negotiated productivity improvements. Under the new job-security programme workers displaced for any of these reasons will be placed into a reserve pool (bank) and receive full pay while waiting to be transferred or retrained for jobs elsewhere in GM. The programme will draw on a one-billion-dollar fund and will last for six years, which is three years beyond the duration of other features of the contract. This job security programme will not cover workers laid off because of sales volume reductions, and a labour–management committee will have the difficult task of ruling whether any given layoff is covered by the programme or is due to sales declines.

The new job-security programme compensates workers displaced by technological change or outsourcing and thereby creates a financial discentive for the company to initiate actions that create such displacement. But the programme does not explicitly limit management's rights to outsource or introduce new technology which continues the union's longstanding acceptance of technological change. Nor does the new programme commit management to any specific future employment levels. The design of the job-security programme is similar to that of the supplementary unemployment benefits programme by compensating workers, creating financial penalties for layoffs, and relying on fund financing.

The cost and coverage of the job-security programme are fairly modest. The billion-dollar job-security fund can provide expenditures of roughly $475 per GM worker per year or full income and fringe benefit support ($50,000) to roughly 4,000 workers per year. Furthermore, in the face of ongoing technological change, GM in any case would probably have had to spend money training workers to handle this new technology. Consequently some of the expenditures from the new job-security programme may only substitute for other training expenses. Yet like other fringe-benefit programmes the UAW has negotiated, the new job-security programme may expand in scope and resources over time.[33]

The new job-security programme also may prove to be a valuable supplement to labour's and management's cooperative efforts. Workers often fear participation programmes or technological change on the grounds that resulting productivity improvements will jeopardize their job security. More flexible and informal work rules and work organization are feared because they create the possibility that supervisors will exploit workers once traditional contractual rules are reduced in scope. The enhancement of workers' job security and the creation of a more explicit career link between auto workers and their employers may lessen these fears.

The establishment of labour–management committees to decide whether or not workers have been displaced as a result of productivity improvements or outsourcing versus demand factors might have significant long-run implications for the industry's connective bargaining structure. Through the committees, national union representatives may become more involved in plant-level issues. Outsourcing decisions frequently are made only after the failure of efforts by plant management to lower in-house production costs through work-rule or other changes. When a joint job-security committee is called in to decide the cause of a layoff it might be drawn into a debate over which work rules the local union is willing to modify in an effort to keep business in-house and avoid outsourcing in the first place. There are now a number of labour–management committees operating at the plant level, including the joint councils for enhancing job security and the competitive edge (mutual-growth forums) and the joint training committees initiated in the 1982-4 national contracts. It remains to be seen how much interaction occurs across these various committees and the degree to which any such interaction leads to a linking of various issues or to increased national union involvement in plant and local union affairs.

The new job-security programme builds on the guaranteed-income stream programme and the training and development programme introduced in the 1982–4 contracts at Ford and GM, and on the supplementary unemployment benefits (SUB) programme. The combination of all these programmes provides a high degree of income security to autoworkers. These programmes, however, do not guarantee employment levels or protect auto workers from the declines in employment that will follow if the Big Three lose even more of their share of the domestic auto market. The critical determinant of future employment levels is the degree to which the 1984 settlement and other ongoing measures improve the competitive standing of the Big Three.

Some positive effects of industry competitiveness will result from the fact that the 1984 GM–UAW settlement avoided a major strike and seemed to cast a positive tone on labour–management relations. At the same time the wage increases provided in the 1984–7 settlement are unlikely to narrow the gap between US wage rates and those abroad. Furthermore, the structure of the pay increases included in the 1984 contract provides only small movement towards the creation of direct links between pay and company performance. Consequently, improvement in the competitive standing of the Big Three will depend heavily on the extent to which work-rule changes and new forms of work organization are adopted at the plant level, which both lower costs and increase the flexibility of the production process. Constrained by the existing bargaining structure which separates the national negotiation of pay from the local negotiation of work rules, however, the 1984 settlement provides no assurance of future work-rule change. Are the Big Three likely to succeed in making the kind of work-rule changes that are needed to improve their competitive standing? There are a number of key plants that shortly will provide indications of the likely future scope and success of work-rule and work-organization changes.

At GM, the extent of work-rule and work-organization change will be influenced strongly by how local contract negotiations are resolved at two new assembly plants. Since 1983 the Lake Orion (Pontiac, Michigan) and Wentzville (St. Louis) assembly plants have been operating with a team system which includes a single job classification for production workers and a pay-for-knowledge system. Under the terms of the GM–UAW national agreement, management has the right to set a new plant's first work rules, but then must negotiate a local contract with the local UAW bargaining unit once the new plant attains full-scale production. In the autumn of 1984 the Lake Orion and Wentzville plants began to negotiate their first local agreements and at both plants the local union was expressing a high degree of resistance to the team and pay-for-knowledge systems. These plants are critical because they test GM's ability to spread the use of team systems, heretofore primarily used in parts plants, to assembly plants, which traditionally have had more difficult labour–management relations and where the threat of job loss to outsourcing is less severe.

Additional indications of the likely future scope of work-rule and work-organization reform will come from those plants where QWL programmes have expanded to the point that they address basic productivity concerns. There evidence will surface regarding whether labour and management have been able to develop mechanisms linking worker-participation and collective-bargaining processes.

GM's decision regarding the future production of small cars in the United States also will be made shortly and have significant impacts on the course of labour-relations reforms. In 1983, GM created the Saturn project to debate and potentially plan the production of a small car in the United States. GM's intent was to use the Saturn project as a mechanism to redesign production and labour relations so as to enable cost-competitive domestic production of a small car. The Saturn project is noteworthy because it involves union and worker representatives in the planning stage of technology and car design. Workers and union representatives participating in the project have visited Japanese, team, and non-union plants in the USA in an effort to learn about new forms of labour relations and work organization. As part of the 1984–7 GM–UAW contract, GM stated an intent to keep the Saturn project in the United States.[34] Exactly what kind of car and labour-relations practices are included in the eventual Saturn production set-up remains to be decided.

Like the new assembly plants, the Saturn project illustrates that the most far-reaching innovations in labour relations are being introduced in cases where new business is at stake. This represents the same pattern revealed in the course of local work-rule bargaining during the 1979 to 1983 sales downturn; workers' willingness to adjust work rules more readily where these changes explicitly guarantee greater employment. The Big Three continue to face many difficulties in introducing labour-relations innovations in such sites. Yet even if they are able to do so, labour and management still will face the even more difficult task of spreading innovative labour relations practices to existing plants where the connection between labour relations and employment security is less explicit.

SUMMARY

The future course of auto labour relations will be affected by economic developments in the world auto industry. At this point it appears that the economic environment will produce moderate pressure for cost reduction, thus encouraging the parties to choose either a status quo or a cooperative path. If economic pressures turn extreme, then it is more likely that extensive outsourcing or a non-union strategy would be chosen, either of which is likely to induce significant labour–management conflict. Even in the face of the pressures exerted by environmental factors, it should be remembered that the history of auto bargaining shows that labour and management retain a significant degree of choice regarding the direction of labour relations.

Recent events do not reveal consistent movement along one path or another. On the one hand there are some signs of extensive innovation in shop-floor labour relations, particularly in GM's operating team plants. At the same time, the inclination to retain the traditional system and follow the status-quo path appears to be strong, a desire most clearly illustrated by the union's efforts to retain formula wage increases and maintain a separation between worker participation programmes and collective-bargaining processes.

The interconnections and logic of labour relations limit the range of choices available as future options. In the light of those limits, whether they choose the cooperative path or not, labour and management need to develop a clear vision of the path they want, and consistent policies to move auto labour relations along it.

NOTES

1 Related discussions of US auto collective bargaining are in H. C. Katz, *Shifting Gears: Changing Labor Relations in the U.S. Auto Industry* (Cambridge, Mass., 1985); *idem*, 'The U.S. Automobile Collective Bargaining System in Transition', *British Journal of Industrial Relations* 22, no. 2 (July 1984), pp. 205-17.

2 The history of wage setting in the US auto industry is discussed in more detail in F. H. Harbison, 'The General Motors–United Auto Workers Agreement of 1950', *Journal of Political Economy* 58, no. 5 (1950), pp. 397-411; M. W. Reder, 'The Significance of the 1948 General Motors Agreement', *Review of Economics and Statistics* 31, no. 1 (1949), pp. 7-14; A. M. Ross, 'The General Motors Wage Agreement of 1948', *Review of Economics and Statistics* 31, no. 1 (1949), pp. 1-7.

3 There was a 110-day strike at GM in 1945-6 and a 103-day strike at Chrysler in 1950 prior to the adoption of long-term contracts that include the use of the wage formulas. Note, Ford and Chrysler did not use wage formulas until contracts signed in 1950.

4 A chronology of postwar bargaining in the US auto industry is in Bureau of National Affairs, 'Collective Bargaining Negotiations and Contracts: Wage Patterns' (Washington DC, various years) and Bureau of Labor Statistics, 'Wage Chronology – General Motors Corporation, 1939-68, Bulletin 1532, US Department of Labor (Washington DC, 1969).

5 H. M. Levinson, 'Pattern Bargaining: A Case Study of the Automobile Workers', *Quarterly Journal of Economics* 74, no. 2 (1960), pp. 296-317.

6 H. C. Katz and C. F. Sabel, 'Wage Rules: A Theory of Wage Determination', paper presented at the Annual Meeting of the American Economic Association, Atlanta, Georgia, 1979.

7 In the collective bargaining agreements reached between 1948 and 1979, the UAW also acted as an innovative force within US collective bargaining regarding fringe benefits. The major advances included supplementary unemployment benefits, '30 and out' pensions, an extensive medical plan that includes dental

and vision coverage, and nine paid personal holidays per year on top of normal holiday and vacation days. Although it is difficult to provide a full assessment of the costs of thse fringe benefits, one estimate is that total hourly compensation costs to GM for an assembler rose from $1.62 in 1948 to $20.17 in 1981 (322% after adjustment for increases in the consumer price index).

8   L. Ulman, 'Connective Bargaining and Competitive Bargaining', *Scottish Journal of Political Economy* 21 no. 2 (1974), p. 98.

9   R. M. MacDonald, *Collective Bargaining in the Auto Industry* (New Haven, 1963).

10 J. W. Kuhn, *Bargaining in Grievance Settlements* (New York, 1961).

11 Bureau of Labor Statistics, 'Collective Bargaining in the Motor Vehicle and Equipment Industry', Report 574, US Department of Labor (Washington DC, 1979).

12 In addition to chapter 5 in this volume, see N. Lichtenstein, 'Auto Worker Militancy and the Structure of Factory Life, 1937-55', *Journal of American History* 67, no. 2 (1980), pp. 335-53; *idem, Labor's War at Home – The CIO in World War II* (Cambridge, 1982).

13 A. Weber, introduction to A. Weber (ed.), *The Structure of Collective Bargaining* (New York, 1961).

14 Job-control unionism is not synonymous with business unionism. The latter refers to the political philosophy of the labour movement. There are labour movements such as the Japanese that could be characterized as business unionist but not job-control oriented.

15 M. J. Piore, 'American Labor and the Industrial Crisis', *Challenge* 25, no. 2 (March–April 1982), pp. 5–11.

16 V. G. Reuther, *The Brothers Reuther* (Boston, 1976), pp. 248–56; F. H. Harbison and R. Dubin, *Patterns of Union–Management Relations* (Chicago, 1947).

17 Harbison and Dubin, *Patterns*, pp. 48–88.

18 Lichtenstein, 'Auto Worker Militancy'.

19 Harbison, 'GM–UAW Agreement'.

20 The employment figures are for SIC 371 from Bureau of Labor Statistics, 'Employment and Earnings', US Department of Labor (Washington DC, various years).

21 These new agreements also introduced a new job-security programme and lifetime employment experiments, and restricted plant closings. For more details see Katz, *Shifting Gears*.

22 From 1948 to 1978, employment of production workers in the auto industry increased from 632,000 to 760,000. Note, the recent rise in the share of import sales implies that potential employment losses from rigid pattern-following are now greater than in earlier periods when primarily domestic inter-company sales movements were at issue.

23 These observations and those that follow are derived from plant-level interviews conducted with company and union officials by the author.

24 National Ford Department, UAW, *Letters of Understanding between the UAW and the Ford Motor Company*, covering agreements dated 18 February 1982, p. 39.

25 I. Bluestone, 'How Quality of Worklife Projects Work for the United Auto Workers', *Monthly Labor Review* 103, no. 7 (1980), pp. 39–41.

26 Evaluation of the impact of these worker-involvement programmes on plant-level industrial relations and economic performance is provided in H. C. Katz,

T. A. Kochan and K. R. Gobeille, 'Industrial Relations, Economic Performance and QWL Programs', *Industrial and Labor Relations Review* 37 no. 1 (October 1983), pp. 3–17.

27   The team system and some of the problems associated with its implementation are discussed in more detail in Katz, *Shifting Gears*, ch. 4.

28   A. Altshuler et al., *The Future of the Automobile* (Cambridge, Mass., 1984).

29   For more on this subject, see Katz, *Shifting Gears*, ch. 6.

30   W. Streeck and A. Hoff, 'Industrial Relations in the German Automobile Industry: Developments in the 1970s', in W. Streeck and A. Hoff (eds.), *Industrial Relations in the World Automobile Industry – the Experience of the 1970s*, (Berlin, 1982).

31   'Executive Pay: The Top Earners', *Business Week*, 7 May 1984, pp. 88–116.

32   Wages also differ across the Big Three because Chrysler's 1983–5 wage contract with the UAW provides somewhat lower hourly wage rates.

33   The 1984–7 contract also raises pension benefits and provides lump-sum payments to some workers who retire with less than 30 years' service. By creating job openings by increasing retirement rates these provisions may further limit the companies' expenses under the new job-security programme. The Ford–UAW 1984 agreement also includes a moratorium on plant closings.

34   The GM–UAW 1984 settlement included two other commitments that also might lead to the creation of new jobs for displaced auto workers. GM management pledged to devote 500 million dollars to new enterprises into which displaced auto workers could be transferred and promised to consult with the union regarding outsourcing, although the specific consequences of these pledges remain unclear.

13

Labour-Relations Strategy
At BL Cars
Paul Willman

The events at BL Cars during the latter part of the 1970s aroused a considerable amount of both popular and academic interest. The popular interest – which included the professional interest of those practically involved in labour relations – focused upon the successes achieved by the company's management in confrontation with trade unions during Michael Edwardes's period at the company. During this period, when as Managing Director he became visibly involved in industrial relations, it became fashionable to associate developments there with his idiosyncratic managerial style, a fashion perhaps assisted by his own predisposition to regard that period of the company's history largely as a series of zero-sum games resulting in his 'victories' over employee representatives and recalcitrant elements of BL management.[1] This was, then, fundamentally an interest in managerial tactics and style.

The academic interest took the same subject-matter as the starting point for discussion of a number of more general issues – such as the role of government in the reform of industrial relations, the changing role of shop stewards, and the impact and pitfalls of participation. However, perhaps the most general issue of all concerned the characterization of a strategic dimension to the process of change in industrial relations.

Lewchuk, in particular has contrasted the labour-relations strategies of Ford and the indigenous UK car companies over a long period of time: in the events at BL during the late 1970s he identifies 'a belated attempt to move towards a Fordist managerial system'.[2] This proposition is of some interest. It implies that, just as the earlier Ryder plan for BL's recovery contained a labour-relations strategy, so one lay implicit in the later Edwardes Recovery Plan. On this reading, the confrontations of the 1970s represented the working out of a planned approach to labour relations rather than giving evidence merely of astute political judgement. Moreover, since the recovery plan looked to the launch of a new product range, and thus beyond the departure of Edwardes himself, a parallel labour-relations strategy would similarly extend and develop. However, the proposition goes beyond the suggestion that a strategy existed to the suggestion that it was Fordist in nature: Lewchuk bases this suggestion on, firstly, the move to

305

measured daywork at BL in the early 1970s and, secondly, the reestablishment of managerial control in 1980.

In this paper, I shall explore the evidence for the existence of a labour-relations strategy, and examine the extent to which it was coterminous with the Edwardes period of the company's history and Fordist in nature. I shall seek to argue that such a strategy does exist, but that to characterize it as pure Fordism is both misleading and relatively unhelpful. The structure is as follows. The next section provides a brief account of events at BL since the Ryder Report and outlines both the Ryder and Edwardes corporate strategies. The following section examines the implications of these corporate strategies for an industrial-relations strategy. A further section, following the division suggested by Gospel,[3] looks at developments in work organization, trade-union relations and individual effort bargains. Another section discusses the extent to which these elements comprise a strategy, and the extent to which it is Fordist in nature. The final section assesses likely developments in labour relations in future. Throughout, I shall focus rather more on Austin Rover, the volume car division of BL Cars, than on other elements, such as Unipart and Jaguar (now privatized).

CORPORATE STRATEGY 1975–84

British Leyland Motor Corporation had been formed in 1968 in the last of the series of defensive mergers between UK car producers which had characterized the postwar scene. The dynamics and consequences of this final merger have been the subject of substantial interest: suffice it to say here that the merger served primarily to concentrate the target of attack for those concerned to voice the litany of faults of the British car industry. Capital investment was low, as was productivity in comparison with overseas competitors. Despite mergers, the failure to rationalize productive capacity led to the failure to achieve minimally efficient economies of scale. The product range was poor, as were product quality and reliability. The industry was seen as having poor labour relations: in particular, the strike record was bad. Most fundamentally, the quality of management in the industry was poor.[4]

Whether all of these criticisms were justified or not, as table 13.1 shows, the investment record and profit performance of the company in the early 1970s was poor. Escalating losses after the 1973 oil crisis led to effective bankruptcy and the company survived only through a move into public ownership, the government purchasing the bulk of the existing equity in 1975 after accepting a plan for the survival of British Leyland (as it now became) presented in the Ryder Report.[5]

The particular interest of the Ryder Report here is that it presented a coherent labour-relations policy as part of the strategy for corporate survival. Included in plans for the development of a new product range, production rationalization and management reorganization were specific

Table 13.1 British Leyland Performance 1968–83

Year	Vehicles sold (thousands)	Profit after tax (millions of pounds)	Employees (thousands)	Productivity (vehicles per employee)	Capital per employee*	Investment per unit of output*
1968	1,050	20.3	188	5.6	100	100
1969	1,083	20.8	196	5.5	84	84.9
1970	984	2.3	200	4.9	101.2	114.4
1971	1,057	18.4	194	5.4	72	73.5
1972	1,127	21.1	191	5.9	56.9	53.7
1973	1,161	27.9	204	5.7	72.6	71.1
1974	1,020	(6.7)	208	4.9	106.1	120.4
1975	845	(63.2)	191	4.4	79.2	99.8
1976	981	46.5	183	5.4	87.7	91.1
1977	785	(5)	195	4	92.7	130.3
1978	797	(10.9)	192	4.2	136.4	183.2
1979	693	(118.5)	177	3.9	144.7	205.9
1980	587	(390.7)	157	3.7	151.6	226.1
1981	525	(339.2)	126	4.2	119.5	159.9
1982	519	(229.5)	108	4.8	146.9	149.4
1983	564	(74.3)	103	5.5	158.7	161.6

Note* index at 1968 prices; 1968 = 100.
Source: Company Reports.

suggestions for the reform of payment systems and collective bargaining and the introduction of industrial democracy. The concern with payment systems arose because of the perceived failure of the move to measured daywork in the period 1971–3: as table 13.1 shows, an essentially unproductive expansion of employment had followed the change which had offset any efficiency consequences. The principle recommendation on collective bargaining was the specific suggestion that the number of bargaining units be reduced. In 1976, the 34 plants of BL Cars contained 58 hourly-paid bargaining units with renewal dates in nine different months of the year: BL as a whole contained 246.[6]

The pattern of competitive bargaining generated by this structure was seen to contribute substantially to the company's poor strike record. The recommendation on industrial democracy consisted of a proposal for a thoroughgoing participative structure, based on joint management committees at plant, divisional and corporate levels. But the Report rejected trade-union proposals for worker representation on the Board, and indeed the general purpose of the scheme was economic, i.e. 'to increase the effectiveness of the operation of Leyland cars to the mutual benefit of all its employees'.[7]

The Ryder strategy itself grew out of previous initiatives. The concern to devise a labour-relations strategy appropriate to the rationalization of production within BL goes back as far as the original merger of the car companies into BLMC in 1968. In addition to proposing a transition from piecework to measured daywork which itself was concerned with the reduction of shop-steward influence on the shop floor, the strategy developed by 1970 included proposals for the reform of collective bargaining, a new range of consultative methods and a concern to establish new forms of direct communication with employees, perhaps including the use of ballots.[8] In the early 1970s this strategy had fallen into disrepair with the evident failure of payment-system reform to 'solve' the productivity problem. By 1975, the strategy needed to be presented anew.

The problem with the Ryder labour-relations strategy stemmed broadly from the failure of the corporate strategy which embraced it. Between 1977 and 1979 the company operated a participation scheme and planned to centralize collective bargaining against a background of mounting losses and falling output (see table 13.1); employment too began to fall steeply from 1978, and the company closed one of its Speke plants. This set up substantial tensions. While the company during this period focused mainly on getting capital invested, rationalizing products and production and reorganizing management structure, there was a drastic loss of market share – from 25 per cent in 1977 to below 20 per cent in 1979.[9]

The end of the Ryder approach to labour relations came with the substitution of the Edwardes Recovery Plan for the Ryder corporate strategy. Whereas the Ryder Plan had been essentially expansionist, projecting output volumes of 900,000 units and a market share of 33 per cent by 1980, the Edwardes Plan called for a programme of capacity reduction involving the loss of 25,000 jobs and the closure or contraction of 13 factories. The immediate stimuli for the change included a second energy crisis and an extremely strong pound which hit the company's exports, as well as the wider impact of the 1979 road haulage and engineering disputes. However, the essence of the problem – the absence of new models and of rationalized productive capacity – would have been familiar to the Ryder Committee.

The Edwardes contraction plans were to be the precursor of a 'product led recovery' which was projected to lead to an output of 950,000 units per year 'during the 1980s'.[10] Hence, as table 13.1 shows, the period 1979–82 was one during which the capital intensity of operations increased markedly, even though employment and output both contracted. The success of the strategy depended upon the occurrence of a turning point in performance, and the 1983 figures show improved productivity and output, some slowing down in the rate of job loss and a less lamentable profit performance; cars operations actually made a small profit. It is too early to give a more definite view of the prospects for the company's survival.

Currently, the corporate plan for the Austin Rover volume cars business contains a number of specific targets: these include a minimum 15 per cent return on assets and a 20 per cent UK market share; at 1982 UK sales volumes, this implied UK sales of 328,000.[11] Other goals include the continuing improvement of productivity, product quality and production technology, and the further establishment of collaborative arrangements such as those currently operating with Honda and VW.[12] Whereas in the Ryder era corporate and labour-relations strategies were explicitly linked, from 1979 onwards, one must establish the links between the two. Two problems arise here. The first is the isolation of necessary rather than contingent links: to establish which parts of the labour-relations strategy necessarily followed from corporate strategy and which did not. As Thurley and Wood note, 'many aspects of personnel policy and industrial relations policy may be "neutral" in relation to the precise business strategy followed and compromise over such policies does not necessarily compromise the strategy itself.'[13] The second, to some extent related, is to distinguish strategy from tactics: this presupposes certain core elements of policy which may be distinguished from particular devices designed to achieve lesser ends. Such distinctions are particularly important for an analysis of BL from 1979 onwards since, taken on its own terms, the Edwardes Recovery Plan proposed a period of contraction during which concerns with divestment and cost minimization would be important, followed by a period of recovery in which new product launch and productivity were the main issue. The implication follows that there may have been several phases in the labour-relations strategy. I shall explore this possibility in the next section.

LABOUR PRODUCTIVITY AND THE PRODUCT-LED RECOVERY

From the discussion of the previous section, it is clear that two broad strategic goals persist throughout the Ryder and Edwardes periods: the launch

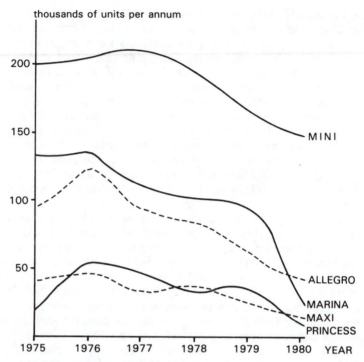

Figure 13.1   Production of Selected BL Models 1975–80
Source: Calculated from K. Williams et al., *Why are the British Bad at Manufacturing?*
(London, 1983), pp. 270–3.

of a new model range and the raising of labour productivity. The issues
involved here can be presented very simply with the aid of company data.
Figure 13.1 gives production totals for the five main BL models from
1975–80: taking these as a surrogate of sales it is clear that all were in the
final phase of the product life cycle, and that the entire model range was
dating at once.[14] The product-led recovery required the launch not of one
or two cars but of a whole model range. As table 13.1 shows, the
productivity figures for BL were alarmingly low: contemporary figures for
US or Japanese producers would show in excess of 20 cars per man-year.
But perhaps more alarming was the nature of the factors underlying low
productivity: these had to do not only with awkward car design, poor
equipment layout and low levels of technology in the late 1970s but also
with poor logistics and labour organization.

Figure 13.2 allows this point to be elaborated. It presents a number of
productivity comparisons made by BL in the late 1970s with similar Ford
models in the UK and FRG. Differences in standard hours per car are
generated by the design and the production technology: the lower box shows
that Ford models tended to be produced with rather less labour time.

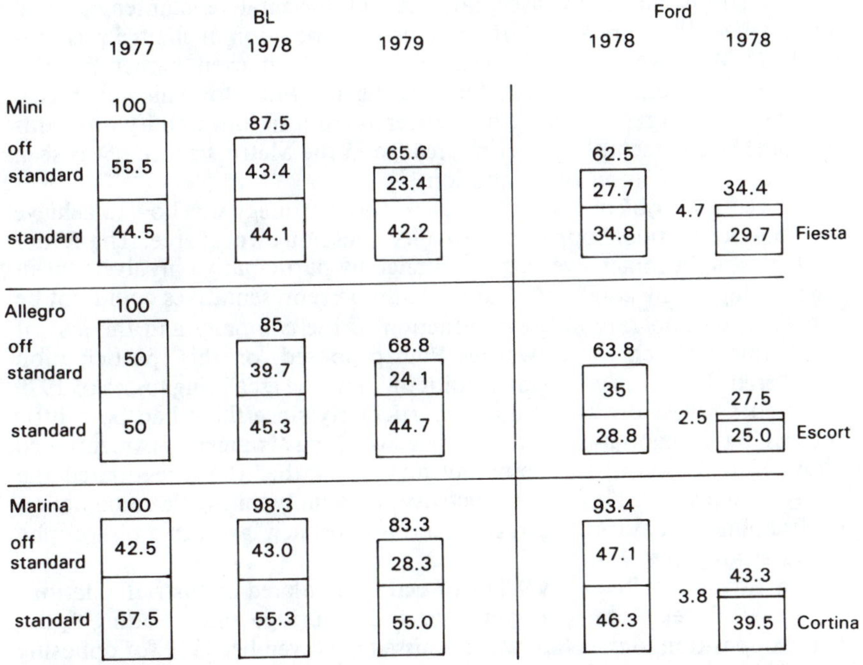

Figure 13.2   Productivity Comparisons Ford and BL 1978

Notes: Includes press shop, body-in-white, paint, trim, final assembly and preparation for sales. Base is 1977 = 100%. Comparison of 1977 base levels is Mini = 100, Allegro = 125%, Marina = 94%. For illustration, the LC8 projected man hours figure in 1977 was 54.4% of that of the Mini.

Source: P. Willman and G. Winch, *Innovation and Management Control: Labour Relations at BL Cars* (Cambridge, 1984).

However, the greatest discrepancies in 1978 tended to be in off-standard hours comparisons, particularly with Ford-Germany. Off-standard hours are generated by mechanical breakdown, materials shortage and rectification work. However, in BL at that stage, a greater source of such lost time lay in disputes, absenteeism, slow workpace and early finishing.[15]

The new product strategy thus implied some reform of the system of labour utilization. This became clear at the planning stage of the first new model, the Metro, when the decision was made to invest heavily in new technology in order to 'maximize automation opportunities and reduce direct man hours per car to the lowest level possible'. As early as 1976, the planners sought levels of efficiency which would require substantial changes in current working practices involving 'greater flexibility, multi trade supervision, elimination of the stint system of working, eliminating late starts and early finishing, eliminating restrictive practices, the acceptance of some jobs currently done by indirect workers being carried out by direct workers (e.g. tool adjustments) the acceptance of full preventative maintenance and many others.'[16] A great deal of workforce cooperation in change was thus implied. Moreover such cooperation achieved an even higher priority because of the concern with product *quality*. The Mini, for which the Metro was the planned replacement, had suffered from serious quality problems in paint, body assembly and trim areas, and the Metro's success was seen to be dependent upon their solution.[17]

The central problem for the labour-relations strategy was how to achieve a highly productive, cooperative quality-conscious workforce. The Ryder strategy sought to achieve this sea change by participative involvement in the running of the company. But trade-union representatives could not be expected to cooperate in the contraction of the company and the loss of employment which the Edwardes Plan proposed: on this, participation foundered. From the company's point of view, the escalating losses of 1979 required a rather drastic solution, particularly since there had been little success in the negotiation of the changed working arrangements mentioned above.[18] In practice, the company imposed rather than negotiated the changes, and secured higher productivity and quality through a combination of discipline and automation. Behind this approach lay both a philosophy and a strategy.

The Edwardes Recovery Plan directly stimulated industrial relations problems. Derek Robinson, convenor at Longbridge and a leading figure in the opposition to the plan, was dismissed in November 1979 for opposing the Edwardes plan in print. In December 1979, a document entitled 'Management in BL' circulated to managers at all levels in the company. The document stated that 'It is managers who have the responsibility for managing, leading and motivating employees and for communicating on company matters . . . shop stewards have the right to represent and to communicate trade union information to their members at the workplace but only within the rules and procedures jointly established.'[19] In a clear statement of the 'agitator' theory of conflict the document pointed to 'the small minority who would like to see BL fail', but committed the company to 'acknowledge and respect constitutional trade unionism wherever it operates within the company'.

The company's willingness to act upon this philosophy was not restricted to the Robinson dismissal. A comprehensive package for changing working practices was circulating from autumn 1979 onwards, and was eventually imposed in April 1980: it was circulated to employees as a 'Blue Newspaper'. The document was explicitly intended to 'supersede all other agreements, customs and practices' and it finally established centralized bargaining, a job-evaluated pay structure and an incentive scheme. However, the key parts of the Blue Newspaper were designed to re-establish managerial control on the shop floor.

The key item was the removal of 'mutuality' – the requirement that the company reach agreement with stewards about change before implementation. Prior to the Blue Newspaper, most plant procedures had contained the status quo clause of the 1976 Engineering Employers' Federation/Confederation of Shipbuilding and Engineering Unions (EEF-CSEU) agreement, which ran: 'It is agreed that, in the event of any disagreement arising which cannot be disposed of, then whatever practice or agreement existed prior to the difference shall continue to operate pending a settlement, or until the agreed procedure has been exhausted.' The two most important areas of application were work allocation and working pace. In both of these areas, change was radical. The Blue Newspaper established the company's right to use all recognized industrial engineering techniques at all times to establish workspeeds and manning levels: complaints were to be processed through a grievance procedure, but no status quo clause operated. For negotiated redeployment of labour, the document substituted the following: 'any employee may be called upon to work in any part of his employing plant and/or to carry out any grade or category of work within the limits of his abilities and experience, with training if necessary.' Whereas previously such changes would have required negotiations with stewards, after the Blue Newspaper they were to follow from management decisions.

The available evidence suggests that the new regime was established quite quickly, although not without resistance in some plants.[20] As I have noted elsewhere, the company experienced a number of large disputes over issues of workpace and effort levels, first at Longbridge then at Cowley, associated with the launching of new models. As table 13.2, listing the major stoppages in BL Cars between 1980–3 shows, similar issues tended to recur. Large disputes at Longbridge accounted for 20.5 per cent of working days lost in motor vehicles as a whole in 1980, and 25.7 per cent in 1981: those at Cowley accounted for 24 per cent in 1983.

The events of 1979–80 have been popularly characterized as Edwardes's victory over the trade unions. However, as this section implies, this is fundamentally misleading in two respects. In the first place, it was not wholly

Table 13.2 Strikes at BL 1980–3

Date	Working days Lost	Issue	Location
April 1980	239,100	New working practices	Several plants
April 1980	26,900	'Togging up' dispute	Longbridge
June 1980	26,800	Tea break dispute	Longbridge
November 1980	14,200	Seat building 'riot'	Longbridge
December 1980	21,500	Dismissal of 'riot' leaders	Longbridge
May 1981	44,500	Production targets	Longbridge
November 1981	87,200	Pay dispute	All areas
November 1981	148,300	Rest allowances	Longbridge
December 1982	14,100	'Bad workmanship' dispute	Cowley
March 1983	6,200	Job Assignments	Cowley
March 1983	125,700	Early Finishing dispute	Cowley

Source: Department of Employment Gazette, 1980–3.

attributable to Edwardes's approach. The company's pursuit of high productivity and high quality on new product lines through automation and the reform of working practices had been established as early as 1976 in the planning stages of the Metro project: the concern to remove mutuality goes back at least as far as the 1968 merger, and may, according to Turner et al., go back even further. They suggest that progressive automation of the manufacturing process generated pressures for high-capacity utilization which are fundamentally inconsistent with the practice of fractional bargaining.[21] The peculiar emphasis on management rights and shop-floor discipline pervading Austin Rover in the early 1980s may have owed more to a particular style of management than to the demands either of the product market or the technical system of production, but it is difficult to reconcile shop-floor autonomy and local bargaining with the perceived productivity requirement set by competitive standards. The style was that of Edwardes, but the strategy had deeper roots.

The second misconception is that the strategy was anti-trade-union or that some victory over unions was involved. In the first place, it is important to stress that the Blue Newspaper involved simultaneously an attack on shop-steward organization in BL while reaffirming the company's commitment to what it termed 'constitutional' trade unionism, identified by adherence to an institutionalized separation between in-plant consultation and corporate-level collective bargaining. It is perhaps best seen as an attempt to mould trade-union organization to fit the radically restricted scope of collective bargaining. As a consequence – and this leads to a discussion of the development of the strategy – BL sought, after the imposition of change, to re-establish procedural arrangements with the unions.

The form of such arrangements is of considerable interest. The new procedure agreement, signed in April 1982, did not simply set out to write a constitutional basis for constitutional unionism. It affirmed the company's commitment to trade-union membership for hourly-rated employees and established check-off arrangements on a company-wide basis. Moreover, it specified the duties and rights of shop stewards in some detail: except when carrying out union duties, the steward shall 'in all other respects conform to the same conditions of employment as other employees': permission of the appropriate supervisor is required before a steward leaves his or her place of work; facilities such as telephones, time off with pay and the possibility of full-time shop stewards are also included. However, the agreement also reintroduced the idea of consultation: after the confrontational phase of 1979–80, the company sought to secure workforce cooperation by manifesting its commitment to *a particular form* of unionism. The consultative arrangements were intended to secure 'the provision and discussion of relevant information so that the views of the Unions may be taken into account in the management decision making process'. This was seen as important because 'Employees and their union representatives have a major contribution to make to the success of the business. To make the most effective contribution, they need to know and understand the main facts concerning the performance and plans of the Company.'[22] This, of course, was a similar logic to that supporting the previous Ryder participation scheme; however this was to be consultation rather than joint decision-making. Committees were to be established at both corporate and plant levels. At both, they were to 'build upon established collective-bargaining machinery' and to involve union representatives.

The two phases of the Edwardes Plan thus had counterparts in the labour-relations area: contraction, and the laying of the groundwork seen as necessary for the new product launch bred confrontation and the imposition of change, while the product-led recovery itself required a cooperative workforce producing high-quality output, for which a commitment to a more open labour-management style was seen as appropriate. These phases were not discrete: current labour-management practice in Austin Rover is an inconsistent amalgam of the disciplinary practices seen as necessary for high productivity and cost minimization and the employee-involvement exercises seen as necessary for high-quality output. I shall have more to say about these incompatible elements below.

Edwardes himself saw the establishment of the 'right to manage' as the '*sine qua non* of survival';[23] in 1983 the chief executive of Cars Division remarked that the labour-relations strategy underlay the company's improved performance. The strategy itself has, on several indicators, been relatively successful. The company lost less than 1 per cent of working time through disputes in 1983, compared with 5.1 per cent in 1979, while productivity has risen substantially: a recent survey suggested that Longbridge has the highest productivity of any plant in Europe.[24] However, it is important to emphasize that the strategy of firm discipline was only one possible solution to the problems of product range and productivity identified by Ryder. It is difficult to avoid the conclusion that mutuality would have to disappear to secure targeted productivity levels but the goal of a productive and cooperative workforce is conventionally assumed to be achieved by a rather greater reliance on consultation and negotiation than was in existence in 1979–80. It may well be that the rapid deterioration of the financial position in autumn 1979 effectively obliterated other options, but it needs to be stated that the labour-relations strategy, while bearing a clear relation to corporate strategy since 1979, was not the only one available in the circumstances. In fact, as the next section will show, it has a certain instability.

WORK ORGANIZATION, INDUSTRIAL RELATIONS AND THE
EFFORT BARGAIN

The purpose of this section is to demonstrate that, in each of these three areas, the company is pursuing contradictory goals. Because of inconsistencies in the labour strategy, labour-relations practice is effectively a balancing act, involving the possibility of expensive and explosive conflict. I shall look at each area in turn.

The organization of work

The inconsistencies within BL's approach perhaps emerge most clearly in the preferred pattern of work allocation and organization. Prior to April 1980, in most of the major plants of BL Cars, these matters were subject to mutuality: afterwards, they were to be established unilaterally on the basis of industrial-engineering standards. Although automated body-assembly techniques involve some changes to both direct and indirect job content, as I have argued elsewhere, this procedural change was, in the short term, far more significant than substantive ones.[25] However, as the deliberations of the planners quoted above illustrate, a great deal was required from employees which could not be secured merely through the enforcement of tight work standards. In the terms used by Offe, the new product strategy implied not only the avoidance of 'preventative' negative influences on the production process: it required a more positive 'initiatory' influence, particularly in the area of quality.[26] This can perhaps best be illustrated by discussing the idea of production teams.

The central principle of the team concept is the organization of operations within a given production zone around a foreman. All resources required for production within the zone came under the foreman, and responsibility for output lies with him. Under the foreman, a team structure as depicted in figure 13.3 operates on most of the new product lines. Within the teams, there is little demarcation between jobs, and a certain amount of job rotation. Teams are responsible for rectification work and the performance of routine maintenance tasks. As well as being a unit of production, the team is also a unit of accountability and, more significantly, the zone within which the team operates is the employee's unit of attachment to the company. 'The concept is designed to ensure that problems within a zone are discussed and resolved within the zone. It is therefore inevitable that the zone will become more and more a focal point of communication to and involvement with employees.'[27] The logic of teamwork is of course the pursuit of productive efficiency. The zone concept maximizes labour flexibility, helps prevent downtime of expensive capital equipment and provides a framework for measuring labour input. However, the teams themselves lack autonomy: they are hierarchical in nature, built around the disciplinary function of the foreman. It is here that several problems arise since foremen must enforce high work rates *and* secure cooperation.

These problems periodically emerge in the form of disputes; some of them quite large. Some, such as that at Cowley in November 1982 and Longbridge in May 1984 explicitly involve problems between workers and individual supervisors over the enforcement of discipline or working standards. Others, particularly smaller ones, involve the degree of mobility or flexibility required: on the company's own figures. 91.5 per cent of working days lost

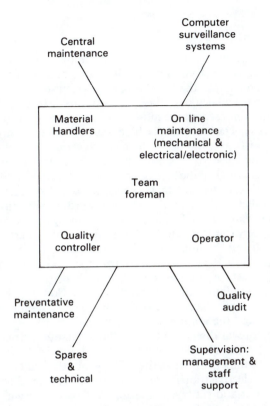

Figure 13.3   Structure of Production Teams at British Leyland
Source: Willman and Winch, *Innovation and Management Control*.

at Cowley Assembly plant in the first quarter of 1984 involved disputes over redeployment or new work assignments.[28] Both aspects featured in the resolution of the 'early finishing' dispute at Cowley. The joint inquiry into industrial relations at the plant set up in the aftermath of the dispute considered complaints from employees both about abuse from supervisors, and about the degree of mobility required. The committee recommended both that 'Senior management must ensure that the normal standards of management–employee relationships are observed in all circumstances', and that in future in the redeployment of labour 'subject to the over-riding operational requirement being met, management must take into account other factors including health, length of service, and age.'[29] Teams do not exist in all BL plants, and objections to supervisory practice and redeployment are almost certainly not confined to teamwork areas. But the team-concept does serve to illustrate the contradictions involved here between cooperation and enforcement. As I shall show below, very similar issues are involved in the involvement-security trade-off for individual employees.

Industrial relations

The principal issue in relations with trade unions concerns the latters'
observance of 'constitutional' activity. It will be recalled firstly, that this
involved close control over the activities of shop stewards and the restriction
of bargaining, particularly over pay, to corporate-level negotiations, and
secondly that this represented the most substantial change from the position
prior to April 1980. The ambivalence here was between the company's desire
to control stewards and the desire to have stewards control employees.

After the imposition of the Blue Newspaper, steward numbers and
facilities were lessened at both Longbridge and Cowley, the two main
manufacturing locations: in fact events at both plants show rather
remarkable parallels. The assault on shop-steward organization effectively
began with the dismissal of Robinson at Longbridge in November 1979.
At Longbridge, between 1980 and 1982, the number of stewards halved from
about 800 to 400 and the number of full-time stewards was reduced from
eight to two. In April 1982, both the chairman and secretary of the works
committee were subject to disciplinary action because of their public
disapproval of company policy.[30] Similarly, at Cowley, withdrawal of
steward facilities took place in 1981–2. Five deputy senior stewards lost
full-time status, and the number of stewards fell. In 1981 the convenor at
the assembly plant was disciplined for calling an unauthorized meeting. In
November 1982 Alan Thornett, a steward and activist, was dismissed.[31]

Overall, the number of stewards fell. At both plants, the primary
mechanism was selective transfer of employees to new product lines where
facilities were poor and supervision close. At Cowley Assembly plant, by
autumn 1983 52 per cent of constituencies had no electoral nominees, and
very few elections needed to be held.[32] The stewards' role had been made
very difficult to perform: steward release from regular work had to be
authorized by the industrial relations department and the supervisors of
any zones involved.[33]

However, steward organization survived in most plants, not least because
the company's labour strategy required it:[34] at no time do managers appear
to have planned dealings with an unorganized workforce. But the
simultaneous experience of rapid change and a reduction in steward
availability caused problems. At Cowley in the first quarter of 1984 22 per
cent of disputes occurred over the unavailability of a steward. During one
of the larger stoppages of the period, the company complained both that
senior stewards appeared to have little control over sectional action and
that they could not secure a return to work.[35] An open letter in May 1984
from the plant director calls for an end to unconstitutional stoppages,
remarking that 'Often against the wishes and recommendations of the senior
stewards, small numbers of employees have stopped work and lost pay for
themselves . . . your officials and your PLC are fully in agreement with
the need to abide by . . . procedure.'[36] Several of these stoppages related

to problems generated by the structure of 'constitutional' union activity. The central element in the company's approach to the latter since 1980 has been to bargain on as few occasions as possible. The bonus scheme is non-negotiable, and the company operated a two-year pay deal to November 1984. As I have shown elsewhere, pay in the car industry generally has continued a long-term decline against national averages into the 1980s; between 1972 and 1982, average hourly earnings in the industry fell from 123.3 per cent to 103.2 per cent of the average for all industries and services.[37] Dissatisfaction with bonus earnings has been the source of periodic conflict particularly at Cowley, and clearly a regressive spiral of conflict can be easily set up under the present labour strategy: discontent over low bonus leads directly to strike activity, since no negotiation is possible, which further lowers bonus levels and raises discontent. As I shall show below, the system is vulnerable to the same sorts of tensions which affected the old decentralized bargaining system.

Effort bargains

The contradictions in the labour strategy are similarly evident in the area of individual renumeration and involvement. Although I have discussed discipline in the previous two sections, it goes without saying that a harsh disciplinary regime and frequent transfers create individual problems: the structure of industrial relations in any event prevents a collective response. But the major tension in this area is between the pure production-efficiency basis of the effort bargain and the attempt to secure employee involvement. The effort bargain is dominated by the bonus scheme, so it is best to begin with a brief account of its operation.

The scheme, which operates at plant level and is non-negotiable, was introduced as part of the Blue Newspaper package: in theory, it can account for up to £30 per week, which in 1983, was over 25 per cent of the top skilled basic rate. At its core, there are two calculations. The first calculates the *current efficiency* of the plant by the ratio

$$\frac{\text{actual hours clocked}}{\text{standard hours of work produced}}$$

The denominator in fact refers to a quantity of work rather than a time elapsed: it describes the volume produced per hour at standard effort, i.e. that assessed on a non-negotiable basis by industrial engineering techniques. The current efficiency then becomes the denominator in the calculation of the efficiency index, as follows:

$$\text{efficiency index} = \frac{\text{bonus threshold target}}{\text{current efficiency}}$$

The bonus threshold target at the outset was based on 1977 performance – it thus produced anomalies between plants. Subsequently individual plants transferred over to audited-plant status, wherein the bonus threshold was established by independent central industrial-engineering audit. When the above ratio exceeded 1, bonus became payable, on the basis of average performance over the previous four weeks.

A number of points need to be made here. The first, and most obvious is that there are two ways of increasing bonus earnings on this calculative basis: one is to increase output, the other is to cut manpower. Secondly, since it is plant-wide, and covers plants which are links in the production chain, it leaves the individual's bonus earnings vulnerable to the actions of others. Thirdly, it commits the company only to payment for cars sold (since the calculations are based on standard hours *shipped*) thus it does nothing to shield individuals from product-market fluctuations. All of these things introduce the potential for instability either of employment or of earnings.

In practice, the scheme operates very differently between plants: the situation is relatively complex and it is perhaps best to deal with the problem chronologically. Table 13.3 shows average bonus earnings for the three largest plants – Cowley Body, Cowley Assembly and Longbridge – for the first three years of the scheme. In terms of the (then) available maximum, bonus earnings were relatively low in the first year, rising relatively steadily to November 1983. Throughout, bonus earnings at Longbridge, where output is dominated by Metro production, have been higher than the average. The lower bonus performance of the Cowley plants is probably connected to the later launch of new models: whereas the Metro was launched in October 1980, the Maestro was not launched until April 1983 and the Montego in April 1984. The figures show also the sales success of Jaguar being transmitted through to earnings: however Unipart, despite its profitability, does not generally experience high bonus payments.

The table understates both increases in earnings and the implied efficiency improvements. The November 1982 annual agreement provided for the consolidation in both November 1982 and 1983 of £3.75 into basic rates, and for the raising of the efficiency index threshold above which bonus is earned to 1.101 and then 1.151. Consolidation thus allows for earnings

Table 13.3   Bonus Earnings, BL Cars 1980–3 (£)

Period	BL Cars Average	Unipart	Jaguar	Longbridge	Cowley Assembly	Cowley Body
November 1980–1	7.17	5.31	3.47	11.01	6.87	6.59
November 1981–2	16.80	9.96	16.68	20.08	12.66	17.21
November 1982–3	20.80	10.95	24.12	22.13	18.82	20.18

Notes: Years are November–November, i.e. between pay reviews; for explanation see text. Excludes bonus consolidation.
Source: company documents.

improvement but a given bonus level becomes harder to achieve. It is this aspect which led an official of the Transport and General Workers Union (TGWU) to refer to the scheme as 'a greasy pole': a BL manager referred to it as 'moving the goalposts back'.[38]

Employee remuneration is thus almost entirely dependent upon short-term plant efficiency. This did not necessarily lead to earnings instability *before* the move to audited-plant status (APS), since the three major Austin Rover plants, for example, overshot maximum bonus efficiency by variable amounts but always earned the non-APS maximum of £22.50: this was the situation at Longbridge from February to October 1982 and at Cowley Assembly from July 1982 to the early-finishing dispute in March 1983. However, earnings have been variable under APS. Figure 13.4 shows the clear seasonal pattern of bonus variation of the Longbridge plant in the pay-year 1982–3. The year was one in which levels of industrial conflict were quite low but industrial action in November and March exerted a downward effect on bonus levels.

I have argued elsewhere that the introduction of APS at Longbridge assisted the reduction of levels of conflict.[39] The plant was at the time highly productive, and a move to APS caused this to be reflected in earnings levels. However, the fall in July and August reflects bonus earnings and output: weekly bonus earnings in August were only 30 per cent of those of June. The workforce remains vulnerable to shifts in demand for different models in the very short term. Moreover, to this earnings-insecurity must be added employment- and job-insecurity. I have already dealt with the latter: short-notice transfer has been a source of grievances since April 1980 in a number of plants. But bonus improvements at Longbridge have also been associated with employment contraction. In the period since 1981, annual decreases in hourly paid employment in the plant have been of the order of 25, 6 and 8 per cent respectively.

This sits rather awkwardly with another aspect of labour-relations policy, namely employee involvement. The concern with direct communication of company plans, of course, goes back for a considerable time. Speaking of the period 1979–80 the (then) personnel director stressed the importance of the fact that 'every employee knew our side of the story at every stage.'[40] However, the zone system of working allowed a rather more systematic approach: monthly talk-ins, suggestion schemes and, at Jaguar, the introduction of quality circles all bear testimony to the concern to secure high-quality output through employee commitment. The employee's response to this of course depends on the extent to which it can be viewed as a credible performance. The company have argued that 'Employees have responded enthusiastically because they recognise that the Company has embarked upon a long term principled plan to improve the working lives of individual men and women.'[41] However, there have been no moves to support this through the establishment of long-term earnings- or employment-security schemes: despite the development of teamwork there has been no further move towards the development of internal labour

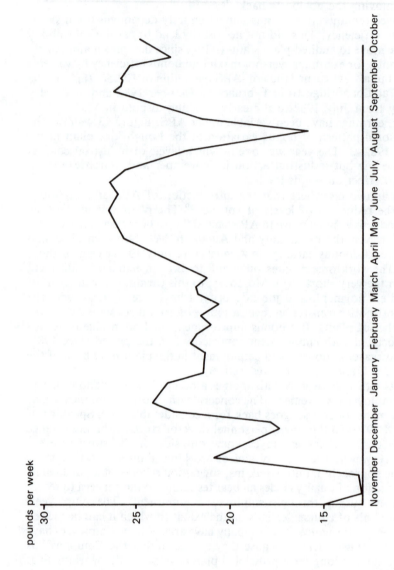

Figure 13.4   Bonus Variation at Longbridge November 1982–3
Source: company documents.

markets. It is difficult to resist the conclusion that, through the bonus and through the form of involvement without influence chosen by the company the concern is to attach the employee to the success and life cycle of the product rather than the provision of longer-term security and earnings stability.

The argument of this section is summarized in table 13.4. In each policy area, there exist contradictory objectives and instruments: since the threefold division into work organization, industrial relations and the effort bargain is for presentational convenience rather than a mirror of reality, it can be seen that the core problems are common to all three areas. On the one hand, the goals of productive efficiency can be served by Taylorian work organization, intensive supervision, output related payments and an attempt to keep trade-union activity out of the plants. On the other, the requirements of high-quality output and production uninterrupted by disputes imply individual employee involvement, some form of team organization and problem-solving activity by shop stewards. One might almost say that the two separate concepts of efficiency compete: the former is essentially an engineering conception which approaches labour relations with industrial-engineering techniques, the latter acknowledges the non-technically determined or 'x-efficiency' component of labour relations success.

FORDISM AND LABOUR-RELATIONS STRATEGY

Although these divergent goals are contained in a single approach to labour relations, this approach does have a clear strategic component and relationship to the business strategy. The latter has itself contained tensions, in the need rapidly to contract certain areas of activity while simultaneously investing at an unprecedented rate in new products. Thurley and Wood argue that the notion of a labour strategy is only credible where it relates to 'a

Table 13.4 Contradictions in BL's Labour Strategy

| | Objective | |
| | (Cooperation) | (Control) |
Element of Strategy	Quality	Output
Industrial relations	Development of consultative arrangements	Removal of restrictive practices; management control of shop floor
Work organization	Teamworking, zone concept	Assertion of discipline; use of industrial engineering
Effort bargains	Involvement programme	Non-negotiable bonus

clear and acceptable business strategy'.[42] The strategies pursued within BL Cars have been clear, but not acceptable to the unions involved.

However, the strategy does look very similar to that being pursued by Ford. The 'After Japan' campaign has a similar set of concerns: namely automation, process efficiency and high quality. As with BL, the approach sets minimum financial and marketing targets: in this case, they are a minimum return on sales of 5 per cent, and on assets of 10 per cent, a break-even point for plants at 60 per cent of capacity and a minimum European market share of 14 per cent. Along with this goes a concern to achieve the highest standards in performance and design of all volume car manufacturers. As with BL, Ford have pursued a combination of discipline and involvement. The tighter disciplinary code introduced in 1980 has been accompanied by a number of stoppages over disciplinary issues. Quality circles, introduced initially at Dagenham, but frustrated elsewhere by union opposition, were similarly seen as necessary in the context of increased flexibility requirements and routine maintenance responsibilities for production operatives. Moreover, the concern has also been to improve the productivity of labour time by reductions in rest allowances and the imposition of bell-to-bell working while reducing numbers employed.[43]

In short, and not for the first time, BL and Ford UK business and labour strategies bear considerable similarities: but is it then reasonable to say that BL pursue a Fordist labour-relations strategy? Fordism classically involves a combination of machine-pacing, close supervision, fragmentation of tasks and high day-rate payment.[44] In retooling both main plants between 1979 and 1983, particularly in the investment in new body-assembly techniques, the company has certainly become more capital intensive, but direct work has been machine-paced for a generation, hence the current technological innovations involve no fundamental change. Similarly, direct labour tasks have been fragmented for a considerable period, and although the intensity and pace of work – particularly in assembly – appears to have increased, the available evidence suggests that the proportion of direct workers falls substantially:[45] a smaller proportion of the workforce are thus subject to machine-pacing. The introduction of teamwork also does not appear to fit within the Fordist conception. However, perhaps the biggest discrepancy lies in the operation of the bonus system. Earnings in the car industry have fallen, relative to national averages, over the last decade, and guaranteed basic rates at BL are even lower.[46] The allegiance to the bonus scheme reflects both the company's misgivings about the measured day-work experience of the early 1970s and the longer-term commitment of UK car manufacturers to piece-rate systems. The Fordist exchange of high pay for intense degraded work is not occurring.

A more accurate description of the labour strategy appears in Braverman. His remarks that 'work itself is organised according to Taylorian principles, while personnel departments and academics have buried themselves with the selection, training, manipulation, pacification and adjustment of 'manpower' to suit the work processes so organised'[47] describe the sets of tension presented above. Fordism relies heavily on the role of financial and disciplinary factors in securing continuity of production, and takes no account of the other measures used to secure positive commitment. In fact, one can argue that Fordism is an implausible description of current labour-relations practice because it relies on an inadequate description of current business strategy. Fordism developed as a labour strategy appropriate to a single-product strategy, based on competitive success through cost-minimization and elimination pricing: the Model T did not compete on quality. However, as Abernathy and Wayne have shown, changes in demand for cars made this approach redundant: the inflexibility of production led to costly retooling in 1926 and a subsequent permanent loss of market leadership.[48] The successful strategy adopted by GM, and referred to by Black as 'Sloanism' involved the annual change of a differentiated product.[49] In the postwar period, just as BL has tended to imitate Ford UK, so in the USA both Ford and Chrysler have tended to imitate GM in both product and labour strategies.[50]

Under current product-market conditions, referred to by Abernathy et al. as a second phase of 'dematurity',[51] product and labour strategies are in a state of considerable flux. Rapid process and product innovation, substantial innovation and the impact of Japanese competition produce the conditions under which demand is extremely sensitive to changes both in product price and quality. A strategy such as that adopted by BL, which seems to minimize labour cost while maximizing all aspects of labour performance, is thus an explicable response to product-market demands: but it is not simply Fordism. The possibilities for its success depend upon the management of the tensions involved. These impose themselves upon individual employees and their representatives. Stewards are subjected to close control and withdrawal of facilities, but the expectation remains that they will control members' grievances. Employees are required to work at a more rapid pace and simultaneously to ensure high quality: their earnings do not only depend on their ability to do so but on the proclivity of others to cooperate. These sorts of problems have contributed to the difficulties of negotiating the new procedures and the generation of divergent expectations about labour's role and share in the future of the company.

NOTES

1   M. Edwardes, *Back From The Brink* (London, 1983).
2   W. Lewchuk, 'The British Motor Vehicle Industry, 1896–1982: The Roots of Decline', in B. Elbaum and W. Lazonick (eds.), *The Decline of the British Economy* (Oxford, 1986). See also *idem*, 'Fordism and British Motor Car Employees', in H. Gospel and C. Littler (eds.), *Managerial Strategies and Industrial Relations* (London, 1983); A. P. Black, 'Long Run Theories of Economic Growth, with Reference to the American and British Automobile Industries', London, Ph.D. thesis, 1981.

3 H. Gospel, 'Managerial Structures and Strategies', in Gospel and Littler, *Managerial Strategies*, pp. 1–24.

4 See House of Commons Expenditure Committee, Fourteenth Report, *The Motor Vehicle Industry* (London, 1975). For a review of the voluminous literature on BL during this period, see P. Willman and G. Winch, *Innovation and Management Control: Labour Relations at BL Cars* (Cambridge, 1985), pp. 17–43.

5 Ryder Committee, *British Leyland; The Next Decade* (London, 1975).

6 Willman and Winch, *Innovation and Management Control*, p. 70; Ryder, *British Leyland*, pp. 59, 16.

7 'Employee Participation in BL Cars', company document, 1975.

8 H. Totsuka: 'A Case-study on the Transition from Piecework to Measured Daywork in BLMC', *Annals of the Institute of Social Science*, no. 22 (Tokyo, 1981). P. W. Ford, 'Changing the Wage Payments System at a Car Factory', Warwick MA thesis, 1972.

9 Source: Society of Motor Manufacturers and Traders, Monthly Statistical Review.

10 Quoted from employee communication from company chairman, 10 September 1979.

11 Actual UK sales in 1982 were 281,600. The 1983 company accounts recorded Austin Rover UK sales at 346,600, exports at 91,000 and UK market share at 18 per cent.

12 'BL Limited', evidence to the Industry and Trade Committee, House of Commons (London, HMSO, 1982).

13 K. Thurley and S. Wood, 'Business Strategy and Industrial Relations Strategy, in K. Thurley and S. Wood (eds.), *Industrial Relations and Management Strategy* (Cambridge, 1983), p. 221.

14 K. Williams, J. Williams and D. Thomas: *Why are the British Bad at Manufacturing?* (London, 1983).

15 J. Hartley, *Management of Vehicle Production* (London 1981).

16 Both quotes are from company documents, 1976.

17 In these areas the percentage 'right first time' averaged 50 per cent on the Mini; targets for the Metro – achieved by 1981 – were 85 per cent RFT.

18 Willman and Winch, *Innovation and Management Control*, pp. 110–29.

19 This and subsequent quotes are from 'Management in BL' n.d. but circulated in December 1979.

20 R. Chell, 'B.L. Cars Ltd: The Frontier of Control' Warwick MA thesis, 1980. Willman and Winch, *Innovation and Management Control* pp. 129–49.

21 H. A. Turner, G. Clack and G. Roberts, *Labour Relations in the Motor Industry* (London, 1967), pp. 86–92.

22 All quotes from BL Cars Procedure Agreement, Hourly Paid Employees, 1982. The consultative arrangements appear at Appendix D.

23 Edwardes, *Back From The Brink*, p. 52.

24 Reported in *The Engineer*, 9 February 1984.

25 Willman and Winch, *Innovation and Management Control*, pp. 149–79.

26 C. Offe, *Industry and Inequality* (London, 1976), p. 36. A similar distinction, between 'consummate' and 'perfunctory' cooperation, appears in O. Williamson, *Markets and Hierarchies* (Glencoe, 1975).

27 Communication to Employee Representatives, November 1983.

28 The other major losses were from disputes over the availability of stewards and support for the TUC day of action.

29 Inquiry Report, 21 May 1983.
30 Willman and Winch, *Innovation and Management Control*, pp. 159–61.
31 Source: TGWU records. The issue of withdrawal of facilities at the assembly plant went to the extended plant conference stage of the procedure, with the company offering no case.
32 TGWU document, November 1983.
33 Procedure effective from 1 March 1982.
34 Willman and Winch, *Innovation and Management Control*, pp. 149 ff.; Chell, 'BL Cars', pp. 60 ff.
35 Company document 22 February 1984.
36 Letter, plant director to all employees, 11 May 1984.
37 P. Willman, 'The Reform of Collective Bargaining and Strike Activity at BL Cars', *Industrial Relations Journal* 15, no. 2 (1984), pp. 1–12.
38 Quotes from interviews, 6 December 1983 and 25 June 1984.
39 Willman and Winch, *Innovation and Management Control*, pp. 164–7.
40 Quoted from the *Guardian*, 10 July 1980.
41 Company document, April 1984.
42 Thurley and Wood, *Business Strategy*, p. 223.
43 Employment in Ford UK fell from 73,200 in 1980 to 61,000 in 1983 (company reports).
44 Lewchuk, 'Fordism and British Motor Car Employees', p. 83.
45 On the Mini and Allegro lines at Longbridge 74.6 per cent of hourly paid employees were on direct production: in the Metro, only 58 per cent were (Willman and Winch, *Innovation and Management Control*, table 8.5).
46 Willman, 'Reform of Collective Bargaining', p. 10.
47 H. Braverman, *Labor and Monopoly Capital* (New York, 1974), p. 87.
48 W. J. Abernathy and K. Wayne, 'Limits of the Learning Curve', *Harvard Business Review*, September-October 1974.
49 Black, *Long Run Theories of Economic Growth*, pp. 256–60.
50 R. M. McDonald, *Collective Bargaining in the Automobile Industry* (New Haven, 1963), pp. 311–55.
51 W. J. Abernathy, K. B. Clark and A. M. Kantrow, *Industrial Renaissance* (New York, 1983).

Index

Abernathy, W. J. 233, 325
absenteeism 21, 30, 80, 271, 311
aerospace industry 112, 122–3
Alfa Romeo 6, 76–8, 82–5, 86,
  89–93, 209, 210–15, 218–30
All-Japan Automobile Workers'
  Union (AJAWU) 173, 176–7
Amalgamated Engineering Union
  (AEU) 45, 46–50, 52, 101
Amalgamated Society of Engineers
  (ASE) 41, 46
Amalgamated Union of Engineering
  Workers (AUEW) 101
American Federation of Labor
  (AFL) 7, 99, 108, 130
American Motors 124, 204
Annual Improvement Factor (AIF),
  see collective agreements
apprentices 172, 176, 180, 278
Armstrong–Siddely 47, 49
assembly line 2, 5, 9, 30, 33, 37–8,
  57, 60, 62, 71, 80, 85, 86, 87,
  104–5, 127–9, 149, 152, 157,
  162, 163, 217, 218, 219, 235,
  238, 240, 261–2, 263, 264, 265,
  268, 269, 270, 271, 272, 273,
  277, 324
  see also flexibility; Fordism
Audi 198, 209, 216, 258, 262, 270,
  271, 277
Austin Motor Co. 3, 14, 32, 46, 103,
  107, 228
  see also British Leyland (BL);
  British Motor Co. (BMC)
Austin Rover, see British Leyland
automation 16, 17, 18, 20–1, 63,
  153, 160, 161–3, 178, 194, 199,
  258–78, 311, 313

see also flexibility, Fordism
automobile industry
  in Brazil 16, 17, 245, 255
  in France 3–4, 6, 7–8, 14, 19, 29,
    33, 52, 57–73, 78, 79, 91,
    197–8, 215
  in Germany 4, 6, 10–11, 12, 19,
    20, 78, 84, 149, 161, 197–8, 209,
    215–16, 245, 258–78
  in Italy 3–4, 6, 8, 9–10, 11, 14,
    15, 19, 33, 58, 76–93, 144–3,
    197–8, 208–9, 220
  in Japan 8, 10–11, 12, 14–21,
    168–86, 199–202, 218, 220,
    224–2
  in Mexico 16–17, 244–56
  in Nigeria 245
  in Soviet Union 57, 84
  in South Africa 245, 255
  in Spain 19, 84, 255
  in Sweden 12, 20
  in UK 3, 6, 7–8, 9, 10, 15, 18–19,
    29–53, 89, 99–107, 108, 110,
    112–13, 197–8, 209, 305–25
  in US 1–21, 29–33, 34, 36, 40, 52,
    57, 59–61, 69, 70, 73, 76, 78,
    80–1, 86, 93, 99–102, 105,
    107–13, 121–39, 196–7, 202–5,
    220, 225, 226, 282–302
  in Yugoslavia 255
Autonomia 158, 160

banks 199
BMW (Bayerischer Motor Werke) 6,
  208, 209, 210–15, 216, 258, 262,
  265, 276, 277
Bedaux system 39, 68, 84–5, 86,
  88–9, 92

328